THE LAST PLAY

Books by James Ridgeway

THE CLOSED CORPORATION

THE POLITICS OF ECOLOGY

THE LAST PLAY

THE LAST PLAY

The Struggle to Monopolize
the World's Energy Resources

JAMES RIDGEWAY

E. P. Dutton & Co., Inc. | New York | 1973

Published simultaneously in Canada
by Clarke, Irwin & Company Limited, Toronto and Vancouver

SBN: 0-525-14355-6
Library of Congress Catalog Card Number: 70-179854

For David Andrew

ACKNOWLEDGMENTS

I particularly wish to thank Elizabeth Boorman who did much of the complicated research for this book. She prepared the elaborate cross tables in the profile section and made the charts showing control of energy companies by different financial institutions.

Among others who have helped and to whom I am grateful are Vic Reinemer and Sally Foulis of Senator Lee Metcalf's staff; Jake Lewis and Peggy Rayhawk of the House Banking Committee staff; Larry Hobart at the American Public Power Association. Christopher Joyce and Frances Lang helped with various aspects of the research. John Fincher kindly criticized the section on Southeast Asia. Davitt McAteer was most helpful both in terms of information and criticism. Thomas Field patiently explained coal taxes. The staff at the American Committee on Africa opened their resources to me. The American Petroleum Institute and American Gas Association kindly allowed the use of their libraries. I am especially indebted to the Institute for Policy Studies which helped support this work, and particularly to Robb Burlage who encouraged it. In addition, the Fund for Investigative Journalism provided me with assistance. Bettina Conner typed the manuscript and offered valuable criticism. The book could not have been written without the patience and encouragement of my wife, Pat.

CONTENTS

PART I
MONOPOLY IN ENERGY

1: THE ENERGY CRISIS

In recent years the oil companies and their consorts in the utilities business have bombarded the public with facts and figures about the growing "energy crisis," what they perceive to be a serious shortage of oil, gas, and coal, the fuels on which our economy is based.

These companies know, as the average citizen does not, that the energy crisis could be the most important political and economic issue of the last quarter of the twentieth century. Not only does the production, distribution, and use of energy underlie the entire environmental movement, but also energy is the foundation of the modern industrial state.

The world economy is based on fossil fuels (coal, oil, gas). According to M. King Hubbert, a former Shell oil geologist writing in *Scientific American,* fossil fuels will last only a few centuries longer. Hubbert says that most of the earth's remaining coal will be extracted between 2000 and 2300; that 80 percent of all oil in the United States will be used up in the 65 years from 1934 to 1999—less than the span of a human lifetime, and that for natural gas the peak production "will probably be reached between 1975 and 1980."

Within the last decade a few international corporations, most of them oil companies, quietly carried forward their own industrial revolution, effectively reorganizing and staking out control over the remaining natural resources of the world.

For more than a generation seven international oil companies controlled two-thirds of the world's oil. Much of that oil was located in the Arab countries of the Middle East. But as those countries adopted increasingly militant, nationalist politics, and as long-term concessions began to run out in such places as Venezuela, the oil companies shifted their strategies. They drew back within the North American continent and, at the same time, branched out so that they might also control development of other fuels, coal, uranium, and gas.

The result is that the oil companies still dominate the international oil markets, effectively controlling two-thirds of the oil and natural gas, but within the United States they also account for more than a quarter of coal and uranium production.

The control is more stark than these figures suggest. One company, Standard Oil Co. of New Jersey, is the single largest supplier of oil and gas on the North American continent. It dominates the petroleum industry of the United States, Canada, and Venezuela. Jersey Standard now has major uranium deposits, is fabricating nuclear fuel, and has assembled the largest block of coal reserves in the nation.

As a result a handful of corporations are in a position to determine the development of the remaining fossil fuels, the rate at which they will be produced, and the uses to which they can be put.

While these firms have built up a new energy industry within the North American continent, they also have moved across the world to stake out remaining deposits of oil, gas, coal, and uranium. In what amounts to a diversionary tactic against Arab nationalism, the major companies have developed large-scale oil and gas deposits in Southeast Asia, where with the assistance of the Indonesian government, they now are laying supply lines to Japan. They also are on the move across the Arctic regions in search for oil and gas, and are actively engaged in drilling for oil and gas on the subsea territories around the world.

In the process these multinational companies have reopened old base camps and made resource colonies of those safe, white islands of colonialism created by the British in the nineteenth century—Australia, Canada, South Africa, the Appalachian region of the United States. At the same time, the companies entered into new relationships with third world countries, acting in effect as their diplomatic agents with major powers in return for exploiting their oil and gas deposits.

The oil men themselves are very much aware of these changing currents. Writing in 1971, George T. Piercy, senior vice-president of Jersey Standard, provided this appraisal:

> As for the consuming nations, there are now new realities in energy that they must face.
>
> First, foreign oil is no longer cheap oil. The trend of foreign oil prices may serve as an answer to the many industry critics who asked for years why the United States did not depend more on foreign oil instead of domestic.
>
> Second, there will be strong pressures in every consuming nation to expand domestic supplies of energy. Growth can be expected in nuclear power, tar sands, oil shales and synthetics. Work will be accelerated to design methods of burning coal without creating air pollution. In the United States, imports of Canadian natural gas will be increased. There will, of course, be a significant amount of imported liquified natural gas. Synthetic gas will come into its own. Already seven plants have been announced.
>
> Thirdly, we can expect further efforts to disperse the dependency upon imports. Many countries, I think, will be re-assessing the diversity of their supplies. And they will probably be willing to pay substantially for increased diversity.

Within the United States this industrial realignment was carried forward with cooperation, indeed, encouragement of the federal governments under both Republicans and Democrats, spanning the administrations of Eisenhower and Nixon.

Historically the Connally hot oil act, passed in the 1930s, first formally allowed the oil industry to set its own rate of production through creation of state "conservation" agencies. In this way the oil men on conservation agencies have been able to influence supply and demand. In the 1950s when large amounts of oil became available in the Middle East, Eisenhower established the oil import quotas to further protect this market system, in effect, ensuring that cheap foreign oil would not be dumped into the United States, driving down prices. Most of the major United States oil supplies lie on the outercontinental shelf, which under law is administered by the Interior Department for the federal government. But even here the government routinely turned over administration of oil production rates to the industry-dominated state regulatory commissions. Thus, in the case of oil, the major market mechanisms are in the hands of industry.

The situation is much the same with respect to natural gas. In 1954 the Supreme Court ordered the Federal Power Commission to begin regulating the price of natural gas at the wellhead. Much gas is produced in connection with oil, and the oil companies were bitterly opposed to what they saw as an opening wedge of regulation in their business. For nearly ten years, the FPC simply ignored the Court's order. Then in the early 1960s the commission established a pricing mechanism. Soon thereafter oil companies, claiming the prices had been established at too low a rate, warned of an impending gas shortage. They insisted the only way to avoid such a shortage was to increase prices, thereby spurring the industry on in its search. There is little way of knowing the extent of a gas shortage because the data on gas reserves is provided by the industry. The government itself does not make estimates of reserves. It accepts the industry information, and, in fact, will not divulge this information publicly because by doing so it might violate proprietary rights of the firms involved. Rather than conduct its own independent gas studies, the FPC, therefore, accepted the statements of the industry, determined there was a gas shortage, and raised the price of natural gas. The Commission also encouraged the gas industry to introduce new high-priced synthetic gas made from naphtha or coal to meet the "shortage." And it permitted increasing flows of costly liquified natural gas (LNG) from abroad to help provide additional supplies of gas. In effect, after ten years of feeble efforts to regulate gas prices, the commission virtually decontrolled the price of gas.

Most of the nation's untouched supplies of coal are located on public lands in the West. These lands are administered by the Bureau of Land Management, a section of the Interior Department. Although there has been an increasing demand for coal to supply electric utilities with fuel, the bureau routinely parceled out coal to oil companies, without requiring competitive bids. The oil companies then sat on the land, holding it out of production, contributing to the scarcity of coal and driving up the price.

In the mid-1960s, the Internal Revenue Service, acting on its own initiative, issued private rulings which provided the single most important impetus toward development of a new energy industry. The IRS allowed oil and mining companies to buy coal firms without paying taxes on the money used for the acquisition. At the same time, the antitrust division of the Justice Department could find no reason to block the growing concentration in energy and allowed the major mergers to go forward without opposition. In Congress, there simply was no opposition to this merger policy until long after the basic realignments had taken place. In part the committees responsible for such matters were taken up with other problems, and in part, the senior members of Congress in charge of natural resources were architects of the policies that encouraged industrial realignment and concentration.

The effects of this concentrated ownership do not represent mere accumulation of wealth by a few individuals or corporations. This private government of energy affects every citizen in the nation. The price of energy is a major cause of inflation in the economy. Not only have rising energy prices contributed to the general increase in prices of all goods and services, but also they have resulted in substantial increases in the costs of electricity, oil, and gas to residential customers.

Some of the effects are more subtle. For example, since the early 1960s the electric utilities in the nation routinely assumed that their supply of future power would come from nuclear power. The electric utility industry never has conducted much research on its own, and the utility executives took the Atomic Energy Commission's (AEC) word for it. Questions were raised about the safety of nuclear power plants, but because the AEC dismissed those questions as groundless, so did the utilities. As it turns out, there are serious technical questions involving safety of nuclear power plants, such serious questions that in some instances environmental groups have succeeded in blocking further construction of the plants. The delays in construction increase the cost of the plants. At the same time, however, completely apart from environmental issues, the AEC and the utilities had misjudged the real cost of nuclear power. Throughout the 1960s, the AEC cheerfully predicted that the cost of nuclear power would steadily decline in comparison to coal and oil. But the prices did not go down. They went up, and with the advent of the environmental challenges, the costs skyrocketed. As a result there is speculation as to whether the utilities may have to abandon nuclear power over the near future.

Since the utilities, FPC, AEC, and committees of Congress all accepted without question the assumptions of nuclear power, which now appear to be seriously mistaken, they are left without an energy policy.

With no real fuels policy alternatives, the utilities have begun to burn up larger and larger quantities of oil and probably will use increasing amounts of synthetic fuels. In effect, they are a captive market for fuels sold to them in the kind and at the rate determined by oil companies. The cost of this foolish, mistaken planning will simply be passed along to the consumers of electricity.

It will be passed along to certain particular classes of consumers, particularly low-income residents of metropolitan areas. The uses and costs of electricity provide an example. In general residential consumers of electricity account for about one-third of the total market, while industry and commercial users take up two-thirds of the market. Studies made in 1972 by the Fairfax County (Va.) Community Action Program indicate that residential consumers use less electricity but pay more for the power than does industry. The analysis concerns rates charged by Virginia Electric Power Co., which operates in the Washington, D.C. suburbs as well as throughout much of Virginia, and it indicates that low-income families who do not use large amounts of electricity actually subsidize industrial customers. The average VEPCO rate per kilowatt-hour is $0.94 for industry and $2.02 for residential. Poor people pay more than three times as much for electricity as industry does, and more than twice as much as large residential consumers. The study concludes, "This inequality persists despite the facts that cost of service in low-income areas is generally low, industrial demands for cheap power are the main reason for costly plant expansion, environmental problems and rate increase requests, and demands for expensive undergrounding of lines come from high-income residential areas rather than low-income neighborhoods."

The same situation can apply to gas. In Boston, where the gas is supplied by Boston Gas Company, a subsidiary of Eastern Gas & Fuel Associates, the rate schedules are instructive. Gas used in Boston comes from Texas Eastern, a major interstate pipeline company which secures supplies from the Southwest and offshore. Texas Eastern buys gas from producers for $0.175 per thousand cubic feet (mcf). Texas Eastern then sends the gas to New Jersey where it is transferred to Algonquin, a pipeline which Texas Eastern owns jointly with Eastern Gas & Fuel Associates, for $0.48 per mcf. Algonquin pipes it 229 miles to Boston and sells the gas to Boston Gas for $0.64 per mcf. Finally Boston Gas sends it through the mains to 315,000 customers for an average price of $2.22 per mcf.

These different transactions represent a 1,200 percent price increase between supposedly independent companies. But with the exception of the initial transaction, where Texas Eastern bought the gas from the producer, Gulf Oil, all the transfers were among companies either owned separately or jointly by Texas Eastern and Eastern Gas & Fuels Associates.

This situation first came to light in Boston, when a local poverty group received a call from a neighborhood resident whose gas was shut off in the midst of an illness. On looking into the situation, the poverty group discovered that during 1970 Boston Gas had shut off service to more than 17,000 households, most of them in the poor or working-class sections of Dorchester and Roxbury.

Both the Boston and Virginia examples illustrate the process through which the "energy companies" maximize profits through concentrated ownership and control over rate mechanisms. They suggest how use of fuels could become a rich man's luxury.

Not only are the small consumers bled through dubious rate procedures, but also, because of the enormous amounts of interest paid to banks and dividends paid to stockholders, electric utilities can be effectively prevented from building the new plants required to produce more electricity. To put it another way, profits in utilities go first to pay off interest, then to stockholders in the form of dividends, leaving little money to be used in modernizing old equipment. One result of this process is that the old plants break down, producing more blackouts and brownouts and thereby add to the propaganda promoting the "energy crisis."

The "energy crisis," as orchestrated by the major oil companies, already has begun to produce even more subtle results, by leading to a growing disparity between rich and poor. The "crisis," as noted above, forces residential consumers to pay more for electricity and gas, while industry pays less. There are other ramifications: Oil companies maximize profits, which means that they need to produce fuels as cheaply as possible. The government reinforces profit maximization policies by providing the energy industry special tax advantages at the production level. The simple result is that while the average citizen paid out taxes at the rate of 20 percent or more in 1970. Gulf Oil's federal tax rate was 1.8 percent. On a local level, the energy companies have taken care to control county tax operations, so that in coal rich counties of Appalachia they pay small amounts of taxes. The counties of eastern Kentucky contain some of the most valuable coal in the world. Yet they are so poor they cannot even afford to maintain decent public schools.

Production of energy necessitates ever-increasing amounts of money for heavy, semiautomated machinery. Declining amounts of money are spent to employ people. Cheapest coal is strip mined, with a few men working expensive equipment, not deep mined with many men working underground. Census maps show the richest energy resource counties of the United States are economically the poorest while the energy consuming counties of the Northeast and West are the most well to do. The latter areas use energy supplies to develop a far more varied economy, one where many more people are employed at decent paying, less dangerous work. Thus, the peoples of coal-rich Appalachia, oil-rich Southwest, find themselves in a position analogous to that of people living in the Middle East, in Canada, and in South Africa. In their cases, development of energy minerals results in a downward economic spiral, leading to poverty.

In still other ways the energy crisis affects the ordinary citizen by providing an entirely new dimension to the pollution problem. To alleviate the gas shortage, oil companies plan to gasify coal in increasing amounts. But gasification of coal requires immense amounts of water. Combined with the coal in gas, this water is exported from the coal mine area. Most of the coal for gasification lies in the mountain states where water is scarce and strictly allotted among agricultural and industrial users. Studies now show that most of the water resources of the area will be required to gasify coal in sufficient quantities to supply utilities in the midwest and western states. If current policies, organized by the energy companies, are pursued, this means an industrial change in the mountain states, a diminution of farming, importation of expensive strip mining equipment, decline in employment. In short, a repeat of the process that 100 years ago ruined the land and the people of Appalachia.

Because of the supposed shortage of natural gas and the increasing price levels approved by the Federal Power Commission, international oil companies have committed large amounts of money to building tankers which can carry liquified natural gas to the United States. This involves the birth of an entirely new form of ocean commerce, great tank ships and port facilities. Serious questions have been raised as to the safety of these ships and facilities, the possible catastrophes in the event of a spill or collision. And yet the government, which makes the studies that raise the issues, is content to accept Shell Oil's own study which indicates there is no environmental danger. Shell has committed more money than any other company to building LNG tankers, and stands to lose most should the new LNG trade be quashed.

It is by now fashionable to investigate the energy crisis. But the government still refuses to exercise its authority under the law to operate the resources in the public domain. Nor will it entertain serious examination of the so-called future fuels, methods for producing energy using means other than fossil fuels, development of solar energy, geothermal energy, and so forth. It has deliberately refused to finance major research into an alternative to the internal combustion engine, which consumes more than one-third of all energy produced. It will not spend money to build rapid-transit systems which are less expensive, more efficient, less polluting, and less consumptive of energy than motor vehicles.

The policies that produced the energy crisis are a function of the corporate social state. They represent part of the process toward centralization of economic and political power into the hands of a few organizations, some business, some governmental, some a combination of both. The overall effect is to lessen the ability of citizens to influence the events that shape their lives, to remove power from their grasp.

This book represents an attempt to set forth a history of some of these policy determinations, and to provide additional dimensions in which the energy crisis can be viewed.

The second part of the book is a guide to the energy industry, providing information on energy resources from several points of view. While it lists fuel resources by major nations, it also attempts to indicate what corporations control the various resources.

One of the basic questions in the United States concerns the influence of ownership over corporate affairs. Part II attempts to provide additional information on this subject, both by providing detailed data on stock ownership of major energy corporations, and through a tabulation which shows holdings of securities in energy corporations by major financial institutions.

In preparing Part II the author meant to provide citizens' groups information which could be used in challenging corporations in rate cases, on electric utility franchise extensions, environmental and safety matters, and in general on corporate maneuvers in the energy industry.

2: LEWIS AND LOVE

Any understanding of the modern energy industry must begin in Appalachia, the source of the coal which built the modern American industrial engine. An instructive point at which to begin the search is the year 1950, when two of the major antagonists of labor and industry opposed one another for the last time. On one side was John L. Lewis, president of the powerful United Mine Workers, a dominant figure in the history of the American labor movement. Opposing him was George Love, Princeton educated, Pennsylvania blue blood, a man accustomed to wealth and power, who by 1950 had put together the most important coal company in the country. With his silent partners at the M. A. Hanna Company, Love was well on his way toward reorganizing the archaic coal business into a modern industry.

These two men forged an alliance that laid the foundation for a new era of energy trusts, a new national economic plan, based on the domination of energy supplies by a handful of major corporations.

After college, George Love worked for a short time as a bond salesman, then accepted an uncle's invitation to return to Pennsylvania to help out with the ailing family coal enterprise, called Union Collieries. This company managed three mines northwest of Pittsburgh, and Love first became assistant to the president, then in 1933 assumed the presidency himself.

During this time the coal industry was in perpetual chaos, with 5,000 different companies, many of them marginal enterprises. The business fluctuated widely because of overproduction. One of the first things Love did was to mechanize the Union Collieries mines; he treated the coal, washing and preparing it for the market, which made it more attractive and fetched a higher price. He also was anxious to conduct experimental research on future uses of coal, and eventually became interested in the development of coal into gas and gasoline.

One of the Union Collieries properties, the Renton Mine, was next door to a mine owned by the M. A. Hanna Company, the investment company originally managed by industrialist Mark Hanna. Love persuaded George Humphrey, president of Hanna, to join operations, and Hanna traded the mines to the Loves in exchange for an equity interest in Union Collieries. Humphrey joined the Union Collieries board of directors. The deal marked the beginning of a long and fruitful business relationship between Love and Humphrey.

In 1942, Humphrey was approached by officers of the National City Bank who wanted to sell the Hanna company a sizable piece of stock in Consolidation Coal Company. Previously owned by the Rockefellers, Consolidation was not regarded as a particularly successful business, but the firm did have sizable coal reserves in northern West Virginia. Humphrey told First National City he would buy the stock if Love could be persuaded to manage the operation. The deal was consummated, and within a year Consolidation had responded to Love's management techniques so well that he merged Union Collieries into it.

At about the same time, the Mellons, who ran Pittsburgh Coal Co., approached Consolidation with an offer to merge their company into Consolidation. Hanna bought out the Mellons, obtaining a majority interest in Pittsburgh Coal.

By this time Love had gained a considerable reputation

within the coal industry. Looking back on Love's career in 1962, *Fortune* was to rhapsodize:

> What George Love did in the coal business was not only to restore a series of sick companies to sound health and profitability, but by the force of his example lead a whole ailing and archaic industry into the light of modern ways. This is not hyperbole. In the early 1940s, when George Love (with George Humphrey at his shoulder) set out to acquire control of and to merge Consolidation Coal Co. and Pittsburgh Coal Co. those two venerable companies between them had, over the years 1925–40, lost the fantastic sum of $100 million. In Love's first year, 1946, as head of the merged company he turned in a net profit of $5,600,000. He has never had a losing year, and in the past five years Consol's net has averaged $20 million. But the important thing about the performance is the imagination that went into it, and the odds against which it was accomplished, for coal is an industry in a chronic condition of oversupply, and its traditional markets are prey to the increasing incursion of cheap residual oil and natural gas.

Love had a determined vision of what the coal industry was to become: "We had a dream," he told *Fortune*. "The trouble with the coal industry was that it was fragmentary in its organization, and wasteful in its technology. We reasoned first that if we could get our hands on enough properties, we could close down or sell off the bad mines, exploit only the good ones. A company with the best thirty to forty million tons could capture the top three to five percent of the market and could make money on that market which is exactly what Consol did."

By 1950 Love was president of the largest coal company in the nation, and with his partner, George Humphrey, who remained in the background with 25 percent of Consolidation's stock, Love was in a position to carry forward his theory for reorganizing the coal industry.

The major obstacle in his path was John L. Lewis, president of the United Mine Workers. Lewis had fought the coal operators for half a century, in the process building a powerful union. At the height of the war with the Allied armies pressing across Europe against the Germans, and the United States in desperate need of coal to keep the advance moving forward, Lewis filed notice that his mine workers were about to strike. (In fact, the strike never took place.)

The quarreling among industry, government, and the UMW reached a chaotic level at the close of the war and continued that way until 1950. During the war the government had seized the mines three times. In 1946, Truman took them over, and the government ran the industry for a year. Lewis bitterly opposed passage of the antiunion Taft-Hartley Act in 1947, and the day it was enacted over the President's veto, he sent the miners out on strike.

A week later he declared a national vacation period. That summer a new contract was signed, but Lewis, insisting the coal operators had dishonored it, struck again. This time the Justice Department went to court and obtained a restraining order. Lewis ignored it. It was not until the Supreme Court upheld the restraining order a few weeks later that the miners went back to work. Lewis was sadly beaten. In June 1949 there was another strike, this one called to help stabilize production. At the end of this strike, Lewis ordered the miners back on a three-day work week. Miners struck in September, went back to work in November, struck again in December, then embarked on the three-day work week. As the year ended they were out on strike again.

Finally after a special inquiry ordered by President Truman had determined that there were but two weeks' supply of coal remaining in the country and that the railroads did not have enough coal to keep going, the President asked Congress for the power to seize the mines.

With this threat hanging over their heads, the industry and union came together and negotiated a pact, the National Bituminous Coal Wage Agreement, signed March 6, 1950. This agreement brought an end to chaos in the coal business, and allowed for a decade of orderly growth and reorganization. Most importantly, it was the first time the workers and industry had negotiated an industry-wide contract. It marked the beginning of a curious partnership between George Love, the chief industry spokesman, and John L. Lewis, the leader of the mine workers.

Before 1950, the UMW negotiated contracts with three major groups: the Northern Coal Operators Association, representing Pennsylvania, northern West Virginia, Ohio, Illinois, western Kentucky; the Southern Coal Producers Association, representing southern West Virginia, Virginia, eastern Kentucky, Tennessee, Alabama; and the captive mines, those coal operators owned by steel companies that did not trade commercially but sent their supplies to captive owners.

Following the signing of the 1950 contract, Love tightened his hold on the coal industry. The northern operators, which he represented, made a pact with the captive mines, which were led by Harry Moses of US Steel. As a result the two groups created the Bituminous Coal Operators Association. The members of this new group outproduced the southern operators two to one and accounted for about half the coal produced in the United States.

(Love always insisted he had little influence at the Bituminous Coal Operators Association, which was run by his colleague Moses. But a close look at the inner workings suggested otherwise. Votes were distributed on the basis of one vote per million tons of coal produced. There was a total of 110 votes. Consolidation Coal produced 15.5 million tons, and Love represented companies with 37.5 million more tons. Thus, he controlled outright 52 of the 110 votes. If that were not enough, he could always call upon his colleagues at US Steel, who had 19 votes.)

While Lewis and Love were often portrayed as enemies, symbols of deep animosity between the union and industry, in many essential respects they shared common positions. Both men realized the industry suffered from oversupply, which created wide price fluctuations and resulted in unpredictable layoffs. Lewis himself had urged the government to regulate the production policies of the industry, while Love had urged control of the market through dominance of the major companies. Both Love and Lewis agreed on mechanization, which would increase production and reduce employment. In looking back on the battles of the 1950s, Lewis said the union never had opposed mechanization provided it was the "union machine." And he went on, "Because we recognized that in this free enterprise system that exists in the United States, investment for profits, reward for incentive, capitalism, call it what you may, could only endure in the world of international competition if it could expand its processes . . . . we just had to improve the processes of mining coal, and we accepted the machine."

And with the large oil finds in the Middle East and development of natural gas, loss of the locomotive market to oil, there were other common enemies which brought the warring labor and industry groups together. Lewis himself was later to remark, ". . . if the coal industry hadn't lowered its cost to increase productivity per man employed, it would have succumbed to its competitor. . . . To wit, oil, gas, diversified fuels made from either coal or petroleum bases, the world competition. So it was necessary for the coal industry to sell its wares in a market that critically looked at prices always and turned to substitutes if the prices didn't suit the way of the market place."

In earlier years the UMW had written contracts on the basis of regional discrepancies, in effect, allowing for differences in wage scales and company practices, thereby attempting to avoid placing undue pressure on small operators who might not be able to meet the terms of a formal national contract. But beginning with the 1950 pact between the mine workers and the operators, the union and companies increasingly sought to apply the contract on a national basis. That meant, for instance, the UMW enforced provisions for payment by operators into the welfare fund, while the industry refused to buy or sell coal or otherwise deal with mine operators who did not honor the terms of the contract. In this way, the big companies applied the squeeze to the smaller operators.

The actual dimensions and workings of the Lewis and Love partnership are not yet clear. What we know of it was brought forth in the courtrooms of Appalachia, developed in large part by John Rowntree, Knoxville attorney, who defended coal operators who felt themselves squeezed out of the coal markets in the 1950s and 1960s.

A sort of populist detective, Rowntree poked through the Appalachian past, reconstructing, ordering a history of the region's political economy. The trial records in his cases consist of thousands of pages of detailed technical, economic, and political information. For weeks Rowntree would patiently instruct the jurymen in the different aspects of their own political and economic history, then ask the members to ponder the results of these historic forces.

Using Rowntree as a guide, we can begin to unravel and understand how Lewis and Love, the union and operators, grew deeply involved in an intricate relationship.

One part of the story involves the Tennessee Valley Authority, the largest utility in the nation, and the single largest consumer of coal. Throughout the 1950s, for its own reasons, the TVA was taken up with efforts to organize the coal industry so that it could acquire sufficient amounts of coal to produce low-cost electricity.

During the 1950s in the midst of the cold war armaments race, the Atomic Energy Commission's operations throughout the nation were expanded. In particular there was a large increase in the production of enriched uranium, used in hydrogen bombs. The process by which uranium is enriched requires large amounts of electricity, indeed such large amounts that the AEC is the single largest consumer of electricity in the nation.

Much of this electricity is and was provided by the publicly-owned TVA. It sends power to the AEC plants in Kentucky.

As the single largest producer of electricity, TVA is an important factor in the fuels market. Historically it created electricity by using water power, building dams along the Tennessee River, which provided irrigation and recreation, and opened the way for industrial development. But during the 1950s, the TVA was not able to meet the demands of the AEC uranium enrichment plants, and in order to do so, TVA built coal-fired electric generating plants. It chose coal rather than gas or oil because it was adjacent to the major Appalachian coal fields, in the Tennessee Valley and west Kentucky, and also in reach of supplies as far away as Virginia in the east and Illinois in the west.

As it turned out, this was a fortuitous event for the coal industry. It was then badly depressed, having emerged from a series of debilitating strikes, losing railroad and home heating business to oil and gas. TVA's appearance as a major coal buyer, eventually the single largest purchaser of coal in the nation, was of great importance. It meant that TVA unavoidably would take a major role in structuring the coal business. In 1951, TVA was buying a little over one million tons of coal a year. Almost all of that coal went to create electricity for the AEC. Between 1951 and 1956 the demands for power from the AEC were twice as much as all the productive capacity of the TVA hydroelectric projects.

Because it was under pressure to produce low-cost electricity, TVA worked hard to persuade the mine operators to mechanize, cutting costs wherever possible, and thereby reducing the price of the coal.

To that end, the TVA instituted a system of long-term contracts under which small mine operators as well as large companies would be guaranteed business if they could deliver coal on certain terms. These contracts were meant to prod the small operators forward, guarantee the TVA a coal supply, and in the process, by providing this guarantee, give the small operators financial security, in effect assuring them a market, and thereby enabling them to borrow money to mechanize. In this way, then,

TVA began to exert increasing pressure on major suppliers in Tennessee and Kentucky, in effect organizing the industry.

Deciding whether to buy Tennessee or Kentucky coal was a tricky business. The southern Tennessee coal was near TVA plants and much less expensive to transport. It had a lower ash content and contained less moisture and sulphur than did coal from western Kentucky, all of which were in its favor. But the coal in Tennessee ran in fairly thin seams, less than three feet high in some cases, compared to the six-foot-high seams in western Kentucky. The thinness and irregularity complicated mining, and made it more difficult for the Tennessee operators to respond to the demands of TVA for mechanization.

Through the mid-1950s, the Tennessee fields remained basically competitive with western Kentucky, but because of mechanization problems, Tennessee operators eventually fell behind. Even so, in bidding for the TVA contracts, the Tennessee operators had other advantages that enabled them to stay in business. For one thing, the United Mine Workers, with which many of the operators had contracts, maintained different types of contracts in different regions. Thus, in Tennessee, the UMW did not enforce the requirement that operators pay 40 cents a ton of coal produced into the welfare fund. However, in the late 1950s, the UMW took a much stiffer position and began to enforce the payment provisions in eastern Tennessee, striking and shutting down mines which did not make payments.

One of the companies involved in this process was Tennessee Consolidated, which supplied TVA under long-term contracts. For years the UMW had excused this company's payments into the welfare fund. Tennessee Consolidated struggled to mechanize, and it held its own in the TVA biddings. But when the union enforced the contract in its full terms, the company had to increase its bids and began to lose business to western Kentucky operators, and in particular to one company, the West Kentucky Coal Co.

By the mid-1950s, West Kentucky Coal was the single largest supplier of coal to TVA, providing about 10 percent of its market. In the late 1950s, its percentage of sales to TVA doubled.

On the surface the struggle between eastern Tennessee and western Kentucky operators for the TVA business seemed to hinge on mechanical and union problems. But as Rowntree explored this matter more fully, he discovered there were other forces at work as well.

In particular, what Tennessee Consolidated did not know was that during the 1950s while the United Mine Workers were for the first time enforcing the full contract terms, the union also was buying stock in the West Kentucky Coal Co. This maneuver was masked through a coalition between the union and Cyrus Eaton, the Cleveland industrialist. The union, in effect, funneled its stock purchases through Eaton, who bought the stock and eventually assumed chairmanship of the company. At the time of the stock purchases, West Kentucky did not have a union contract, and even after the contract was negotiated, West Kentucky was laggard in paying money into the welfare fund.

The effect of these different forces was to hasten the collapse of small mine operators in eastern Tennessee. It was part of a generalized process through which competition was eliminated, unemployment increased, and mechanization brought on—all leading to general economic concentration in the Appalachian coal fields.

Rowntree unraveled another piece of the industry-UMW puzzle in a case he argued and won in behalf of the South-East Coal Co. against Consolidation Coal Co., the industry leader, and the UMW. This case evolves around the fortunes of the LaViers family, which had long operated coal mines in eastern Kentucky. In the late 1950s, LaViers's coal began to run out, and Harry LaViers, Sr., head of the family company, was forced to either invest in a new mine and processing plant or fold up. In order to continue business, LaViers borrowed money from a Louisville bank and The Prudential Insurance Co. But it turned out to be insufficient, and he returned to the bank seeking an additional $1 million. However, the bank would agree to the loan only if interested parties entered into the agreement as well. The interested parties were the Louisville & Nashville Railroad, which serviced the mine, and the Consolidation Coal Co., which marketed the LaViers coal. Both L&N and Consolidation agreed to put up $500,000 between them. In addition to the loan Consolidation bought a 20 percent stock interest in South-East.

Because of the costs of the processing plants, LaViers found himself in deepening financial difficulties, and eventually he went to Washington to meet with Thomas Kennedy, then president of the UMW, in hopes he could persuade Kennedy to modify the union contract, reducing the amounts of money paid into the union welfare fund, or perhaps excusing them for a temporary period. LaViers pointed out that the fund was relatively well-off, and that the unions excused other smaller operators from payment. In addition, South-East Coal was providing employment for miners in eastern Kentucky at a time when industry in general was leaving the place and it was becoming progressively more poverty-stricken. But Kennedy would not agree to a change in the contract, insisting that it be applied across the board.

On his return to eastern Kentucky, LaViers determined he had no choice but to break the union contract and run the mine nonunion. He wrote his employees to this effect, announced the decision to the UMW, and promptly was struck. With his sons and a few other employees he kept the mine open.

Before LaViers actually broke the union contract he discussed the situation with the vice-president for sales of Consolidation Coal. At the time, Consolidation marketed all South-East coal. He later recalled the meeting with the vice-president in Pittsburgh. "He had taken me to dinner at the Schenley Park, I believe it is, Hotel, and it was during the dinner meal that he asked me if it was true that we were going to cancel the contract with the United Mine Workers, and I told him yes, that it was, that I felt I had no other alternative and to protect the interest of the company, I had done everything else I knew to do and that we were going to cancel the contract with the United Mine Workers and attempt to operate the property non-union."

"What was his reply?"

"He said, 'Well, you know if you do that we cannot continue to sell your coal.'"

At that point LaViers decided to organize his own sales company and he got in touch with David Swanson, an experienced coal salesman. Swanson agreed to set up a South-East Sales Company. Shortly after the new company was formed, LaViers and Swanson went to Milwaukee for a meeting with officials of the North Western Hanna Coal Co. As Swanson recalled, "While Consolidation Coal Company was the sales agent, North Western Hanna was . . . the biggest customer, definitely the biggest lake customer that South-East had and naturally we were very anxious to continue shipping them coal."

But the meetings were fruitless. As Swanson later recounted, "They told us that they had talked to their Pittsburgh office the day before we arrived and told Pittsburgh that Mr. LaViers and I were coming up there, and what were they supposed to tell us. They went on to say they weren't to tell us anything, just don't do any business."

(At the trial company representatives denied canceling South-East contracts and disputed the version of events provided by LaViers and Swanson.)

Swanson went on to recount that while South-East was able to make several small sales to Consolidation, they never were able to do substantial business.

South-East hired salesmen, and they repeatedly called on Consolidation offices in Milwaukee and in Cleveland during 1962 and 1963 but without any success. The company obtained Consolidation records enabling it to attempt to sell to Consolidation's customers, which were mostly retail yards and some industrial accounts. But as Swanson recounted, his team of salesmen had great difficulty in maintaining these accounts, and had to reduce prices to hold on to business.

In late 1964, South-East Sales purchased Peerless Coal Co., a coal sales agency based in Columbus. One of the reasons for buying out Peerless was to secure a wider source of supply; the other was to get new customers. One of Peerless's main customers was Consolidation. But Swanson had run up against another stone wall. His testimony:

> Q: After you acquired the Peerless Coal Company did you continue to sell coal through Peerless Coal Company to Consolidation Coal Company?
>
> A: We did for a few months, and then sales stopped entirely. . . .
>
> Q: What were the total sales of the Peerless Company?
>
> A: . . . In the year 1962, Peerless Coals, Incorporated, sold to Consolidation Coal Company $138,922 worth of coal; in 1963, $176,840; in 1964, $132,235; in 1965 when Peerless was a wholly owned subsidiary of the South-East Coal Sales Company, the sales were $6,253.

In 1966 there were no sales.

These two cases then are instructive in the methods employed by union and industry in restructuring the coal industry of Appalachia. On the one hand, the union worked with the industry to buy out competition and gain control of an important market. In another instance, a major coal company used the union contract as a device for shutting off markets to a coal company in Kentucky. The result was concentration of the coal industry into a few large corporations.

3: THE NEW ENERGY INDUSTRY

KING COAL

Probably the simplest explanation for the sudden interest in coal during the early and mid-1960s was the industry's profitability. In 1968, *Fortune* reported a 15 percent profit margin for the industry as a whole, with a 16.8 percent return on invested capital. Independent and industry experts in West Virginia, among the largest coal-producing states, set the profit at between 80 cents and $1 a ton. Taking the lower figure and multiplying it times the tons of coal mined, the total annual profits in West Virginia in 1968 were $116 million.

Profitability in the coal business involves an intricate process of economic colonization through which absentee corporations are provided easy access to the coal, then offered incentives to mine it in the guise of low property and income taxes. They are even provided with hidden subsidies by the state and federal governments in the form of unenforced health and safety laws.

While the tax benefits in the coal industry are not as widely celebrated as those in the oil business they are extraordinary. Sometimes a coal operator can make better use of the tax mechanism than an oil man even though the rates are lower for coal because of the way the taxes are computed.

First, royalty holders are provided with select treatment. This applies to perhaps as few as 1,000 owners, most of them wealthy individuals operating either on their own or through corporations, and organized politically through the Coal Lessors Association. They live far from the coal fields, in New York, Philadelphia, or London. These individuals own coal lands in Appalachia, the mountain states, and elsewhere throughout the nation. They lease the land to various coal companies which mine it. In return these landholders are paid a royalty on each ton of coal mined. A typical figure is 25 cents per ton. Ordinarily royalty income is treated under the tax laws as ordinary income and taxed at the full rate. But the tax laws contain a loophole when it comes to coal. The loophole allows income from coal royalties to be treated as capital gains. In other words, recipients of coal royalties pay taxes on them at half the rate they would otherwise pay.

In actual dollars the government does not lose much money—perhaps $5–$8 million a year. But the coal royalty tax treatment has established an important principle, and one that other groups seek to use as a precedent for easing their own tax status.

In 1969 Wilbur Mills, chairman of the House Ways and Means Committee, sought to knock out the coal royalty loophole from the tax reform bill. In fact, one morning in executive session he managed to get the section killed. But by that afternoon, John Watts, the second-ranking Democrat on the committee and a representative from Kentucky, had written it back into the law. Rather than antagonize Watts, Mills dropped the matter.

In addition to the special capital gains treatment on coal royalties, a coal operator can take advantage of a 10 percent depletion allowance. The tax loss to the government as a result of coal depletion ranges between $40–$50 million a year. (Total depletion allowances for all minerals amount to $1.4 billion.) Here the crucial point is not the amount of the tax deduction, but the point at which the deduction can be taken. For example, in the oil business an operator can take the depletion allowance at the wellhead, the point at which the oil comes from the ground and is sold to a second party. But in the coal business operators can base the depletion allowance to include not only the cost of actually mining the coal, but also the cost of preparing it, breaking and sizing it, and transporting it up to 50 miles. Thus, the cost of a short-haul railroad can be included in the depletion allowance. (Thus far it is not legal to deduct the cost of making coal into synthetic fuel under the depletion allowance, but it seems likely this will be a new demand. Already there is a precedent for such a step. The oil shale lobby won a special tax provision that allows an operator to include the process for turning the shale into oil within the depletion allowance.)

In coal, the depletion allowance can be used to shelter up to one-half the individual's or company's income. The other half of the operator's income can be protected through several other different gimmicks.

For example, one can write off the costs of exploration and development. If a mine operator thinks he would do well to develop another coal seam, he can deduct the cost of dropping a new tunnel into the second seam. In coal that would be regarded as an exploratory expense where in other industries it would be considered a capital expense and written off over the useful life of the new coal seam. Under the exploration and development rule, the cost can be written off over one year. The line between development and ordinary mine costs is a thin one, and most difficult for an IRS official to draw in an audit.

During consideration of the coal mine safety act in 1969, the National Coal Association lobbied for and won passage in Congress for a five-year amortization of new mine safety equipment. This means that the equipment can be written off much sooner than the facts justify. Equipment costs usually are written off over the life of the assets, perhaps 15 to 20 years, not in five years as in the case of coal.

These are the major tax incentives that the federal government extends to coal companies as incentives for them to do business. There are other much more extensive incentives provided on the local level.

West Virginia Subsidies

Records of local coal holdings and taxes paid on them are hard to come by. In an unpublished study of coal in West Virginia (1970), J. Davitt McAteer looked into coal ownership in 14 major coal-producing counties. The 14 counties controlled 82 percent of all mining operations, and produced 88 percent of all coal mined in the state. The counties lie in a band stretching across the state from the Pennsylvania and West Virginia borders in the north to the borders of Kentucky and Virginia in the south. All told, the counties encompass 4.7 million acres, about 31 percent of the total land area of West Virginia. A little less than half the state's 1.6 million residents live there. Under the county lands is half of all the state's unmined coal reserves. By any ordinary gauge, they ought to be rich indeed.

In looking through the land books, McAteer found that most of the land in the area was owned, and had been owned for many years, by corporations in the coal business. The leading 25 landowners owned as much as 44 percent of all the land. And of that amount the largest holdings were by two railroads, which crisscross the coal fields of Appalachia: The Norfolk & Western and the Chesapeake & Ohio/Baltimore & Ohio railroad systems. Through its subsidiary Pocahontas Land Co., the N&W is the largest single landholder in the state, holding 7.2 percent of all land in the 14 counties. Through two subsidiaries, New Gauley Coal Co. and Western Pocahontas Co., C&O/B&O system controls 4.4 percent of the land in the counties.

While more than one thousand coal companies operated in the state of West Virginia during 1966, three-quarters of all tonnage came from 25 of the largest coal firms, which also are among the largest landholders in the 14-county area. Consolidation Coal Co., subsidiary of Continental Oil, is the second largest landholder.

Thus the land in these key 14 counties is dominated, if not controlled outright, by the two major coal-hauling railroads, the leading coal producer in the nation, and by the other 25 corporations, most of them out of the state. McAteer's statistics help to explain why the people of West Virginia have for so long regarded themselves as powerless, serfs of their eastern overlords.

Even so, corporations sometimes contribute to the betterment of those communities which suffer their presence by paying taxes. And it was in the county tax books that McAteer learned his most bitter lesson. The 14 counties in McAteer's survey contain land and buildings which have assessed value of more than $1.3 billion. Under West Virginia's law, the assessed value of property must be 100 percent of its true and actual value. But as McAteer made his inquiry, he learned that the normal assessment in West Virginia was 50 percent of the actual value. The actual value of the real estate in the 14 counties, therefore, was as much as $2.7 billion. On looking further, he found that the assessed value had nothing to do with the riches underlying the 14 counties. Indeed, the tax system worked in reverse; those counties with the lowest assessed value attached to their land are those with the greatest reserves of recoverable coal.

McAteer goes on to instruct:

> Before examining this premise further, however, several points illustrated in other sections of this report should be reiterated. First, Mr. Neil Robinson of Robinson & Robinson Mining Engineers, contends that Geological Survey estimates of recoverable tons of coal in the United States are vastly overexaggerated. He states that in West Virginia, probably only 15 to 20 percent of the reserves estimated to be recoverable by the Geological Survey will actually be commercially minable through the year 2,000.
>
> A second point to be kept in mind in the following discussion is that as shown in the preceding section of this report, the net profit to be gained on a ton of coal probably ranges from eighty cents to one dollar.
>
> Let us now turn to one of our first counties—Boone County —and apply the above consideration. In 1968, the assessed

land value of Boone . . . was $15.7 million. . . . The West
Virginia Geological Survey estimates that there are 4,640,-
764,000 tons of recoverable coal in Boone.

By applying Mr. Robinson's 15 percent, or lower estimate,
it can be calculated that only 696,114,600 tons of the coal in
Boone are actually recoverable with today's technology.

Using this report's lower estimate on profit per ton of coal—
or eighty cents—it can be computed that the coal recoverable
according to Mr. Robinson's estimates would have a net profit
value of $556,891,680.

Under the laws of West Virginia, the maximum actual value
that could have been attached to the land in Boone in 1968
was $31,561,560. This would seem to be less than realistic
when the potential net profit in Boone coal alone—using very
conservative estimates—is actually worth nearly twenty times
as much as the values attached to the land by the county
assessor.

The coal industry's general attitude about taxes was perhaps
best illustrated by an incident at Osage, West Virginia, several
years ago. Osage is a community of about 600 people, located
just outside Morgantown in the coal fields. Most of the men
work at Consolidation Coal mines. There was a move in Osage
to incorporate the town, an act which would give the citizenry
the right to charge property taxes. The industry applauded
the idea, and Julius Singleton, a Morgantown attorney, who
served as an officer of the state coal association, offered to do the
legal work free. Consolidation Coal offered the services of
its engineers to draw up the maps, also free of charge. The
maps were late in being drawn, and presented to the townspeople only a couple of days before the vote on incorporation.
The drawings carefully included all features of the proposed
limits of incorporation except for two indentations, which had
been cut out of the circle that marked the town boundaries.
One indentation excluded the property on which sits the main
office of the Consolidation Coal Co. The other excluded Consolidation Coal's machine shop. The townspeople went ahead
and approved the incorporation; of course, the two indentations

effectively prevented them from ever collecting property taxes from Consolidation, the only real source of benefit from incorporation.

Coal operators in West Virginia are eligible for other subsidies: They draw $1 million a year from the state treasury through the Gasoline Tax Refund. This law provides refunds to certain purchasers—largely coal companies—who buy 23 gallons or more at a time, if no part of the gasoline is used on a public highway. McAteer points out, "It is a double gyp to the state's small taxpayers. First and not by coincidence, the state tax department lacks the resources to check the claims which the coal companies file. Said one state official, 'Sure they use the public roads and do it most of the time. We know they're lying to us but it would cost us too much to check on them.' Secondly, the very excuse for the tax break is a transparent fraud. Since the state gas tax helps to pay for public highways, the coal companies argue, they should not have to pay it on the gasoline they burn on their own private access roads. They fail to add that the state itself built most of their private access roads with public funds."

In 1968 coal operators mined out 145,133,550 tons of West Virginia coal, worth about $725 million. That same year their taxes comprised only 3.8 percent of the state's total revenues, $11,620,000 in state taxes and $6,310,000 in property taxes. Meanwhile West Virginia's small taxpayers were straining small budgets to produce more than that in cigarette taxes alone— $23,047,695. But West Virginia is no exception. The ownership and tax policies in the entire southern Appalachian region are maintained in this colonial fashion.

Eastern Kentucky and Tennessee: In 1965 the *Louisville Courier-Journal* made a study of coal taxes in Kentucky and concluded, "The industry has been able to get rock pile assessments on land loaded with black wealth.

"Thousands of acres of coal land worth $200 to $300 an acre get on the assessment books at $2 an acre," the paper went on to say. "Other thousands of acres are literally hidden from the assessor."

One such instance came to light in Bell County, an eastern Kentucky county, when the Tennessee Valley Authority acquired 8,800 acres of rich coal lands when one of its suppliers was unable to provide coal under a TVA contract. TVA was perfectly willing to continue paying the property taxes on the land, but as it developed, none of this valuable land was on the tax books.

In 1967, James Millstone of the *St. Louis Post-Dispatch* made another survey of property tax payments and found the situation little changed. Harlan County, a major coal-producing region in the eastern part of the state, was in miserable poverty. Many people had deserted in hopes of finding a better life elsewhere. Forty percent of those who remained lived under the poverty level. The county was worse off than 92 percent of all other counties in the country. Harlan County could not raise more than 10 percent of the costs of running its school system. Yet US Steel, a company with $4.3 billion in revenues that year, and operator of two mines valued at $9.3 million in Harlan County, paid taxes of only $34,500.

Harry Caudill, who campaigned against the out-of-state colonizers, described the situation at a hearing of the National Education Association: "I'd like to compare with you, for example, the tax burden of Inspiration Consolidated Copper Company in Arizona with the burden borne by United States Steel Corporation in Harlan County. US Steel operates a very large mine through US Coal & Coke Company. Inspiration Consolidated Copper in 1967, the last year in which I have compared these figures, had listed for taxation in the state of Arizona $49,457,000; it paid property taxes to that state in the sum of $1,727,000. That means that it would require 28½ years to pay that state in taxes an amount equal to the appraised value of its property. Now, if we look at the United States Steel Company, for example, we find that it has an appraised value of $9.3 million on which it paid Harlan County taxes amounting to $34,500. Now, this means that it would require 270 years for US Steel to pay Harlan County and the state an amount equal to the assessed value of its property. Looked at another way this means that if Inspiration Copper's mining equipment had been located in Harlan County, Kentucky, instead of paying $1,727,000 to the county and the state, it would have paid $186,000. It means that if US Steel had been operating that same enterprise in Arizona it would have paid not $34,500 but $310,500. These figures tell you the story of what is wrong with education in Kentucky, of why the playgrounds are muddy and why the teachers are underpaid and why they are in revolt."

When Ralph Nader went after the former Kentucky revenue commissioner, James E. Luckett, for allowing US Steel to get away with this tax avoidance, Luckett claimed Nader was mistaken. Nader wrote back,

> One would expect to find the U.S. Steel Corporation not on the list of those deserving the special sympathy of Kentucky's tax administrators. Yet your portrayal of U.S. Steel's subsidiary, U.S. Coal and Coke's property-tax status in Harlan County reads more like a company press release—which it later became—than the observation of a public official committed to property-tax equity. You assert that this company had paid more in property taxes in Harlan County in 1966 than the $34,500 I had cited. You fail to mention, however, that most of this payment was not to Harlan County as a whole, as was the $34,500; instead it was to a small school district carved out especially for the company, its officers and employees in the town of Lynch—which until recently was virtually a 100 percent company-owned town. In other words, by a neat trick of fiscal gerrymandering, Kentucky has insulated the coal-mining subsidiary of a corporation which had almost five billion dollars worth of sales in 1970, from the urgent educational needs of the children of Harlan County, and has relieved it of the duty to support the schools except those that cater mainly to it alone. It is difficult to imagine a property-tax system more grotesquely warped to the convenience of a multi-billion dollar, out-of-state corporation.

In addition, the bald assessment and tax figures you cite are
no proof whatsoever of the legal adequacy of U.S. Steel's
property-tax payments. The measure of property-tax uniformity
is relative: the law requires that all taxpayers, large and small,
be assessed and taxed at the same percentage of their property's fair market value. So merely to say, as you did, that
U.S. Steel paid a total of $148,520 in property taxes in 1966,
or that its assessment rose from $9.3 million in 1966 to $10.4
million currently, gives not a hint at all of the adequacy of
these assessments and payments relative to the fair market
value of the company's property, or to the burden borne by
other taxpayers in the county.

Knott County was another coal-producing region from which
people had fled, and those that remained lived in poverty.
Fifty-seven percent were below the poverty line. One of the big
landowners in Knott County was Elk-Horn Coal Corp., head-
quartered at Charleston, West Virginia. Elk-Horn had revenues
of $1 billion in 1966. It paid Knott County $2,750 in property
taxes on 15,107 acres of rich coal properties.

When Millstone inquired into taxes paid by coal operations in
Knott County, the tax commissioner told him, "The coal companies pretty much set their own assessments. We pretty much
have to work with them. We have no system for finding out
what they own. Like they may tell us they own 50 acres at a
certain place when actually they own 500 acres.

"As far as mineral rights are concerned, we can't tell what's
under the ground. If a company says an area is barren or mined
out, we have to accept it."

At Leslie County, the tax commissioner John D. Muncy described his annual arguments with the Fordson Coal Co., a
subsidiary of the Ford Motor Co. Fordson holds mineral rights
to large amounts of Leslie County land. Each year the company submits valuation figures which Muncy considers to be
inaccurate. He counters by raising the valuation. On appeal to
the tax supervisors, appointed by the local county judge, Fordson
always wins. (It is usual in eastern Kentucky for the chairman

of the county appeals board to be an official of a coal or mining company.) In 1966, Fordson lowered Muncy's valuation from $880,000 to $660,000. In 1967 the company's tax bill totaled $5,189.

To set this into context: Leslie County is the poorest of all eastern Kentucky counties, with over two-thirds of its people living below the poverty line. Ford Motor Co. in that year had sales totaling $12.2 billion with a net income of $621 million.

Pike County is one of the richest coal counties in Kentucky. In 1966 its production was 16.3 million tons valued at $65 million. Millstone writes, "But although it is one of the nation's richest coal counties, Pike County could raise only 18.3 percent of the $4.1 million needed to operate its schools last year, also 45.3 percent of its people subsisted on incomes below the poverty level."

In another exchange with Luckett, Nader made these points about Pike County: "You defend the assessment of 'potentially-rich coal fields' in Pike County at the same level as 'poor-to-fair farmland'—$25 to $200 per acre—because of the cost of extracting the coal. In reply, one can only suggest a comparison of the revenues of coal-owners from their property, despite the extraction costs, with the revenues gleaned by tillers of the state's marginal farmlands. And if indeed the assessment of unmined coal is so 'difficult [an] assignment,' why did not the Commissioner offer an easier-to-administer alternative, such as a severance tax, instead of merely holding forth assessment difficulties as an excuse for current performance? (Senator Lee Metcalf of Montana has introduced severance tax legislation into the U.S. Senate, S. 1843, which could yield $25 million annually for Kentucky alone at 1966 levels of production.)"

A survey by the *Nashville Tennessean*, September 1971, disclosed that coal-field owners pay minimal property taxes, and at a lower rate than farmers in that state. Because there is no mineral tax in Tennessee, the state and its counties and cities receive nothing in tax revenue on income from millions of dollars in coal sales. When one county sought to institute a privilege tax on coal mining, the companies ganged together and beat off the tax.

The paper goes on to describe the by now typical formula of colonization: "In 1970, the giant British land company, the American Association Ltd., which owns 44,000 acres in the coal-producing portion of Claiborne County, paid $6,000 in property taxes. Consolidation Coal leases 21,000 acres from American Association. In the fiscal year ended June 30, 1970 Consol produced, according to the Tennessee Department of Labor, 1,257,-240 tons of coal. The market value of the coal that year was about $4.50 a ton. The terms of the lease call for a royalty payment of 15 cents a ton to American Association. This would mean that in one year the firm with 90 percent of its stockholders in London made $198,586 from just that lease. Moreover, Consolidation pays the property taxes on its lease, which was $65,000 in 1970, $19,000 of which was in buildings and equipment from its deep mines." In 1960 and 1962, American Association paid Claiborne County $14,479 in taxes. In 1970, it was only paying $18,000.

Health & Safety

One of the reasons why coal mining is so profitable is that the companies and the union have by and large taken so little care to protect the health and safety of the workers. These safety precautions are oftentimes expensive and tend to reduce productivity. The industry skimps on them. As a result the coal industry is rightly viewed as among the most backward industries in the world, and medieval in disregard of its workers.

In some industries the U.S. government attempts to spur growth through subsidies in the form of outright outlays of cash, tax incentives, and so on. In the coal business one of the silent subsidies has been in the form of state and federal mine safety laws which the industry, union, and legislators know do not work, and indeed, have not bothered to go through the motions of enforcing. It is important to understand just how vicious this system of human exploitation is, for there is nothing in the backward underdeveloped areas of the world that can compare to the way in which we treat the people who each day risk their lives digging the coal that makes the electricity and energy which assure so many of us daily luxury. Since the beginning of the century 100,000 men have died in coal mines. One million others have been injured. Coal mining is the most dangerous industry in the world.

Originally miners got the coal out by hand. They lay on their sides in passageways underground, and undercut the coal with their picks. Then they made a hole on top of the seam, drove wedges into it, and broke the coal out and down that way. The miner then would load the coal by hand and haul it out of the mine.

Machinery gradually was introduced into the mines. Output per man did not reach six tons until 1946. Since then, however, mechanization increased markedly, and output per man climbed to 19 tons a day in 1967.

While there are different ways of mining coal, the most conventional method involves five steps. First, a cutting machine carves out a slot at the base of the coal wall, or face. Then a boring machine drills holes halfway up the face, and the holes are stuffed with explosives. The men retire to safety, blow off the charges, and the coal tumbles down out of the seam. Then loading machines pick up the coal pieces, put them onto conveyor belts which carry the coal to shuttle cars, and the shuttle cars carry the coal to railway cars, which, in turn, take the coal out of the mine.

Beginning in the middle 1950s the so-called continuous miner machines were introduced. These large machines, operated by one or two men, have spinning teeth which gouge the coal out of the seam, depositing it on a conveyor belt which takes it out of the mine.

The most common cause of accidents in coal mines is collapsing roofs. As miners work either with cutting machines or explosives against the face of coal, they must take care to extend roof supports above or else risk the danger of rocks and earth coming down on them. Historically the common practice, and one still employed in smaller mines, was to run timbers overhead as the mining operation moved forward against the coal seam. Experienced miners have a way of listening carefully to the rocks grinding above them, and they can tell whether it is merely the earth working naturally or whether a fall is imminent. The use of roof timbers provides them with a few minutes warning, for just before a cave-in the timber supports will begin to snap with the weight of rock, providing a second or so of warning for the miners to jump back out of the work area.

During the 1950s mine operators introduced a new technique for roofing called roof bolting. After the coal is taken from the face, a member of the crew goes forward, and drills a hole up into the stone roof. Then he inserts a long bolt with an expanding section at its end. The top expands as it tightens, squeezing the rocks together, and, in effect, forming the rocks into a laminated roof.

But before either the bolting or the timbers can be stretched across the top of the working space in a mine, some sort of temporary support should be thrown up for the sake of safety. Yet because the emphasis is all on productivity, some coal operators don't bother with the temporary roofing, and the experienced coal miners come to adopt a casual attitude to working in unprotected areas. They depend on their hearing for the telltale noise of grinding rock.

The continuous miner, which makes possible increased productivity, is another source of danger within the mine. The machine uses large amounts of electricity, and care needs to be taken for it gives off sparks. The sparks can easily ignite the flammable atmosphere of gas and fine coal dust in the mine. In constantly ripping away coal from the face at high speeds the continuous miner itself stirs up a great amount of dust. The operator works amidst this continuing swirl, and because of it has difficulty seeing where he is going with the machine. This is tricky business, for if the miner goes above the coal seam the machine will hit into hard stone, causing sparks, which again can combine with methane and create explosions. Because of the noise of the machinery, the work crews are unable to hear the shifting rocks. Sometimes, much to the annoyance of their supervisors, men shut off the machines and listen for the sound of rocks shifting in the roof above.

Some of the difficulties could be overcome if the mine operators would agree to string electric lights in the working areas, but they are hesitant to put up electric lights in the mines on the grounds they cause additional safety problems. Of course, they use large amounts of electricity to run the continuous miner machinery. So, in many mines the men feel their way about, oftentimes blinded by the coal dust, their way lit only by helmet lamps.

The coal operators are able to get away with these unsafe practices because the state and federal safety inspectors are unwilling or legally unable to enforce effective safety measures. In the state of West Virginia, for instance, state inspectors are not taken seriously because violations often do not carry any penalties. The federal inspectors are more highly regarded, but since neither the industry nor the union encourages safe practices, they often regard their jobs as hopeless. At any rate, the federal inspector is viewed as policeman, and the miner who dares complain to him about conditions is more likely to lose his job than receive any reward.

The contempt in which the coal operators hold the safety laws and the men who are meant to police them is scarcely believable. McAteer reports, for example, how Consolidation Coal Co. took pains to make sure entrances of mines located on the Pennsylvania–West Virginia border opened from the West Virginia side because the laws there were less strict.

Because of the uproar over the government's failure to enforce the coal mine health and safety laws, Congress asked the General Accounting Office (GAO) to make a study of the way in which the Bureau of Mines was carrying out its responsibilities. Released in June 1971, the study revealed that nine out of every ten underground coal mine accidents can be traced to inadequate safety precautions on the part of the mine operators. It charged the Bureau of Mines with outright negligence, and disclosed that only 31 percent of the required safety inspections and only 1 percent of the required health inspections had been made by December 31, 1970.

The GAO further said the bureau had failed to use its power to close mines when inspectors found repeated safety violations. Inspections had been "at times extremely lenient, confusing, uncertain, and inequitable." And the GAO said the bureau had not required operators to take dust samplings, and allowed them to submit erroneous data. There also was little effort made to develop sound methods for roof control and ventilation.

Even where the government penalizes the mine operators for safety infringements, the penalties don't amount to much. The safety act that calls for penalties was passed in 1969, but the General Accounting Office reported that it had discovered that violations between March 30, 1970 and April 1, 1971 were not regarded as real violations because this period was meant to provide an educational experience for the mine operators so that they could get acquainted with the act. (In the 15-month educational period from April 1, 1970 to June 30, 1971, the number of men killed in mining accidents shot up to 309 from 246 in the previous 15-month period.) Reporting in *The Wall Street Journal*, Burt Schorr said Island Creek Coal Co., the third largest coal producer, had drawn 30-odd government citations for unsafe mining conditions which threatened immediate injury or death to miners. According to the Interior Department's guidelines, the usual penalty would be from $5,000 to $10,000 for each such violation. But assessors at the Bureau of Mines actually proposed penalties of only $2,000 each.

In March 1972, the *Miner's Voice* newspaper made an examination of the bureau's handling of safety violations. It discovered that the bureau had canceled more than $2.6 million in fines originally assessed against coal companies, after the managements had protested the fines were too steep. Two years after the safety act took effect the bureau had collected only 11 percent of the fines originally assessed. Only $1.3 million has been collected from operators out of $12.5 million assessed for safety violations. Despite its claim to having adopted a get-tough policy, the bureau still was holding "informal conferences" with operators and reducing fines as a result. Despite provisions which require the bureau to seek criminal prosecutions for continued and willful violations of the act, the bureau had only acted in two cases.

The *Miner's Voice* goes on to describe specifically how the sweetheart arrangements between mine operators and the Bureau of Mines work out. They cite the case of the Shannon Branch mine of Allied Chemical Corp. where a man was killed because the roof fell in on him: "For the period from July 23, 1971 to August 3, the Bureau fined Allied Chemical $12,425 for violations when assessment officials finally got to the case on January 3 of this year.

"On January 25, Jack B. McNicol, an official of Allied Chemical in Bluefield, West Virginia, wrote to Bureau assessment officials and requested that they reduce the fines, stating that they were too high and were unfair.

"Nine days later, the Bureau reduced the fines from the $12,425 originally assessed to $5,915—more than a 50 percent reduction. No single major reduction caused the decrease. Instead, 43 separate violations were reduced or totally vacated. Fines for serious violations likely to cause death to miners originally assessed at $250 were knocked down to $50, $400 fines were dropped to $125, $150 fines were reduced to $25, etc."

Bureau records showed that in only one case was a $10,000 fine levied. Allied Chemical apparently does not have any special sway. Freeman Coal Co. managed to talk the bureau out of proposed fines of $6,975 on October 21, 1971 and got the fines reduced to $1,205. That's a reduction of 83 percent. Freeman had written the bureau, "Heavy fines do not and would not make Freeman any more aware of the desirability of safe operations."

The records of the Bureau of Mines indicate that the bureau discriminates in favor of the big companies and against the smaller concerns. Those records show, for example, that the largest 20 coal companies, which run most of the mines, and produce most of the nation's coal, also have most of the safety violations. Yet they pay only a trifling amount of the total fines. The top 20 companies all told pay 37.6 percent of all fines. The amount of infringements is staggering. Island Creek was assessed $849,075 in fines, about 8.3 percent of the total fines. Peabody Coal had 1,190 violations in 17 mines and was assessed $198,980 for 1.9 percent of the total. Consolidation had 505 violations in 6 mines and was assessed $95,720 or .9 percent of the total.

The Black Lung Fiasco

For the first time the Coal Mine Health and Safety Law of 1969 took cognizance of black lung disease. It established a procedure for compensation and set maximum permissible concentrations for dust in the mines in the hopes of reducing or preventing future cases of the disease. Experts argued that no more than three milligrams of dust per cubic meter of air was acceptable, but when the coal operators insisted that was an impossibly low level, George Schultz, then secretary of labor, retreated and offered a four-and-a-half milligram standard. When the law finally passed it did call for a three-milligram level.

Unfortunately these standards seem to have been an exercise in semantics. In a special report on mines in Kentucky, Robert K. Jones, of the state department of health, said that some miners in that state were breathing 76 times the maximum concentration of coal dust. The study showed that 57.4 percent of the state's underground mines exceeded federal limits as of June 1970.

The law also established a compensation process through which miners disabled by black lung could qualify for compensation. But the Social Security Administration, in whose hands this part of the law was placed, applied a bureaucratic standard for determining compensation. By September 1971 more than half of the 300,000 miners who had applied for compensation on the basis of having black lung disease were rejected. The outcry over the Social Security Administration's handling of black lung was particularly intense in Kentucky and West Virginia. In Kentucky, 68 percent of 31,549 miners' claims were turned down. In West Virginia, it was 54 percent of claimants. Yet in Pennsylvania 70 percent of miners applying were approved.

Part of the problem with the Social Security Administration's bureaucratic red tape was its insistence on the use of x-rays and breathing tests. Experts who have worked with coal miners believe these diagnostic devices are faulty. Dr. Donald Rasmussen of the Appalachian Regional Hospital at Berkeley, West Virginia, and leader in the fight against black lung, claims that gas studies of blood oxygen and carbon dioxide are better ways to detect the disease. He also predicts that the new drilling techniques used in coal mining will produce more cases of black lung and at a much earlier age over the next few years.

Why European Mines Are Safer: Although the U.S. coal industry boasts the American coal miner produces five times as much as a West German and ten times as much as a Russian, U.S. mines are far more unsafe than those in either of those two countries. Over the five years 1965–1969, twice as many miners died in the United States than in all the countries of the European economic community. And the rate was three times as bad as the rates for Britain, Poland, and Czechoslovakia.

Ironically, it is much easier to mine in the United States. Appalachian mines are but a few hundred feet below the surface; the coal can be removed from a seam that runs horizontally, and most of the seams do not dip or pitch much. The seams are from three feet to six feet deep. By contrast most European coal seams are 2,000 to 4,000 feet below the surface of the earth. The seams are often less than three feet thick, and they pitch and dip which makes it doubly difficult to maneuver machinery around. The European mines give off much more gas than do American mines, and miners must be constantly alert in case an electrical spark sets off an explosion. Because of the great depths, roofs are a hazardous problem, with tons of rock and dirt overburden. In one Soviet mine, worked 4,000 feet below the surface, the temperature of the surrounding rocks is over 100 degrees Fahrenheit. Masses of cool air must be pumped down.

European coal is generally mined according to the long-wall system. Under this method, a shaft is sunk down into the earth or tunneled into a hill to get at the coal seam. Then a cutting machine is brought up against the face of the coal seam, and it slices off the coal in a lathelike motion with sharp steel picks. The coal falls onto conveyor belts that run back and forth behind the machine, and the belts carry the coal to passageways at either end of the seam. Above the machine, hydraulic jacks support metal roofing over the work area. As the machine moves forward slicing at the coal, the hydraulic jacks also go forward. In this way a metal roof is constantly over the work area; in effect, providing a steel umbrella. Once the men and machinery have passed over an area, the roof is allowed to collapse into the mined-out areas, or in some instances the mined-out area is filled with debris. In Great Britain 92 percent of all coal is mined by the long-wall method, and it is widely used throughout Europe as well.

But the long-wall method has not caught on in the United States to any great extent. It still is regarded as immensely expensive, and not adaptable to U.S. coal-mining conditions. Still, as the clamor over safety continues, and the demand for coal increases, the U.S. industry has begun to install some long-wall machines. Recently Eastern Gas & Fuel introduced some long-wall techniques. One of Consolidation's mines is long-wall. In all there are 25 long-wall mines in the United States, accounting for some 3 percent of underground coal production.

While the recent interest in long-wall mining coincides with the demands for better mine safety, the introduction of the technique probably has less to do with safety than with a greater interest in recovering more coal. In the commonly employed room and pillar mine, large blocks of coal are left, in effect, as pillars to support the mine as the coal is taken out. Hence as much as 40 percent of the coal remains underground. In the long-wall process, 90 percent of the coal is recovered.

The Europeans employ other techniques to protect miners. Most of the European mines are dangerously full of methane gas. A spark could ignite the gas and cause an explosion. European mine officials are constantly on the watch for methane and, in the Soviet Union and Great Britain, actually have installed methane sensors at the coal face. Once the level of methane reaches 1 percent, all equipment is automatically shut down and stays out of action until fans have sucked the methane out of the mine.

In his excellent report in *Coal Patrol* on European methods, from which much of the above is drawn, Tom Bethel writes, "At the Bazhanov mine in Russia, 41,000-cubic feet of methane is 'outgassed' every hour. When it reaches the surface, the gas is trapped and stored (instead of simply being blown by ventilation fans into the atmosphere, as in American mines), and used as fuel by the power plant that generates the mine's electricity. Thus the gas more than pays for the cost of recovering it. Britain's National Coal Board has sold methane for power plant use since 1957—and the British now install gas removal systems so that they can continue in use after a mine ceases production."

The Europeans also work to keep down coal dust by spraying water on the face and around the haulageways. European mines use explosion barriers to stop fires. They are simply designed platforms hung from ceilings. When an explosion takes place, the wind from the shock waves triggers a release mechanism in the barrier, and water or rock dust is dropped in front of the advancing flames.

The British worked to reduce the incidence of black lung disease, by taking great care to keep down dust. They have reduced the incidence of new black lung cases by 75 percent—

from 8.1 cases per thousand miners in 1955 to 1.9 in 1967. They employ men around the mines to clean up, and, in effect, miners themselves are paid hardship pay for working in mines.

COAL GASOLINE CARTEL

Among the most obvious reasons for the sudden interest in coal by oil companies during the 1960s was their fear that the coal industry might actually make good on its threat to build refineries and turn coal into gasoline. Since the supplies of oil over the long range are small compared to coal resources, such a development might very well be the end of the oil business. The prospect of making coal into gas or gasoline is a real one; and, indeed, constituted such a threat that the major oil and chemical companies actively conspired from the 1930s onward through the creation of a cartel to prevent such an unhappy eventuality. The cartel was created between Jersey Standard and I.G. Farben, the big German chemical company which had discovered a way to make coal into gasoline. The resulting agreements between I.G. and Standard represented a simple agreement not to compete, by recognizing I.G.'s primacy in chemicals, and Standard's primacy in petroleum. In a letter dated July 27, 1936, Frank A. Howard, vice-president of the Standard Oil Development Company, explained the arrangement:

> The I.G. may be said to be our general partner in the chemical business as to developments arising during the period beginning in 1929 and expiring in 1947. The desire and intention of both parties is to avoid competing with one another and by these means to permit their technical organizations to cooperate wholeheartedly to their mutual advantage. This arrangement is set forth very clearly in the Division of Field agreement. It is always dangerous to summarize arrangements which are themselves the briefest possible accurate summary of all the subject matter to which they relate but an understanding of the relationship of the parties involved in this loose general partnership on chemical business is as follows:

1. The assumption is that the I.G. are going to stay out of the oil business proper and we are going to stay out of the chemical business insofar as that has no bearing on the oil business.

2. The implied assumption which is clear to both sides and has been much discussed, that the field of oil specialities, for example pharmaceuticals and insecticides, is one in which the two parties are and necessarily will be competitors, and that there is no help for this and any commitments which they may make with respect thereto would not alter this.

Howard goes on to say,

the general theory of the agreement is that chemical developments which are more closely related to the oil business than to outside chemical business remain in control of Standard with I.G. participating in some manner to be agreed upon at the time with respect to each development, whereas developments which are more nearly akin to the outside chemical industry than to the then existing business of Standard pass to the control of I.G. with suitable participation by Standard.

The following specific question clarifies the situation: "What new chemical development is Standard free to make or acquire without any obligation to bring I.G. into the picture in any way?" The answer to this question is that Standard remains free to enter into any new chemical development it pleases (not originating with I.G.) and without offering any participation to I.G. provided that such development is closely related to the then business of Standard.

What this meant was that I.G. turned over to Standard and to the Shell oil group its world-wide hydrogenation rights except for Germany. Hydrogenation is the process by which coal is changed into petroleum. In the United States they went exclusively to Standard. Through International Hydrogenation Patents Co., Ltd., Standard and Shell gave Imperial Chemical Industries (ICI) the exclusive license for hydrogenation of coal in the British Empire. In return for these patent rights, ICI agreed to limit production, to buy all its oil from Standard and Shell, and to market its products through the two oil companies.

Neither Standard nor Shell had much interest in promoting the use of the hydrogenation process. Standard's policy was set forth as follows:

> IHP should keep in close touch with developments in all countries where it has patents, and should be fully informed with regard to the interest being shown in hydrogenation and the prospect of its introduction. . . . It should not, however, attempt to stir up interest in countries where none exists. If the Management decides that in any country the interest in hydrogenation is serious or that developments in such country are likely to affect IHP's position adversely, then IHP should discuss the matter actively with the interested parties, and attempt to persuade them that its process should be used. . . .
>
> If coal, tar, etc., hydrogenation be feasible from an economic standpoint, or if it is to be promoted for nationalistic reasons or because of some peculiar local conditions, it is better for us as oil companies to have an interest in the development, obtain therefrom such benefits as we can, and assure the distribution of the products in question through our existing marketing facilities.

After obtaining control of the hydrogenation patents, Standard then formed a company, Hydro Patents Co., for the purpose of administering the U.S. rights, and sought to involve other American oil companies in a joint venture, by taking shares in the firm and licenses from it.

Some of these companies evidently took the invitation as a command. Howard said, "Kingsbury (Standard Oil of California) says frankly he thinks the plan rather tough on him since, if used on a very large scale, it will result in very large royalty payments. . . but that, in view of the potentialities of the process, he cannot justify staying out and therefore expects to come in. He says he believes that, if other people speak with equal frankness, they will tell the same story and I think he is exactly right. All of these great companies are going to kick like steers at the prospect of paying any substantial running royalties. . . . My hope is, however, that they will all feel as Kingsbury does, i.e. that they cannot afford to be left out."

In one sense, Standard's hydrogenation licenses became a means for controlling other developments in the oil business. To obtain licenses other companies were required to turn over their own technical developments to Hydro Engineering & Chemical Co., the organization established by Standard to provide engineering advice. Standard deliberately constructed a broad definition of hydrogenation, so broad that it seemed all inclusive. Howard himself declared, "The definition of the term 'hydrogenation process' is not an effort to define the scope of any patents which we own, but rather an effort at defining the field of our present and future inventions, within which field all parties must cross-license one another."

Standard's domination over hydrogenation process was challenged by a new method. Howard urged Standard to get involved right away: "We must try to move our Fischer [originator of new method] negotiations as fast as we can if we expect to have a part in this picture. In my opinion we ought to have a part in it. If we let the foreign governments proceed. . . without any cooperation on our part the outcome will be that we shall wind up in a very large proportion of our markets with the governments actively interested in the oil business in competition with us rather than in cooperation with us."

Eventually Standard, Shell, and I.G. won a main share of the world markets. Howard said in 1938, "The high points of the matter are that Jersey and Shell acquire sufficient effective control of the hydrocarbon synthesis process in the world outside of the United States so that their position as leaders in the entire field of synthetic petroleum production is assured."

While there seems little question but that Standard's agreement with I.G. greatly assisted Standard in policing and strengthening its control over the oil industry, the company stoutly maintained that the hydrogenation process as it applies to coal was uneconomic.

Among the enthusiasts for changing coal into gasoline or gas was George Love. In a September 1962 article, *Fortune* describes Love's interest:

> In 1947, Love contracted with Standard Oil Development, New Jersey, for joint research on the gasification of coal, and for some years thereafter the business world was agog at the revolutionary prospect of coal being burned close to the minehead, producing a gas that could be piped directly as a cheap domestic and industrial fuel or converted into gasoline and chemicals. A $300,000 pilot plant was built, a successful public demonstration of the process staged, and plans were announced for the construction of a $125 million refinery to be in operation by 1951. But Consol never quite managed to get the economics of the process in line with competitive fuels prices, and when the vast new oil fields in the Middle East began opening up in 1950, Love grimly ordered the gasification project shelved. Consol keeps on top of the technology, however, and Love thinks he'll live to see the day when a Consol plant is turning Consol coal into gas for the pipelines in the winter, and into liquid gasoline in the summer.

PRODUCTION PAYMENTS

There were still other more pointed reasons that pulled the oil and coal industries together. Among them was a series of unpublished private rulings by the Internal Revenue Service that made it possible for minerals companies, particularly oil firms top-heavy with accumulated cash, to buy other minerals companies and pay no tax in the process. These rulings, couched in metaphysical tax jargon, involved what was known as an "ABC transaction."

What that means is that an oil company or some other minerals company can buy another minerals producer with money that has never been subject to taxation. In contrast, ordinary business (like ordinary taxpayers) must at some point have paid tax on the income they use to make purchases of other firms or assets.

Here essentially is how an ABC transaction works: The seller of a mineral property ("A"), say a coal operator, requires the purchaser ("B"), say an oil company, to make a small down payment on the property. The seller ("A") then conveys to the purchaser ("B") the "working interest" in the property (in effect, ownership), whereupon the purchaser operates the property as if it were his own. "A" retains a "production payment," which is a right to a specified share of the future income from the property.

"A" then sells his retained production payment to a bank or another financial institution ("C"). "A" then owns the mineral property, subject to an obligation to pay "C" a fixed share of the income for a set period of years. "C," the bank, has an asset which is substantially the same as any other outstanding loan. The whole arrangement is similar to the purchase of a home subject to a mortgage—except that a home owner must pay tax on the income he uses to pay off his mortagage, whereas the purchaser of a mineral property in an ABC transaction uses tax-free money to satisfy his obligations to the bank.

These rulings by the IRS were a virtual invitation to monopoly, and the process was employed to accomplish two of three major takeovers in the coal business.

Technicians within the IRS felt compelled to issue these private rulings for different reasons. For one thing, they persuaded themselves that such treatment was fair because of prior rulings made in the oil industry. In reaching this decision they were egged on by skillful attorneys for the minerals companies, among them John Nolan of Miller & Chevalier, who during the 1964–1965 period was a chief advocate of the then proposed merger between Continental Oil and Consolidation Coal. The IRS eventually concluded in favor of extending the ABC treatment to the Continental-Consolidation deal, and despite vigorous opposition at high levels of the Treasury Department, the private rulings were issued. That opened the sluice gate for oil companies grabbing coal companies.

(The story has an ironic twist. Nolan left private practice from 1969 to 1972 to become the deputy assistant secretary for tax policy in the Treasury Department. During his tenure at Treasury he was instrumental in persuading the Congress to reverse the private rulings he had a few years before so skillfully helped engineer. Nolan was meant to become commissioner of the Internal Revenue Service, but his tough views on tax policy ran afoul of Peter Flanigan in the White House. Flanigan wanted to pursue more relaxed industrial tax policies. Nolan thereupon left the government.)

THE MERGERS

These conditions—taxes, hidden government subsidies, history of cartelization—separately, or in conjunction with one another, were factors that influenced the move by large mining and petroleum companies into the coal business. The effect of these industrial realignments was to create a new energy industry in which large minerals companies owned oil, gas, coal, and uranium, and indeed, were in a position to supply the economy with its total energy requirements.

The major mergers or acquisitions of coal lands began in the early 1960s. Looking back on these developments from the vantage point of 1971, Carl Herrington, an official of Standard Oil Co. of New Jersey, described for Congress how his company became involved in coal: "Our studies of the nation's energy requirements indicated that utilization of all of the nation's energy resources would be needed to meet increasing demands. We concluded that coal mining and the marketing of coal as a utility fuel offered an attractive long-term investment opportunity which draws upon Humble's [the Jersey Standard subsidiary] experience in exploring for minerals and its established management and technical resources. Humble recognized concurrently that coal at some future date could become a suitable raw material to supplement crude oil and natural gas as an economically attractive source of hydrocarbons."

Jersey made its own investigation of coal lands, determined that two-thirds of the reserves were under control by other companies, and determined it could amass enough commercial reserves in Illinois and the Rocky Mountain states for a commercial operation. In 1964, a mining consulting firm confirmed Jersey's decision, and in the fall of 1965, Jersey Standard quietly began to buy coal lands in Illinois as well as in North Dakota, Montana, Wyoming, and Colorado. The company ran its coal operations through a company called Monterey Coal Co., owned by Carter Oil, in turn a Jersey subsidiary.

In October of 1965, Continental Oil Co., then the twelfth largest U.S. oil company, announced an agreement in principle to purchase Consolidation Coal Co., the nation's largest coal producer. Consolidation dominated the eastern markets, and had recently acquired substantial reserves in the west as well. Moreover, Consolidation was actively involved in research, sponsored by the federal government, which held out promise for turning coal into gasoline.

In announcing the merger, Continental's president, L. F. Mc-Cullum, explained why the two companies were coming together: "We have made intensive studies of trends and potentialities of the coal industry, and of the properties and coal reserves and businesses of Consolidation. As a result we are convinced that the coal industry has attractive long-term prospects, particularly in supplying increasing requirements for generation of electric power. Acquisition of Consolidation Coal reserves will strengthen the basic energy raw material position of the company."

One of the men who negotiated the merger was C. Howard Hardesty, Jr., then an executive vice-president of Consolidation Coal, and now senior vice-president of the Continental company. For the benefit of a congressional committee, he reviewed the reasons for the merger:

> Continental acquired the Consolidation Coal Co., I think for a whole series of reasons. The most important of which I think would be the fact that it recognized at the time that the supplying of energy to this nation just would not turn around

solely on oil or gas, but would certainly rely to an ever-increasing degree on coal and coal conversion to synthetic gas and liquids.

I think it also looked upon it that coal will have an important role in the future of this nation and that as such, it was a wise investment for our shareholders.

I think it accepts the fact it has been proved a fact and proven since that time, there is a synergism between the talents that are necessary to work in both industries. There is a flow back and forth that has been beneficial to both, whether it be from environmental or safety or all of the things that we can do as a company. And these briefly, Mr. Chairman, would be the reasons why we took this step.

Before the merger was finalized, the antitrust department of the Justice Department looked into the possible anticompetitive effects of the merger. As Donald Turner, then chief of the antitrust division, remembers it, they could find no fault with the proposed consolidation:

> Only insignificant amounts of Continental's gasoline are sold in Consolidation's market areas. Although natural gas and residual fuel oil—which Continental produces—may sometimes compete with coal, Continental sold these products for use only in areas of the country in which Consolidation does not operate and Consolidation did not sell in areas in which Continental's product was sold.
>
> Moreover Consolidation and Continental are not significant potential competitors. Heavy residual fuel oil requires water transportation, if it is to be shipped far from where it is produced. It is thus unlikely that Continental could expand its residual fuel oil sales into Consolidation's markets. Similarly transportation costs made it unlikely that Continental's natural gas would be sold in Consolidation's markets or that Consolidation's coal would be sold in Continental's markets.
>
> We were, of course, fully aware that Consolidation was trying to develop a process for making gasoline out of coal. Even if it develops such a process, however, it is unlikely that it would have competed significantly with Continental. Consolidation operates primarily in Pennsylvania, West Virginia,

and Kentucky, and presumably would sell gasoline in that area. Continental's sales in that area account for only eight-tenths of one percent of its total domestic gasoline sales. There is no indication that either company intends to expand its marketing territory significantly. Moreover, if Consolidation succeeds in converting coal to gasoline, it should be anticipated that other companies can do the same and are potential competitors in the gasoline market to the same extent as is Consolidation. In our judgment, therefore, the removal of one of them as a potential competitor was unlikely to affect significantly the behavior of companies that now sell gasoline or have any significant adverse long-run effect on competition.

One junior member of the antitrust division staff objected to the merger, but, according to Turner, all the others agreed there was no reason to object. Turner said he received no evidence of interest by the White House. Turner, however, did receive a letter from Richard Solomon, then chief counsel at the Federal Power Commission, urging the department to intervene. Turner subsequently met with Solomon, but remained unconvinced. In addition, questions were raised by Treasury Department officials with the Federal Trade Commission, but resulted in no action.

(Actually there is some question as to whether Turner's factual understanding might not have been amplified. In a study, *Coal: The Captive Giant,* Laurence D. Beck and Stuart L. Rawlings maintain that Continental Oil sells 18 percent of its gas and oil east of the Mississippi in Consolidation's markets. Included in this figure is 80 percent of the company's total heating oil sales in the states of New Jersey, Rhode Island, Connecticut, Massachusetts, and Pennsylvania. Consolidation has sales offices in the Midwest and mountain states. In addition, before the merger took place Consolidation obtained substantial coal reserves in the mountain states with an eye to developing coal mines which could feed mine mouth power stations.)

At any rate, the antitrust arguments may have diverted attention away from a central issue of the case. That was the Internal Revenue Service's ruling on the ABC production payment. Under that "private" ruling, then in existence, Continental purchased Consolidation, making a down payment of approximately $63,875,000 to Consolidation and agreed to satisfy a retained production payment of $460 million. In addition, the company agreed to pay another $235 million to cover interest costs. Then Consolidation sold the "production payment" worth $460 million plus the $235 million interest through a "straw." (Because of restrictive New York state banking laws, these transactions often run through companies other than banks, thereby keeping the bank's name out of the deal. In this instance, William Coal Corp., controlled by Lehman Brothers, bought the production payment after borrowing funds from a group of institutional lenders headed by the First National City Bank of New York.) At that point Consolidation Coal Co. was liquidated, and distributed its assets to the stockholders. A new Consolidation Coal Co. was created as a subsidiary of Continental Oil Co.

The same sort of maneuver was employed shortly thereafter by Kennecott Copper in its purchase of Peabody Coal Co., the second largest coal producer. The merger, however, is still contested within the Federal Trade Commission on grounds of its anticompetitive effects. Looking back on it, the IRS ruling and to a lesser extent the antitrust section approval, provided the green light for the surge in fuels mergers that subsequently took place. Other major mergers occurred during the latter half of the 1960s. Among the more prominent: Occidental Petroleum purchased Island Creek Coal Co. in January 1968, and then Maust Properties in August 1969. Standard Oil of Ohio bought Old Ben Coal and Enos Coal in August 1968. By 1970, it was argued, the oil industry controlled the coal industry, with two of the three largest producers owned outright by oil companies, and the largest single block of reserves in the hands of Jersey Standard.

ROCKY MOUNTAIN COAL FEVER

Because of the great demand for coal by electric utilities, and the pressure placed on them by conservationists to meet air pollution standards, there has been an increasing interest both by electric utilities and the large oil companies that now dominate coal in developing the country's largest coal reserves, which are located in the western mountains. There, where the population is relatively scarce and where there are vast tracts of stripping coal to be had for pennies an acre, the idea has been to construct an immense dynamo which with equal ease can throw electricity across the Rockies to California or back east across the Great Plains to Chicago. Variations of this general plan have been discussed from time to time in government; the planning is going ahead more intently and utility plants are actually under construction or in operation. The Four Corners power plant in New Mexico, a major source of pollution, is the most prominent of literally hundreds of similar electric utility operations. More than a dozen new electric utility plants are planned for the state of Utah. The Interior Department is discussing a $700 million plan to build aqueducts that can carry water to 42 different mine mouth power plants in Montana, Wyoming, and North Dakota. At the same time there is growing interest in building gasification plants, changing coal into natural gas, and in that way ending the pollution issue by creating a relatively pollution-free fuel.

Much of the coal is in the public domain, administered through the Interior Department by the U.S. Geological Survey. Because of the imminent development there is rampant speculation in land. A great deal of it by oil companies.

The leasing system used by the Interior Department has been an open invitation to speculation. Under the Mineral Leasing Act of 1920, anyone may prospect for coal on federal lands in blocks up to 5,000 acres for a total of 46,000 acres in any one state. The prospector must apply to the Interior Department, then pay $10 for each 5,000-acre block as well as 25 cents an acre rent each year for five years. In the sixth year, the rent goes up to $1 an acre. If a prospector actually mines the land, the government gets a royalty of 17 cents a ton for the coal.

According to Congressman William Kastenmeier of Wisconsin, who has made a study of this matter, there has been a great press for leases, and in 1970 the number of leases granted by Interior doubled. In all, the government has leased out 767,902 acres of public lands in the western states for coal mining. Oil companies control about 24 percent of the leases outright, and may actually control more land through other companies. There are 520 leases outstanding, but only 73 of them are producing any coal. Ninety percent of all coal leases are unproductive.

In fact, at a time when demand for coal is outstripping supply and coal prices are at their highest level in years, the coal production on public lands is declining. It decreased from a peak of 10 million tons in 1945 when 75,000 acres were under lease to 7.5 million tons in 1969 when 725,000 acres were leased out.

The center for much of this activity lies in a swath of land running from southeastern Wyoming through eastern Montana to western North Dakota. The Interior Department estimates the coal resources of this area at one trillion tons, about 5 percent of which is recoverable by strip mine methods. These beds account for more than one-third of all remaining coal resources in the United States, and they are in demand because so much of the coal can be stripped.

In 1971, two companies had tied up large amounts of the coal. Peabody Coal Co., a subsidiary of Kennecott Copper and second largest coal company in the country, has three billion tons of coal reserves in Montana and Wyoming. Reynolds Metal Co. is drilling on 40,000 acres at Lake DeSmet, Wyoming, and its reserves are in excess of two billion tons. Another major factor in coal is the Union Pacific Railroad, which owns every other section of land in a strip 40 miles wide, across the state of Wyoming.

Water is crucial to coal operations. It requires about 20 acre feet of water per megawatt to run a mine mouth power plant. Two big public water projects along the Bighorn River can now provide water for coal operations in the North Dakota–Wyoming–Montana area. They are the Yellowtail Dam on the upper

Bighorn in Montana and the Boysen Reservoir downstream in Wyoming. Much of the water is contracted for by oil and mining companies. The Bureau of Reclamation establishes the number of acre feet of water for industrial use, then contracts for it over a 40- to 50-year period at the inexpensive rate of $9 to $11 an acre foot. The price is cheap, considering that newly developed water would run up to $125 an acre foot. Of the two reservoirs, the Yellowtail Dam is the larger with 640,000 acre feet allocated for industrial use. As of August 1, 1971 the Bureau of Reclamation had contracted for 80 percent of that water. In Montana most of the water went to three oil companies, Kerr-McGee, Shell, and Jersey Standard. In Wyoming it went to mining companies, including Reynolds, Peabody Coal, Westmoreland Coal, and to oil companies including Shell. In the Boysen Reservoir, where 135,000 acre feet are up for contact, Sun Oil has taken 35,000 feet. Other contracts were pending at this writing, in spring, 1972.

The allocation of most existing water at cheap rates to a handful of corporations could very well determine the outcome of the energy game.

Whether or not the oil industry is involved in some concerted strategy to control markets, it is interesting to note that while the demand for coal has greatly increased, actual production of coal in the last three years has remained relatively stable and actually decreased in 1968. (Production, 1967, 552,626 million (m) tons; 1968, 545,255 m tons; 1969, 554,051 m tons.) At the same time, Kastenmeier found that the Interior Department was handing out more coal leases than ever before, but that production on those leases was declining, not increasing.

URANIUM

While nuclear power accounts for less than 1 percent of all electric power, the Atomic Energy Commission tirelessly predicts that the industry will soon rapidly expand and by the end of the century provide 50 percent of all electricity.

Oil companies control 45 percent of all uranium resources in the nation. Eighteen of the top 25 oil companies are involved in uranium, either through actual production or in research. One firm, Kerr-McGee, provides 27 percent of all uranium; two companies, Kerr-McGee and Allied Chemical, have monopolized another crucial stage of the business, changing the processed ore into a gaseous state. It is necessary to change the uranium into a gas so that it can be put through the AEC's gaseous diffusion plants where it is enriched for use in nuclear reactors.

There are various steps in processing raw uranium into an enriched fuel that can be made suitable for use in a nuclear power plant, and the tendency has been for the oil companies to become involved in mining and milling, then to gradually expand their functions in a vertical manner through manufacture of the large nuclear power plants themselves. Gulf and Jersey Standard both have announced their intentions of entering the manufacturing and fabricating end. Thus, they will be in direct competition with four electrical heavy-equipment manufacturers, General Electric, Westinghouse, Combustion Engineering, and Babcock-Wilcox, who are also entering the mining, milling, and processing stages of the business.

Control over the manufacture of the power system can be a crucial aspect of the nuclear business for several reasons. The manufacturer of the system also often designs and provides the finished fuel core. This is not only a big piece of business, but also, more important, ties the manufacturer to the utility over a long period of time during which the core must be serviced and eventually renewed, thereby establishing a profitable association between manufacturer and electric utility. It is also possible that the utility will not own the core outright but lease it from the manufacturer. Utilities are generally regulated and required to disclose business dealings, at least to some extent. But one area of operations which is seldom disclosed is the price paid to a manufacturer for a power plant. Often there is no competitive bidding. Thus, it becomes a prime area for price increases. Manufacturers reportedly make more money when they build a nuclear power plant than if they build a fossil-fuel power plant. Thus, it would seem to be in their interest to push nuclear power.

The United States does not have a monopoly on uranium ore. Canada and South Africa both have large reserves. So do the former French colonies of Africa. And the Soviet Union and China are believed to have substantial supplies of ore. But of the "free world nations" the United States alone has had the ability to enrich uranium. Rather than sell or license this technology to other countries, the AEC in the past rented its gaseous diffusion service to foreign nations, taking in raw ore, and handing back enriched fuel for a toll cost. At the same time, the United States through the Export-Import Bank loaned large amounts of money to friendly nations so that they might build nuclear power plants utilizing enriched uranium. (The Export-Import Bank reportedly has $2 billion available for such loans.) This process, of course, was meant to tie development of nuclear power abroad to U.S. technology, providing a market for the four heavy-equipment manufacturers, and producing business for the AEC's gaseous diffusion plants, which with the decline in manufacture of bombs run the danger of turning into expensive, obsolete ornaments.

In the early 1970s, President Nixon sought to remove the federal government from the nuclear business by selling the gaseous diffusion plants to private industry. But this move was blocked by the Joint Committee on Atomic Energy. Reportedly there was little serious industrial interest in buying the expensive plants. One explanation for the lack of interest was the development abroad of different nuclear power technologies, which appeared to be more efficient. In particular, there was considerable interest in the European plans for a centrifuge system.

In 1972, the United States managed to stave off the threat of this competition at least temporarily in Japan by forming joint ventures with the Japanese by which they would enrich uranium in the United States in conjunction with the U.S. government.

That succeeded at least for the near future in tying Japan, which expects to use large amounts of nuclear power, to the United States.

Within the United States nuclear power has not grown as fast as the AEC or the FPC had predicted. In part that is due to conservationists' attacks and suits, which held up construction of some plants, thereby adding to their costs. In addition, the AEC apparently is faced with serious scientific questions concerning catastrophic accidents should the radioactive core of a power plant melt and break out of the protective covering. Such an accident would result in deaths for several miles. These safety obstacles postpone plant development even longer, adding more to their cost, and suggest that new plants may be required to operate at lower rates of production, which would increase costs even further.

From the industry's point of view the most serious questions concerning the future of nuclear power were raised by Philip Sporn, former chairman of American Electric Power Co., in a 1969 report to the Joint Committee on Atomic Energy. Sporn is an acknowledged and respected authority on electric power. In his study, Sporn argued that nuclear power was losing the fight against coal. While the cost of coal was rising, the cost of building nuclear power plants had risen even more steeply. Nuclear plants, scheduled to come in at 3.5 mills per kilowatt-hour of electricity, actually would end up costing nearly double that amount. Sporn pointed out that because of the dismal economics involved, one of the two projected nuclear power plants had been canceled; others were delayed. Still other utilities had set aside plans for building nuclear power stations and were pushing coal fired plants instead. "It is obvious that we have a slowdown in the ordering of atomic generating capacity," Sporn worte. "As against a peak of 25,780 Mw (megawatts) placed on order in the three years 1966–1969, orders declined in 1968 to 16,044 Mw and in 1969 to 7,190 Mw."

The Sporn report presented the most serious economic questions to the atomic energy establishment, that loose coalition of the AEC, Joint Committee on Atomic Energy, utilities, and the American Public Power Association. Comments were solicited, and together with the report they were published by the committee in December 1971.

In December 1970 Sporn brought his original report up to date. He pointed out that the trends originally noted had accelerated, not decreased. He had originally predicted cost of nuclear power at seven mills per kilowatt-hour, but one year later, in 1970, the cost had risen above eight mills.

In his initial report Sporn's overall conclusion was that nuclear power would be seriously set back, and that instead, utilities might well find themselves turning to oil. He speculated on the amounts of oil coming from the north, from Alaska and Canada.

Despite Sporn's work, and the atomic energy establishment's inability to deal with the criticisms he raised, the government goes along cheerfully predicting rapid development of nuclear power.

In one sense these predictions merely reflect the difficult bind which the nuclear power establishment finds itself locked into. On the one hand, Europeans are challenging the nuclear technology built up in the United States, thereby threatening billions of dollars of investments. On the other hand, utilities finding themselves blocked by environmentalists are turning, as Sporn predicted, to oil. They will probably use increasing amounts of LNG and synthetic gas.

The government's major response to criticism of the nuclear power program has been, as in the past, to threaten private power with public nuclear power programs. Thus, the AEC has announced it will finance a joint venture between the TVA and Commonwealth Edison for a prototype breeder reactor.

Viewed from the standpoint of the oil industry, the delays in nuclear power carry a certain ambivalence. The oil companies own most of the uranium, so that when it is used, however it is used, they will stand to make money. On the other hand, the longer nuclear power remains off the market, the keener the demand, and the higher the price to be fetched by the other fossil or synthetic fuels which they control.

THE GAS GAME

For the better part of the century, the oil industry controlled development of synthetic gas or gasoline from coal. In the 1930s the development of a coal gasoline was forestalled in the United States through a formal cartel entered into initially by Jersey Standard and I.G. Farben. An apparently serious effort by Consolidation Coal to build a coal-gas-gasoline refinery in the early 1950s was halted because of the big oil finds abroad. But as the oil supply picture changed, with Organization of Petroleum Exporting Countries demanding more of the take, leases gradually expiring, growing nationalistic tendencies in the oil world, and the demand for petroleum increasing, there was renewed interest in turning coal into gas or gasoline. In his testimony before Congress, Howard Hardesty, senior vice-president of Continental Oil Co., acknowledged that the potential development of gasoline from coal was one of the factors that had excited Continental in its merger with Consolidation Coal.

Since 1970, there has been a quickened interest in coal gas, in part because of the oil industry's alarms over the energy crisis, but also because for the first time the government and the utilities which consume the gas agreed to pay the much higher prices that will permit oil firms to market synthetic gas. In short, synthetic gas is now "economically feasible."

For nearly 20 years the oil companies argued that the policies pursued by the Federal Power Commission were wrongheaded, that restrictions placed on prices of natural gas were onerous and would surely create a shortage of gas. They now say, in effect, the predicted shortage is at hand, that even with much higher prices, there won't be enough natural gas, and that the solution, or at least partial solution, lies in alleviating the natural gas shortage by mixing in coal or other synthetic gas. In many quarters, including most sections of the federal government and Congress, the industry warnings and claims seem to have been justified, and the oil companies appear vindicated.

But there remain unresolved questions as to what extent the industry itself may have promoted the gas shortage. The industry, not the government, maintains statistics on gas reserves, and these are held in private, the details routinely denied to the government agencies which must regulate the price and use of the fuel. The central problem is that there is no independent source of information on which to base an opinion one way or another.

The actual use of natural gas has grown greatly, in particular during the last five years or so because of the pressure for cleaner fuels. Gas now accounts for about one-third of all energy sources. Sixteen percent of all gas is used to create electricity. While there is a great growth in gas for residential home heating, residential uses of gas are not large in terms of the entire market. Most of the gas is used for industrial purposes, and the largest users are the chemical and oil industries.

The real supply of natural gas is unknown, buried beneath the ground. The figures on amounts of supply, or reserves, as they are called, are guesses of one sort or another. As geological techniques are perfected, these guesses become more accurate, and they take into account the production history, knowledge of geological formations, and exploratory well drilling.

The estimates of natural gas reserves are divided into categories. The most common is called "estimated proved recoverable reserves," the quantity of gas that can be expected to be produced with reasonable certainty from known reservoirs. These reserves are generally committed to the market, and thus evidence is bound to be better since money has been invested to transport the gas through pipelines to customers. In addition to the proved reserves, there are categories of "potential reserves." This category is broken down into three subclassifications: "probable," usually extensions to existing gas fields; "possible," supplies associated with similar geologic formations; and "speculative," supplies associated with yet undiscovered fields in areas that have no production history.

The situation is further complicated because the actual known quantity of a reserve may be misleading. In addition to the gas being present, it is essential that there is enough pressure to force the gas out into the pipelines. Without the pressure, it's hard to make the reservoirs produce.

Although gas has been found in various parts of the country, the principal fields on which the gas business depends have been in the southwestern part of the country. There are five of these. The Permian Basin area, including west central Texas and southwestern New Mexico, is the primary supply for the southwestern states, southern California, Arizona, and New Mexico. In recent years the Permian Basin became a secondary source for the middle western markets. The Hugoton-Anadarko area, including northern Texas, the Oklahoma panhandle, and the state of Kansas, is an old producing region, and gas from this area goes to the central and middle western parts of the country. The Texas Gulf coast, until the early 1960s, was the major source of supply to the East Coast. Then South Louisiana and offshore Gulf coast came into production and began to send gas to the East Coast.

The northwestern part of the country is largely dependent on Canadian gas, and some of that Canadian gas also goes to the upper Midwest.

There are other producing regions, but none of them so important as the five mentioned above. There are gas fields in the lower peninsula of Michigan, the Appalachian area, and in Utah, Colorado, Nebraska, Wyoming, and California.

In part the oil industry's argument over a gas shortage is suspect simply because the oil men have been claiming there was a gas shortage since the 1950s. In fact, there has never been one. Their claims of shortage coincided with each decision by the courts or the Federal Power Commission limiting their prices. In testimony before Congress Charles Wheatley, Jr., of the American Public Gas Association, outlined the history of this cat-and-mouse game, and the following historical sketch relies on much of his testimony:

In 1954 the Supreme Court held in the Phillips Petroleum case that producers of natural gas should be allowed to charge no more than a "fair and reasonable" price for gas, and that the Federal Power Commission should oversee their producing activities. The producers thereupon introduced legislation in Congress that would once more make them exempt. The producers argued that if the price of gas were not controlled then shortages would occur. A. P. King, Jr., representing the Texas Independent Producers Royalty Owners Association, declared in 1955, "The supply of natural gas available in years past—at least in large part—was priced artificially low at the well and will rapidly fall short of growing demand unless allowed to reach normal competitive levels." And the Independent Petroleum Association of America sent along a resolution, introduced into the hearings, which said, "the consuming public has benefited from competitive exploration and development of this great natural resource. On the contrary, Federal regulation of natural gas will inevitably result in diminishing supplies and higher cost of this essential and desirable fuel."

Wheatley pointed out, "In 1955 the reserve figures for 1954 were put out by the AGA Reserve Committee. Even the venerable industry publication, the *Oil and Gas Journal,* was shocked when the AGA data showed a decline of 10.8 trillion cubic feet in addition to reserves despite what producers had considered a remarkably successful year. The journal editorialized that the 'joint reserve committee muffed a big chance to serve the industry by failing to explain its puzzling reserve figures.' It was perhaps a coincidence that these 'puzzling reserve figures' were released in the same year the big push was on in the Congress to obtain exemption from regulation."

President Eisenhower vetoed this bill on the grounds there had been undue lobbying by producers. But throughout the 1950s, and into the early 1960s, producers fought regulations, and the FPC in general sided with them, refusing to implement the Supreme Court's order in the Phillips case. Finally during the early 1960s, under the chairmanship of Joseph Swidler, the commission set about establishing a scheme for controlling producer prices.

The industry always had been anxious to avoid disclosing actual costs in finding gas, and finally the commission allowed that preserve to remain, and established instead area-wide prices for gas. The rate-making cases came out of the commission and were challenged in the Supreme Court. The current gas shortage claims of the producers coincide with the Supreme Court's decision in 1968 affirming the Federal Power Commission's 1965 decision in the Permian Basin Rate case and in the first Southern Louisiana Area Rate case. These cases set prices in the major gas-producing sections of the country, and the producers were vigorously opposed to them, claiming that reserves were declining in terms of production. In its Permian Basin decision, the Supreme Court said, "Nor can we hold that the Commission has underestimated the deficiencies of current programs of exploration. The producers' argument has been uniformly premised upon the assertion that the ratio of proved recoverable reserves to current production is an accurate index of the industry's financial requirements. The producers urge that this ratio has dangerously declined, and conclude that any reduction of prevailing field prices will jeopardize essential programs of exploration. There is, however, substantial evidence that additions to reserves have not been unsatisfactorily low, and that recent variations in the ratio of reserves to production are of quite limited significance. Nothing in the record establishes as proper or even minimal any particular ratio."

After this decision, producers and pipelines filed motions to rehear the case, some of them warning of impending shortages of gas unless producers received higher prices than the commission had granted them.

Wheatley says, "At this time, i.e. late 1968 and early 1969 after the Permian and first Southern Louisiana cases, it was clear there was no shortage of available gas reserves to interstate pipelines. Mr. H. D. Borger, chairman of the board of the vast Consolidated Natural Gas System having distribution, transmission, and production operations, and chairman of the United Distribution Companies group, testified he did not believe there was a shortage of available gas for purchase prior to the fall of 1968.

"The industry reserve committee of the American Gas Association subsequently in May 1969 reported for the first time that production exceeded additions to reserves in 1968 and issued a similar report in May 1970 for calendar year 1969."

Because of the producers' requests for a closer look at the federal offshore leases in southern Louisiana, the commission ordered its staff to make an inquiry. The order said, "In order that the issues involved herein may be properly determined, offshore leasees are hereby directed pursuant to the provisions of Section 8, 10, and 14 of the Natural Gas Act to grant authorized members of the staff of the Federal Power Commission during regular business hours, free access to their property and access to and the right to inspect and examine all of their accounts, records, and memoranda including, but not limited to, the books, papers, correspondence, contracts, agreements, maps, reports of engineers, logs, and other data pertinent to the investigation herein authorized, and upon staff request shall furnish copies of such material to the staff." Thereupon the staff of the commission set about preparing a series of questionnaires which might produce the information that could be used to iron out the differences of opinion. One of the most important questions was, "What is the extent of the existing reserves and of potential reserves in the federal domain available to provide natural gas to meet the demands of the jurisdictional interstate market," and it said, "Staff proposes to secure itself or have other participants in the case prepare necessary costs and gas reserves information. Our draft questionnaires would impose on the respondents thereto . . . the responsibility for reporting the required data."

But by August 1969 it was apparent the producers would not voluntarily produce the cost and reserve data by leases. A spokesman said, "Staff counsel had accurately stated that producers are unalterably opposed to that proposal." The staff pointed out, "The allegations of gas supply shortage ought to be and are being taken seriously. But the key to supply remains the amount of reserves found for a given amount of effort. Furthermore, assuming that gas supply is price responsive (otherwise increased rates are meaningless), the costs of production must be known if the commission is to judge the necessary price to elicit needed gas supplies. Thus, the refusal of respondents to supply meaningful gas reserve information itself prevents granting the relief they seek." On December 15, 1969, the commission denied the staff request to send out its questionnaires. By this time some people were beginning to think the gas crisis was phony. Bruce Netschert, an independent economist employed by electric utilities, made a study which showed that there were some 500 gas wells shut in offshore Louisiana, containing enough gas to supply one-quarter of the entire home heating market. Netschert also found out that because the Interior Department does not carefully administer the leases, oil companies find it easy to reduce production on leases. More to the point, the FPC's staff began to rebel. On February 12, 1970, Haskell Wald, the chief economist, sent a memo to John Nassikas, chairman of the commission, pointing out they had compared two sets of industry data on gas reserves, the American Gas Association estimates and the statistics reported to the commission each year by the gas pipeline companies. "This comparison revealed some surprisingly large differences between the two sets of estimates."

The next day Nassikas got another note from Edward McManus, chief of the commission's producer division, which began, "It is believed the reliability of gas reserve estimates for any specific reservoir or field initially is suspect." McManus went on to say that while "certainly initial reserve estimates are not necessarily reliable for concluding a gas supply shortage exists, but that a statistical series such as the AGA reserves studies consistently compiled over a period of years and revised as additional information is obtained, is reliable as a signal or trend to alert the commission and the industry of a gas supply problem.

On February 19, Wald wrote Gordon Gooch, the commission's chief counsel, again voicing his concern about the reliability of the AGA statistics, and setting forth questions that could be asked the gas association. But Gooch wouldn't take the advice of the Office of Economics, and instead of building questions for testimony, he wanted to set up a private meeting between the economists and the gas men, to try to iron out the discrepancies. Wald stiffly rebuked Gooch, "I am not at all convinced that the meeting's broadened purpose is entirely consonant with the staff's role as an adversary party to the proceedings. In effect, we will be holding a 'moot court.' Not only will the AGA witness be clued in on various problem areas which he should be prepared to discuss in his testimony, but he may also gather suggestions on how he should shape his reponses on cross-examination. No other witness will be given this advantage of trying out his answers on the staff and using the experience, if he wishes, to sharpen his defenses in advance of the hearing. Is it proper for the FPC staff to engage in an activity which may help an outside witness build his case? Will the fact that it will be done behind-the-scenes create an impression of collusion? Isn't there some advantage in eliciting spontaneous responses during cross-examination instead of well-rehearsed ones? After all, our interest is in full and accurate disclosure, which may not be Mr. Jacobs' primary motivation, since he may wish to build the best possible defense of the AGA statistics."

In the midst of the wrangling within the commission between the staff and the commissioner's office over the accuracy of the gas reserve statistics, Senator Phillip Hart, chairman of the Senate antitrust subcommittee, discovered the dispute, and wrote Nassikas about it. In September 1970 Nassikas replied that the industry-supplied reserve statistics "closely parallel trends and projections based on national statistics." He said, "The staff has also made specialized reports and conducted investigations into the gas supply problem as a matter of our continuing regulatory responsibility apart from formal evidence in rate proceedings." But he never said what the staff position was, instead leaving the impression the staff agreed with him, which was the opposite case.

On November 13 Nassikas got another memo from Wald informing him that the FPC gas reserve statistics and those provided by the industry through the gas association differed by 42 percent in one instance. A week after that Nassikas told Metcalf the industry figures were "reasonably reliable."

In preparation of the final opinion, the commission refused to insert footnotes to statements on reserves by the Office of Economics. And in July 1971 the FPC found: "We thus find a critical shortage of gas in the United States." The commission, thereupon, allowed a series of rate increases which increased the price of gas by as much as 50 percent. For real or imagined reasons the commission took the position that there is indeed a gas shortage, and that the most sensible way to rectify this situation is to offer to producers incentives in the form of higher prices to search more diligently for gas. Consequently, in 1971 the commission approved price increases for natural gas at the wellhead by 54 percent.

But according to both the commission and the industry there is no certainty that these price increases will produce enough gas to meet the demands of the country by 1980, let alone 1990. Hence, major producers, with commission agreement, propose to supplement the supplies of natural gas in gradually increasing amounts with a synthetic gas or liquified natural gas. Over the short term this synthetic gas will come from naphtha and it will be supplemented by LNG, imported from Africa and Latin America. Over the long term, the oil companies propose to devote a substantial portion of their coal holdings to manufacture of synthetic gas.

There is nothing new in the process of making gas from coal

or naphtha. The British manufactured synthetic gas from naphtha generally, and it was not until fairly recently when natural gas was discovered in the North Sea that synthetic gas declined in use there. In the United States, before World War II, gas was made from coal. Natural gas, generally discovered in association with oil, was flared at the well, or burned off. After the war, the government turned over large pipelines, originally used to bring oil from the Gulf coast to the eastern seaboard, from oil to natural gas pipeline companies. From World War II onward, neither the big pipeline companies nor the petroleum companies, which produce the gas, showed much interest in synthetic gas.

Indeed they showed little interest in synthetic gas until the Federal Power Commission approved general price rises for natural gas. Those price increases made it possible to sell synthetic gas or imported LNG at even higher prices. The synthetic gas is used by utilities and other industry as so-called peaking or shaving gas, in effect a sort of backstop at times when there is a great demand. The expensive gas is blended into the pipeline with the cheaper gas, and the cost increases passed along to the consumers are not so staggering that they revolt. At any rate, certain customers rely so extensively on gas that they are locked in to the market and would find it more costly to shift from gas than pay the price. Residential customers, for instance, probably would rather pay higher prices than go to the trouble and expense of installing a new type of furnace. Automobile manufacturers, which use gas in paint-spraying operations, have no choice. They can either pay the increased prices or change technology. That is why the natural gas market is so appealing. It offers, over the long term, a market of individuals and corporations which will pay very high prices for the fuel.

With the basic gas prices raised, the oil companies and the pipelines are in the process of building up this high-priced market, and it is to this market that they hope to commit larger and larger quantities of coal. Jersey Standard predicts that total coal devoted to gasification will amount to 100 million tons by

1980. That is almost one-fifth of the total market in 1970, and will be about one-tenth of all coal produced at that time.

When the prices rose, the companies began to announce their plans for synthetic gas and liquified natural gas imports. El Paso Natural Gas Co., for example, announced completion of a deal with the Algerian government which would permit importation of 1 billion cubic feet of liquified natural gas a day to the East Coast United States.

The LNG trade from Africa to the East Coast is not exceptional, but is part of a trend developed by the international oil companies. Since 1967 Phillips Petroleum has been shipping Alaskan gas to Japan, and there has been movement of African gas to England and southern Europe since the mid-1960s. It is expected that there will be efforts to sell gas to the United States by the Soviets, Venezuelans, Nigerians, and others. Ironically the trade with international gas-exporting countries will provide a substantial supply of gas, and it will precipitate demand by the U.S. international oil companies, increasingly protectionist, for development of coal gas on the grounds that we are too dependent on unstable governments.

The El Paso deal was a bellwether; for once it was disclosed, El Paso announced plans for development of a commercial coal gasification plant near coal lands it owns jointly with Continental in Oklahoma. The El Paso LNG deal, with its high prices, made it now commercially feasible for the oil companies to do what they had hitherto refused to do, develop their coal gasification.

But LNG is expensive, and over the near term it is more likely that the most popular synthetic gas will be made from naphtha under a process long used by the British. In response to a run on naphtha, U.S. oil companies moved the price up. Thus, across the board the price for gas and substitute gas was pushed ahead.

A CORNER IN ENERGY?

By 1970 it was made plain that the oil and gas and coal companies had reorganized themselves into what was called an "energy industry," and were off on a new tack. Not only had the coal industry become more concentrated with ten firms controlling more than two-thirds of all production, but also nearly two-thirds of the top fifty companies were owned by companies in other industries.

Seven of the leading 15 coal producers were oil companies, including 5 of the largest. In the previous five years oil companies had increased their share of the national coal production from 7 to 28 percent.

But even these figures are on the conservative side. S. Robert Mitchell, former Justice Department economist, points out in his memorandum to the American Public Power Association that the major coal producing companies also market coal produced by other companies. "These companies either buy coal from the other producers for resale or act as brokers for other companies in the sale of their coal. This effectively increases the control of the large companies that engage in such purchasing and brokerage activities, since the coal that is involved is produced by smaller companies."

Mitchell continues. "Consolidation Coal, for instance, reported that it purchases and resells, or sells as an agent, coal mined by other producing companies (Report to Shareholders dated May 16, 1966). Recent data are not readily available, but Consol reported that it distributed 3.1 million tons of such purchased and agency coal in 1965. Consol's production in 1965 (including affiliates) totaled 48.6 million tons. The total volume of coal actually marketed by Consol in that year amounted to 51.7 million tons, therefore, or 6 percent more than the production figure.

"Kennecott Copper's annual report for 1969 indicates that its sales of brokerage coal produced by other companies totaled

10 million tons in that year. Kennecott's coal production amounted to 59.6 million tons in 1969. Thus Kennecott actually controlled the sale of 69.6 million tons, or about 17 percent more than its production. Peabody (Kennecott's subsidiary) is considered to be the largest coal broker in the United States."

Mitchell concludes, "Thus, these 13 large companies actually control somewhat more than 60 percent of the coal marketed in the United States on a commercial basis."

Because of the increasing demand for electricity, the demand for coal increased. Yet production remained fairly stable, and in one year actually declined. (Production in 1967 was 552,626 million tons; in 1968, 545,245 million tons; and in 1969, 554,051 million tons.) As Congressman Kastenmeier had discovered, the Interior Department was handing out more and more coal leases in the western public lands, but actual production on the federal leases was declining.

Meanwhile, as production remained steady or in certain instances declined, prices rose sharply, and during a period when there was no major labor distress which could cause the price of coal to move forward.

Among the substantial influences in the structure of the coal markets has been the growth of the long-term contracts, pioneered by TVA, as one instrument for organizing the coal business. The long-term contract generally requires the producer to sell coal to a consumer over a period of from five to 30 years. Prior to the 1960s, coal was sold primarily in the spot markets, or on the basis of short-term contracts for periods up to one year. In his memorandum, Mitchell comments, "Despite the widespread use of long-term contracts by the large coal companies, the short-term or spot market has been and will undoubtedly continue to be an important source of supply for many coal consumers, particularly electric utilities that for various reasons have not desired to enter into long-term contracts. However, the withdrawal of nearly all of the tonnages of the large coal producers from the spot and short-term market has severely restricted the available supply for these consumers and their demands for the limited tonnages being offered have resulted in a very sharp upward movement in prices charged in this market during the past year [1971]." He notes that the National Coal Association's publication, *Bituminous Coal Facts,* says investors will not lend money for the development of new coal mines unless long-term contracts have been obtained to cover the expected output of the mines, and then to underscore the point says, "Coal men are confident that if their customers will agree to long-term contracts, to assure the necessary financing, they can produce the coal the nation needs."

Mitchell notes, "The shortage of coal supplies for the spot or short-term market was no doubt the basic cause of this sharp price advance, but this situation appears to have been artificially created by the recent shifting of tonnages that ordinarily would have gone into this market to take care of newly negotiated, long-term contracts, as previously pointed out. Moreover, it is possible that coal was actually withheld from this market for the purpose of inducing customers who had not yet signed long-term contracts to do so if they wanted to be assured of receiving future supplies. There may have been collusive activities in this connection."

While information on coal profits is scant, particularly where coal operations are part of oil and gas corporations, Mitchell says, "Information is available for several of the largest independent coal companies which clearly indicates that the increased prices contributed substantially to higher profits and were, therefore, far greater than necessary to cover increased costs. For instance, Pittston's return on sales (net income as percent of sales) was 6.9 percent in 1970, which was substantially above its return of 4.1 percent in 1969 (Standard Corporation Records). Similarly, Westmoreland's return was 3.9 percent in the first three-quarters of 1970 as compared with only 1.2 percent in the first three-quarters of 1969 (data for the last quarter of 1970 is not yet available).

The Tennessee Valley Authority best illustrates the effects of this coal price increase. TVA is the single biggest power system in the country, serving 5.5 million people in seven states, and it influences the lives of many others because it sells or exchanges electricity with other systems as far away as Chicago, Miami, Kansas. Eighty percent of TVA's electricity is created by burning coal. It burns 32 million tons of coal each year, and is the single largest purchaser in the nation. As indicated previously, TVA played a major role in structuring the coal industry during the 1950s through the introduction of long-term contracts.

As the oil men bought out the coal companies, TVA found its business was changing. Of the top ten coal suppliers, which provide over 80 percent of all the utility's coal, six companies accounting for 65 percent were owned by oil or mining firms.

TVA generally attempts to keep 60 to 75 days of coal at each plant in case of an emergency, and there was little difficulty in doing so until 1968. Within that year supplies were cut in half. TVA entered the winter of 1970 with only 11 days' supply on hand. Aubrey Wagner, TVA's director, explained the situation to a House committee: "There are a number of reasons for this decline but the basic one is that the production of coal—nationwide—has not kept pace with the expanding consumption. The reserve piles of all industries which use coal, according to the Bureau of Mines, declined by 12 million tons in the three years from 1967 to 1969. This included an eight-million-ton drop in the stockpiles of electric utilities. This decline is all the more serious because it came at a time when the utilities were increasing their generation and the need for reserves was growing. We understand that there is at present a deficiency of 40 million tons in the normally desirable coal reserve of the utility industry."

Most of the TVA contracts were long-term, and most utilities buy on such contracts. Thus, it was not possible that a short-term demand for coal could shorten supply. "While we in TVA were among the first in the industry to offer and obtain very long-term contracts, we find now that we are receiving only about 80 percent of the coal for which we have contracted. If this deficiency were remedied, we would be able to carry our loads and to restore our stockpiles on a gradual basis."

TVA could not get enough coal: "With one or two exceptions, we have received almost no response to our invitations to bid on new long-term contracts such as would require opening of new mines. The TVA Act ordinarily requires us to buy our coal under competitive bidding except in cases of emergency. Competitive bidding for the TVA market has declined appreciably and we are now compelled more frequently to resort to the emergency procedures of direct negotiation with individual companies in order to assure future deliveries."

Along with the shortage of coal, prices rose. TVA announced a price rate rise of 23 percent in October 1970. "We estimated that fuel bills of the power system in this fiscal year will be $60 million more than we had anticipated 18 months earlier. Another factor is the rise of interest rates."

Wagner went on, "We estimate that the average cost of fuel to be burned in our system in fiscal year 1971 will be somewhat more than 27 cents per million BTU, an increase of about 53 percent over our cost of 17.69 cents per million BTU in fiscal year 1965, and more than 26 percent greater than fiscal year 1970's average cost of 21.44 cents per million BTU. . . . At our Shawnee steam plant in western Kentucky, for example, the purchase price of coal in 1967 and 1968 was running about 19 cents a million BTU, or about $4 a ton delivered. . . . Prices under new contracts arc now about 37 cents a million BTU, or about $7.50 to $8 a ton at that plant, depending on quality.

"At Widows Creek plant in northern Alabama, the price ranged from 21 cents a million BTU in 1967 and 1968 to about 23 cents last year. The price for new coal has now gone to about 39 cents—a jump from about $4.50 a ton to nearly $9."

The coal industry insisted that whatever little rise in prices was the result of additional costs brought on by the mine safety laws. But as Wagner makes clear, that argument does not make much sense from the point of view of TVA. "TVA represents a market for at least 35 million tons a year for a good many years into the future. We are willing to enter into long-term contracts for that coal—contracts that can serve to back up the financing of the heavy investments needed to open new mines. We expect to pay prices that will cover costs of mine operations including necessary costs of safety for miners. We expect to pay prices that will cover costs of strip mine reclamation and environmental protection. And we expect to pay prices that will allow a fair profit—a fair profit but not an exorbitant profit. In the normal operation of American business, it seems to us that this should provide the incentives for opening the needed new mines and expanding coal production to meet market demands."

Before another congressional committee, James Watson, TVA's director of power, said that when TVA had approached coal companies they would only open up new mines if it could be done on the basis it would provide "the same returns that we might get from investing in petroleum production anywhere in the world."

TVA's rebellion against the coal price increases did not produce great results. Tennessee Congressman Joe Evins held hearings, a group of TVA supporters persuaded the government to reopen the Continental-Consolidation merger case by removing it from the Justice Department and sticking it in the Federal Trade Commission. TVA itself began to hedge against the coal corner by planning a much larger percentage of its future production in nuclear plants. It made an alliance with Commonwealth Edison Co., the big Chicago utility, and won AEC support for construction of a breeder reactor, while at the same time casting about for the possibilities of obtaining uranium leases, before they too were totally consumed and controlled by oil.

Consolidation Coal Co. never had been willing to sell coal to TVA, and in a way its quiet animosity toward TVA was finally vindicated, for the energy industry broke down the single biggest consuming force in the coal industry.

Although a good deal of the haggling over prices is couched in the public relations cant of the oil industry, there are times when the naked politics come out in the open. On one such occasion, Brice O'Brien, vice-president of the National Coal Association, lost his temper at a meeting of Tennessee Valley utility officials in December 1970 and told them, "We raised the hell out of the price of coal . . . you gotta pay it. Don't sue us—you're wasting your time."

"The days of cheap energy are gone," O'Brien said in explaining why the cost of coal had gone up $2 a ton. "So we are going to charge $3. To hell with TVA." While O'Brien later apologized for his outburst, neither he nor the National Coal Association denied its content. An association public relations man said the remarks were made "off the cuff," but that O'Brien's comments were made in the context that "we have other operating costs and we have to get a fair return. The context was that we won't sell $4 coal for $3.90 a ton anymore."

In 1951 George Love was talking about building a refinery to turn coal into gasoline, and considering the possibility of turning coal into gasoline during the winter, and gas in the summer. The prospect that Consolidation could take gasoline out of coal was one of the reasons for the merger. Yet by 1970, everyone concerned lost interest in the project, which year by year had seemingly become more and more complicated, seemingly impossible to run. It is worth remembering that during World War II the German air force was supplied solely from 13 synthetic fuels plants, which produced 90 million gallons of synthetic gasoline a month.

At the time of the Continental-Consolidation merger, the Bureau of Mines claimed studies showed gas could be made from coal at costs ranging from $0.105 to $0.13 a gallon. At the time it cost $0.125 to $0.14 to refine crude oil into gas. Not only did the coal gas appear to be cheaper, but also because the world's reserves of oil are limited, and coal reserves are much larger, it seemed to suggest a major shift in the energy business from oil to coal. Ironically enough after the merger, Project Gasoline, as the research project was called, never reached fulfillment. The initial contract signed in August 1963 called for the government to spend $9.9 million By 1971, the government had paid Continental $20 million and the plant still did not work. (In 1971, they managed to get it going for two days.) Indeed, the Interior Department had renegotiated the contract letting Continental off the hook entirely, continuing to provide them more funds so that the plant could be used for desulphurization of oil.

C. Howard Hardesty, the coal man who had foreseen a rosy future for changing coal into gasoline during the merger negotiations, had changed his mind by 1971, and was talking about making coal into gas instead.

In an exchange he had with Congressman Neal Smith, who wanted to find out why Continental had changed its mind on liquefaction, Hardesty explained it this way.

> HARDESTY: And I say that for one reason. It is economics. At the present time, one of the problems of coal liquefaction that gasoline has is the fact that gasoline prices have continued almost level. They have not escalated up as have other costs of goods and services that this nation has experienced during the period of inflation.
>
> As a consequence, instead of a moving target that we were competing in conversion of coal to gasoline, we have been competing against a stable type of thing and I think that had costs of gasoline conversion gone up proportionately, we would be closer today.
>
> SMITH: Why?
>
> HARDESTY: Why? Well because we after all have to be competitive and if they can from the conversion refining of liquid crude produce gasoline below what our economic target is and it remains stable, that two to three cents makes a big difference.
>
> SMITH: It seems to me that you are saying substantially what your critics have been saying, that you have the incentive to work the hardest in areas where you make the most money.
>
> HARDESTY: We don't. No sir. We are a very minor part, Mr. Chairman, of the whole marketing enterprise of this nation on gasoline products. But we cannot escape an economic fact that whoever, whether it be a coal company, whether it be

an oil company, or whether it be somebody entirely divorced from it, they have to look at the economics of coal liquefaction. The competition that they have from liquid fuels has remained rather constant and this two or three cents makes a difference.

4: MARCH INTO THE CANADIAN NORTH

As the major economic satrapy of the United States on the North American continent, Canada is expected to provide a growing share of energy resources through the end of the century. In recent history the United States has come to regard the place as a sort of resource storage bin into which we dip as we feel the need.

The policy is simple enough: As fuels are depleted in the United States, thereby driving prices upward, the American petroleum and mining industries, which dominate the Canadian resource economy, will find it economically feasible to open up the Canadian north by the end of the century, just as the railroads opened up the Canadian west in the previous century. The abundant supplies of oil and gas in the Canadian north will be drawn into the United States to meet our shortage. This is euphemistically referred to as the "continental" approach, and involves establishment of "free trade" zones. All that means is that the United States seeks formal recognition of current practices where it takes what it wants.

Crosscurrents of economic nationalism are on the rise in Canada, buoyed as one might expect by a natural resentment at the arrogance of U.S. policy. But the continental policy is so deeply ingrained, it will be difficult for the Canadians to challenge the policy without endangering other aspects of their economy. From the Canadian point of view, the situation is frustrating and likely to become more so as the United States tightens its squeeze.

The extent to which Canada functions as a U.S. resource colony is not sufficiently understood in this country. Before describing the current energy "play" in northern Canada, it is worth looking briefly at some economic history to set the current politics in perspective.

A useful guide in this regard is *American Capital and Canadian Resources,* published in 1961 by Hugh G. J. Aitken. Aitken attempted to trace the flow of capital into Canada since the beginning of the nineteenth century. The paragraphs below contain a brief sketch of his major points.

By the middle of the nineteenth century the British accounted for the most substantial investments in Canada, generally in the form of bonds used to finance canals and then railroads. But Britain's interest in Canada was insignificant compared to its investments in Europe or the United States. At mid-century the U.S. investments in Canada were estimated at about $15 million.

In the last half of the nineteenth century the British interest in Canada heightened, and investments, again mostly bonds, increased five-fold. Most of this money went to expand the country westward, and much of it was spent in building the Canadian Pacific railroad.

Meanwhile, United States investments increased from $15 million in 1867 to $160 million by 1899. In contrast to the British, the Americans spent money in direct purchase of land, timber or mineral rights or else toward establishment of corporate subsidiaries and branch plants. About one-third of the U.S. money was invested in mining with another third in manufacturing. (Only 3.75 percent went to oil development.)

U.S. investments in Canada rose sharply during the early years of the twentieth century. By 1925, they had grown 265.5 percent from $880.7 million in 1914 to $3.2 billion. During this period, British investments began a steady decline. For the first time the United States became Canada's principal foreign creditor. More than 70 percent of total investment was for mining and manufacturing, as compared with 50 percent in 1914.

By 1932, U.S. interests controlled manufacturing firms which produced 23 percent of Canada's total manufacturing capacity, and 38 percent of all mining production. By the end of 1958, U.S. investments amounted to $14.6 billion, or 77 percent of the total. By that year, U.S. companies controlled 43 percent of all manufacturing and 52 percent of mining and smelting.

Aitken points out, "While investment in Canadian manufacturing rose by 250 percent over the period and remained the largest single category in 1957, investment in Canadian minerals increased by no less than 1,543 percent. Most of this increase reflected United States participation in Canadian petroleum and natural gas development after the important Leduc discovery in Alberta, but investment in other minerals was also significant, rising from $251 million in 1939 to $1,312 million at the end of 1957."

By 1964, 80 percent of long-term foreign investment in Canada was from the United States. Canada accounted for 31 percent of all U.S. direct investment abroad, more than the total U.S. investment in Europe.

Aitken's figures, then, give a shorthand picture of both the change from British to U.S. investment in Canada, and point up the difference between the two types of investments. They are a help in providing some perspective to Canadian political economy, but they need be set into wider context. In the eighteenth and nineteenth century, Canada provided Britain with a set of staples, furs for the fashion industry in Europe, lumber to replace Baltic timber Britain had hitherto relied upon, and breadstuffs made possible by technological breakthroughs and development of transportation systems. The industrial raw materials that Canada now exports to the United States were not resources until technologies could be developed to exploit them and until the United States was faced with depletion of its own vast supplies.

A change in geographic alignment also was important. Aitken writes, "Historically, the Canadian nation was constructed along an east-west axis: From the days of the fur trade onward, expansion took place by a series of westward advances from an eastern base. All the older staples, with the partial exception of the lumber trade, reinforced this alignment. The Canadian transportation system, the waterways and later the transcontinental railroads, gave it physical expression. The protective tariff helped to make it an economic reality by building up an industrial sector in central Canada to serve the staple-producing sectors elsewhere. The creation and maintenance of this simple, linear structure was, and to some extent still is, the primary economic responsibility of the Canadian federal government. Imports of capital from Britain helped to finance its building, and the export of staple products to Britain was its basic rationale. Any map of the Canadian transportation system illustrates the point: So does any map of Canada's population distribution. Immense though it is in total land area, economically and socially Canada *is* a series of narrow strips of inhabited territory joined together at the ends."

During the last 50 years the map has been overlaid with crisscrossing lines running north and south. Nearly 70 percent of Canada's imports come from the United States, and a little over 10 percent are from Great Britain.

Canada greatly depends on her exports. They represent 15 percent of her gross national product. And three-fifths of those exports go to the United States. Seventy percent of that amount is raw materials for U.S. industry.

Within the last few years there have been several reports on foreign ownership in Canada. The most recent of these studies, by Herb Gray, was prepared for the Cabinet. The Gray report tends to confirm or restate conclusions of previous reports, among them the Watkins report of 1968 and the Wahn report of 1970.

It points out that foreign participation is greater in mining than manufacturing: Almost 63 percent of mining assets, 60 percent of sales, 55 percent of profits, and 48 percent of taxable income are accounted for by nonresident-owned firms.

One result of foreign ownership in the resources industry has been to emphasize capital over labor. While the jobs are often high paying, there are relatively few of them. Mineral production in 1970 accounted for about 7 percent of the GNP, but only 1.4 percent of the labor force was employed in mining. Hence, the emphasis on mining is criticized as one of the factors that has produced the stagnant unemployment situation which hovers between 7 and 8 percent in Canada.

In an effort to stimulate investment, and thereby promote economic growth, successive Canadian governments since the late 1940s have held out enticements of various tax incentives. These include forms of rapid depreciation, where a company can write off its taxes the cost of equipment at a much more rapid rate than the equipment will be used up. It is possible to write off taxes two-thirds of the cost of equipment with an estimated life of 15 years in the first five years. Ordinarily, the company would depreciate this equipment at some steady rate over the life of the equipment. Firms have been offered incentives by being allowed to write off research costs at 150 percent of actual amount spent. The government allows corporations to defer payments of income taxes through various accounting methods. This deferment, a sort of loan made at no interest, is estimated to total $3.5 billion by the Canadian government. That makes the government the largest lender in the country.

These tax provisions are part of the reason that U.S. firms with subsidiaries in Canada no longer need invest much capital in Canada for the purpose of expanding their facilities. As Eric Kierans, Trudeau's former minister for communications, points out, "Investment incentives (depreciation, depletion, three-year exempt mining income) apply precisely in those industries where foreign ownership is most ˉconcentrated, i.e., mining, petroleum, and manufacturing. Total sources of funds for American subsidiaries in Canada in 1968 amounted to $2,611 million.

Funds from the United States amounted to $127 million or less than 5 precent. Within Canada was provided $1,027 million in net income, $864 million in depreciation, and $539 million from Canadian financial institutions. Legislation to inhibit further inflows would be useless. Our tax laws are such that increasing ownership, takeovers, and control of Canadian firms can be entirely financed within our own economy."

And Kierans adds, "If foreign ownership dominates the mining and petroleum industries, our tax system has clearly invited this concentration. We have not only extended a warm invitation to foreign capital, but we have told it where to go. If you invest in the service industries, we say, you will have to pay taxes on 87 percent or 90 percent of your profits. On the other hand, in metal mining you will only have to pay on 13 percent and in petroleum on 5.7 percent of your profits. The invitation says, in effect, 'Come and gut us.'"

While taxes for corporations generally declined in the last decade, those for individuals were increased. Again quoting Kierans, "In 1961 and 1962, 35 percent of the tax revenues collected by the federal government came from persons. Of the taxes it now collects, 41.4 percent come from people and most of that is taken on the day they receive their cheque. On the other hand, ten years ago 23.5 percent of all money collected in taxes by the federal government came from corporations. Today that has decreased to 19.5 percent and will decrease even lower when we put through some of the things being asked of us."

Kierans's argument was summed up in a speech in Commons September 9, 1971, in discussing the U.S. 10 percent surtax then recently announced by President Nixon.

What is the United States saying to Canada in particular by imposing the 10 percent surtax? When they impose the surtax just on manufactured goods they are saying, "We do not want your manufactured goods but we will take all your oil and gas and all the metal mine exports that you can give us. There is no tax on those commodities and we will take them." They say we will take them because as [George] Schultz said, "Out of every dollar we give to you we get 71 cents back." What are they saying to Canada when they say that they are going to give the American corporations in the United States an investment allowance to apply to new capital equipment that they buy, on condition that that equipment is built in the United States and nowhere else. They are saying to us, "We do not want any of the output of your machinery and equipment factories." What are they saying with their DISC program, the Domestic International Sales Corporation program? They are saying, "We want you to take our manufactured exports." They are also saying, on the other hand, "We will take the exports of your resources. We will take all the resources that you can give to us." And what does this add up to?

I have seen this mentioned in many newspapers recently. It adds up to the following: that you can have growth in Canada because, "If our economy expands," says the United States, "we will require more resources and you will have more growth." Well, if we have growth and an expansion in our resource industries that outweighs the decline in our manufacturing output, I suppose you could say that we will have a net increase in our gross national product. But, do we then have a net increase in employment? The answer is no. Will we get a net increase in taxes? Again, the answer is no. We tax firms in the oil and gas industry on less than 6 percent of their profits. We tax manufacturing firms, on the average, on 63 percent of their profits. In the metal mining industry, we tax firms, on the average, on only 13 percent of their profits after you add up all the accelerated depreciation, depletion allowances, and other privileges. So, we could have growth in the economy with a decline in employment. We could have growth with a decline in tax revenue and we could have growth, really, with a decline in the division of profits that takes place in the oil and gas industry; because, given its concentration and the way dividends go, there would be an outflow. Our dollar value, similarly, could remain exactly the same. We could substitute $1 billion worth of oil and gas exports for $1 billion worth of manufactured exports and the pressure on the dollar would remain high; but the effect within the economy could be virtually disastrous.

To conclude, the Canadian economy, once dominated by indirect investment and trade patterns with Britain, is now tied in direct investment and trade to the United States. The area of greatest U.S. concentration is in the Canadian resource industry. U.S. companies no longer need export capital to Canada, but can finance the takeover of the Canadian economy through the advantageous tax policies provided by the Canadian government. Their expansion has not resulted in more jobs, but rather tied up capital in nonlabor-producing industries.

The purpose behind the American march into Canada is the capture of natural resources. While the U.S. government may indulge in trade talks, discussions of auto pacts, and other such niceties, what's involved at base is a naked play for Canadian resources, in particular, future resources in the Arctic regions.

The Arctic Play

Canada's oil and gas industry is dominated by U.S. companies. This influence can be measured in different ways. By 1965 total direct U.S. investment in Canadian oil and gas amounted to $3.6 billion, compared to $930 million from all other foreign sources. In 1963, U.S. corporations were reported to control 62 percent of all oil and gas in the country.

In a speech at the Mid-America World Trade Conference in Chicago, March 1972, Jean-Luc Pepin, the Canadian minister of industry, trade, and commerce, said that Americans controlled majority shares in Canadian-based companies accounting for 51 percent of all assets in mining in Canada; 67 percent of all assets in mineral fuels production; and 76 percent in petroleum refining.

According to a 1971 *Oil Daily* report, "According to official U.S. sources, about 81 percent of the capital needs of the Canadian petroleum industry are now being supplied by foreign sources with American investors providing 70 percent of that total."

The ten leading oil producers were U.S. companies, led by

Imperial Oil, Jersey Standard's Canadian subsidiary which has the biggest operations of any company in the country.

The same sort of pattern is repeated in the gas industry, which as elsewhere is inseparable from oil. The leading producers are U.S. companies, led by Gulf and Phillips.

Most of the oil and gas heretofore has been found and produced in Alberta province, then transported to the population and industrial centers of Ontario by means of pipelines. The gas pipeline is Canadian-owned. But the oil pipeline is controlled by Imperial. Jersey Standard has been criticized for refusal to extend the pipe beyond Toronto to Montreal, the country's second major industrial center. Rather oil companies prefer to supply Montreal with oil from subsidiaries in Venezuela or the Middle East. It is shipped up the east coast to Portland, Maine, and sent by pipeline to Montreal.

During the Eisenhower, Kennedy, and Johnson years, Canada was exempt from import quotas, with the result that imports of Canadian crude increased while those of Venezuela and Middle East declined. There was speculation that Canada was not included in the quota program because the government had threatened to build a continental oil pipeline that would have threatened the interests of companies operating from Venezuela. At any rate, Canadian oil did not flow entirely freely because importation of Canadian oil did not help domestic producers get more quotas for purchase of the much cheaper Middle Eastern and Venezuelan oil. In 1967 there was a gentlemen's agreement not to flood the U.S. markets with Canadian oil.

Canada exports about as much oil as she imports. Much of the refining is done below the border, which means that job-producing industries are created in the United States, not Canada. As for gas, about half of all the gas is piped into the United States, much of it purchased by utilities in the northwest.

In 1970, the year the United States discovered its energy crisis, these arrangements began to change. U.S. utilities were put under pressure by environmentalists to reduce air pollution, which they could best do by switching from coal or high sulphur oil to gas. At the same time, supplies of gas were short-ened, whether by industry design or natural cause. The result was to drive prices higher. At this point, the U.S. producers and the U.S. government took a more serious look at the Canadian natural resources. There was talk back and forth between Walter J. Hickel, then Secretary of the Interior, and J. J. Greene, then the Canadian energy minister, about a continental fuels policy. The Shultz report on oil quotas formally proposed har-monizing Canadian-U.S. fuels policy.

U.S. gas pipeline companies simply assumed they could take down more gas from Canada, and without waiting for permis-sion from the Canadians, the Federal Power Commission ap-proved a pipeline company request to build a $37.2 million gas line from Michigan and Wisconsin to Canada. In August, the Canadian National Energy Board approved gas exports totaling 6.4 trillion cubic feet, on the grounds that there were sufficient Canadian reserves to supply the remaining Canadian market. In commenting on this decision at the time, Jean-Luc Pepin said, "It would be crazy to sit on it. In maybe 25 to 50 years we'll be heating ourselves from the rays of the sun and then we'd kick ourselves in the pants for not capitalizing on what we had when gas and oil was a current commodity."

Quite apart from the question of draining off Canada's gas, the increased exports to the United States could produce a serious reaction in Canada, leading to a spiraling of prices. In a continental market, the Canadian gas would move upward in price toward the U.S. price, which as already noted has been forced ahead. Industry officials predicted that higher prices could price western Canadian gas out of the Canadian market. Moreover, the gas exports threatened to make it more difficult for Canadian industry to switch to the nonpolluting fuel.

A year later, under pressure from utilities in Ontario which were changing from coal to gas to reduce air pollution, the energy board blocked a request to export 2.6 trillion cubic feet. There were immediate hysteric cries from the United States that the spigots had been turned off.

Now the lines of the energy game have changed, with the major play being concentrated on long-range supplies in the Arctic.

Proved resources of oil and gas lie in the Mackenzie delta region, a part of the Northwest Territories and Yukon lying above the lower Canadian provinces. These finds are most likely to be developed before others, and they are controlled by the major international oil companies, Imperial, Gulf, etc.

While the policy lines remain vague, one theory holds that Alberta supplies should be saved for Canada; foreign capital should develop the Mackenzie delta region, and Canada should export much of this gas as well as whatever oil the United States will take. This could involve a gas pipeline down the Mackenzie River to the Chicago area of the United States, with connecting links to the northwest. It might be possible to bring down supplies of Alaskan crude oil and gas through such a piping system. Indeed, such a pipeline apparently is the most economic way to market Alaskan gas.

(There is more than usual interest in this plan within Canada, for the residents of Vancouver are alarmed at the prospect of oil pollution along the coast when the trans-Alaskan pipeline is built. That pipeline will run from Prudhoe down the coast to Valdez where the oil would be put into ships, and hauled down through the western islands into Seattle.)

Above the Northwest Territories and the Yukon lie the Arctic regions, and in this territory the major operator has been Panarctic Oils, Ltd., a consortium of oil companies, 45 percent owned by the Canadian government.

Panarctic in a sense functions as the outrider in what the industry calls the Arctic play. It takes all the chances, but it is unclear how much of the finds are reserved for Canadians. Thus, Panarctic is actively involved in drilling programs in the western Arctic islands and has found both gas and oil. While there are severe technical difficulties in getting this petroleum out and to market, the difficulties probably can be overcome. To make these explorations, Panarctic needed $75 million. But instead of asking for this money from the Canadian government, it made a deal with Tenneco for the $75 million. Under that arrangement, when gas is found, Tenneco has first call on it. So as in so many other instances, the Canadian government hires out to the United States.

While Panarctic's finds were considered to be fairly far away from market, the situation changed dramatically in early 1972 when the company brought in oil on Ellesmere Island, an island in the eastern Arctic. Unlike its western Arctic finds, this one is near the open sea, which means that oil not only can be brought out and put in tankers, but also it is in close proximity to both the Canadian and the U.S. east coast.

The oil companies in Canada divide their time between the Arctic play and operations off the coast of Nova Scotia.

In 1971, Mobil, which has leases off the coast, announced a commercial gas well, and followed that up with claims that it had oil as well at Sable Island, Nova Scotia. The entire eastern coast of Canada is leased out, and there are several companies working up and down the coast as well as off Labrador to the north. Mobil's gas find may go to eastern Canada, or it may well go down to the northeast of the United States.

The problem here involves a dispute over control of the shelf between the government of Quebec and the federal Canadian government. The Quebec government wants to sell oil and gas to the United States. The central government, through its energy department and the energy board, is much less apt to take such a course.

An earlier dispute between the provinces and central government involving western offshore waters was settled by the Canadian courts in favor of the central government. The current dispute is now before the courts.

While there is no clear practice in the case of either oil or gas, the Trudeau government appears willing to sell off gas and oil in the north, and it will be through this means that the "continental" energy policy will be affected, perhaps by U.S. capital financing the activities of Panarctic with the stipulation that the United States recovers a certain set supply first before it can be used elsewhere.

Electricity for the United States

Oil and gas are not the only energy resources in which the United States has an interest. There have been efforts to harness the rivers and lakes of Canada to produce electric power for the United States, and this raises another sore point in Canada, for it is argued that the country's abundant supply of hydro-electric sites should be used to develop cheap electricity for the Canadian economy, not for sale to the United States.

The most grandiose and widely debated of the electric projects is the so-called James Bay Project in Qubec. The provincial assembly of Quebec approved this scheme in July 1971; it would involve harnessing five of Quebec's rivers flowing into James Bay. The ultimate capacity would be about 10.6 million kilowatts. The complex would be the largest in Canada and supply the equivalent of a quarter of Canada's current total generating capacity.

While the precise plans remain vague, James Bay is projected to cost about $6 billion. Quebec hopes that most of the power would be exported to the United States, to New York State, and in particular to Consolidated Edison. Con Ed, of course, is feverishly casting about for ways of producing electricity because it has been blocked in expanding nuclear plants by environmentalists, and is, at the same time, under strict pollution orders.

The Prudential Insurance Co. claims to be interested in part of the financing, and the Quebec government made the rounds on Wall Street, but so far financial plans remain distant.

The Quebec Hydro-Electric Commission, which is in charge of James Bay, is the major customer and a shareholder in another enormous hydroelectric scheme, the Churchill Falls Corporation, which operates a gigantic hydroelectric project in Labrador. The Churchill Falls development illustrates a central aspect of the recolonization process in Canada. Fifty-seven percent of

Churchill Falls, in turn, is owned by an investment company called Brinco, Ltd. The major holdings in Brinco are shared primarily by Rio Tinto Zinc Corporation, a leading London-headquartered international mining company, and Bethlehem Steel Corp. Through Brinco, both RTZ and Bethlehem are anxious to explore all possibilities for developing hydroelectric power in Canada. Churchill Falls itself will finally result in the largest man-made lake in Canada; in addition to that, they are working on a second project downstream, and mapping hydroelectric schemes in British Columbia.

The money for Churchill Falls was raised mostly in the United States through the sale of bonds, and the whole scheme is credited to Winston Churchill, as an example of the best sort of imperial spectacular. The deal was put together by the London branch of the Rothschild family, which has taken an active part in the operations of RTZ.

The RTZ company itself has other holdings in Canada which are connected to the hydroelectric plans. One of these is Rio Algom Mines, the largest uranium producer in Canada. Together with the United States and South Africa, Canada has the world's richest supplies of uranium. While there is a glut of uranium at this writing, it is expected to become relatively in short supply by the middle or late 1970s, and hence Rio Algom's position over the long term could turn out to be most advantageous. Especially so since Rio Tinto Zinc, the parent company, is interlocked through a directorate with the big South African uranium producer, Anglo American Corporation of South Africa.

Until recently, much uranium needed to be sent to the United States for enrichment treatment before it could be used in nuclear power plants. The United States kept close hold of the enrichment process because of the arms race. Hence, countries using the predominant type of reactors would buy uranium, have it enriched in the United States, then make fuel out of it. Canada has developed nuclear power plants that use raw uranium, that is, nonenriched uranium. But even though the Canadians don't need enriched uranium for their own uses, RTZ and its partners in Churchill Falls are investigating the possibility of using some of that large amount of electricity to enrich uranium for other countries. This represents another curious attempt to exploit Canada's resources for export, mining her uranium, enriching it with hydroelectric power, and selling it off overseas.

Exporting Canadian Water

Canadians also worry that in the long run the United States will demand and subsequently take their water. The government insists the water is not for sale, but past events suggest the government is malleable on the matter.

Under the Columbia River treaty, signed between the United States and Canada in 1964, the United States paid the Canadians $344.4 million to build dams for control of the Columbia River above the U.S. border. Once this control was established, the United States was able to harness the water below the border and to build hydroelectric installations which provide electricity to utilities in the northwest.

It was an advantageous deal for the United States. Stewart Udall, then secretary of the Interior, set the value of flood control and power at $710 million if the United States had undertaken it alone. The flood control alone would have cost $500 million. As it turned out the United States paid the Canadians $69 million for that. General A. G. L. McNaughton, of the International Joint Commission, said in a speech at the time, "The studies in the International Joint Commission and elsewhere have shown that the benefits to stream flow control which Canada can provide to the United States are so large that to match them within their own territory the United States would need to expend close to a billion dollars even if they could obtain permission to use the sites for the works required."

And none of these estimates took into account the payments that needed to be made to people who were dispossessed from their homes and businesses, communities that were flooded, and loss of productivity of land flooded.

While the treaty stipulates that the United States will consult Canada about flood control procedures, it makes clear that in the final analysis, the United States has the say in how the project is managed within Canada.

Had they had to harness the Columbia River, the Canadian engineers would have done it much differently. In opposing the treaty in a Commons speech, Tommy Douglas, then the New Democratic party leader, read from James G. Ripley's article in the *Engineering and Contract Record,* September 1963: "The present treaty places three of the four major dams (high Arrow, Libby, Duncan) virtually on the American border, where they are absolutely useless for any purposes except regulating U.S. flows. As the value of this regulation declines . . . we eventually are left with three useless structures. We cannot produce a kilowatt of at-site power for Canada at any of these dams. The fourth dam (Mica) will produce some power but will always sacrifice part of its potential output because the treaty says it must be operated primarily for U.S. regulation."

He adds, "McNaughton would develop the Canadian half of the Columbia in precisely the opposite way by putting all major storages as high in the mountains as possible. (This is also the way the United States would develop the river if there were no international boundary.) He would eliminate high Arrow and Libby, and replace them with dams at Bull River, Luxor, and Dorr. The net effect would be that this water could be run through 1,280 feet of Canadian head before it reached the border. The Americans would get the same water, but Canada would use it first and would control the regulation."

In opposing the treaty, Douglas summed up the argument in Commons: "The most important thing the United States will get out of this treaty is tremendous quantities of water, and water at flow rates dictated by the needs of the United States. The Americans have been 40 or 50 years ahead of us in recognizing that the day will come on this continent when water will be more important than gold. That is why the United States have spent the last 30 years impounding water. That is why the United States today pipes water hundreds of miles down into states like California, because the Americans know that unless you have quantities of water you cannot have agriculture, you cannot have industry, and you cannot have large urban centers. I do not think the Americans are worried about the power, I think they are worried about flood control; but what they are primarily concerned about is to control a great volume of water, and this is what we are giving them by turning over to them the resources of the fourth largest river on this North American continent. And we are doing it, I may say, for a measly $344.4 million which is going to be used to build storage dams primarily to help the United States."

As James Laxer points out in *The Energy Poker Game,* the Columbia River treaty, a bungled bit of work from the Canadian point of view, is of long-term significance in that by considering the Columbia River as a continental resource, it attacks the concept of the International Joint Commission, established in 1909, to work out differences between the two countries on questions of boundary water. The commission had relied on the so-called Harmon doctrine, which held that in deciding disputes, the upstream country has a right to "exclusive jurisdiction and control over the use and diversion . . . of waters on its own side of the line which in their natural channels would flow across the boundary or into boundary waters." Without approval of the commission, the downstream state was prevented from construction of any works that would cause the level of the water to be raised on the other side.

Subsequent to signing the Columbia River treaty, the Canadians became apprehensive over another U.S. scheme to tap their water, called the North American Water and Power Alliance (NAWAPA). The NAWAPA plan was put forward by Parsons Engineering Co., a Los Angeles engineering company, and won support from legislators in the water-scarce mountain states. Senator Frank Moss of Utah, for instance, became a convert. On its face, the plan is an engineer's spectacular. It would involve building large dams in Alaska and the Canadian Yukon to trap the waters of the rivers in those areas. These waters would be channeled into a man-made reservoir 500 miles long, built up around the Rocky Mountain Trench. That would necessitate constructing a series of connecting tunnels, canals, lakes, dams, and lifts. At the northern end of the trench, Parsons would dredge out a 30-foot canal to carry water to Lake Superior, and hence on to the rest of the Great Lakes, which need fresh water. Another section of canal would feed water into the upper stretches of the Mississippi and Missouri rivers.

In his book, *The Coming Water Famine*, Congressman Jim Wright explains how the system would work: "A series of dams and power stations would lift the water up to the three-thousand-foot altitude of the Rocky Mountain Trench, a natural geological defile in southwestern British Columbia, from five to 15 miles wide, which stretches for a length of about nine hundred miles. The site for the big storage reservoir would be the five hundred downstream miles of the southern end of the Trench.

"From the Trench Reservoir water would be pump-lifted to the Sawtooth Reservoir in northwestern Montana. From this point the water would flow by gravity, via linked canals and tunnels, throughout the western part of the system, passing the Sawtooth Mountain barrier through a tunnel eighty feet in diameter and fifty miles in length.

"This water would help mightily to meet the needs of the western states for irrigation, industry, power, recreation, and municipal conservation."

The late General A. G. L. McNaughton vigorously opposed this plan in a speech before the Royal Society of Canada:

> Of course, NAWAPA has nothing to do with the maximum development of these rivers or resources in Canada. Its purpose is to flood the valleys in Canada, and to drain off the water in regulated flow for beneficial use in the United States.

But the valleys themselves are of vital importance to British Columbia, because they contain the level land which is so vitally needed for road and railways, for industries, for people, and for agriculture. Whitehorse and Prince George would be submerged, and their land with them, as would countless miles of railway and highway. These irreplaceable assets would be destroyed in the name of trans-mountain navigation. In my address to the Canadian Club of Montreal in October 1965 I referred to some of the serious legal and political implications of the NAWAPA scheme. I observed at that time that this is a monstrous concept, not only in terms of physical magnitude, but also in another and more sinister sense, in that the promoters would displace Canadian sovereignty over the national waters of Canada, and substitute there for a diabolic thesis that all waters of North America become a shared resource, of which most will be drawn off for the benefit of the midwest and southwest regions of the United States where existing desert areas will be made to bloom at the expense of development in Canada.

. . . To me it is obvious that if we make a bargain to divert water to the United States, we cannot ever discontinue or we shall face force to compel compliance. There is nothing in our experience to date which indicates any change in the vigor with which our American friends pursue objectives which they deem in their national interests, however much this may hurt a neighbor who has unwittingly made a careless bargain in other circumstances.

But as Laxer points out, the scheme to drain water out of Canada is harebrained. Canada's own percentage of electric power produced by hydroelectric power will diminish from 82 percent in 1966 to 45 percent in 1990. In populated Ontario province, hydroelectricity will account for only 20 percent. And he quotes Trevor Lloyd's article in *Foreign Affairs* in July 1970. He states, "Fresh water is a renewable resource that is attracting increasing attention in the drier parts of North America where the supplies have been polluted or depleted. The landscape of much of the far north includes a rich variety of lakes, ponds, and rivers and gives an impression of providing a reserve of water which might become available for use elsewhere. The impression is misleading. Precipitation over much of the north is low, although evaporation is also low and the permafrost beneath prevents the water from draining away. While information is still incomplete, it suggests that the northern water reserves can contribute little or nothing for export southward."

Since initial adverse reaction to the Parsons plan by Canadians, there has been little activity toward its implementation in Congress. Senator Moss, a main supporter, hopes to produce some sort of legislation that can commission a serious study of the possibilities. The NAWAPA proponents at Parsons eagerly anticipate some sort of favorable Canadian study which will then allow them to push on with their dream.

While the NAWAPA plan at first glance may seem grandiose, it should be taken seriously. For not only does the United States expect to be short of water by the end of the century, but also its exacerbated fuels problems may merely hasten the coming of the drought. For example, major plans now are to develop the mountain states coal reserves. These enormous coal reserves can be strip mined, at which point they may be burned in power plants creating electricity which can be shipped to markets in the West or Midwest. In that case they will require large amounts of water to process the coal and cool the power plants. A far more ambitious scheme, however, is to strip mine the coal, then turn it into gas, and ship that gas either through pipelines, or burn it, creating electricity for markets in the West and Middle West. If the coal is turned to gas, the only known commercially economic process requires vast amounts of water. Unlike the power plants, which simply use the water, returning it befouled to the river beds, gasification removes the water from the area. Thus in addition to shipping gas, say, to Chicago, we will also be exporting water from the water-scarce areas of the mountain states. Already the government has plans for immense new reservoir and aqueduct schemes in the mountain states. The increasing demand for water will almost surely reawaken our interest in Canadian water.

It is difficult to believe that Canadian water is not for sale. John Diefenbaker, the Canadian prime minister who made the Columbia River deal, told Eisenhower on signing the treaty, "My hope is that, in the years ahead, this day will be looked back on as one that represents the greatest advance that has ever been made in international relations between countries." Lester Pierson, the next prime minister and a Liberal, said during the 1965 election, "The United States is finding that water is one of its most valuable and is becoming one of its scarcest resources. . . . the question of water resources . . . is a continental and international problem. We have to be careful not to alienate this resource without taking care of our own needs and we will be discussing this with the United States, who are very anxious to work out arrangements by which some of our water resources are moved down south. This can be as important as exporting wheat or oil."

And in February 1970, on the same day that J. J. Greene, the energy minister, told Commons Canada would not sell water, Trudeau was being asked some questions about natural resources, including water, on television. He said, "I don't want to be a dog in the manger about this. But if people are not going to use it, can't we sell it for good hard cash?"

As Laxer notes, "One rather frightening aspect of the government's bargaining posture with respect to water is the fact that it regards its ignorance as a major diplomatic strength. The government has said that since it does not know what Canadian water needs are, or what our resources amount to, we cannot bargain with anyone on the subject. This head-in-the-sand approach will hardly suffice when in mid-decade the Americans begin to bargain seriously about water. By that time, we had better have found something stronger than the ignorance of a Liberal government to rely on if we wish to assure a future for the people of northern and western Canada."

The Continental Policy

Within the last five years there has been renewed speculation and discussion for solidifying and formalizing the policies that now exist between Canada and the United States. In 1970, the Schultz report (The Oil Import Question: A Report on the Relationship of Oil Imports to the National Security) worried about possible boycotts among Middle Eastern or African countries, which would shut off oil to the United States. Canada, on the other hand, was viewed as a safe source of supply. "The risk of political instability or animosity is generally conceded to be very low in Canada. The risk of physical interruption or diversion of Canadian oil to other export markets in an emergency is also minimal for those deliveries made by inland transport." The Schultz report, however, believed Canada's east coast supplies, dependent on Venezuela, to be more vulnerable, and it urged the government to replace its support on Venezuela with safer arrangements, probably bringing the pipeline across from the west. In exchange the United States would open the market to Canadian oil. Shultz puts it this way, "A large U.S. tariff preference for Canadian oil is difficult to justify while eastern Canada continues to import all of its requirements from potentially insecure sources. In case of a supply interruption, Canada could be expected to turn to the United States to furnish those imports, or to compete for whatever supply is available, and thereby to subtract from the security value of the U.S. imports from western Canada. Some provision for limiting or offsetting Canadian vulnerability to an interruption of its own oil imports should therefore be made a precondition to unrestricted entry of Canadian oil into our market. Full realization of the security benefits implicit in such a preferential arrangement is also dependent on the development of common or harmonized United States-Canadian policies with respect to pipeline and other modes of transportation, access to natural gas, and other related energy matters. Pending the outcome of discussions on these subjects, the United States must decide what arrangements it is prepared to make unilaterally."

In his special message on energy of June 4, 1971, President Nixon had this to say about the Canadian situation: "Over the years, the United States and Canada have steadily increased their trade in energy. The United States exports some coal to Canada, but the major items of trade are oil and gas which are surplus to Canadian needs but which find a ready market in the United States.

"The time has come to develop further this mutually advantageous trading relationship. The United States is therefore prepared to move promptly to permit Canadian crude oil to enter this country, free of any quantitative restraints, upon agreement as to measures needed to prevent citizens of both our countries from being subjected to oil shortages, or threats of shortages. We are ready to proceed with negotiations and we look to an early conclusion."

Laxer points out, "As the [Shultz] report says, 'The economic infrastructure of the United States is and can be far more integrated with that of Canada than with the economy of any other country in the western hemisphere.' Anyone who imagines that a greatly increased sale of our oil to the United States can take place without great pressures for us to purchase more American industrial and manufactured goods should ponder the conclusion of the task force carefully. Obviously the supposed benefits of the energy deal in terms of jobs and tax dollars begin to vanish if it would bring in its train simply larger remittances of profits to the United States and greater imports of U.S. goods— goods which if manufactured in Canada would provide far more jobs and tax revenue than the export of raw products. The relationship between raw materials exports from the hinterland country and the import of finished goods from the metropolis is not lost on the task force; it should not be lost on Canadians either."

5: SOUTHEAST ASIA CO-PROSPERITY SPHERE

To an undetermined extent the outcome of the "energy crisis" in the United States will depend on international political and economic forces centered in Japan. In recent years the Japanese economy has been the fastest growing in the world, and it is largely based on importation of fuels. Japan produces little coal, oil, or natural gas and the country's growth has been dependent on petroleum which provides 70 percent of all energy requirements. Most of that oil comes from the Middle East and 90 percent of it is supplied by international oil corporations.

As a result, major international oil companies together with a net of other mining firms organized to supply the dynamic Japanese markets.

Now, however, these economic networks are under stress, both because China and the Soviet Union are emerging as major competitors to the U.S. supply companies, and because of a slowly rising wave of discontent, even rebellion, in Japan's resource colonies.

The Japanese are uneasy about their dependence on international corporations, particularly in the petroleum industry, where firms can fix prices and control supplies. And it makes them all the more uneasy because the oil supply mostly comes from the Middle East where the Organization of Petroleum Exporting

Countries (OPEC) has raised prices and threatened boycotts if the internationals do not grant them an ownership role.

In the year ending March 31, 1970, Japan imported three million barrels of oil a day. By 1975, when oil will account for 73 percent of the country's total energy requirements, crude oil needs are expected to be 6.2 million barrels a day, and by 1985, when oil as a source of energy will have declined to 68 percent, 13 million barrels a day will be needed. The biggest oil supplier is Caltex, the combine of Texaco and California Standard. It alone provides 15 percent of Japanese crude oil. Jersey Standard and Shell provide 11 percent each. Arabian Oil Co., a Japanese company, provides 10 percent. That means 37 percent of the basic Japanese energy sources are provided by three international corporations, two of them American.

(In geographical terms, 87.4 percent of all oil comes from the Middle East, with only 11.2 percent from Indonesia. Of the Middle Eastern oil, 32 percent is from Iran. Saudi Arabia is the second largest supplier. The search for oil on the Japanese offshore shelf is increasing, and three international corporations— Royal Dutch Shell, Caltex, and Indiana Standard—are all in joint ventures with Japanese companies.)

The statistics above help to show why the Japanese consider themselves something of a pawn in the energy game. For these reasons they have attempted to pool capital through cartels, and to build for themselves an oil-producing industry which can compete or at least hold its own with the Seven Sisters— Standard Oil of New Jersey, Royal Dutch Shell Group, Gulf, Texaco, Standard Oil of California, Socony Mobil, and British Petroleum. So far these efforts have not been terribly successful. The Arabian Oil Co. did find oil in Kuwait, but the oil is high in sulphur content and not particularly useful within Japan, where the demands are to reduce sulphur and cut air pollution. The oil explorations in Alaska were not successful. In Indonesia, where Japanese companies made oil finds, they apparently lacked sufficient capital for development, and wound up making agreements with big international oil companies to develop the petroleum.

To an uncertain degree the Japanese native oil industry and the internationals are allied in their efforts to develop petroleum resources throughout Southeast Asia. So far most of the activity has centered around the accommodating Indonesian government, in Malaysia, off the coast of Indochina, and on down to Australia, where Jersey Standard has begun to discover some fairly substantial amounts of oil. At the same time, the international oil companies have sunk considerable capital into development of new sorts of tankers that can transport liquified natural gas from Malaysia and Australia to Japan. Heretofore, gas was burned off at the wellhead, but with recent technological developments of the LNG tankers, whereby gas is captured, frozen, and thereby condensed, it can be transported by ship. The Buckley family companies discovered what appear to be substantial gas fields in northwestern Australia, and eventually this gas may find its way to Japanese markets.

In one sense the frantic exploration throughout the shallow seas of Indochina is within the joint interests of the international companies and the Japanese, meant to provide both with a diversified source of supply clear of the OPEC Middle Eastern regions, as well as to provide the needed additional supplies for Japan.

Yet the Japanese are in a constant squeeze trap. While they may want to get clear of OPEC, they cannot shake their everpresent partners, the big U.S.-based international oil companies, or the politics they drag along with them.

For example: Should the Communists win in South Vietnam and there turned out to be substantial amounts of oil in the Vietnamese territorial waters, then there might well be a source of petroleum in Southeast Asia outside the control of the international oil companies. That prospect is what makes the American companies so anxious about securing leases under the current regime. Whether or not there are large amounts of oil off

South Vietnam is really beside the point. The major companies naturally would like the oil for themselves, but as Michael Tanzer, the oil economist, points out, they may also want to prevent others from getting it, thereby threatening their control over prices. To maintain their high price structures, the international companies not only will want to get the oil, but also to maintain the South Vietnamese concession-granting government. In the case of South Vietnam, the large military apparatus provides a sizable market for oil, now mostly supplied by Jersey Standard and Shell. Jersey Standard has plans to expand its refinery in South Vietnam and it could, as in other areas, add a fertilizer plant. In order to protect their ventures, the American oil men may form joint ventures with the Japanese, a usual practice elsewhere in Southeast Asia. The result of such a political maneuver would be to tie both the international companies and the Japanese to the South Vietnamese military apparatus, a ruinous eventuality from the Japanese point of view.

The oil play in Japan grows progressively more complex for it involves both China and the Soviet Union. Until recently most of China's petroleum supplies lay along the Soviet border, far from major population and consumption centers, and because of their proximity to the border they were regarded as strategically vulnerable. Within the last year, however, the Chinese are reported to have made substantial discoveries of oil offshore, in the mouth of the Yellow River. If this oil can be developed, it will be of considerable advantage because it is so much closer to consuming centers. More important oil discoveries off the Yellow River are suggestive of far greater amounts of oil that lie under the Chinese outer continental shelf.

The China shelf is the center of considerable controversy, with the major international oil companies, the governments of South Korea, Taiwan, and Japan maneuvering for control. The U.S. Navy's oceanographic office believes the continental shelf off China, Korea, and Japan is "potentially one of the most prolific oil reserves in the world." According to the UN organization Economic Commission for Asia and the Far East (ECAFE), one shallow stretch of sea between Japan and Taiwan "may contain substantial resources of petroleum, perhaps comparable to the Persian Gulf."

By 1972, three sets of conflicting concessions were made by the governments of South Korea, Taiwan, and Japan without any consultation with China.

The largest, most controversial tract is under lease to Gulf Oil in an area between Japan and Taiwan, and it is thought to hold the most valuable resources. In the middle of Gulf's concession is a chain of uninhabited islands, called the Taioyutai, known in Japan as Senkaku Gunto. This chain of islands is about 120 miles southwest of Okinawa. Historically the islands belonged to China. Geologically they are part of the Chinese continental shelf.

But Japan, which made surveys around the islands, claims they form part of the Ryukyu Island chain of Okinawa. Thus, the Japanese are claiming them as part of their military sphere.

China began to make an issue of her sovereignty over the islands and their subsea resources in early December 1970. On December 29, 1970, the Chinese press specifically warned the international companies to stay clear of them. The U.S. State Department, in an effort to avoid raising diplomatic obstacles to discussions with the Chinese, thereupon announced in early April 1971 that the United States would not intervene in the event U.S. exploration ships were seized by China.

China's intervention followed meetings in November 1970 at which Japan, Taiwan, and South Korea all agreed to set aside their differences over concessions and cooperate in joint development of the shelf areas. On March 3, 1972, the Chinese UN delegate one again reasserted the claim to the offshore shelf area:

> On behalf of the government of the People's Republic of China, I hereby reiterate: China's Taiwan Province and all islands appertaining to it, including Taioyu Island, Huanqwei Island, Chihwei Island, Nanhsiao Island, Peihsiao Island, etc., are part of China's sacred territory. The sea-bed resources of

the sea around these islands and of the shallow seas adjacent to other parts of China belong completely to China and it is absolutely impermissible for any foreign aggressor to poke his fingers into them. No one whosoever is allowed to create any pretext to carve off China's territory and plunder the sea resources belonging to China. And no one will ever succeed in doing so.

The delegate went on to argue this principle:

We hold that it is within each country's sovereignty to decide the scope of its rights over territorial seas. All coastal countries are entitled to determine reasonably the limits of their territorial seas and jurisdiction according to their geographical conditions, taking into account the needs of their security and national economic interests and having regard for the requirement that countries situated on the same seas shall define the boundary between their territorial seas on the basis of equality and reciprocity.

We maintain that all coastal countries have the right of disposal of their natural resources in their coastal seas, sea-bed and subsoil thereof so as to promote the well-being of their people and the development of their national economic interests.

We maintain that the seas and oceans as well as their submarine resources beyond the limits of territorial seas and national jurisdiction are in principle commonly owned by all the peoples of the world. Questions of their use, exploitation, etc., should be settled through consultation by all countries jointly, both coastal and land-locked, and manipulation and monopoly by one or two superpowers are absolutely impermissible.

The question then is how this will affect the domination of petroleum in the Pacific Basin by the major oil companies. Will China permit any one of these companies to enter into an arrangement for exploitation of her oil? In exchange for capital or technology, for instance, will China give oil to the international cartel to be marketed under the cartel's control? It seems unlikely, for China has taken a position strongly backing the OPEC nations. What seems far more likely is that the international companies will shortly face a serious threat to their control in the Pacific in the Japanese markets from China and OPEC.

At the same time, the resource politics in the Pacific Basin are made much more complicated because of longstanding discussions between the Japanese and the Soviet Union, also involving imports to Japan of large amounts of coal, oil, and, most important, natural gas from the vast gas fields of Siberia. Such an agreement would necessitate building a long gas pipeline across Siberia and down to Japan. The discussions have been going on for considerable time, and while plans have been laid, the projects still are tentative. An agreement with the Soviet Union on fuels could jeopardize possible stepped-up trade relations between Japan and China.

Other basic raw material staples for the Japanese economy, such as iron ore and coal, which are the ingredients that enabled the country to have become the world's second largest steel producer, are provided through another industrial network which Japan has organized together with American and British corporations. Most of the operations are carried out in the "safe" old dominions of Canada, Australia, eastern United States, and South Africa. In August 1969, *Fortune*, by way of giving some advice to investors, described the growing reliance on the old dominions: "The major risks to today's mining companies are likely to come from the movement of great political forces. When large powers had their way with their colonies, there were few nationalizations or expropriations. Today even small countries, spurred by a growing sense of autonomy and nationalism, are demanding either a greater share of the profits from foreign mining operations, or outright ownership of them. . . . A not surprising consequence is that mining firms are poking around more assiduously these days in the 'stable' countries."

To satisfy demand in Japan, a few international corporations therefore have carried forward a sort of recolonization program, the worst results of which are apparent in Canada, but which also takes place in Australia, Appalachia, and South Africa. Ironically, this recolonization is encouraged throughout the dominions, as we have seen in Canada and Appalachia, through national policies of taxation and subsidy.

The process is at a fairly early stage, but it may presage new international relationships in which corporations, nations, and parts of other nations create new sorts of power alliances. The Canadians know very well what it is to be a resource colony of the United States, yet they may not realize the extent to which they also are a colony of the Japanese. The Japanese and Americans compete with one another in manufacture of steel, and yet part of the United States, indeed some U.S. steel companies, actually supply the Japanese with the coking coal that makes the steel which undercuts the U.S. steel market. The common agents in these transactions are international corporations, most of them domiciled in the United States, but increasingly in a position to play off nations against one another.

What follows is an attempt to look at parts of this process in operation, and some of the participants in the play.

THE JAPANESE IN APPALACHIA

Within the last few years the Japanese have had a substantial influence in organizing the coal industry of southern Appalachia, and hence carry considerable sway in the economy there. While it is difficult to be precise about the Japanese influence, it is nonetheless formidable.

Among the most profitable parts of the U.S. coal industry is the export trade, which produces about $1 billion in revenues a year. More than one-quarter of that trade is with Canada: coal fields in Pennsylvania and northern West Virginia produce steam coal, which is shipped by rail and boat to Canada where it is burned in electric utilities in Ontario, mostly around Toronto.

But the other more lucrative part of the coal export business is centered in southern Appalachia, in the triangular area encompassing southwestern Virginia, eastern Kentucky, and southern West Virginia. This area holds the world's most valuable deposits of coking coal, the coal that is turned to coke and becomes an ingredient in the manufacture of steel. In the United States, steel companies historically own their own captive mines which produce coking coal, as well as buy some additional supplies from coal companies. In addition, a few corporations specialize in selling coking coal abroad to steel mills. Historically they have sold the coal to Europe, particularly to Italy, France, and West Germany. In recent years, the trade with Japan has doubled, then trebled, as the U.S. coal miners labored to produce sufficient supplies of coal to supply the growing Japanese steel industry.

(The coal export trade is substantial. In 1970, a bumper year, the United States exported 70.9 million tons of coal, worth $950.2 million. The single largest customer was Japan, accounting for 38.9 percent of all coal exports, valued at $407.5 million. The second largest customer was Canada, which took 26.3 percent of the coal. Most of that was less expensive utility coal, valued at $197.9 million. In other words, about half the coal export trade went to Japan. The importance of the Japanese markets was even more apparent in 1971, when because of the slump in the Japanese steel industry exports fell off by 25 percent, according to preliminary figures.)

This is a special but important trade, for not only has it had a growing influence in the economy of Appalachia, but it has also had serious effects on other parts of the United States. Basically the export coal trade is organized by the railroads, and in particular the Norfolk & Western railroad.

The N&W is among the most profitable railroads in the country. Through Pocahontas Land Co., a subsidiary, the N&W owns large tracts of coal lands. The railroad is prohibited by law from mining the property, so it leases the holdings to coal companies. It then services the mines with its railroad cars. The most important part of its business is hauling coal out of the southern Appalachian triangle to its pier at Norfolk, Virginia. There the coal lies in an immense rail yard, then is loaded aboard ships for foreign trade.

To a much lesser extent, the other major coal-hauling railroad, the Chesapeake & Ohio, does the same thing. It also hauls to Norfolk, as well as to Philadelphia, for transshipment abroad. But the N&W has the biggest pier facility and does the most business carrying coal to port.

Executives of both these railroads are constantly on the move abroad, attempting to stir up business for their railroads, and for the mines on the railroad property. And in this sense the railroads act as brokers for the Japanese steel industry, putting together deals. They can buy coal for the Japanese and arrange long-term contracts.

While the railroads, on the one hand, have played an important role in tying the southern Appalachian districts to Japan, the Japanese agents themselves are in constant operation throughout Appalachia. Representatives from one or another of the big trading companies visit mines. They go through them, make diagrams, take pictures, meet the employees. Then with this information in hand, they return to Tokyo to work out a deal.

While it is hard to measure the real impact of the Japanese operations, and dangerous to make generalizations about it, it is possible to observe the extent of this business by looking at recent agreements. Consolidation Coal Co., the industry leader, produces about 10 million tons of metallurgical coal a year, and of that total now sells 3.5 million tons to the Japanese steel business. Island Creek, Occidental's subsidiary, is building one mine with Japanese financing, and is discussing a second mine in Virginia. The output in both instances would go to Japan under long-term contracts. The Pittston Co., fourth biggest U.S. coal company, sells two-thirds of its production abroad, and of that amount two-thirds goes to Japanese steel companies. The Japanese are Pittston's biggest single buyer. Eastern Gas & Fuel Associates, another major coal company, sells large quantities of coal abroad to the Japanese. In Alabama, U.S. Pipe & Foundry, a subsidiary of Jim Walters Corp., struck a deal to sell the Japanese large amounts of coking coal over the long term. George Wallace provided backing in the form of legislation to deepen the Mobile port so that the coal could be moved out.

Alabama has steadily increased shipments of its low sulphur metallurgical coal abroad. In 1970, 1.2 million tons were sold abroad, a 20-fold increase over the tonnage shipped during the 1960s. Coal executives were predicting sales might exceed 10 million tons by 1975. With some grades of coal selling for $21 a ton in Japan, compared to $9 a ton in the United States, coal executives in Alabama were all aglow at the prospect of more Japanese business. President Nixon came down in the spring of 1971 to dedicate a proposed waterway linking the Tombigbee and Tennessee rivers. Rivers now link the Mobile port with Alabama coal fields, but if this new quarter-of-a-billion dollar project is completed, Mobile could also serve coal fields of Tennessee and Kentucky.

The influence of the Japanese business is difficult to gauge because of its subtlety. For example, TVA, which during 1970—the year of growing Japanese imports—was pushed hard to find sufficient supplies of coal, lost one of its suppliers because the Japanese had persuaded the company to drop the public power system and, primed with cheap financing, redirect its mining operations to the Japanese markets. Part of the difficulty in obtaining coal by utilities during 1970 was a shortage of railroad cars. On investigation it was discovered that thousands of cars were sitting on the sidings at Norfolk, waiting for the Japanese ships to come in and take off the coal. Those cars could have been used to haul coal from Appalachia to utilities desperate for fuel. In that same year, some coal companies did not meet their contract requirements with electrical utilities; because the export market was more profitable, they directed their activities at developing mines for those markets.

In early 1972, coal company officials in Virginia glumly speculated on a further slowdown in some mines and possible shut-down in others because of expected continuing declines in the Japanese steel industry.

Meanwhile, the Japanese incursion into Appalachia has other ramifications as well. David Francis, chairman of the Princess Coal Sales Co., of Huntington, West Virginia, ran up against the ecology movement when he sought to mine coal for the Japanese in 1970. After some initial exploring on the Shavers Fork River, Francis leased what he believed to be valuable coal lands, containing two seams of Sewell-type coal, and determined to open a mine. As he recalled the situation, "In May of this year [1970], we were approached by representatives of Nippon Steel Co., who expressed an interest in the joint development of large reserves of Sewell coal. When we explained that we had under lease about 100 million tons in 30,000 acres with a railroad there to serve us, they showed immediate interest. As a result of three months of intense discussions and negotiations, in early July we finalized a contract for the development of the Linan area. The Japanese agreed to lend us $1.6 million and we agreed to produce approximately 500,000 tons per year. The Japanese loan was for development of roads, mine sites, purchase of underground equipment, outside conveyor belts, bins, bath houses, etc. The Japanese intent was for us to develop Sewell coal production up to a rate of three to four million tons per year for their account."

Francis went on to recount how he called the West Virginia governor Arch Moore from the Japanese offices in New York to seek his permission for a water pollution permit. The governor had recently returned from a trip to Japan where he had held talks with the president of Nippon Steel, who, the governor later told the press, had assured him the Japanese were anxious to buy up more West Virginia coal.

But because of protests by local ecologists, Francis did not get his pollution permit, and the proposal for the new mine ran down into a bitter local argument between the ecologists on the one hand, worrying about stream pollution, and Francis on the other, who claimed the new mine would create more jobs for unemployed people. As a result, the mine project was postponed, while Francis appealed the pollution permits through the courts.

There are other dimensions to the Japanese influence in Appalachia. Among the most promising future markets for U.S. coal exports are Brazil and Argentina. In Brazil the steel industry is expected to double capacity by the middle of this decade. Such expansion will mean considerable growth for U.S. coal exports there. While the steel industry in Brazil is owned in the majority by the government, both Japanese and U.S. steel firms have minority interests in steel production. In this instance, U.S. and Japanese steel companies work together in influencing the economy of southern Appalachia.

More ironically, US Steel, which has its own captive mines, sold some of that coal to the Japanese. This seemed a particularly bizarre maneuver since US Steel coal became Japanese steel, which could compete with US Steel products in American or other foreign markets.

While the U.S. coking coal is considered to be the most valuable in the world, neither the Japanese nor Europeans can afford to use it exclusively. Thus, they generally blend the good coal with some lesser quality material. In the case of Japan, that lesser quality coal may come from Australia, its second biggest supplier, or western Canada, its third largest supplier. Japan also on occasion uses South African coal.

These other coal sources are organized for the Japanese steel industry by a handful of U.S. or British domiciled international corporations.

AUSTRALIA AND CANADA

Both Australia and Canada provide major supplies of coal to the Japanese steel industry. The mining activities in both these countries are dominated by a few international corporations— chief among them, Kaiser Industries; Utah International Resources, a San Francisco firm; and Rio Tinto Zinc, the British mining conglomerate.

In western Canada, Kaiser Industries is building enormous strip mines to supply the Japanese. In fact, Kaiser pretty much established and dominates the Canadian coal-mining industry, the production of which is scheduled for export to Japan. The Canadians have not placed controls over coal exports, and in fact they encouraged the project by spending upward of $25 million to build Robert Bank, a superport near Vancouver, where the coal can be transshipped to Japan. The Canadian mining tax incentives apply to this venture, and as previously noted, the result is to import mechanized industry, which exports and exhausts raw materials without creating many jobs.

Because of its abundant raw materials and proximity to Japan, Australia provides Japan with major supplies. The country provides 40 percent of all the Japanese iron ore and large quantities of coking coal for steel making. Both iron ore and coal are the country's major exports, and as agriculture declines in relative significance, mining seems likely to expand. (Indeed, there have been approaches to China for sale of iron ore.) As in the case of Canada, Australia is attractive to the Japanese because much of the mining can be done by machinery in strip or open pits. Thus labor costs are low, or conversely the extraction of raw materials is not a major factor in providing employment. Because of the run on Australian coal, there has been criticism within the country that the resource may be exhausted within 35 to 55 years.

In Australia, Kaiser and Rio Tinto Zinc formed joint ventures which result in their dominance of the aluminum industry and iron ore production. They also mine coal. The coal industry is largely dominated by U.S.-based companies. For example, Peabody, Kennecott's subsidiary, second ranking U.S. producer, with most of its mines in the Midwest or Rocky Mountains, is a major coal producer in Australia with its output going to the Japanese markets. Daniel Ludwig, the American who controls a large tanker fleet, is involved in coal mining in Australia through Clutha Development Corporation.

Perhaps the most interesting Japanese coal supplier in Australia is Utah International (formerly Utah Mining and Construction), which until recently was controlled by the Eccles family of Salt Lake City. Utah is ranked as the fifth largest uranium producer within the United States, and it operates the world's largest coal strip mine in Arizona. But the company is best known for its shrewd activities in the Pacific Basin. It owns various mining properties in Latin America and Australia, and makes a business of mining the ores, then hauling them to Japan. For example, Utah has extensive iron ore holdings in Australia where it is engaged in mining the ore. A subsidiary, based in Panama, markets the iron ore, and arranges for another subsidiary, this one based in Liberia, to carry the ore. If the harbors are not deep enough for Utah's modern supertankers, then the company calls in yet another subsidiary which has deep-water dredges to open up the port.

In Australia, Utah's most impressive project is a vast coal strip mine in the Boonyella section of Queensland. This mine has contracts with the Japanese for $1 billion worth of coal, and is involved in building a port, railroads, and a company town.

JAPAN'S NEW ALLY IN SOUTH AFRICA

South Africa might well emerge as a major fuels supplier for both Japan and Europe. Mining always has been a staple of the South African economy, although its future depends on an increased rate of industrialization. Much of the industry in recent years has come from U.S. firms, which set up base camps in South Africa, then push out into developing Asian markets. Thus, auto makers establish headquarters in South Africa, then set up parts and assembly operations in other countries where labor is inexpensive. The products are finally sold in Japan. Ironically, the South African government's apartheid policy is hindering industrial development by keeping blacks out of skilled jobs at a time when there are not enough skilled workers. But apartheid does reinforce the traditional South African mining industry, which depends on masses of poorly paid black workers. Thus, apartheid benefits the Japanese and European purchasers who recently completed contracts for South African coal, not because South Africa has so much coal or because it is of high value, but because it is cheap. In the past, South Africa depended on gold mining, but gold is declining in prominence and other minerals are taking its place. The greatest boost for South African mining came a few years ago when Rio Tinto Zinc, an international mining corporation based in Britain, put together the large Palabara copper mines. Uranium is produced as a by-product of gold mining, and the country has the world's third largest reserves. For the time being, there is a glut of uranium, but the Japanese are writing contracts for the mid-1970s, when stockpiles are expected to decline. In addition, South Africa supplies West Germany's nuclear reactors, and the Germans have provided them with scientific help in nuclear technology. In 1971, the South African government claimed it found a way to enrich uranium and said it would build a pilot uranium enrichment plant. If true, this development will enhance the country's position, placing it in line to get part of the $1 billion nuclear fuels market. South Africa has never signed the nuclear nonproliferation treaty.

URANIUM MONOPOLY

By the end of the century, much of the electricity in the world will be produced by nuclear energy. Despite the safety problems, the United States is resolutely pursuing the goal of nuclear power, and Japan, dependent on the various suppliers of oil and coal, is moving fast to create nuclear power plants. Nuclear power depends on production of uranium, and one result has been to create a headlong race among the international corporations for control of uranium supplies. Outside of the Soviet Union and China, the most important economically inexpensive uranium supplies are in Canada, the United States, and South Africa.

As with the international coal trade, the pattern is repeated, with a few major companies moving to dominate the uranium supplies. In the United States one oil company, Kerr-McGee, controls 27 percent of the uranium market. Kerr-McGee is relatively small among oil companies, and within five or ten years it may be overtaken by one or another of the major oil firms which have moved into coal. Gulf, for instance, is fast developing major uranium supplies. In Canada and South Africa, however, uranium production is dominated through interlocking mining companies. Two of these are preeminent: Rio Tinto Zinc (RTZ) and Anglo American Corporation of South Africa, both of which are interconnected through their directorates; Anglo American holds an interest in RTZ.

Both of these organizations hold extraordinary positions in the international fuels business. Rio Tinto Zinc is a London-based mining conglomerate which modestly declares in the annual report that it aims to discover and exploit the natural resources of the world. Rio Tinto is not large by U.S. standards (sales of only $1 billion) and is ranked well down in *Fortune*'s list of 200 international corporations. Still the company is of considerably greater importance than these figures suggest. The company is an amalgam of copper interests in Spain, tin holdings in Australia, and vast borax deposits in Nevada. More recently, RTZ became deeply involved in copper mining in southern Africa. The Rothschilds are important backers of the company. A 1970 annual report shows that Baron Guy de Rothschild and D. Colville, both partners of N. M. Rothschild & Sons, held more than 600,000 shares of stock. RTZ is of considerable importance in Britain because it maintains a large holding in British petroleum.

Aside from the United States, Canada and South Africa have the largest uranium deposits in the world. Through a subsidiary, Rio Algom, RTZ controls seven of the 11 uranium mines in Canada, and is by far and away the largest producer, supplying the British Atomic Energy Commission and various Japanese customers. In addition, RTZ and affiliated companies explore for uranium in the United States, have discovered large uranium finds at Rossing in southwest Africa, and control Mary Kathleen uranium works in Australia. RTZ is important in South Africa because it supplied the impetus to build up copper exports through the Palabara mine. It is of considerable importance in Australia, being part of the venture which recently made the first major iron products sale to China.

A growing force among the international fuels corporations is the Anglo American Corporation of South Africa. Anglo American is the vehicle for the activities of Sir Harry Oppenheimer, the gold magnate. Until his death in 1970, Charles Engelhard, the American who ran a precious metals empire through Engelhard Minerals and Chemicals, had associated himself with Oppenheimer in various ventures. Shortly before Engelhard's death, the Engelhard family sold most of their holdings in Engelhard Hanovia to Anglo American, providing Oppenheimer with control of the company.

In South Africa, Anglo American accounts for about one-third of all production. Much of Anglo American's uranium holdings are committed to the Japanese. In addition, Anglo American has several coal mines, and the business is brisk because of increasing exports to Japan.

If South Africa becomes a basic fuels supplier to the Japanese, Anglo American's fortunes will rise. Equally important, however, are the various Anglo American investment holdings. Most of the company's investments outside of Africa are handled through an affiliate based in London, Charter Consolidated. Charter Consolidated, another company stitched together by the Rothschilds, maintains a sizable but undisclosed holding in Rio Tinto Zinc, with which it is involved in different mining operations in southern Africa.

THE PACIFIC RIM

In the past it has been usual to perceive Japan's relation to the United States through its military relationships, resulting from the occupation at the end of World War II, and extending through first a 1954 and then a 1960 mutual security pact with the United States, which since 1970, either side can abrogate with one year's notice.

Within the framework of successive mutual security agreements, the Japanese and American companies developed a "military-industrial complex," modeled after the U.S. lines, whereby U.S. firms licensed Japanese counterpart companies in military areas to build planes, ships, and other equipment, and hence tie Japan to the United States through the military-industrial complex. These historic arrangements reached even further, however, for from the early 1950s onward, the United States objective in Southeast Asia was to prevent the Asian markets from falling to the Communists. Herbert P. Bix describes the situation in the *Bulletin of Concerned Asian Scholars:*

> The key agreement of the period of the first American military alliance with Japan was the U.S.-Japan Mutual Defense Assistance Agreement (MDA), signed by the Yoshida government on March 8, 1954, after a year of lengthy negotiating. Yoshida himself, it should be noted, had desired the rearmament of Japan to follow rather than accompany the completion of economic reconstruction, and therefore disagreed with Dulles over the speed at which rearmament should proceed.
>
> On the basis of the MDA, Japan's modern armed forces were organized: laws were enacted setting up the Japan Defense Agency (JDA), equivalent to a ministry of war in all but name, and the Self-Defense Forces; the police system was recentralized to bolster internal security; a Defense Secrets Protection Law was enacted; and other laws were passed to consolidate the defense industry. Underlying the MDA, however, was a U.S.-Japanese understanding on matters that were other than military in nature.
>
> The MDA was negotiated during a time of profound crisis and confusion in American policy toward Asia. The French were on the verge of defeat in Indo-China and the American objective was to prevent that region from falling into the hands of the Communists, i.e., genuinely nationalist forces who would not be subservient to the interests of American

capitalism. Such an eventuality, by cutting Southeast Asia off from the world capitalist market, would not only deprive the American empire of vast raw material resources, but also force newly independent Japan to normalize relations with her natural trading partners, her Communist neighbors. The American-sponsored rearmament of Japan was thus paralleled by the economic objective of fitting Japanese exports into the agricultural economies of Southeast Asia. Consequently, while the Self-Defense Forces were being reorganized and equipped with American weapons, the "Society for Asian Economic Cooperation" (Asia Society) was launched under the aegis of the Foreign Office to facilitate Japan's economic penetration of Southeast Asia.

During the Korean war the United States forced a trade embargo with China on the Japanese, and Japan backed up the United States in taking a tough stand against China. Bix writes, "One explanation lies in the fact that after 1954 the United States pressured other nations in its alliance network to open up markets for Japan 'in return for increased opportunities in the American market.'

"At a closed regional meeting of American ambassadors in Asia in early March (1955), Secretary of State Dulles outlined American diplomatic strategy, a major goal of which was to develop markets for Japan in Southeast Asia in order to counteract Communist trade efforts and to promote trade between Japan and Southeast Asian countries. Dulles must also have been aware of the pressure at that time from within Japan for increased trade with the People's Republic of China."

Actually, of course, the military alliance of Japan and the United States, in Southeast Asia did become a sizable undertaking, but instead of working together, the two military allies found themselves in competition.

As Japan grew progressively stronger militarily, the military alliances with the United States grew weaker, and hence the economic alliances and networks became more important. In effect, the economic ties became the means by which the United States could continue to control military policy in Japan.

The energy alliances and trade described above provide some idea of the basic trade networks in the natural resource area. A group of West Coast businessmen have concocted a much more ambitious theory for Pacific Basin trade, which envisions a type of common market trading network among the nations of the Pacific rim. The members of this group cluster around Stanford University, and the group involves members of mining firms, banks, the petroleum industry, shipping, farm products, and so on. The politics are not particularly subtle. What they have in mind is a "common market" that will provide them incentives to dredge out iron ore in Peru or Australia, ship it to Japan for processing, and then market it through other multinational corporate members of the Pacific rim community. In one sense it represents an American intrusion into the old Japanese Southeast Asia Co-Prosperity Sphere.

The Pacific rim concept helps to set into perspective some of the energy industry operations. But perhaps the best example of it in fullest rendering is to be found in the automobile industry. Expansion by U.S. auto companies into Southeast Asia, for instance, is a natural extension and development of the existing natural resource industry networks.

The three major automobile makers have been anxious to get a grip on the Japanese auto markets and they fantasize capturing control of "mass" markets in Asia as well. Generally they pursue a common strategy which runs as follows: Manufacturing operations are based in the old dominions of South Africa and Australia, which now serve as springboards into Asia. These base plants are supplemented by parts and assembly operations in other Asian countries where wages are particularly low. U.S. companies bought into Japanese auto makers with an eye to capturing part of the Japanese luxury car export sales, most of them in the United States. Finally the fantasy is for the big three auto makers to begin mass production of inexpensive automobiles and trucks in poor countries of Asia in order to develop and capture this market.

If successful, the overall result of the strategy will be to cir-

cumscribe independent auto development in Asia and keep
control of the world auto industry in Detroit.

So far the U.S. companies have met with some success.
Ford's subsidiary, Ford Asia Pacific & South Africa, with headquarters at Melbourne, is in charge of coordinating activities
of the basic Ford plants in Australia and South Africa with
assembly operations in the Philippines, Singapore, New Zealand,
and Thailand. Ford negotiated to purchase a 20 percent initial
interest in Toyo Kogyo Company, the Japanese auto maker that
sells Mazda cars and trucks. In resisting this investment, the
company president warned that holdings of more than 25 percent "would be tantamount to being taken over by the U.S.
company." But Henry Ford insisted he doesn't want to take
over Toyo. In March 1971 when he was in Japan, he declared,
"We would have representation on the board of directors and
initially one or two residents in Hiroshima. We would expect
to participate in major operating and policy decisions, but we
would not have any positive authority—that would continue
to reside with Mr. Matsuda and the Japanese management."

But after nearly three years of talks the deal between Ford
and Toyo fell through. The Japanese feared Ford was seeking
a wedge in Southeast Asia to use against them. The *Japan
Economic Journal* reported, "Toyo Kogyo President Matsuda
said that the biggest problem had been that Ford sought management control and the two companies decided that it was
fruitless for both to keep on continuing the talks."

Ford also apparently objected because of the high price of
Toyo stock. *Japan Economic Journal* added, "Another factor,
informants felt, was that Ford was anxious to secure Toyo
Kogyo's technology on producing rotary engine autos in entering into a capital tie-up but the Japanese auto maker completely
was against exchanging technologies."

Ford also wants to build cars on its own for the Asian mass
markets. Henry Ford has said, "In South Korea, Taiwan, and
Indonesia we see promising markets and an attractive supply
of cheap labor." Tentative plans call for developing a car which

could be sold for as little as $800, built from materials by Asian workers. Eventually such a vehicle could be assembled in such places as Cambodia, Laos, or Papua-New Guinea. One idea is to make a plywood body with a rugged frame and a two-cylinder engine.

GM Operations, also based in Melbourne under General Motors Holdens Pty., Ltd., is in charge of activities throughout Asian, Pacific and South African theaters. GM maintains assembly plants in Malaysia, the Philippines, and New Zealand. New assembly plants are scheduled for opening in Indonesia and Taiwan. GM was prepared to settle for a 20 percent investment in a Japanese auto maker, but the Sato government, apparently fearful of offending the company, announced GM was expected to demand a 35 percent investment in Isuzu Motors Ltd., a big truck maker. On learning this, GM immediately pressed for and apparently will receive a 35 percent interest.

A Chrysler subsidiary in Australia coordinates activities in Asia, but is under control of Chrysler International in Geneva. Chrysler bought an initial 15 percent interest in Mitsubishi Motors. The amount is less than the GM and Ford investments, but that may reflect Chrysler's own sliding fortunes in the United States. At any rate, the investment is scheduled to increase to 35 percent by 1973. Under the terms of the deal, Chrysler is marketing Mitsubishi's small passenger car, the Dodge Colt, in the United States. It is also making Mitsubishi autos in South Africa and Australian plants, and Mitsubishi hopes Chrysler will make available facilities in France and Britain as well. Next fall, Mitsubishi will begin importing Valiants into Japan from Chrysler plants in Australia.

These takeover maneuverings are long-term arrangements. For the time being the Japanese auto makers are in a bad slump. Overcapacity is such that the Japanese industry could produce at least one million more vehicles than it now does with existing plants. Domestic markets are thoroughly saturated and likely to stay that way. The solution is foreign expansion: In 1967, 12 per cent of production was exported; in 1971 nearly one-quarter of all autos produced were exported, most to the United States.

The Japanese are anxious to sell more vehicles to China, which in 1970 announced its intention to purchase "several tens of thousands" of trucks and buses from Japan. This wouldn't amount to much when set against the 400,000 units exported each year to the United States. However, the China market is likely to increase, and it is one way out of the Japanese auto glut.

6: THE NEW ALLIANCES

The Japanese supply net of multinational corporations that poach on the old white dominions may have a parallel in new relationships that are taking place between U.S.-based multinational companies and governments of the third world. The proposed arrangement for importation of natural gas from Algeria into U.S. East Coast ports by the El Paso Natural Gas Co., largest U.S. gas pipeline company, may foreshadow other similar energy alliances. It is worth looking at in some detail because the El Paso deal raises new political issues, of both domestic and international scope.

For years El Paso has monopolized the gas supplies of California, controlling the major pipelines from the southwestern gas fields into the rich southern California markets. In addition, it has controlled spur lines through the mountain states and into the northwest, where they connect with Canadian fields. Since 1961, the company has ignored the Supreme Court's order to divest itself of this northwestern pipeline. The Supreme Court sought by this order to restore some semblance of competition to the gas business in the West. El Paso has countered by presenting special interest legislation which would circumvent the Supreme Court order.

El Paso has various other operations including international holdings in both oil and gas, real estate development schemes around Houston, and coal fields it holds jointly with Consolidation. It eventually plans to develop this coal into synthetic gas.

Since 1964, El Paso has discussed with the Algerian government various schemes for developing the vast gas supplies of Algeria by liquifying the gas, then shipping it either to southern Europe or to the United States. In 1968, it formally proposed to purchase one billion cubic feet of gas per day from the Algerian government for importation into the gas-scarce U.S. East Coast markets. The arrangement would run for 25 years. The gas will be liquified, then shipped in specially constructed tankers to East Coast utilities which are both short of gas and in need of a clean fuel because of increasingly strict air pollution regulations. In all, this deal will cost $1.7 billion.

Even before the final arrangements were completed, the El Paso-Algerian deal had stirred considerable repercussions. Because the imported LNG will cost much more than gas piped from fields in the southwestern part of the United States, it contributed to the pressures resulting in higher gas prices within the United States. Indeed, it might be considered to have established a threshold level for this sort of gas. After the FPC had granted preliminary approval, there were announcements of other LNG negotiations, and El Paso, and others that had been insisting that synthetic gas made from coal was economically unfeasible, took a more optimistic view of that business, and announced plans to build gasification plants.

For its part, the maneuver represented a skillful strike into new U.S. markets by El Paso, which heretofore had monopolized the West Coast, and now was attacking the East Coast from sea. The Algerian gas deal, if finally approved, will supply as much as 15 percent of the total East Coast gas supply during the 1980s. Thus, El Paso is offering a strong challenge to the other major pipelines—Texas Eastern, Tenneco, and Transcontinental—which historically have served the East Coast markets through long-range pipelines extending north from the gas fields of the Southwest. And this threatened competition without doubt has hastened their interest in both LNG, and more important, synthetic coal gas. The existing pipeline companies are better able to exploit coal gas because their pipelines extend through major Appalachian coal fields.

The Algerian LNG deal will introduce for the first time U.S. traffic in the new cryogenic gas tankers. There is considerable question about the safety of these new tank ships, which may turn out to be floating bombs. A 1972 report by the Bureau of Mines says that in case of a spill the odorless gas would pour out of the ship, at first forming flammable layers along the top of the water, then dissipating into an even more dangerous flammable cloud. While the bureau experts don't want to be alarming, it is not difficult to visualize the dangers: If an LNG tanker should collide in, say, New York harbor, a gas cloud might well bathe Manhattan in a sea of flames.

There is little experience in dealing with LNG. But the Bureau of Mines experts remember what happened in Cleveland during World War II, when an LNG storage tank opened and burning gas poured into the streets and sewers causing explosions and killing 128 people. Flames reached half a mile into the sky. The bureau, which is making a study for the Coast Guard, attempted to simulate conditions of a spill in an earlier test made in 1970. A little LNG was dropped into an aquarium, blowing it up. Then gas was dropped into a pond, and there were thumping explosions. The report concluded, "Unfortunately the study raised questions on one aspect of the problem for which no answers are yet available. Small scale explosions occurred when LNG was poured into water; no explanations can be offered that these explosions could not scale up to damaging proportions in a massive spill."

In 1972, one LNG tanker made calls at Boston, bringing in gas from Algeria to Distrigas Co. Other shipments passed through lower New York harbor on their way to the oil and chemical complex along the Arthur Kill at Staten Island. If El Paso's current proposals are approved by the Federal Power Commission, half a dozen other tankers will be constructed to import Algerian LNG to east coast U.S. ports. And there is a good possibility that LNG may be imported from the Soviet Union, Nigeria, Venezuela, and Libya. Ships now ply the Pacific carrying LNG from Alaska to Japan. Other tankers soon will be transporting gas from Malaysia and Australia to Japan.

But the safety problems are not the least of the ramifications to the El Paso-Algerian deal. Negotiations for the venture were unusual. Since the United States and Algeria do not maintain diplomatic relations, Algerian agents in the United States employed the law firm of Clark Clifford to represent them in complicated negotiations at the State Department and before the Federal Power Commission, which must give final approval. The U.S. Export-Import Bank agreed to underwrite part of the cost. A group of American banks, led by Manufacturers Hanover will finance other aspects of the deal.

The deal initially was opposed by major U.S. oil companies, including Standard Oil Co. of New Jersey. These companies made it clear they would block serious negotiations until Algeria paid off some $40 million in claims pending since Algeria nationalized the oil business. Once the Algerians agreed to pay off the claims, the major companies dropped their resistance. Still the deal met objections by independent U.S. oil and gas men, who feared the foreign competition, and by the utilities, the major gas purchasers, because they did not want to pay such high prices. In Algeria there was opposition within the government on grounds that the proposed deal tied the nation's economy too closely to the United States.

The most serious objections apparently came from the French, who diligently sought to dominate the Algerian economy since independence. The French, for example, have blocked World Bank loans to Algeria which might have provided a measure of economic independence. When Algeria nationalized the oil industry, the French threatened to sue other countries that bought Algerian oil. When the El Paso deal was put together the French apparently sought to block it. According to Algerian sources, the French first schemed among the Arabs, attempting to convince them that by selling gas to the United States, Algeria was casting in with Israel's principal ally, and that the deal should be opposed on this ground. In the United States, the French attempted to convince Zionist groups that the deal represented a collusion between the United States and the Arab enemy.

Originally, El Paso had been in negotiations for an LNG project to ship the gas to southern Europe, but this project was cut short by the Soviets.

The Soviet Union scheme to turn its large oil reserves into a major export item had never worked out, but the Russians had successfully developed large-scale gas reserves in Siberia and built a pipeline to the Moscow area. The pipes then were extended down into Europe. And the Soviets aggressively began to market gas among the French and West Germans. They won a major deal in Italy, arranging to provide the Italians with large amounts of Siberian gas through an extended pipeline system. All along, the Soviet Union was meant to be Algeria's ally, helping the developing country break the bonds of French colonialism. But in Europe the Soviets regularly undercut all Algerian initiatives in building a gas trade. In Algeria the Soviets were regarded with growing bitterness. Their role in blocking European gas sales was among the subtle forces which contributed toward moving Algeria away from the Soviet Union, closer to the United States on the one hand, and toward the Chinese on the other.

Thus, among all the other implications, the El Paso-Algerian arrangement is widely regarded as a substantial breakthrough by the United States in establishing diplomatic and trade relations with a third world country, but also as a coup in breaking the Algerian economy away from the French influence, and from the Soviet.

The Algerian arrangement may well come under attack from the environmental movement within the United States. By the spring of 1972 certain aspects of the arrangement were questioned by environmentalists. That would be an ironic turn of events. Ecologists have applied much of the pressure which is causing electric utilities to use more gas. They have pushed hard for strict air pollution regulations, limiting the amount of sulphur emissions, and thereby virtually excluding coal as a fuel. (The market for low sulphur coal is tight, and there is no practical way of getting sulphur out of coal.) At the same time, ecologists successfully blocked a variety of nuclear projects. As a result, utilities are forced to search harder for gas and to convert to oil.

The project raises other questions of a more subtle nature. An environmental challenge to the Algeria-El Paso deal, for instance, might be perceived as pitting the American, white upper-middle-class environmental movement against the interests of a developing third world nation. For the radical community in the United States, Algeria's relationship with El Paso Natural Gas Co. holds other poignant ironies. Here is a new nation of the revolutionary third world, having secured its independence from France, breaking from oppressive economic dependence and now replacing that relationship with partnership with a U.S.-based utility, which, as much as any other company, has worked to exploit the "energy crisis" for the profits of its stockholders. In that sense Algeria has escaped the French to become a junior partner in the international oil cartel, which through history has systematically drained the world's natural resources.

7: CONCLUSION

The politics of the energy trusts are destructive. The El Paso Natural Gas-Algeria liaison may well represent the beginning of a process which not only will result in further drain of natural resources, but also will raise new environmental questions, and ultimately lead to new alliances between the multinational corporations and nations of the third world. In Canada we have observed how U.S. pressure to draw down oil and gas has a regressive effect, contributing to a stagnant political economy, causing unemployment, engendering a deepening bitterness by Canadians to the United States. The domination of oil, gas, coal, and uranium by large energy trusts has helped to create its own energy crisis, raising prices, changing markets, carving out new resource colonies, leading to growing disparity between rich and poor. But the process does not stop here. For what the energy companies now predict is that after having exhausted the people and resources of Appalachia, they can move on to the western mountains where the new coal reserves lie, and in due course exhaust those resources and those people in imitation of the ruinous process applied in Appalachia.

There are other approaches for dealing with the "energy crisis" than the ones proposed by private industry—but they demand fundamental political and economic change, essentially involving the expropriation of the nation's energy resources by democratic processes and destruction of the current apparatus through which the private government of energy operates. A proposal for how the changes might began to be carried out is sketched below.

The major U.S. energy resources which now are being developed or shortly will be developed are either owned by state or federal governments. In the case of oil and natural gas the major new deposits lie under the sea on the outercontinental shelf. Coal and uranium deposits are on public lands in the mountain states, as is the case with oil shale. State and federal agencies have allowed the bureaus in charge of these properties to become instrumentalities of the industries themselves. Thus, the Interior Department has allowed production of oil in offshore waters, controlled by the federal government, to be dictated by state regulatory commissions which usually are industry-dominated bodies. There has been no effort to plan development of coal resources, except as the companies come forward with one or another of their own schemes for exploitation. Although the U.S. Geological Survey is supposedly an agency of the U.S. government, it answers largely to the petroleum companies which provide it with details of oil and gas reserves. The Geological Survey keeps those reserve statistics private in order to protect the interests of the competing companies. The Federal Power Commission, as already indicated, follows the lead of the Geological Survey and the industry, refusing to make its own independent estimates of natural gas reserves. Congressional committees with a purview over energy resources spend their time attempting to work out technical difficulties which permit the industries to get on with their work, i.e. ensuring that gas prices will be increased, helping to spur industrial growth, and so on.

The first, basic step required before any further action can be taken on energy would be to establish independent agencies within the federal government to oversee and administer natural resources. The most important part of this process would be to conduct independent analyses of the nation's energy resources. As of this writing, spring 1972, there is no sign that such a policy will be established either by government or within the Congress. Hence, it remains for citizens acting through the courts to block further sale or lease of energy resources in the federal or state domains unless and until government undertakes its basic responsibilities under the law and conducts independent public surveys of energy resources on which some sort of rational energy policy can be based. In various areas environmental groups have succeeded in holding up offshore lease sales, but the attacks need to be much more systematic, aimed at halting the entire Interior Department lease sales operation.

Such a relatively simple step could have important consequences, for it would equip citizens groups with information they now lack to challenge the contentions of the energy trusts that there is an "energy crisis."

A second step would be to reorganize energy resources, replacing the private government of energy with truly public institutions. Such a reorganization might include the following possibilities: The Congress would create a federal energy board, which could supervise overall energy policy within the country. The board would provide an umbrella for regional plans, which in turn would carry forward different schemes. On an international level, the energy board could negotiate and make purchases of oil, gas, and other fuels in world markets.

Under the broad aegis of the government's energy board, certain energy regions within the United States would be created. Within each region, public elected agencies would establish economic plans, binding on development within that region. These plans would necessarily determine how much of a region's energy resources were required to execute the overall plan. In addition, such a planning agency would determine energy surplus or deficiency, then arrange to purchase or sell supplies through the national board.

The idea of a regional energy agency would be to develop

binding economic plans for the area. For example, in the north-east part of the country such a regional agency would weigh the necessity of developing offshore oil and gas in terms of the fuels end use. If the petroleum were to be refined into gasoline, then the analysis and decision would take into account air polluting effects of motor vehicles, whether for example it would make more sense to develop rapid transit. If the petroleum were to be used principally in the manufacture of electricity and the electricity would go to a large new office complex in downtown New York, the regional plan would determine whether that building complex was necessary, what useful purpose it would serve.

Under federal law each region would be eligible for sizable federal loans, the proceeds of which could be used to develop energy resources. The resources themselves would be broken down into tracts with every other tract reserved for development by the regional agency either on its own or on contract to a public nonprofit organization. Determination of the winning bidder would be made on the basis of his potential ability to produce the resource, taking into account various strict environmental and technical requirements. The federal loans would be made available to different sorts of public nonprofit groups, so that an organization's financial resources would not be a factor in determining its acceptance as a winning bidder. In practice, this might mean that a group of townspeople, a community corporation, etc., could successfully bid to produce oil or gas or coal for a stated purpose within the regional plan. A community corporation in an impoverished section of West Virginia, for instance, might be provided the funds and the coal reserves to develop mines that would produce coal to make electricity for the town. In Logan County, scene of 1972's disastrous flood, such a community organization of survivors and miners might well apply for and win control of the five Pittston Co. mines in order to meet provisions of the regional plan; in this instance, that plan would involve rebuilding the communities of Logan County and introducing into them some nonmining industrial and service industry. To put it another way, the revenues and profits which would ordinarily accrue to Pittston, would rather be redirected to the communities which suffered the mines. The men who work the mines, and whose lives are directly affected by them, would control the mines, and they would work the mines to develop their own communities, not to meet criteria developed by Pittston to suit Japanese buyers in Tokyo.

As the resources were developed according to the regional plan they would be fed through existing marketing installations of private industry—investor-owned utilities, refineries, gas stations, pipeline systems, gasification plants, etc. But all these facilities henceforth would be treated as public utilities required to handle resources from all sources at some established fee, and managed through the regional plan. To be more specific, if such a program were adopted, the American Electric Power Co., biggest privately owned electric power concern in the nation, would be administered under one or two regional plans.

Turning the marketing mechanisms of the fuels industry into public utilities would provide immediate and immense savings to consumers. The 1,200 percent gas price increase from producer to consumer in Boston, for example, would be eliminated. Since there would be no stockholders, there would be no dividends, and whatever nominal interest was paid would be paid the government on loans, not to banks. Thus, two of the major drags on the utility industry would be eliminated. (In an interesting analysis, "Who Rules the Corporations" published in *Socialist Revolution*, Robert Fitch and Mary Oppenheimer point out how financial institutions can bleed electric utilities:

> Electrical power failures in New York City and other eastern cities are the unintended consequence of long-range financial planning. A reading of Con Ed's income accounts will show that power failures are inevitable. Beginning in 1964, the year before the epic blackout, Con Ed received about $100 million in net income. By 1969, net income had grown about 27 percent, to $127 million yearly. But while net income was

growing at about five percent a year, deductions from income were growing even faster. Dividend payments increased about 28 percent; payments to holders of Con Ed's long-term debt increased more than 45 percent—about nine percent a year. The result is that while the amount paid to capital holders amounted to 88 percent of Con Ed's total income in 1964, by 1969 their share had reached 93 percent. It is no wonder that the absolute amount spent on additions to plant *declined* nearly 10 percent between 1964 and 1969. Given increasing demand for service and decreasing investment in facilities for producing it, New York City power failures are as natural occurrences as the summer heat waves that precede them.

But why do the directors choose not to accumulate capital in utility plants? The answer lies in Con Ed's rate of profit on invested capital. In the utility sphere, rising profits are greatly dependent on political institutions: on utility commissions granting rate increases, on tax assessors valuing utility property at bargain rates. In New York City, the political climate has not been notably favorable. The result is that Con Ed's profits on invested capital are comparatively low and show no upward trend. This makes accumulation of capital in the industrial sphere unprofitable; it makes credit harder to get and facilitates the withdrawal of industrial profits by the financing institutions whose representatives serve on the board of directors. The surplus value earned in the industrial sphere is channeled back to financial institutions where it is used as loan capital. Additional investment in utility capacity to take care of peak demand periods represents dangerous irresponsibility from the standpoint of finance capital.

Even under this sort of scheme, the northeast region of the United States would still lack energy resources. Some oil and gas resources might be developed off the coast in accordance with procedures outlined above. The northeast would also utilize the federal energy board as a marketing mechanism for purchase of petroleum gas abroad. In addition, the national energy board could allot certain tracts of known oil production territory off the Louisiana gulf for energy-scarce regions. Part of the federal energy board's loan fund would involve considerable expenditure for development of future fuels, solar energy, geothermal, etc.

There are other possibilities which might help the northeast become less vulnerable in terms of its energy resource problems. The northeast planning region might initiate an energy arrangement with Canada that could open the way for a serious continental energy policy. Thus, it might be possible to obtain oil from Alberta in exchange for installation and training in Alberta of a technologically advanced industry, say, a Xerox plant. Such a turnkey arrangement could lead to diversification and development of various Canadian provinces, in exchange for export of set amounts of oil.

The federal energy board would administer the U.S. government's foreign policy as it pertained to fuels. The board would be the central mechanism through which regions purchased or sold supplies in world markets, and it would function as a sort of mass market sorting house in this regard. Oil import quotas, of course, as well as other constraints the United States places in the way of international energy trade, would be eliminated. The board would deal with foreign governments, state companies, and where governments were captives of multinational corporations, with those corporations.

These new public bodies might well make bad plans. There is nothing to assure they would not do so. Public planning often turns out to be inefficient, detrimental to the environment, stagnating, fouled in red tape. On the other hand, it is difficult to imagine public planning being any worse than the current policies of private industry. The regional planning boards would additionally provide a focus for the activities of the environmentalists, consumer and labor groups, etc.

At the least, the governors of the regional plan would be held publicly accountable. They would be elected officials, with limitations on their terms in office. While in office they would not be permitted to hold other jobs, receive other incomes, or own securities of any corporations. The process of determining the plans themselves would be public.

It is important to understand that these plans might produce quite different approaches to the energy situation. The overall schemata might result in irrational methods for handling energy in the sense that regional plans could end up working against an integrated national energy system. But these matters can be bargained among regions, and between regions and the federal board.

The most important aspect of this scheme is the process, that literally requires the American people to participate and be held accountable in a political process which affects their lives. At least there will be no excuse for their not participating. Unless the people of the nation themselves seek to develop a rational energy policy, one that allows for the greatest amount of freedom and development, we cannot begin to build a new society; instead we will remain observers as our existing order is gradually extinguished.

NOTES

CHAPTER 1

M. King Hubbert, "Energy Resources of the Earth," *Scientific American*, September 1971. Statement by George T. Piercy, senior vice president, Standard Oil Co. of New Jersey, *Oil Daily*, November 16, 1971. Data on Virginia Electric Power Co. from "Subsidy of Industry by Poor Persons through Electric Rate Structure," Fairfax Community Action Program, March 21, 1972. Information on Boston Gas prepared by People's Coalition for Peace and Justice, 2 Brookline Street, Cambridge, Massachusetts 02139. For correlation between energy-rich counties and poor people, see map, Families with Income under $3,000 in 1959 by counties of the United States, 1960, prepared by the Bureau of the Census, U.S. Department of Commerce.

CHAPTER 2

For early history of Love and the Hanna Company see *Fortune*, September 1962, p. 102. For an excellent review of the Rowntree suits, see T. N. Bethell, "Conspiracy in Coal," *The Washington Monthly*, March 1969. See trial record, *Tennessee Consolidated Coal Co.* v. *United Mine Workers of America* (U.S. Court of Appeals, 6th District), particularly testimony of Paul Callis, p. 155 of the trial transcript; reading from exhibits 44 and 45 concerning loans made by the union to business enterprises, p. 508; testimony of Roland Kampmeier, on history of TVA's efforts to secure coal, p. 1418. Deposition of Cyrus S. Eaton, taken in Cleveland, Ohio, November 11, 1960, p. 522 of the trial transcript.

Also trial transcript, *South-East Coal Company* v. *Consolidation Coal Co.* and *South-East Coal Company* v. *United Mine Workers of America* (U.S.

Court of Appeals, 6th Circuit). Testimony of Harry LaViers, Sr., p. 329, David H. Swanson, p. 678, and testimony of John L. Lewis, p. 1078.

CHAPTER 3

Federal tax rules for coal: see Section 631 (c), Internal Revenue Code of 1965 for coal royalties; section 613 of the code for coal depletion allowances; section 617 for rules on coal exploration and development expenses. General interpretation and explanation of tax laws as applied to the coal industry were provided by Thomas Field, executive director, Taxation with Representation, a public interest tax lobby. Field is a former Treasury Department official who worked in this area.

For detailed studies of coal mining, see J. Davitt McAteer, ed., *Coal Mining Health and Safety in West Virginia,* July 1970. For information on landholdings and tax assessments see Appendix B, pp. 453–503. Quotation from Robinson, p. 457. For information on Kentucky tax policies see James C. Millstone, "Kentucky's Method of Taxing Coal Lands Is Woefully Inadequate," *St. Louis Post-Dispatch,* November 20, 1967. James C. Millstone, "East Kentucky Coal Makes Profits for Owners, Not Region." Also *St. Louis Post-Dispatch,* November 18, 1967. Nader's remarks were contained in a letter from him to Honorable James E. Luckett, January 11, 1972. Tennessee tax information is from "The Ugly Mark of Strip Mining," a series of investigative reports by William Greenburg, *Nashville Tennessean,* reprinted by the paper. The stories in the reprint appeared from September 12, 1971 through September 29, 1971.

For details on safety problems in mines see McAteer report, Chapter II, pp. 65–82. Burt Schorr's article was reprinted from *The Wall Street Journal* in the *Mountain Eagle,* Whitesburg, Kentucky, August 8, 1971. The GAO report is quoted in *Health/Pac Bulletin,* No. 33, September 1971, in an article, "Ole King Cole," by Des Callan. Assessment information is from a compilation of Bureau of Mines records by McAteer, March 1972. *Miner's Voice* quotes February–March 1972, "Law and Order at the Bureau of Mines," by Don Stillman. Black lung comments are from Bob Harwood, "Coalfield Clash," *The Wall Street Journal,* September 24, 1971. For details on European coal mining practices see *Coal Patrol,* No. 19, January 24, 1972.

Information on production payments is contained in a memorandum prepared by the Treasury Department for Congress, 1969, "General Explanation, Carved Out Production Payment Transactions, and ABC Transactions." Further explanation was provided by Thomas Field, then a Treasury official, who handled this matter within the government.

For details on coal gasoline cartel, see Robert Engler, *Politics of Oil,* Macmillan, 1961, pp. 96–105. Also George W. Stocking and Myron W.

Watkins, *Cartels in Action*, Twentieth Century Fund, 1947. See Chapter II, "The Role of I.G. Farben," pp. 491–504.

Letter to Johnson from Howard is exhibit No. 372, Investigation of National Defense Program, hearings before a special committee investigating the national defense program, U.S. Senate, 77th Congress, first session, Washington, 1942.

For a good general summary of the merger problem see "Concentration by Competing Raw Fuel Industries in the Energy Market and Its Impact on Small Business," hearings before the Subcommittee on Special Small Business Problems of the Select Committee of the House of Representatives, July 12, 1971. Jersey Standard's position is summarized from statements made in those hearings by Carl G. Herrington, vice-president Humble Oil & Refining, p. 129. Statements attributed to Howard Hardesty occur in the same hearings, p. 98. Turner's statement on Continental-Consolidation merger: Letter in answer to queries printed in Hearings before the Senate Select Committee on Small Business, part 2, March 15–17, 22, April 6, 1967, pp. 766–768. See also Laurence D. Beck and Stuart L. Rawlings, *Coal: The Captive Giant, a Report on Coal Ownership in the United States*, published in 1971 by the authors, pp. 153–154. Kastenmeier's findings on western leases appear in the *Congressional Record*, March 17, 1971, p. H 1696 and *Congressional Record*, July 19, 1971, p H. 6883. Details of water problems are contained in *Montana-Wyoming, Coal Resources for Electric Generation*, a study by Ken Holum Associates, Washington, January 1970. See also "Water-Coal-Industrial Development," paper by Harold Aldrich, regional director, Region 6, Bureau of Reclamation, delivered at American Institute of Mining, Metallurgical and Petroleum Engineers, New York City, March 1, 1971.

Summary of gas production techniques is from George E. Boner, "Gas Supplies for U.S. Consumers," New York State Department of Public Service, Albany, New York. Wheatley's testimony is contained in the House Small Business hearings, "Concentration by Competing Raw Fuel Industries," pp. 344–359. The FPC staff memoranda were first exposed by Jack Anderson in 1971, then made public, and can be obtained from the Federal Power Commission.

Mitchell's comments are contained in "Artificial Restraints on Basic Energy Sources," a memorandum prepared for the American Public Power Association, April 26, 1971, pp. 58–89. Aubrey J. Wagner's statement was made in hearings before the Subcommittee on Special Small Business Problems of the Select Committee of the House of Representatives, October 6, 7, 8, 1970, pp. 141–157. Information on German synthetic fuel plants during World War II is from Strategic Bombing Survey, September 30, 1945. Summary report, p. 8.

CHAPTER 4

Valuable books on links between the U.S. and Canadian economies, particularly as they apply to natural resources, include: Hugh G. J. Aitken, *American Capital and Canadian Resources*, Harvard University Press, 1961; James Laxer, *The Energy Poker Game*, New Press, 1970; Kari Levitt, *Silent Surrender*, Liveright, 1970; *The Gray Report*, New Press, 1971.

For recent news on Canadian energy, the *Oil Daily*, with correspondents in Alberta, is an excellent source.

The summary of Aitken's data and arguments comes mainly from *American Capital*, Chapter 2, pp. 19–65. The quotation concerning east-west axis is from page 126. See page 19 of *The Gray Report*. For detailed analysis of tax advantages offered U.S. firms see Luncheon address, annual meeting, 1971, Canadian Economics Association, "Contribution of the Tax System to Canada's Unemployment and Ownership Problems," by Eric Kierans. Quotations are from pages 11 and 16 of that speech. Also see Kierans's speech in Commons, September 9, 1971, p. 7675 of Commons Debates. Also at pp. 7672–7676 of September 9 Commons Debates. Jean-Luc Pepin, Canadian minister of industry, trade, and commerce, made his speech at the Mid-America World Trade Conference, Chicago, March 1, 1972. The *Oil Daily* of July 9, 1971, is quoted on Canadian capital needs. In *The Energy Poker Game*, Laxer provides a good description of import quota background, p. 29. In the same book, page 34, Laxer describes how the U.S. gas companies determinedly stepped up their take of Canadian gas. From a somewhat different point of view, see also, Robert Smith, "Canadian Gas Export Policy–An Updating," *Public Utilities Fortnightly*, February 3, 1972, p. 40. The *Oil Daily* quotes Mobil officials confirming their Sable Island find, November 12, 1971. For details on James Bay, see the *Last Post Resources Report*, p. 14. Also see Consolidated Edison Co.'s twenty-year plan, 1971–1990. For details on corporate schemes at Churchill Falls, see the 1970 annual report of the British Newfoundland Corporation, Ltd. Also in connection with Churchill Falls and Canadian uranium, see the 1970 annual report of the Rio Tinto Zinc Corporation, as well as "RTZ Explained," a booklet prepared by the company, December 1969. For Canadian opposition to the Columbia River Treaty, see Tommy Douglas, House of Commons debates, March 3, 1964. In *The Energy Poker Game*, Laxer sums up the water program. I have relied on his sections pp. 35–42 for description of plan. NAWAPA is described in *The Coming Water Famine* by Jim Wright, pp. 218–224.

CHAPTER 5

For general information bearing on Southeast Asia see Michael Tanzer, *The Political Economy of International Oil and the Underdeveloped Countries,* Beacon, 1969; Chitoshi Yanaga, *Big Business in Japanese Politics,* Yale, 1968. Also Jon Halliday, "Washington V. Tokyo, Wall Street V. Marunouchi," *New Left Review,* No. 67 (May–June 1971), p. 39; Jim Peck, "Why China Turned West," *Ramparts,* May 1972 p. 42; Malcolm Caldwell, "Oil and Imperialism in East Asia," *Journal of Contemporary Asia,* Vol. 1, No. 3, 1971, p. 5.

Detailed information on Asian and Japanese economic news is hard to come by. Good general material is contained in the *Far Eastern Economic Review,* Hong Kong. Also the *Bulletin of Concerned Asian Scholars* will carry an occasional piece. The best systematic rundown on Asian business transactions is carried in *Pacific Basin Reports,* a bimonthly newsletter published at Custom House, Box 26581, San Francisco. Another detailed, official source is *Japan Economic Journal,* a weekly from Tokyo. The other standard source is *Foreign Broadcast Information Reports,* published daily by the Central Intelligence Agency.

For information on Japanese petroleum demands and supplies see *Japan Economic Journal,* January 11, 1972, p. 20; January 18, 1972, p. 24; February 1, 1972, p. 20; February 8, 1972, p. 30. Also Dr. Toshiaki Ushijimu, "Japan's Vigorous Oil Search Widens," *World Petroleum,* December 1970, p. 34. Japanese inabilities to capitalize big oil in Indonesian waters are reported in *Pacific Basin Reports,* May 1, 1971. For description of politics and maneuvers over Vietnam oil see *Pacific Basin Reports,* April 15, 1971, p. 96. Also June 1, 1971, p. 144. For China oil developments see *Pacific Basin Reports,* February 1971, p. 39. The statement from China at the UN was made on March 3, 1972, by An Chih-yuan, at the UN Committee on the Peaceful Uses of the Sea-Bed and the Ocean Floor Beyond the Limits of National Jurisdiction. Typical of Chinese support for OPEC was a March 15, 1972 statement from Peking by Hsinhua, approving OPEC's victory in forcing Aramco to give producing countries 20 percent participation rights. Detailed analysis of Soviet minerals industry, including proposed Japanese deals, is contained in Robert E. Ebel, *Communist Trade in Oil & Gas,* Praeger, 1970. For recent discussion of proposed Japanese-Soviet gas pipeline see *Pacific Basin Reports,* February 1971, p. 53.

Coal export statistics and information are from *World Coal Trade,* published by National Coal Association, Washington, D.C., 1971. Railroad sales activities were described in interviews with the author by executives.

For details of export trade see annual reports, 1970, of Continental Oil, Occidental Petroleum, and Pittston. Also the Bureau of Mines officials provided details. *Washington Post* story on Alabama sales, June 10, 1971. David Francis is quoted and a speech contained in the *Inter-Mountain,* Elkins, West Virginia, October 28, 1970. For details of Kaiser in Canada see 1970 annual report, prospectus, July 22, 1971; *Forbes,* April 15, 1968; *Coal Age,* December 1970. Details on Roberts Bank development, *Business Week,* September 27, 1969, p. 120.

For general information on Japan and its energy resource suppliers, see *World Petroleum,* December 1970, "Japan in the World of Mining." For information on Utah Mining, see prospectus, 1969; company annual report, 1970; and proxy statement, January 11, 1971. South African mining, see *Financial Times,* London, "South Africa Survey," June 14, 1971. For description of enrichment process, see *The Wall Street Journal,* October 23, 1970, p. 16. General information on U.S. corporate involvement, see *Apartheid and Imperialism: A Study of U.S. Corporate Involvement in South Africa,* American Committee on Africa, September–October 1970. See the Rio Tinto Zinc 1970 annual report for information on that company. Also "RTZ Explained," December 1969. See 1970 annual report of Anglo American Corporation. Bix quotation is from Herbert P. Bix, "The Security Treaty System and the Japanese Military-Industrial Complex," *Bulletin of Concerned Asian Scholars,* January 1970, p. 30.

Adventuring in the Asian car markets is described in *Pacific Basin Reports,* December 1970; March 15, 1971; May 1, 1971; May 15, 1971. Breakdown of talks between Ford and Japanese, *Japan Economic Journal,* March 14, 1972. Henry Ford is quoted in *Pacific Basin Reports,* December 1970.

CHAPTER 6

See official report, Federal Power Commission, in the matter of Columbia LNG Corporation, Southern Energy Company, Consolidated Gas Supply Corporation, Vols., 7, 8, 9, April 14–16, 1971. George D. Carameros, Jr., "Where El Paso-Algerian LNG Project Stands Now," *Oil Daily,* November 15, 1971. El Paso Natural Gas Co. annual report, 1970; company prospectus, September 2, 1970.

For safety problems involving LNG, see "Hazards of LNG Spillage," in *Marine Transportation,* a report prepared by the Bureau of Mines, 1972. Subsequent research, 1972, was not published at this writing, but results were obtained in interviews between author and Bureau of Mines officials.

Algerian reaction to LNG scheme was provided the author in several private interviews.

CHAPTER 7

Robert Fitch and Mary Oppenheimer, "Who Rules the Corporations?", *Socialist Revolution,* Vol. 1, Nos. 4, 5, 6.

PART II
A GUIDE TO THE ENERGY INDUSTRY

1: OIL

Over half the known oil reserves are in the Middle East. Another 10 percent are in North and West Africa. With the demand for fuel in Japan, there is heightened interest in developing oil and gas in the South China Sea area and of the shallow waters off mainland China.

Seven major oil companies dominate the oil business. They are Standard Oil of New Jersey, Royal Dutch Shell Group, Gulf, Texaco, Standard Oil of California, Socony Mobil, and British Petroleum. Their percentage of the market has dropped from 90 percent in 1955 to 70 percent in 1969. While there is a somewhat more aggressive effort by Middle Eastern and African exporting nations grouped together in the Organization of Petroleum Exporting Countries (OPEC) to take more profit, and to share management of the oil industry, it is uncertain how this will affect the Seven Sisters, as the major oil companies are called. They still control most of the world tanker fleets, refineries and retail outlets. They are leading chemical producers, are active in land development, and control other major fuels.

Nonetheless, the increasing OPEC demands probably contributed to the quickened interest in developing oil in the shallow waters off Southeast Asia, and spurred exploration in the Arctic, and will lead to development of other offshore areas, including the eastern seaboard of the United States.

The Soviet Union's hope to become a major oil exporter seems, at least for the time being, to have been stymied. The demand at home is intense, and the Soviet Union appears more likely to become an oil importer, as is the case with Eastern Europe. China's oil industry is still in a stage of early development, but from all accounts, it is proceeding ahead fairly rapidly.

What follows is a breakdown of major oil-producing countries, showing concessionaires and markets.

UNITED STATES: Historically most oil came from the southwest, but in the future it will probably be drawn from the arctic region of Alaska and Canada, and from the underwater areas on the outer continental shelf surrounding most of the continent.

Total proved crude reserves in the United States were 29.6 billion barrels in 1969, according to the American Petroleum Institution. Total production in 1970 was 9.1 million barrels a day.

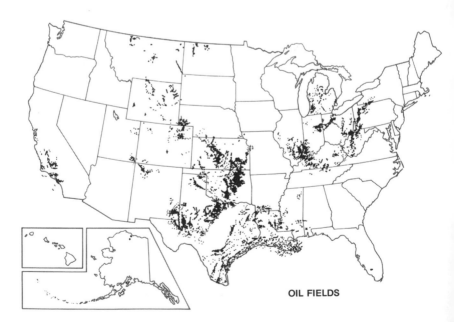

OIL FIELDS

THE ARCTIC
OIL AND GAS

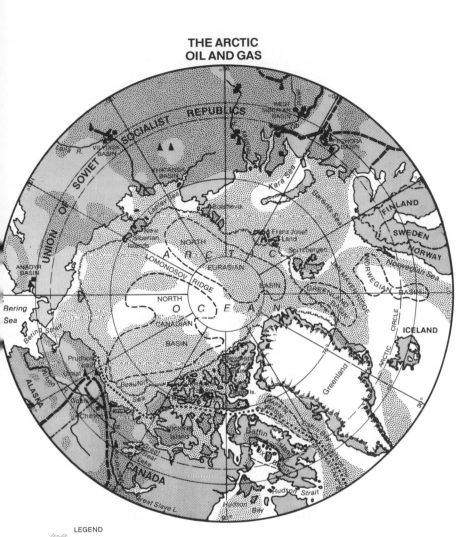

LEGEND

Sedimentary basins locally favorable for petroleum

▲ Oil field

■ Gas field

— Existing pipelines

-- Pipelines, proposed, or under construction

⌐⌐ Submarine depressions

Areas of permanent polar ice

Permanent ice pack

About 34 percent of all the oil came from Texas, 24 percent from Louisiana, and 11 percent from California. Oklahoma produced 6.7 percent and Wyoming 4.3 percent.

Imports of oil are restricted by the import quota system established under President Eisenhower. In 1968, 472.3 million barrels were imported. Of that total, 169.4 million barrels came from Canada, 125.7 million from Venezuela, and 41.5 million from Libya. The quotas are being relaxed as the demand for oil increases.

Gasoline is the biggest oil product. Of a total 4.7 billion barrels of oil products manufactured in 1968, gasoline accounted for 1.9 billion. Fuel oil and residual oil (used by electric utilities) are the second and third largest categories.

The largest consumers of gasoline are California, 206.1 million barrels; Texas, 135 million; New York, 129.8 million; Ohio, 104.3 million; and Illinois, 102.6 million.

In 1969, the ten largest U.S. oil producers were Jersey Standard, 867 million b/d; Texaco, 752 (est.); Gulf, 602; Shell, 540; California Standard, 472; Arco, 454; Indiana Standard, 452; Mobil, 350; Getty, 300; Union, 256.

In terms of refining, the leaders were Jersey Standard, Indiana Standard, Texaco, Shell, Mobil, California Standard, Gulf, Phillips, Sun, Union Oil.

The U.S. oil industry is international in scope, and its future is largely dependent on exploration of arctic regions of the world, particularly the Canadian arctic, as well as further development of the underwater areas. Within the U.S. territorial limits, the major activity is likely to be on the outercontinental shelf.

On September 28, 1945, President Truman issued a proclamation which declared that the natural resources of the subsoil and sea bed of the continental shelf contiguous to the coast of the United States were regarded as under jurisdiction and control of the United States. The Submerged Lands Act of May 22, 1953, returned to the coastal states jurisdiction over the submerged lands to a distance of three geographical miles from their coastlines into the Atlantic and Pacific oceans and up to three marine leagues into the Gulf of Mexico under certain conditions. The Outer Continental Shelf Lands Act of 1953 provided for jurisdiction and control over the submerged lands lying seaward of those granted the states. The act authorized the secretary of Interior to grant mineral leases on the outercontinental shelf.

The boundaries of the OCS have not been defined. The seaward limits remain undefined and the location of the shoreward boundaries, particularly in areas of high mineral value, is generally a point of dispute between the federal government and the coastal states. For example, several New England states are suing the federal government, claiming their colonial treaties give them control of the shelf beyond the three-mile limit.

The continental shelf of the United States measures 875,000 square miles, or about 560 million acres, and is relatively undeveloped. Of this area, 290,000 square miles, or about 186 million acres, lie in the Gulf of Mexico, offshore from the Atlantic seaboard, and in the waters of the Pacific off the coasts of the states of California, Oregon, and Washington. As of December 31, 1970, of the 186 million acres off the mainland of the United States, approximately 2 percent, or 4.3 million acres, were under lease on the outercontinental shelf. The Interior Department periodically holds lease sales on the shelf. So far it has sold leases off Santa Barbara, California, and in the Gulf off Texas and Louisiana. Within the next decade it will auction leases to other sections of the Gulf, around the Florida west coast, off Alaska, and in the Atlantic.

Drilling off the populous East Coast in the Atlantic is a subject of growing interest. The U.S. Geological Survey estimates that 7.7 billion barrels of oil and 46.2 trillion cubic feet of gas may be located off the nation's east coast. Prime sites for exploration are southwest of New York City off New Jersey and Long Island, in the waters around Cape Hatteras off North Carolina, and at the edge of Georges Bank running up to Canada.

Drilling off North Carolina's coast has been underway since 1946, when Jersey Standard sunk a hole off Albemarle Sound in state waters. In 1965, Mobil drilled three wells off Albemarle and Pamlico sounds, all of them in state waters. In 1971, two companies held all the leases to North Carolina's state waters. Cities Service held one lease which covered two million acres including sounds and bays, as well as open ocean. This is the first lease North Carolina awarded, and to hang on to the territory Cities Service must drill 12,000 feet every two years. The company currently is drilling two holes on land to meet the lease terms. Colonial Oil & Gas Co. holds the other lease, which includes approximately 400,000 acres of state submerged lands. North Carolina state geologists report that major oil companies were exploring the outercontinental shelf. They say the work involves some preliminary drilling of 1,000-foot holes.

In the summer of 1971 a consortia of 33 oil companies led by Jersey Standard made an exploration in two areas—one 100 miles off Cape Cod and the other in a swath stretching from the tip of Long Island to Delaware Bay. The consortia subsequently reported finding oil and gas in commercial deposits on the continental shelf 30 miles off the coast of Long Island. The oil companies believed wells could be drilled as close as 30 to 50 miles offshore, and up to 200 miles off the coast. Most of the consortia's studies were conducted in a depth of 250 feet, but some were made at a 10,000-foot level.

So far drilling on the outercontinental shelf has been restricted to areas off California, Texas, and Louisiana. Federal leases have not been given in the Gulf off the Florida coast, but the state has leased the submerged lands it controls, and as a result, oil companies are creeping around the southwestern tip. Gulf, California Standard, and Mobil have drilled wells on the southwest Florida coast. The Interior Department plans to lease the outercontinental shelf in the Gulf off Florida in 1973. The department will hold environmental impact hearings in preparation for leasing the Atlantic outercontinental shelf, and the actual lease sale is scheduled to take place sometime before 1976. The sale must await court resolution of differing state claims on jurisdiction and will probably be tied up in court because of environmental group opposition. Usually states control submerged lands out to the three-mile limit, with the federal government taking control from that point out to 12 miles. But in Florida the state claims jurisdiction to 10.5 miles; Maine claims 80 to 100 miles on the basis of a 1606 charter granted the colonial government. Most New England states support Maine. Maine has leased sites in what it considers its ocean territories to King Resources, Inc., of Denver.

The Georges Bank, one of the choice oil sites, is the center of large-scale commercial fishing by many nations. The oil industry insists there will be no environmental disturbance.

CANADA: Canada is the center of an oil rush, with foreign interests, mostly U.S., sinking millions on a gamble that oil will be found and can be brought out of the arctic. Main activity centers around the Mackenzie River delta, the arctic islands to the north, and the seas and inlets around those islands. In addition, oil companies produced the first real oil and natural gas discoveries off the east coast of Canada, and sizable amounts of money are now committed to further exploration of those areas. Finally, there is renewed interest in the west coast offshore areas.

According to the Canadian Petroleum Association, the nation has total proved oil reserves of 10.4 billion barrels of crude oil. It is estimated that the Athabasca oil sands could be made to yield an additional 600 billion barrels, with about half of that being recoverable under known methods. In 1970, total production was 517 million barrels of crude oil.

The potential for oil and gas in the unexplored arctic and offshore areas is considered to be substantial. For example, Charles R. Hetherington, president of Panarctic Oils, Ltd., the quasipublic company that actively explores the arctic, put ultimate reserves in Canada's north, including the arctic coastal plain and the Mackenzie delta, at 260 trillion cubic feet of gas and 43 billion barrels of oil. That potential is more than one and a half times greater than Canada's east coast and nearly three and a half times greater than Alaska's.

The Canadian oil industry is dominated by the major international companies, in particular those domiciled in the United States. The leading producers, in 1970, in order, were Imperial Oil (Jersey Standard), Mobil, Texaco, Shell, California Standard, Hudson's Bay Oil & Gas (Continental), Pacific Petroleum (Phillips), and Arco.

The international companies, led by the U.S. corporations, also control refining. Of a total of 41 refineries listed by the Canadian government in January 1970, 28 were owned by nine U.S. companies. Six were Dutch (Shell), three were British, three Canadian, and one Belgian. Imperial Oil is now consolidating its refineries, closing down small installations, and building the largest refining complex in the country.

Some of the arctic exploration ventures include the following:

Imperial Oil made three discoveries in the Mackenzie delta. Aquitaine Co., Mobil, and Amerada Hess have a joint exploration venture in the Norman Wells area of the Mackenzie delta. French interests, led by Elf Oil Exploration, and including Total and Aquitaine, are exploring at Banks Island. Gulf has a five-year exploration venture in the arctic, with leases in North Baffin Bay. In the Beaufort Sea, Gulf, Imperial, and Texaco all hold substantial leases. Panarctic is exploring intensively in the arctic islands, and has hit gas in two instances. (Panarctic is owned 45 percent by the government; the remainder is divided among several different oil companies.) A September 1971 survey by *Oil Daily* reported there were 44 drilling rigs located in the Canadian north.

Offshore on the east coast, Imperial has 24 million acres of leases. Mobil and Texas Eastern hit oil and gas at Sable Island, a sandbar about 175 miles out in the Atlantic east of Halifax. A group led by Tenneco, and including Amerada and Total, were drilling off Labrador. In 1971 the *Oil Daily* survey reported several rigs working off the east coast: Shell had two rigs, Imperial two, Indiana Standard two, Mobil one, and Tenneco one.

There has been continual speculation about development of the Athabasca oil sands, a 30,000-square-mile area of northeast Alberta. The Japanese evidenced interest in building a complex to process the sands during the early 1960s, but with the oil discoveries at Prudhoe Bay the Japanese turned instead to Alaska. In 1971 representatives from Mitsubishi surveyed the sands and said Japanese groups were interested in their development. Currently the only plant changing the sands into oil is operated by Great Canadian Sands, Ltd., a subsidiary of Sun Oil. In 1971, Syncrude Canada, Ltd., proposed to build a 125,000 b/d capacity synthetic recovery project at a cost of $300 million. Syncrude is a joint venture involving Imperial Oil, Gulf, Arco, and Cities Service. As the cost of fuels increases, synthetic oil seems more possible, and there is speculation about building a pipeline into the United States.

PACIFIC OPERATIONS: Recent oil explorations in the South China Sea, off Indochina in waters surrounding Indonesia and Malaysia, could change the energy picture, as well as influence U.S. foreign policy. U.S. oil companies are exploring what some experts believe to be large oil and natural gas deposits.

The boom is centered around Indonesia, but there is activity from South Vietnam all the way down to Australia. Headquarters for exploration is at Singapore, a major refining center, where thousands of oil workers reside. Most of the oil and gas will go to energy markets in Japan. Japanese demands for oil are expected to jump to 12.1 million barrels daily. The projected increase is encouraging to the big international oil companies for it means the Japanese probably will not be able to provide much of the needed oil through their own companies as they had initially hoped, and instead must rely on American-based internationals.

In 1969 six American companies began to explore the areas. Tenneco, Standard Oil of California, Gulf, Continental, Union Oil of California, and British Petroleum each invested $2 million in exploratory research, according to *Fortune*. Experts also are surveying the China Sea. One report suggests the shallow subsoil between Japan and Formosa may hold the world's richest oil and gas deposits, richer than those in the Persian Gulf. This oil is of particular interest to the United States because it is low in sulphur content.

Following is a rundown of activity as of 1971:

Indonesia and Java Sea Basin: This is the center of the oil boom. In 1961 production totaled 271 million barrels, all of it onshore, and most of it from two long-time Indonesia operators: PT Caltex Pacific Indonesia, 218 million barrels (owned equally by Texaco and Standard Oil of California), and PT Stanvac Indonesia, 17 million barrels (owned by Mobil and Standard Oil of New Jersey). This basic production goes 50 percent to Japan, 20 percent to the U.S. west coast and Hawaii, and 20 percent to Australia.

There were five major oil strikes in offshore waters of the Java Sea, a cuplike basin that draws up along the shores of Java and Sumatra, and controlled by Indonesia. Estimates are that these new finds will soon double Indonesia's production. Groups making the discoveries were:

1. Union Oil of California and Japex Indonesia, Ltd.
2. Cities Service Co., Monsanto Co., Ashland Oil, Inc., Robin Loh Group (Singapore).
3. IAAPCO, a subsidiary of Natomas Co., Reading & Bates Offshore Drilling Co.
4. Atlantic Richfield and Natomas.

Gulf Oil paid $1.5 million to get one of the largest concessions in the Java Sea Basin. An area as big as the state of Oklahoma, this territory runs from the Borneo coast to Sumatra and Singapore. Under the agreement, Gulf gets 40 percent of all production to cover costs at U.S. prices, and thereafter participates in refining, shipping, and distribution profits.

Shell recently bought into Natomas, agreeing to pay $116 million in exploration costs.

Brunei/Sarawak: Royal Dutch Shell Group, long the mainstay of oil activity in the Pacific, produces nearly 200,000 barrels a

day from wells offshore the island of Borneo, in waters off
Brunei—the British-protected sultanate—and off neighboring
Sarawak, East Malaysia. Forty percent of the oil is refined at
Shell's Sarawak refinery. This makes Shell's Brunei/Sarawak op-
eration the third biggest oil producer in Asia, after Indonesia and
China. New fields are now opening. Shell has combined with
Mitsubishi to transport LNG to Japan at the rate of four million
tons a year. Other companies are now challenging Shell's monop-
oly of these waters. Groups drilling are headed by Sun Oil and
Ashland Oil.

South China Sea: Most of the Thai continental shelf has been
parceled out to six oil companies, five of the United States, one
British. They include Tenneco, Inc., (Marathon, Phillips, ENI),
British Petroleum, Amoco International (subsidiary of Standard
Oil of Indiana), Gulf, Continental Oil (with Mitsui), Union Oil
Co. of California.

South Vietnam: Ampex Corp., in a contract with Saigon, conducted two different sets of exploration treks off South Vietnam
in 1969 and 1970. The results were sold to an unidentified group
of oil companies. United Nations sponsored surveys were made
off the southwest coast near Cambodia. Bidding was expected to
begin for offshore leases early in 1971, but was delayed by the
Saigon government. North Vietnam protested the lease sales.
    Shell Oil Group has potential plans for a 40,000-barrel-per-day
refinery at the east coast port of Nha Trang. The refinery would
be run by Shell (40 percent), Esso Standard Eastern (24.75 percent), and Caltex Petroleum Corp. (5.25 percent). Esso now
controls petroleum in South Vietnam, supplying the military and
operating gas stations. The French government received initial
permission to search for oil off Cambodia.

Singapore Oil Refining Center: Singapore is the center for a
fast growing refining operation, which takes in crude oil from
the South China Sea area, then sells different marketable prod-

ucts to Japan, and elsewhere. Standard Oil of New Jersey and the Royal Dutch Shell Group lead in running refineries. Esso is building a $65 million refinery on an island offshore Singapore, and a $30 million lubricating oil plant. The refineries are served by a new large mooring terminal which can handle tankers up to 250,000 tons. The refinery will handle Middle Eastern crude oil, up to 80,000 barrels a day.

The Shell refinery can process 230,000 barrels a day. It is the biggest complex of its sort in that part of the world. Shell is also building a new refinery for lubricant base oil, and expects to invest from $65 to $100 million over the near term.

Other refineries are owned by Mobil and British Petroleum. British Petroleum and Shell account for about 60 percent of Singapore's domestic petroleum requirements. A new refinery is to be built by a Standard Oil of Indiana group.

NORTH SEA: In 1964, the major finds were natural gas, but in recent years the interest has switched to oil in the heavily prospected British area: 450 wells have been drilled and $500 million spent. A succession of oil wells has established the North Sea as a major oil-producing province. British Petroleum, Phillips, and Shell-Esso have major finds in the Ekofisk and surrounding areas. While no one believes these finds will replace the Middle East or North African dominance as European suppliers, nonetheless they are important for Norway and the United Kingdom. On the conservative side the North Sea may be producing one million barrels of high-quality oil by the mid-1970s. By the end of the decade the figure could be as much as two or three million barrels with as much as 40 percent coming from the United Kingdom. According to a *Financial Times* survey, "the cost of alternative imports from the Gulf and Libya already averages a landed price of $2.75 per barrel, with further rises to come under the OPEC agreements. The cost of North Sea supplies, after tax and royalties, could well be 50 or 60 cents per barrel less than this." In August 1971 the British government accepted high bids for 15 exploration blocks in Britain's sector. Britain has yet to award 421 other North Sea tracts. They are to be given out on the basis of administrative decision. Jersey Standard and Shell, in a joint venture, made the highest winning bid, $50.5 million.

The Conservative government has reversed the policy of the Labour government and dropped the rule of compulsory partnership with the state enterprise. The government is considering installing a system of auction bidding. For the time being, blocks are distributed on the basis of work programs put forward by applicant companies.

SOVIET UNION: While no data has been published since the 1930s, "explored" reserves are estimated by *World Oil* at 4,500 million tons. According to Robert E. Ebel, a U.S. expert on Soviet petroleum, "explored" reserves are perhaps 50 percent higher than "proved" reserves, the figure usually cited in other parts of the world. During the 1960s, crude oil production rose from 148 million tons in 1960 to 353 million tons in 1970. During the early part of the decade most of the production came from the Urals-Volga field, and toward the end of the period production slackened in that area, but sharply increased in the new fields of western Siberia.

While exports to Western countries more than doubled to 840,000 b/d in 1970, the net exports to the West actually declined slightly. This reflects pressure on the Soviet Union to supply increasing amounts of oil for its own economic uses, as well as to fulfill its plans for exporting oil to Eastern European countries. Not only was there a cutback in sales to the West, but also recently the Soviet Union suggested that Eastern Europe also look elsewhere for oil.

As a result of the pressure to get more oil, the Soviet Union is turning more aggressively to the Middle East, where together with Eastern European countries it has struck deals with Iraq, and has deals pending with Kuwait and Iran for both oil and gas. In 1971, British Petroleum signed a ten-year contract with

Poland to supply three million tons of crude oil annually from the Persian Gulf. In addition, both Hungary and Austria negotiated for construction of a pipeline from the Adriatic.

The Soviet Union sent a team of geologists to Bolivia to prospect for oil. It represents a form of technical aid requested by the Bolivians since, following the nationalization of the Bolivian Gulf Oil Co., it could not obtain technological assistance from capitalist countries.

At the World Petroleum Congress, held in Moscow in 1971, the Soviet Union revealed it had been conducting geological surveys in the offshore areas on the Soviet side of the Bering Sea, which reaches to Alaska. Soviet geologists also discussed "the most certain" prospects in the Caspian and Black sea areas. In another paper, Soviet experts described the use, on two occasions, of underground nuclear explosions to increase oil and gas production. A Soviet official said, "No radioactive contamination of the atmosphere and the territory of the oil field has resulted from the explosions. After the explosions the products from the wells displayed no contaminants."

At the same time, the Soviets intend to drill wells nine miles deep—much deeper than ever before. They will be sunk into the Baltic shield in northern Russia, around the Caspian, and possibly in the Sea of Japan.

In his discussion, Alexander Sidorenko, minister of geology, said the Soviet Union would spend much greater effort in developing oil and gas in the European part of the country. "Since 1966 the scope and extent of oil and gas prospecting work in the European part of the country have been enlarged. More than half the deep drilling works for prospecting purposes carried out by the U.S.S.R. Ministry of Geology alone have been devoted to oil and gas. . . . The search for oil and gas has been undertaken on a vast scale on the entire plain of European Russia."

U.S. businessmen are anxious to sell refining processes and oil exploration equipment to the Soviet Union, but they were prevented from doing so by the Commerce Department.

The future for Soviet oil production depends largely on its ability to successfully drill wells and transport oil out of the arctic regions. There the problems with the permafrost and tundra are similar to those experienced in Alaska.

In October 1970 the president of North Slope Oil Co., a consortium of 30 Japanese companies, visited Moscow to propose a cooperative venture for exploration and development of the continental shelf off Sakhalin Island and the Kamchatka Peninsula. Under one previous proposal the Japanese suggested that they provide oil field equipment and pipelines, and buy oil if the Russians would do the actual work of developing deposits. The Soviets have not replied to this proposal, but have done testing in the area. One company in the North Slope consortium, Idemitsu Kosan Co., has been buying Soviet oil for ten years. The Russian oil is of considerable interest in Japan because it is of low sulphur content. In 1972, U.S. oil companies—Gulf, Jersey Standard, Bechtel—approached the Japanese and Soviets to participate in explorations.

IRAN: Persia let its first oil concessions in 1872. W. K. D'Arcy was granted a 60-year monopoly to explore and exploit oil resources in 1901, with the exception of the five northern provinces which were then in the Russian sphere. Oil was discovered in commercial quantities in 1908, and the Anglo-Persian Oil Co. was formed. It was renamed Anglo Iranian in 1935 and British Petroleum in 1954. The company dominated the country's principal oil fields in the south, and built up the world's largest refinery complex at Abadan. After a longstanding series of disputes between government and company, the oil industry was briefly nationalized in 1951 after the revolution. When the Mossidiq government was in turn overthrown, the current Iranian oil consortium was established, allegedly with the scheming of the Central Intelligence Agency. The consortium is called Iranian Oil Participants Ltd., and it produces 92 percent of all oil and refines 83 percent of it. Membership is mainly divided among American, British, and Dutch interests, as follows: British Petroleum, 40 percent; Shell, 14 percent; Gulf, 7 percent; Mobil, 7 percent; California Standard, 7 percent; Jersey Standard, 7 percent; Compagnie Française des Petroles, 6 percent. The remaining 5 percent is divided among several American companies: American Independent Oil Co., Arco, Signal Oil & Gas, Getty Oil, Ohio Standard, Continental Oil.

The consortium created two operating companies, organized under Dutch law: Iranian Oil Exploration and Producing Co. and Iranian Oil Refining Co.

Ownership of oil is held by the Iranian state company, National Iranian Oil Co. It arranges for development of oil, gas, and other minerals outside the consortium territory. Consortium agreements run to 1979 with the possibility of extensions for 15 years more.

Iran is the fourth largest crude oil producer in the world and the largest producer in the Middle East. Total production in 1969 averaged 3.3 billion barrels daily. Petroleum exports account for 85 percent of all foreign exchange earnings and provide $1.1 billion in revenues to the government.

In recent years Iran has constructed deep water facilities for shipping oil at Kharg Island in the Persian Gulf, and has built new refineries. The country's plentiful supplies of natural gas are used to run the refinery as well as for other consumer purposes in Tehran. In the future much natural gas is to be sent by pipeline to the Soviet Union. In 1972 Iranian officials warned the country must have a greater interest in managing oil operations in the future, and there was talk of nationalization.

KUWAIT: Closing of the Suez Canal and demand for low-sulphur content oil temporarily hurt Kuwait. The canal closing forced development of a new tanker port in the gulf, and requirements for low-sulphur oil (main Kuwait fields produce oil with 2.3 percent sulphur content) necessitated building special processing plants. Most all the country's production (87 percent) comes from Kuwait Oil Co., which is owned by British Petroleum and Gulf Oil. Kuwait's Burgan oil field is believed to be the world's largest oil reserves, with some 62 billion barrels.

The state-owned refining company, Kuwait National Petroleum Co., is negotiating with the Soviet Union to reach a products exchange deal. The plan was for Kuwait to supply Soviet customers in the Indian Ocean, including India, with its crude, while the Soviet Union supplied Kuwait's customers in Europe with refined products. Kuwait's main customer in Europe is West Germany.

Other companies operating in Kuwait include: American Independent Oil Co. in partnership with Getty Oil; Arabian Oil Co., a Japanese firm in partnership with the governments of Saudi Arabia and Kuwait; and Kuwait Shell Petroleum Co. In addition, there is also the state firm, Kuwait National Petroleum Co., with 60 percent government participation.

Crude oil production in Kuwait is associated with large production of gas, approximating 10 million tons annually, and only 20 percent of this gas is used, mostly for generating power, water distillation, refinery use, and reinjection into oil fields to maintain pressure.

SAUDI ARABIA: The major producer is Arabian American Oil Co., owned by Jersey Standard, 30 percent; California Standard, 30 percent; Texaco, 30 percent; and Mobil, 10 percent. The country's oil concessions were originally granted to California Standard in 1933. In 1936, Texaco bought into the operation, and in 1948 Jersey Standard and Mobil were included. Aramco initially held 672,864 square miles of territory under concession, but this will soon be reduced to 20,000 square miles. At the end of 1968, Aramco's proved reserves were 84 billion barrels. Aramco owns the big Tapline pipe system, which extends 1,068 miles from the company's oil fields to the Mediterranean port of Sidon, Lebanon. Guerrillas have blown up Tapline on several occasions, but in only one instance did this result in a long-term breakdown. That occurred in 1970 when a Syrian farmer drove a bulldozer into the pipeline. Syria refused to allow repairs, until 1971, when Aramco agreed to pay more for traversing Syrian territory. Actually, Aramco has discussed abandoning the line altogether. A major tanker port has been built in the Persian Gulf at Ras Tanura, which gives the company the option of going by sea around the Cape of Good Hope, or chancing it across the desert by pipe.

IRAQ: In recent years most of the oil in Iraq was produced by Iraq Petroleum Co. (IPC), a consortium of British, Dutch, French, and American companies, owned 23 3/4 percent each by British Petroleum, Shell, Compagnie Française des Petroles; 11 7/8 percent each by Jersey Standard and Mobil; and 5 percent by a Panamanian company controlled by the Gulbenkian interests of Paris. (Caloste Sarkis Gulbenkian, an Armenian entrepreneur, was instrumental in forming the original oil exploration company, created before World War I and called the Turkish Petroleum Co.) However, in 1972 Iraq nationalized IPC holdings.

In 1961, the Iraq government passed Law 80 which restricted the IPC to actual producing oil fields, equivalent to about 0.5 percent of the previous areas. The remainder of the concession was withdrawn. Haggling between the government and company proceeded until 1964, when Iraq created a state company, Iraq National Oil Co. (INOC), which was given rights to all areas except those left to IPC under Law 80. INOC can operate jointly with foreign companies so long as no concessions are made. It has an arrangement with Enterprise de Recherches et d'Activites Petrolieres (ERAP), the French state company, under which ERAP will explore for oil. If oil is found INOC will own it all, but ERAP can buy at a privileged price.

Recent major developments surround an agreement with the Soviet Union to develop the long dormant North Rumaila oil field. The Iraqis have lacked expertise to begin oil production, and until recently there was no real demand for oil. They now, however, are involved in several agreements with the Soviet

Union for development of various oil fields. The Soviets will provide equipment and technical teams to aid in exploration.

Iraq wants to exchange oil for goods: Bartering with the Czechs to establish a refinery in exchange for oil, promising the Spanish oil in return for cement and construction of pipe rolling plants. Hungary is to drill wells. Iraq claims to have $200 million worth of business lined up in Eastern Europe.

Iraq has crude reserves of 28.5 billion barrels, fifth among the seven nations which hold 70 percent of the world's crude oil reserves.

LIBYA: Esso made the first oil finds in Libya in 1957, but it wasn't until 1966 that Occidental brought in its enormous well. Emergence of Libya as a major oil producer took on considerable importance with the closing of Suez, because it was ideally placed to supply European markets. Its oil is low in sulphur content. At the same time, the nationalist government has taken initial steps toward taking over the oil industry. The government pressed for a higher share of the take, setting standards now imitated by the rest of the Middle Eastern exporting countries (55 percent of the take), a higher royalty rate, and perhaps most importantly over the long term, the Libyan government insists that the foreign oil companies train Libyan personnel to fill jobs. It has also forced the oil companies to cut down production on the grounds that oil resources are not to be drained away over a short period, and has attacked the common Western practice of flaring gas found in the search for oil. The government insists the companies catch the gas, and it orders them to conduct active, aggressive oil exploration programs.

The government has taken over domestic marketing operations of three foreign oil companies and turned them over to the new Libyan national oil company. In general, when Western oil companies balk, the Libyan government begins to talk about letting the Soviets come in.

The groups operating in Libya include Occidental, with production of 700,000 b/d; Esso, 446,000 b/d; (Esso Sirte, Inc.,

Grace Libya America Oil Co.), 118,000 b/d; Oasis (Marathon, Continental, Amerada Hess, Royal Dutch Shell), 818,000 b/d; Mobil/Gelsenberg, 222,000 b/d; Amosease (Texaco and Standard Oil of California), 284,000 b/d; British Petroleum Bunker Hunt, 217,000 b/d; and Acquitaine Group, 18,700 b/d.

VENEZUELA: Venezuela is the largest oil-exporting country in the world, producing 3.5 billion barrels a day during 1969. Companies owned by U.S. firms produced about 73 percent of the total, with Creole Petroleum Corp., a subsidiary of Standard Oil of New Jersey, alone accounting for 43 percent. Two-thirds of all production comes from fields in the Lake Maracaibo district. Fifty private oil companies operate in Venezuela. In addition to Creole, they include cia Shell de Venezuela, subsidiary of the Royal Dutch Shell Group; Mene Grande Oil Co., subsidiary of Gulf; and affiliates of Sun Oil, Socony Mobil, Texaco, Phillips, Standard Oil of California. Corporación Venezuela del Petroleo (CVP), a new government company, now controls 33 percent of all internal marketing.

2: NATURAL GAS

Until recently the United States was the one country in the world which deliberately developed and used ntaural gas, largely because pipelines could be built from oil fields of the south and central parts of the nation to markets in the East, mid-continent, and West Coast. In recent years, however. the Soviet Union and thc Netherlands have become major suppliers of natural gas to the European continent. The Soviet Union is negotiating to supply the Japanese as well.

World reserves of natural gas are listed at 1,144 trillion cubic feet, but these statistics are not to be relied on. The major fields are in the United States, along the Gulf of Mexico and on the north slope of Alaska, in the North Sea, onshore in the Netherlands, and in the eastern part of the Soviet Union.

Technological advances make it possible to freeze natural gas, and in a liquified state (LNG) ship large quantities of it in tankers. This development enables Middle Eastern and African oil-producing countries, which once burned the gas discovered with oil, to capture gas and ship it to markets. The trade in LNG probably will become an important factor in the energy business over the next few years. The existing routes extend from Algeria and Libya to the United Kingdom, Spain, France, and Italy. Routes are being opened from North Africa to the East Coast United States. A net of routes converge on Japan, with gas shipped from Alaska, Brunei, and Abu Dhabi. Gas trade is expected to soon commence between Japan and Australia. Other possibilities involve LNG shipments from Nigeria and Venezuela to East Coast United States, and there is the prospect of traffic in LNG from Soviet ports to the United States.

Until introduction of wide diameter pipe at the time of World War II, gas was manufactured from coal. European countries, including Germany, and South Africa still make gas from coal. In the United States, natural gas pipeline companies now are anxious to supplement short supplies of natural gas with synthetic gas made from coal in the western states. This promises to be a major development in the gas business. The price of synthetic coal gas is believed comparable with LNG.

In most parts of the world, the gas trade is dominated by the major international petroleum companies. In Europe, for example, Jersey Standard and Shell compete for growing markets with the Soviet Union. In the United States, Jersey Standard is the largest producer, with five times as much reserves as Indiana Standard, its nearest competitor. Through holdings in Imperial Oil in Canada and Creole Petroleum in Venezuela, Jersey Standard virtually dominates the fuels industry of the North American continent. In Asia, Shell is providing major LNG supplies to Japan from its Brunei fields. El Paso Natural Gas, a large U.S. company, in combination with Sonatrach, the Algerian government oil and gas agency, will carry gas from Algeria to U.S. East Coast ports.

UNITED STATES: Nearly one-third of all energy in the country is created by natural gas, which is in increasingly keen demand because it is relatively low in air pollutants, does not require high capital expenditures, and is fairly easy to handle.

In 1970, 22 trillion cubic feet of natural gas was consumed. Most of the gas was produced by oil companies in Texas and Louisiana. About 779 billion cubic feet was imported from Canada. According to the Potential Gas Committee of the American Gas Association, the industry trade group, current proved

reserves are estimated at 290 trillion cubic feet. Taking into
account recoverable but not yet identifiable reserves of gas in
the ground, the U.S. Geological Survey estimates gas reserves
recoverable under current technology to be about 2,100 trillion
cubic feet. The gas association, however, places the figure at
1,178 trillion cubic feet. Because the government has not itself
measured the gas resources, all statistics and estimates are essentially the industry's own.

Historically, natural gas was discovered in the search for oil,
and until after World War II was burned off at the wellhead.
The industry is dominated by oil companies. Largest U.S. producers, based on 1968 figures (million cubic feet per day), were
Jersey Standard, 5.2; Texaco, 3.2 Phillips, 3.1; Gulf, 2.9; Mobil,
2.7; Indiana Standard, 2.7; Shell, 2.2; California Standard, 1.4;
Continental, 991,000; Tenneco, 520,000. Jersey Standard had 113
trillion cubic feet of gas reserves, compared to Indiana Standard,
second largest reserve holder, with 20 trillion cubic feet.

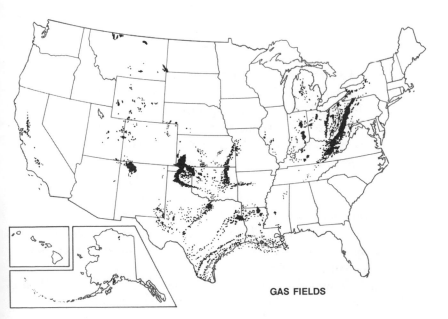

GAS FIELDS

Producers sell gas at the wellhead to pipeline companies for shipment either within the state or for interstate commerce. Before gas goes into the pipeline, it is usually stripped of other components, such as sulphur, which are then recovered for other uses. If the pipelines conduct interstate business, they are regulated by the Federal Power Commission. Pipeline companies sell gas to industrial customers or to utilities which distribute it locally. One-third of gas consumed is used for heating homes; one-sixth goes for making electricity, and one-half is consumed by industry. Industrial uses of gas include chemicals, 13.2 percent; petroleum refining, 10.9 percent; food, 6.4 percent; stone, clay, and concrete manufacture, 4.9 percent; and paper, 3.7 percent.

The big pipeline companies that buy and sell gas tend to be conglomerate operations, maintaining interests in other major fuels, with holdings in shipping, engineering, and land development as well.

Tenneco, among the largest pipelines, is also an important international petroleum producer with holdings in the North Sea, Canada, and Southeast Asia. In addition, it manages farms, including the largest grape vineyard in California, makes farm machinery, builds ships, and controls an insurance company. El Paso Natural Gas is building a fleet of LNG tankers and has large coal holdings. Texas Eastern is intertwined with Brown & Root, the big Texas engineering firm with projects around the world. El Paso and Tenneco are developing residential communities on their landholdings in various parts of the country.

Electric utilities also sometimes own gas pipelines and have a stake in oil, gas, coal, and uranium producing properties as well. Pacific Gas & Electric Co., the utility that supplies northern California with electricity, owns Pacific Gas Transmission Co., a major gas pipeline supplying California from Canada. Pacific Lighting, a gas company which supplies Los Angeles, has a stake in Canadian gas wells.

Pipeline interests are sometimes interlocked through their boards of directors. Transcontinental and El Paso have two directors in common, for example. Reports by the companies of their ten largest security holders to the Federal Power Commission reveal a pattern of control by major financial institutions and individuals. For instance, Puritan Fund, a Boston mutual fund, is reported as the eighth largest stockholder in Texas Eastern, the fourth largest holder in El Paso, and the eighth largest holder in Tenneco. Alfred C. Glassell, Houston, is the fifth largest stockholder in Transcontinental and the sixth largest holder in El Paso. First National City Bank of New York has interlocks with both El Paso and Transcontinental. Chemical Bank New York Trust Co. has one interlock with Tenneco, and manages trust funds with substantial holdings in both Tenneco and El Paso. Mellon National Bank & Trust is interlocked with El Paso and Pennzoil (United Gas pipelines) and Bank of New York is interlocked with El Paso and manages trust funds with substantial investments in Texas Eastern.

Insurance companies, including Metropolitan, John Hancock, Equitable, Aetna Life, Prudential, and New York Life are major holders of pipeline company long term debt.

Under the 1954 Supreme Court Phillips decision, the Federal Power Commission is charged with regulating the price of natural gas at the wellhead. In 1954, when the decision first came down, the FPC opposed jurisdiction, and for nearly ten years made little effort to regulate gas prices. Finally, in the 1960s, it began to establish a series of gas pricing schemes for the different gas regions of the United States, and these proceedings still drag on. In 1970, the industry and its proponents on the commission argued that the price of gas should be raised in order to encourage companies to search for more gas, otherwise there would be a shortage. But critics claimed the shortage was promoted, if not concocted, by the gas industry in a drive to escape federal regulation and establish higher prices. For example, it was revealed in congressional testimony that over 500 gas wells offshore Louisiana had been shut off by the lease operators, never connected to pipelines which could take the gas to market. At the same time, operators in Texas diverted

75 percent of new gas away from interstate markets where prices are regulated, and instead sold it within the state where prices are not regulated. In Louisiana, the second biggest gas-producing state, 40 percent of all gas was held for intrastate sale. In Kentucky, a pipeline company deliberately closed valves on wells in a major field to give the impression the wells had run dry. In this way the company hoped to persuade local residents to give up control of valuable land. The staff of the Federal Power Commission questioned the industry figures, but John Nassikas, chairman, and the other members, accepted the gas industry's general statistics.

In the future the Interior Department expects much gas to come from offshore drilling on the outercontinental shelf, over which it has jurisdiction. Moreover, the substantial Alaskan natural gas fields, with reserves estimated at 327 trillion cubic feet, will probably be connected by pipeline to the main U.S. markets, as will other gas fields in the Canadian arctic. LNG shipments will provide additional gas. The oil companies themselves appear to have speculated heavily on synthetic gas made from coal, and they have bought up coal resources in the western mountains. The Atomic Energy Commission through Project Plowshare is anxious to help in the search for gas. In projects Rulison and Gasbuggy the AEC blew off nuclear explosions underground for Austral Oil and in that way opened large reservoirs of natural gas. But this gas was radioactive. To supply one trillion cubic feet of gas a year would require more than 50 nuclear blasts a year, and the project is regarded with skepticism.

The British propose to manufacture a synthetic gas of pipeline quality from naphtha. They insist naphtha gas would be competitive with LNG. Power-Gas Corp. of America, part of the Davy-Ashmore group, said it could build plants capable of making 100 to 250 million cubic feet of gas a day at a cost of from 64 to 69 cents per 1,000 cubic feet. Crude oil contains about 20 percent naphtha, and while in the United States most of this is used either in gasoline or for manufacture of chemicals, the major product in foreign refineries is heating oil, thereby creating a large stock of naphtha. The British group claimed naphtha could be imported from the Middle East or Africa at a cost of about six cents a gallon on delivery to the United States. Naphtha could be carried in small tankers, and would not require the large cryogenic tankers used for LNG.

CANADA: Canada's natural gas industry is controlled by U.S. oil companies; about half of total production is shipped to the United States, and while there is growing demand for a restriction on exports, especially by utilities in Ontario which have switched from coal to gas because of pollution, U.S. companies are steadily expanding their grip on Canadian resources. A group of U.S. utilities in combination with Canadians have contracted for most of the available new reserves discovered in the Northwest Territories. More important, they are anxious to begin construction of a 2,500-mile gas pipeline which will carry gas from north slope Alaska and the Canadian arctic down through the Mackenzie delta to markets on the west coast and mid-continent.

Canada's proved natural gas resources are increasing, and in 1970 stood at 52 trillion cubic feet. Ultimate gas reserves are estimated at about 700 trillion cubic feet. Of that some 250 trillion cubic feet are in the Canadian arctic.

Most of the natural gas is produced in Alberta, where the leading producers in order are: Gulf Oil, Shell, Pacific Petroleums (Phillips), Hudson's Bay Oil and Gas (Continental Oil), Imperial Oil (Jersey Standard), Amoco (Indiana Standard), Central del Rio (Canadian Pacific—controlled by U.S., Canadian, and British interests), Canadian Superior (Superior Oil of California). Of a total 1.6 trillion cubic feet production, 778 billion cubic feet were exported to the United States, a 15 percent increase over the previous year. Major important companies were El Paso Natural Gas, Midwestern Gas Transmission, and Pacific Gas Transmission. One-quarter of gross revenues comes from the United States.

Major centers for new gas exploration are offshore east coast and in the Canadian arctic. In 1971, Mobil hit gas at Sable Island off Nova Scotia. Tenneco was drilling off Labrador. With the Mobil find activity was expected to pick up amidst predictions that offshore east coast areas would soon begin producing gas for Canadian and U.S. east coast markets within the next few years.

The main search, however, centers around the Mackenzie delta in the Northwest Territories and in the islands of the Canadian arctic. Panarctic Oils, Ltd. (owned 45 percent by the government, 55 percent by 20 private companies) developed gas wells on Melville and King Christian islands in the arctic. It then formed a consortium with five U.S. utilities to carry out more drilling. The venture, a five-year endeavor, involves $75 million, with Tenneco, which put up half the money, Columbia Gas, Texas Eastern, and Northern Natural Gas Co. In addition, Pacific Lighting Co., which services the Los Angeles area, contracted for other gas in the area. The Canadian government formed a pipeline subsidiary through Canadian National Railways and joined the group listed above, which is called the Canadian Arctic Study Group. This group of companies is thought to be in a good position to build the pipeline out of the arctic to California and Chicago.

At the same time, Imperial Oil, Jersey Standard's subsidiary, began negotiations with west coast utilities for development of potential gas supplies located in the ten million acres of land it holds in the Canadian arctic, and these negotiations could lead to alternate pipeline proposals.

NORTH SEA: Gas discoveries in the United Kingdom's sector of the North Sea have resulted in a radical reorganization of that country's energy markets, leading to a sharp increase in the use of gas. Amoco U.K. (Standard Oil of Indiana) is operator for a group including British Gas Council, Amerada Hess Corp., Texas Eastern Transmission Corp., with interests in the U.K. sector of the North Sea encompassing 2.7 million acres. The

Amoco group has two gas fields, and controls more gas reserves in the U.K. sector than any other group of companies (1.1 billion cubic feet a day). Others operating gas fields in the British sector include Atlantic Richfield, Phillips, BP, and Continental Oil (400 billion cubic feet a day). Current gas production in U.K. waters is about 1.5 billion cubic feet daily, and is scheduled to increase to about 4 billion cubic feet by 1975. By that time, gas from the North Sea is likely to replace all manufactured gas in Britain and account for 15 percent of the country's energy supply, and thereby necessitate further exploration for gas. Gas finds in nearby Norwegian waters may also benefit Britain. Gas may be piped ashore in Britain because of the deep fiord system paralleling Norway's coast, precluding construction of pipelines from the shore out to the fields. Because of the growth in use of gas, Britain is reorganizing the gas industry, abolishing the Gas Council, and creating in its place the British Gas Corporation.

NETHERLANDS: With the discovery of the big gas fields at Groningen, the Netherlands have become one of the two major gas suppliers to the European continent. The other supplier is the Soviet Union. In 1969, production totaled 773 billion cubic feet; reserves are estimated at 60 trillion cubic feet. Almost half of the amount produced is exported.

Shell and Standard Oil of New Jersey are the dominant factors in gas production. They share ownership in Nederlandse Aardolie Maatschappij (NAM), which until 1969 accounted for production of all gas and oil. Recently two other combines were allowed to explore for gas in the Netherlands. One is French, led by ERAP, and will develop gas for France. The other group is led by Standard Oil of Indiana; it is developing gas on the west coast for sale to West Germany.

Under current terms the government has the right to buy up to 40 percent in any exploration permits. Also, companies with gas production must first offer the gas to the Dutch marketing organization, Gasunie. Gasunie is owned by Shell, 25 percent;

Jersey Standard, 25 percent; state mines, 40 percent; and the state, 10 percent. Gas for export is handled by NAM. In 1970, the Netherlands and Italy signed an agreement providing for 4.2 trillion cubic feet over a 20-year period beginning in 1974.

SOVIET UNION: Gas reserves as of January 1970 were reported to be 12.1 trillion cubic meters. Perhaps as much as one trillion cubic meters more were added during 1970. (These reserves are listed as "explored," a category which is probably about twice as much as the term "proved" used in the West.) More than half of all gas reserves are in western Siberia. Development of gas dates from 1955. At that time, gas accounted for 2.4 percent of all primary energy produced in the Soviet Union. In 1968, it accounted for 18 percent.

Current production is about 200 billion cubic feet, somewhat below anticipated levels. In part this can be attributed to an embargo on wide diameter steel pipe by NATO countries. The embargo, now lifted, slowed pipeline development.

Exports of natural gas could turn out to be an important factor in increasing the Soviet Union's foreign exchange position, and in light of its failure to produce and export large amounts of oil, gas is viewed with considerable importance.

Along with the Netherlands, which has the sizable Groningen gas fields, the Soviet Union is in an unusually good position to supply Europe with natural gas. The Russians have built 33,000 miles of natural gas pipeline from the central part of the country to Moscow and down through Europe where it will connect with an Italian line. (The Soviet lines also supply Eastern Europe.) Most of the pipe comes from West Germany, although future supplies also will be made in Italy and France. Canadian experts who visited the Soviet arctic in 1971 reported the gas pipes were laid out on ground with only wooden planks to support and insulate from the permafrost. The Canadians said the Russians were aware of the ecological problems but built the pipes anyway and will worry about the problems later. The Soviet gas deals in Western Europe involve an exchange of pipe and equipment. The Soviet Union began providing Austria with 1.5 billion cubic meters a year (through 1990) in 1968, in exchange for $115 million worth of pipe and gas industry equipment. In 1969, the Russians made agreements with the West Germans and Italians for importation of gas over 20-year periods. West Germans will take 3 billion cubic meters a year, representing about 7.5 percent of the natural gas consumption. In exchange for gas the West Germans provided credits for purchase of large diameter pipe.

The Italian agreement provides for annual importation of six billion cubic meters, as much as 25 percent of total Italian consumption. The Italians also are to supply pipe and gas equipment in exchange. The negotiations with Italians dragged on for some time, but Italy was in a difficult position. Italy now requires ten billion cubic meters a year, with the demand expected to double during this decade. The situation is difficult because the main Po gas fields are expected to run dry by the end of the 1970s, and thus Italy is very much interested in making long-term arrangements for importing natural gas. Ente Nazionale Idrocarburi (ENI), the state petroleum company, hit gas in the northern Adriatic, and discovered a field in the Nile delta. In addition, Jersey Standard has a contract to supply Italy with Libyan LNG. While these arrangements reduce the pressure for Italy to make an all-conclusive deal with the Soviet Union, sizable imports were nonetheless required.

In 1971, the French signed a gas agreement with the Soviet Union, providing for imports of 2.5 billion cubic meters annually over a 20-year period beginning in 1976. In exchange the French will provide equipment for the Soviet gas industry.

Japan and the Soviet Union concluded recent large-scale gas deals. With gas reserves running out and demand increasing, Japan in 1967 originally struck a deal with two U.S. firms, Marathon and Phillips, for importation of Alaskan LNG for Tokyo Electric Power and Tokyo Gas Co. In 1971, the Soviet Union and Japan reached basic agreement on terms of an important natural gas project for running a pipeline from Soviet fields on Sakhalin Island and fields in Yakutsk in the Soviet far east to Japan. Two gas pipelines will be built across the Soya Strait between Sakhalin Island and the northern Japanese island of Hokkaido. The first pipeline will have a capacity of 85 billion cubic feet of gas a year. The second pipeline, which the Japanese are committed to building in the future, will carry gas from the Soviet far east fields of Yakutsk on the Lena River in eastern Siberia to Magadan, the Pacific port where the gas could be liquified and then shipped to Japan. U.S. companies—Gulf and Jersey Standard—may also become involved in this project.

Actually, for the time being, the Soviet Union is a net importer of gas. (In 1970, it was a net importer by about 3.7 billion cubic meters, but by 1975 will be a net exporter by 7.9 billion cubic meters.)

It imports natural gas from Iran and Afghanistan into gas-deficient regions of the country. In 1966, after the United States had refused the Iranians a steel mill, the Soviet Union offered Iran a steel mill complex in exchange for gas. Possession of a steel mill was an Iranian dream and they agreed. The price of gas to the Russians is cheap, so inexpensive that it will barely cover the cost of the pipeline. In future years, however, the Iranians will siphon gas off the pipeline for use inside Iran, and prices for this gas will be much higher than those quoted the Soviets. Thus, Iranian consumers, conceivably including big U.S. and British oil and petrochemical works, will help subsidize the Russian line. By 1975, the Iranian and Afghanistan pipelines will be sending up to 14 billion cubic meters of gas into the Soviet Union.

Over the short term, the Soviet Union gas imports from the Middle East made possible exporting gas into Europe. Over the longer term, the Russians should become a major gas exporter. Eventually Soviet gas may be shipped to Baltic Sea ports where it can be liquified and sent abroad as LNG to compete for markets in East Coast United States.

In mid-1972, three U.S. companies, Tenneco, Inc., Texas Eastern Transmission Corp., and Brown & Root, Inc., division of Haliburton Co., were in negotiations with the Soviet Union for potential development of Siberian gas reserves. The field for which the companies negotiated contained 120 trillion cubic feet of gas, about half the amount of total U.S. gas reserves. Tenneco probably would build the tankers to carry the LNG if the deal went through. The companies would barter for the gas, exchanging products made by other divisions (construction equipment from Brown & Root, farm machinery from Tenneco, etc.) in exchange for the gas. They also would be prepared to back up the Soviet deal with another stream of gas, either made synthetically from naphtha or coal, or brought from the Canadian arctic (where both Texas Eastern and Tenneco are financing exploration) by pipeline.

ALGERIA: Algeria has been in the midst of complicated negotiations with U.S. interests in an effort to arrange a large-scale export of LNG to east coast U.S. ports. Under a contract signed with Sonatrach, the state company, El Paso Natural Gas would import LNG from the Algerian oil company and sell it to three U.S. firms: Southern Natural Gas Co., Columbia Gas Systems, Inc., and Consolidated Gas Supply Corp. El Paso is to provide nine specially built tankers for transporting the gas at a cost of about $450 million.

Three of the tankers already have been ordered at French shipyards. Algeria is to build a liquefaction plant for gas at her own expense, but she applied for a $250 million loan from the U.S. Export-Import Bank to finance purchase of the required equipment. The contract calls for exporting 365 billion cubic feet of gas a year for 25 years, starting in 1975. The contract was first bitterly opposed by the French on the grounds that the United States should not do business with Algeria because it nationalized French oil installations without providing payment, and by U.S. oil and gas interests which opposed dealing with a Communist country, thereby threatening their control of the industry. The contract approval was temporarily held up by

White House aide Peter Flanigan, who stopped letters of approval from the Defense and State Departments going to the Federal Power Commission. The deal was eventually approved.

At the same time, the Federal Power Commission approved, with State and Defense department concurrence, a much smaller contract between Sonatrach and Distrigas for importing LNG into the U.S. to use for supplying electricity in peak periods. The contract calls for annual imports equivalent to 15.4 billion cubic feet annually for the next 20 years. Distrigas says it is considering a three-fold increase in imports after 1975. Distrigas is owned two-thirds by Cabot Corp. of Boston and one-third by Gazocean SA, which is controlled by French interests.

LIBYA: Esso (Standard Oil of New Jersey) scheduled loadings of LNG for Italy and Spain were delayed because of pipeline explosions. It will provide natural gas to Spain for the first time, and boost Italy's natural gas supply by one-third. Esso is to build four special tankers for the trade. Occidental also has announced plans for a $60 million LNG plant in Libya. The government is insisting that oil companies stop flaring gas from the oil wells, an historic practice, and instead capture the gas for sale.

VENEZUELA: Philadelphia Gas Works and CVP (Corporacion Venezuela del Petroleo), the government-owned company, are in a joint effort to determine economic feasibility of importing LNG to east coast U.S. markets. CVP plans to build two LNG plants by 1974. They would have a total capacity of 1.3 billion cubic feet a day. The government has specifically reserved LNG for the government-run company, barring foreign firms from the business. Even so, Creole, Jersey Standard's subsidiary, announced plans for building an LNG plant and speculation was that Creole would seek an accommodation with the government allowing for participation in the trade.

SOUTHEAST ASIA: A sizable LNG trade is beginning to take shape in Southeast Asia and Australasia. Shell, which will soon have the largest fleet of LNG tankers in the world (seven are on order) will begin in 1972 to ship four million tons of LNG a year from Brunei to Japan. The deal was made through Mitsubishi. At the same time, Shell is investigating the export of natural gas from a sizable field in New Zealand.

Australia, which until recent years was virtually dependent on petroleum imports, is fast becoming an important producing area. In 1968, natural gas production totaled only 216 million cubic feet. One year later, 9.3 billion cubic feet of natural gas was produced, and gas began to flow to domestic and industrial markets in Brisbane, Melbourne, and Adelaide. Recoverable reserves were estimated at 15 billion cubic feet. The Australian government will not permit exports of natural gas where it is in easy reach of markets, but gas fields in the northwest, far from population centers, are not included in the prohibition.

Tokyo Gas is interested in gas reserves offshore northwest Australia in the Bonaparte Gulf. Mitsubishi also is investigating the possibilities in this area, and held exploratory talks with Atlantic Richfield, which holds major leases. A Japanese consortium, headed by Okura Trading Co., announced in 1971 it was prepared to invest $750 million to develop natural gas in the northwestern Australian desert. The gas would be piped out to a port in northwestern Australia, frozen and transported by ship to Japan. The extensive Australian gas wells are held by a consortium, dominated by the Buckley family interests in New York. Another member is Freeport Sulphur Co.

3: URANIUM

About half of all uranium produced is now processed into fuel for nuclear power plants, and nuclear power is likely to provide the major and increasing market for uranium well into the 1980s. At that time, the Atomic Energy Commission believes breeder reactors, which utilize plutonium or thorium, may be in service.

Production of uranium from ore into a nuclear fuel involves a fairly intricate process, and a complex industry has sprung up to do the job. Most of the uranium ore that is mined contains 0.23 percent of the desired U_3O_8. Vast quantities of it must be mined, then milled into U_3O_8 or "yellow cake" as it is commonly called. (In the United States alone nearly six million tons of ore must be mined each year to produce 12,000 to 15,000 tons of U_3O_8.) The yellow cake is then changed into UF_6, a gaseous state. In this form it can be introduced directly into gaseous diffusion plants where uranium is enriched. In this process the fissionable isotope U-235 is concentrated. After enrichment the fuel is fabricated, changed into fuel elements to meet specific requirements of different power plants.

WORLD RESERVES: In 1970 the total world market for uranium was about 30,000 tons, half of which came from the

United States. The other major producing countries were Canada and South Africa.

Three corporations dominate the uranium industry. In the United States Kerr-McGee, an oil company, produces 23 percent of all uranium. In Canada the largest uranium producer is Rio Tinto Zinc, a British firm, and in South Africa, Anglo American Corporation of South Africa is an important producer. Rio Tinto and Anglo American are interlocked through various joint ventures; an Anglo American subsidiary owns parts of the Rio Tinto complex.

According to a joint report of the European Nuclear Energy Agency and the International Atomic Energy Agency, world reserves of uranium have increased somewhat in recent years because of intensified exploration. In 1967 estimated reserves of U_3O_8 recoverable below $10 a pound stood at 700,000 tons. But as of January 1, 1970, those estimates were revised upward to 840,000 tons. The increase was the result of intense exploration carried out in Australia, Canada, Central African Republic, Gabon, Niger, and the United States. These agencies believe that further analysis of data may show the reserves to be even larger. The United States accounts for over half of all known reserves. Other major reserves are in Canada and South Africa. The survey did not include the Soviet Union or China or the eastern European states. Sizable uranium resources exist in the U.S.S.R., East Germany, and China although few details are available.

While there is actual overproduction of uranium at this time, the report anticipates supplies will shrink as nuclear power plants increase in number, and that by 1975 or 1976 there may be a shortage of uranium.

UNITED STATES: In February 1967 the AEC estimated total U.S. reserves of U_3O_8 to be 875,000 tons. At that time the agency estimated basic uranium requirements for nuclear power at 170,000 tons through 1980. In addition, the AEC believes the industry should be equipped with an eight-year reserve of uranium. So, it sets the total uranium requirements at 600,000 tons.

To make nuclear power economical, uranium must be recovered at $10 or less a pound. In 1969, the AEC published a breakdown of uranium resources as follows: It believes there are 161,000 tons of U_3O_8 recoverable at $8 a pound, and another 320,000 tons recoverable at $10 or less a pound. In addition, the agency calculated there were some 350,000 tons more that could be mined at $10 or less, and 350,000 tons to be had at prices ranging from $10 to $15 a pound. All in all, estimates of uranium recoverable below $10 stood at 831,000 tons against the AEC's estimate of requirements for one million tons to the end of the century.

Domestic production of U_3O_8 was 12,000 tons during 1970. The AEC ended its purchasing program for uranium during 1970, and of the total production in that year bought only 2,600 tons. The remainder were private sales, mostly for reactors. The

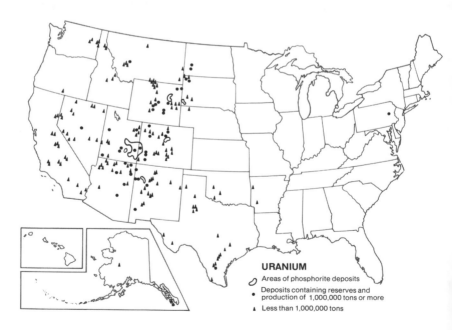

URANIUM

⟋ Areas of phosphorite deposits

• Deposits containing reserves and production of 1,000,000 tons or more

▲ Less than 1,000,000 tons

AEC U_3O_8 stockpile is about 50,000 tons, and there is another 5,100 tons of stockpile in the hands of private industry. The average price for domestic and foreign private sales was about $6 per pound.

Most of the uranium comes from the West with 90 percent of it produced in five western states: New Mexico, which has 50 percent of all recoverable reserves; Wyoming, with 25 percent; Utah, Colorado, and Texas.

In 1967, 124 companies produced ore from 368 mines in the United States. Of these companies, 15 both mined and milled the ore, and together they operated 223 mines and produced 92 percent of the ore. A hundred and nine independent companies ran 145 mines and produced 8 percent of the ore.

Of these major producer-refiners, Kerr-McGee was the leader, accounting for 23 percent of the business. United Nuclear and Homestake Mining in partnership represented another 17 percent of the business. These leaders are followed by Anaconda, Utah Construction & Mining, and Union Carbide. All in all, oil companies control 45 percent of all uranium reserves. Because of a 23 percent depletion allowance, there is an incentive to mill as well as mine; the allowance is available only at the milling stage.

Once the ore is processed into yellow cake, it next must be changed into UF_6 in order for it to be enriched in gaseous diffusion plants. Two companies now run UF_6 plants: Allied Chemical and Kerr-McGee.

In certain respects, the gaseous diffusion plants are at the crux of the uranium business, both domestic and foreign. The AEC owns and operates three gaseous diffusion plants for enrichment of uranium, both for civilian and military purposes. The key processes of these enormous installations are classified. The plants are run under contract by Union Carbide and Goodyear. In 1969, the government announced plans to sell them off to private industry. But after opposition developed within the Joint Committee on Atomic Energy, the plans were shelved. Democrats on the committee opposed selling the plants as a further giveaway to private power interests, and in the end the plan seems to have been dropped because there was little interest by industry. However, the government continues to pressure in subtle ways for the sale. Most recently it denied funds to improve and expand the plant facilities.

When it emerges from gaseous diffusion plants, the enriched uranium must be fabricated into different fuel elements for use in different types of power plants. This work is done mainly by the four major nuclear power systems manufacturers: General Electric, Westinghouse, Babcock & Wilcox, and Combustion Engineering.

CANADA: With known reserves of 232,000 tons of U_3O_8 recoverable below $10 a pound, Canada has the second biggest uranium reserve in the West. Four producers, three in the Elliott Lake region of Ontario, and one at Uranium City, Saskatchewan, accounted for the total 1969 output of 3,500 tons of U_3O_8.

Three Ontario companies produced 75 percent of the total: Denison Mines, Ltd., a Canadian firm; Rio Algom Mines, Ltd., subsidiary of Rio Tinto Zinc, the British mining concern; and Stanrock Uranium Mines, Ltd., a Canadian firm with substantial U.S. interests. The remainder came from Eldorado Nuclear, Ltd. Known contracts for these four companies total 39,000 tons of U_3O_8 through 1983. Deals include 16,300 tons to Japanese utilities by Denison, Rio Algom, and Eldorado. In addition, Rio Algom is scheduled to ship 13,600 tons to the United Kingdom Atomic Energy Authority and 6,300 tons to the Ontario Hydro-Electric Power Commission. The Stanrock output of 12 tons a year was sold to reactor manufacturers in the United States.

U.S., Japanese, West German, Italian, and French interests are involved in Canadian uranium exploration. Rio Algom, the RTZ subsidiary, is by far the biggest producer. Gulf Minerals, Gulf Oil of Canada, and a West German firm, Uranerzbergabau GmbH & Co., formed a group to develop Rabbit Lake uranium property in north Saskatchewan where a large pitchblende discovery was made. Production should begin in 1974. Gulf holds about two million acres of mining claims and exploration permits in Canada and is continuing an active exploration program. Kerr-McGee discovered a large deposit of low-grade uranium ore on acreage held jointly by it and a group of 15 Japanese companies in the Elliott Lake area. Phillips Petroleum is in joint ventures with Denison Mines.

To ward off foreign domination of its uranium resources, Canada is limiting future exploration to companies with only one-third foreign interest. However, the rules do not apply to existing operations.

In general, the uranium markets in Canada reflect small, even insignificant growth, awaiting expected demand in the middle 1970s when the nuclear power business is meant to pick up. In the meantime, the Canadian government announced an arrangement with Denison for stockpiling uranium, thereby preserving the jobs of miners. Otherwise, Denison had threatened to close down some mines.

SOUTH AFRICA: With the third largest uranium reserves, 200,000 tons of U_3O_8 recoverable at below $10 a pound, the industry increased production slightly. As elsewhere it awaits anticipated increase in the middle 1970s. Much of the South African uranium occurs as a by-product of gold mining. Production of U_3O_8 totaled 7,957,765 pounds during 1969, and nearly 40 percent of that was provided by members of the General Mining and Finance Corp., Ltd., a South African company. The Anglo American Corporation of South Africa, which now controls the mining ventures of Engelhard Industries, the U.S. company, accounts for about one-third of total uranium production. (Charter Consolidated, an affiliate of the Anglo American group, owns a substantial interest in Rio Tinto Zinc, the British combine that dominates Canadian uranium operations. Rio Tinto Zinc and Anglo American companies are jointly involved in uranium exploration in South Africa.) Much of the production was stockpiled because of lack of demand.

Three gold mines of the Anglo American group announced

plans to build a joint uranium treatment works, and Nuclear Fuels Corp. of South Africa agreed to supply Sumitomo Shoji Kaisha Ltd. of Japan with 450 tons of U_3O_8.

Uranium is regarded as a most important business in South Africa because of the general decline in gold mining, and because of the building demand for fuels, including uranium, in Japan. At the same time, South Africa announced it has developed its own uranium enrichment process, which could put it in competition with the United States.

AUSTRALIA: The country has relatively small reserves of 21,700 tons, but there is a good deal of exploration, all with an eye to providing the Japanese energy markets. Most of the holdings are British. U.S. companies involved in uranium exploration include Western Nuclear, Standard Oil of New Jersey, and Union Carbide.

FRANCE: France has relatively large uranium deposits (45,000 tons known reserves at $10 or less). French interests organized mining ventures in the former colonies of Gabon, Central African Republic, and Niger, where there is considerable activity.

INDUSTRY NOTES: Forty-five percent of U.S. uranium reserves are controlled by U.S. oil companies, and the key stages of uranium refining and processing are controlled by two oil companies: Kerr-McGee and Atlantic Richfield.

In general the trend is for U.S. oil companies to integrate vertically from mining through construction of nuclear equipment. Hence oil companies are involved in uranium mining, refining, and in the case of Gulf Oil's subsidiary, Gulf Atomic, in the construction of nuclear power plants. At the same time, established equipment manufacturers, General Electric, Westinghouse, Babcock & Wilcox, and Combustion Engineering are moving into mining. Some utilities also have begun to operate their own mines.

Until now the United States had an edge on the world market because it controlled nuclear technology. The government discouraged other governments from building costly uranium enrichment facilities by classifying key processes of the gaseous diffusion operation, and by offering foreign operations the opportunity to have enrichment done by the United States at relatively low prices. As a result, about half the output of the gaseous diffusion plants is for enrichment of fuel for abroad. In addition, the Export-Import Bank has committed $552 million to help other nations build 12 nuclear plants.

U.S. mining and oil companies are deeply involved in uranium mining ventures abroad. Gulf has large uranium fields under contract in Canada, as does Kerr-McGee. In South Africa, U.S. investors are involved through the Engelhard mining interests, now part of the Anglo American combine. And U.S. companies are exploring for uranium in Australia, which is a major supplier of fuels and minerals for Japan.

Looked at from another perspective, that of the multinational corporation, it is clear that a major portion of the world uranium market is dominated by three firms: Kerr-McGee, Rio Tinto Zinc, and Anglo American. The latter two firms are interlocked themselves.

U.S. control over enrichment may be ending. The Germans, Dutch, and British are discussing plans to join forces and build their own enrichment facilities. The Canadians have limited future foreign investment in uranium. The Japanese are discussing their own uranium enrichment scheme, and the South Africans announced they have developed a method for enriching uranium. Rio Tinto Zinc's Canadian subsidiaries are anxious to become involved in uranium enrichment enterprises.

The AEC's publicity and estimates are crucial to the future of the industry. The AEC, through its unilateral decision to add eight years of reserves to uranium needs, estimates a shortage of reserves for the future. In fact, the actual market is glutted with stockpiled uranium. None of the mines in the United

States, Canada, or South Africa are producing at or near capacity. The current world price for U_3O_8 is between $5 and $6 a pound, well below the $10 break-even figure.

Environmental attacks on nuclear power may well drastically change the shape of the business in the United States. Environmentalists have tied up construction of several proposed nuclear plants, and a pending suit by the Scientists' Institute for Public Information in New York seeks to block the development of breeder reactors. Breeders use natural uranium and produce more fuel than they use. The scientists argue they cause serious pollution, and the suit is an effort to begin the sort of controversy which led to the downfall of the SST (supersonic transport).

Nonetheless, the president has asked for an increase in funds for nuclear energy. Tenneco and Westinghouse jointly announced a program to build a floating nuclear power plant, and Public Service Electric & Gas Co., the large New Jersey utility, studied proposals to situate plants up and down the New Jersey coast.

One result may be that U.S. boiler makers and uranium companies will be encouraged to seek markets abroad, especially in Japan, where restrictions for products are less stringent than in the United States.

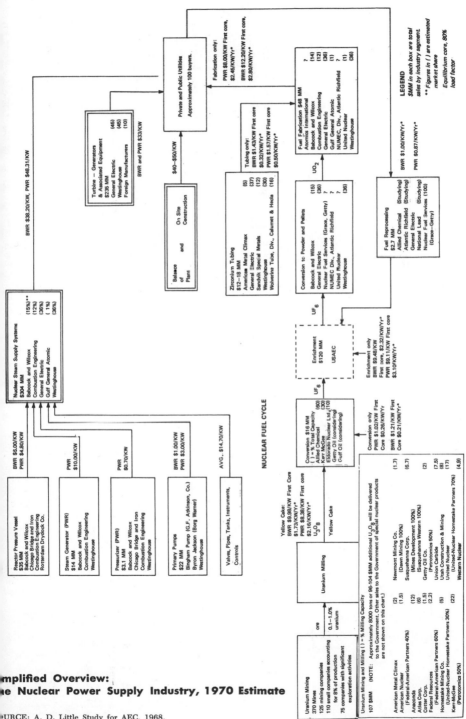

Simplified Overview:
The Nuclear Power Supply Industry, 1970 Estimate

SOURCE: A. D. Little Study for AEC, 1968.

Estimated Resources of Uranium

(Data available April 1970)

Country	Price Range < $ 10/lb U₃O₈ Reasonably Assured Resources (Reserves) 10³ short tons U₃O₈	10³ tonnes uranium	Estimated Additional Resources 10³ short tons U₃O₈	10³ tonnes uranium	Price Range $ 10-15/lb U₃O₈ Reasonably Assured Resources 10³ short tons U₃O₈	Estimated Additional Resources 10³ short tons U₃O₈	Qualifying Remarks
Argentina	10	7.7	22	17	11	33	
Australia	21.7	16.7	6.7	5.1	9.2	6.6	The geological potential is excellent for a substantial increase in resources.
Brazil	1.0	0.8	1.0	0.8			Potential for substantial increase is excellent. Additional resources dependent on phosphate, gold, and niobium production.
Canada	232	178	230	177	130	170	New data based on recent government-initiated study (January 1970).
Central African Republic	10.4	8	10.4	8			New data in view of 1969 decision to exploit deposits.
Denmark					5		As 1967 Report. Resources are in Greenland.
France	45	35	25	19	9.0	15.5	Increased resources following 1967-70 search.
Gabon	13.5	10.4	6.5	5		6.5	Doubled resources following 1967-70

							Remarks
Italy	1.5	1.2					Prospecting 1968–69 did not change reserves; higher priced resources linked to production of other elements.
Japan	2.7	2.1			4.5		
Mexico	1.3	1			1.2		
Niger	26	20	39	29		13	Large increase following prospecting by French CEA. Local milling 1971.
Portugal } Europe	9.6	7.4	7.7	6		15	Prospecting to be renewed 1970 in Angola and Mozambique.
Angola						15	
South Africa	200	154	15	11.5	65	35	Production capability and size of reserves a function of gold production.
Spain	11	8.5			10		
Sweden					350	50	Production will be limited to meeting a portion of Swedish demand.
USA	250	192	510	390	140	300	Does not include 90,000 short tons estimated by-product U_3O_8 from phosphate and copper production in Reasonably Assured Resources up to $ 10. Excludes 90,000 short tons of additional resources at $ 10 estimated in areas other than well-established uranium districts.
Others	3.6	2.8	11	8.5		1.5	
APPROXIMATE TOTAL	840	645				750	

U.S. Uranium Milling Companies and Plants

Company	Plant Location	Nominal Capacity Short tons Ore Per Day	Short tons U_3O_8 Per Year
The Anaconda Company	Bluewater, New Mexico	3,000	
Atlas Corporation	Moab, Utah	1,500	
Continental Oil Co.— Pioneer Nuclear Inc.	Karnes County, Texas	1,700[1]	
Cotter Corporation	Canon City, Colorado	450	
Dawn Mining Company	Ford, Washington	500	
Federal-American Partners	Gas Mills, Wyoming	950	
Humble Oil and Refining Company	Powder River Basin, Wyoming	2,000[1]	
Kerr-McGee Corp.	Grants, New Mexico	7,000	
Mines Development, Inc.	Edgemont, South Dakota	650	
Petrotomics Company	Shirley Basin, Wyoming	1,500	
Rio Algom Corp.	Near Moab, Utah	500[1]	
Susquehanna-Western, Inc.	Falls City, Texas	1,000	
Susquehanna-Western, Inc.	Ray Point, Texas	1,000	
Union Carbide Corporation	Uravan, Colorado / Rifle, Colorado	2,000	
Union Carbide Corporation	Gas Hills, Wyoming	1,000	
United Nuclear-Homestake Partners	Grants, New Mexico	3,500	
Utah Construction and Mining Co.	Gas Hills, Wyoming	1,200	
Utah Construction and Mining Co.	Shirley Basin, Wyoming	1,200[2]	
Western Nuclear, Inc.	Jeffrey City, Wyoming	1,200	
		31,850	19,000

1. Planned for 1972 start-up.
2. Under construction, 1970 start-up.
SOURCE: *Uranium, Resources, Production and Demand*, September 1970, Organization for Economic Co-operation and Development.

4: COAL

Most of the world's coal is located in North America and China. The United States is the largest coal producer in the world, and its major exporter. But because of the Japanese demand for fuel, there is feverish effort by big U.S. and British mining companies to develop the coal resources of western Canada, Australia, and South Africa. North Vietnam has substantial coal mines, but they were badly bombed by the United States. In addition, the Russians are negotiating deals for sale of Siberian coal to the Japanese.

Coal demand outpaces production in the United States itself. There is increasing demand for coal to fire electricity plants, and for export to Japan. The Japanese in tandem with oil companies are developing coal mines in Appalachia.

UNITED STATES: Coal reserves, totaling 3,210 billion tons, are the second largest in the world. In 1969, the United States produced 560.5 million tons of bituminous coal, or 18 percent of the world supply. More than half of that amount—308.5 million tons—was purchased by electrical utilities.

The United States is the largest exporter of coal in the world; in 1969, 56.2 million tons, worth $585 million, was shipped abroad, most of it to Japan, central Canada, and Europe where it is used to make steel or for electricity.

The cumulative production of coal to January 1, 1967, the date of the most recent estimates by the U.S. Geological Survey, amounts to 38 billion tons, half of it burned since 1930. At current rates of use there is enough coal in the United States to last for 400 years. Almost all coal in the past was mined from three major fields east of the Mississippi. (West Virginia and Pennsylvania historically have produced more than half of all coal produced in the United States.) The most developed coal fields are in the Appalachians centering on Pennsylvania and northern West Virginia, a southern field in West Virginia and Virginia, and a field in Kentucky and Illinois. The other major fields, now being developed, are in the Rocky Mountains and northern Great Plains.

Most of the coal in these three developed areas is privately controlled. In the past it was common for steel companies and railroads to own vast tracts of coal lands. Now coal companies are increasingly part of conglomerate corporations or subsidiaries of oil companies.

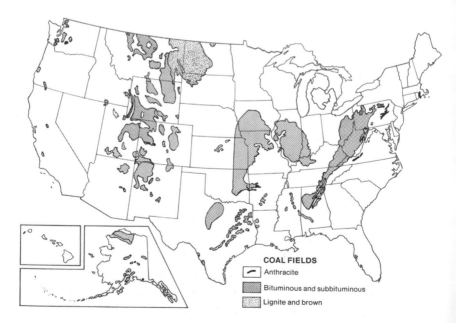

COAL FIELDS
- Anthracite
- Bituminous and subbituminous
- Lignite and brown

Three major companies, two of them oil firm subsidiaries, control 27 percent of all coal production. They are:

1. Consolidation Coal Co., a subsidiary of Continental Oil Co., accounts for 11 percent of the market with an annual production of 60 million tons. Reserves are estimated at seven billion tons.

2. Peabody Coal Co., a subsidiary of Kennecott Copper, also has 11 percent of the business with 60 million tons of production. Peabody's reserves in the West alone are estimated in excess of 3 billion tons.

3. Island Creek Coal Co., a subsidiary of Occidental Petroleum Co., has 5 percent with a production rate of 26 million tons. Island Creek's reserves are 4.1 billion tons.

The major acquisitions of coal companies by large oil companies and other large industrial corporations in recent years are listed below:

Oil Companies	Company Acquired	Date of Acquisition
Gulf Oil	Pittsburgh and Midway Coal	Late 1963
Continental Oil	Consolidation Coal	September 15, 1966
Occidental Petroleum	Island Creek	January 29, 1968
" "	Maust Properties	August 8, 1969
Standard Oil of Ohio	Old Ben Coal	August 1968
" " "	Enos Coal	August 1968
Eastern Gas and Fuel	Joanne Coal	June 18, 1969
" " "	Ranger Fuel (30% Interest)	January 1970
" " "	Sterling Smokeless	April 15, 1970

Other Large Industrials	Company Acquired	Date of Acquisition
General Dynamics	Freeman Coal	December 31, 1959
" "	United Electric Coal	December 31, 1959
Kennecott Copper	Peabody Coal	March 29, 1968
Wheeling-Pittsburgh Steel	Omar Mining	December 1968
American Metal Climax	Ayrshire Collieries	October 31, 1969
Gulf Resources & Chemical	C & K Coal Co.	January 6, 1970
Alco Standard	Barnes and Tucker	July 1970

The following important acquisitions of coal companies were also made by several of the largest independent coal companies during the past decade:

Acquiring Company	Company Acquired	Date of Acquisition
Peabody Coal	Midland Electric Coal	August 1963
Pittston Co.	Eastern Coal	October 1969
Westmoreland Coal	Winding Gulf	November 1968
" "	Imperial Smokeless	January 31, 1969

Another company that is a major factor in coal production is Jersey Standard because it has six billion tons of coal reserves.

Two of the three largest coal producers are oil companies; five of the largest ten are oil companies, and seven of the largest 15 are oil firms. In the past five years oil companies have increased their share of the national coal production from 7 percent to 28 percent. Looked at another way around, of the top 15 coal producers, only three are independent companies. Among the top 50 coal companies, 29 are captives of other industries. The smaller companies are owned by utilities and steel firms. Oil company holdings are all concentrated in the largest 15.

Strip Mining: Much more coal is strip mined now than it once was. In 1917, 1 percent of the coal was stripped; now about 33 percent of 179 million tons is open cut. The technology makes it possible for bigger shovels to scoop out more of the overburden, the layers of soil and rock separating coal from the earth's surface. In 1955, shovels were able to scoop out overburden 42 feet thick. By 1965, shovels were taking out 125 feet of overburden. Still, relatively small amounts of coal resources are strippable. At the current level of technology, stripping away from zero to 100 feet of overburden, it is possible to mine 108,095 million tons of coal, or some 9.6 percent of the estimated total coal resources.

The heightened interest in stripping coal is because the electric utilities need inexpensive coal to burn for electricity. In strip mining, output per man day is 100 percent higher than in underground mining; average recovery is 60 percent higher, and operating costs are 25–30 percent lower. A strip mine operation gets out 80–90 percent of all coal, compared with 50 percent recovery underground.

Gasification of Coal: Historically, coal was used to make gas. The gas industry predates discovery of petroleum and natural gas by many years. Gas was originally used for lighting streets, then was replaced by electricity. Gas was made from coal in several different ways. In producing coke from coal a gas with relatively high heating value is recovered. Other synthetic gases can be distilled from coal. The maximum production of manufactured gas was reached in 1947, when it began to be replaced by introduction of natural gas from the oil fields. Development of natural gas in turn was made possible through introduction of large diameter steel pipe. The Big Inch and Little Big Inch pipelines used to ship oil from Texas to the Northeast during World War II were turned over to natural gas.

During the 1920s and 1930s, the Germans developed methods of changing coal into gas. This provided them with a secure supply of synthetic fuel for the air force. During World War II, German planes were frequently fueled with synthetic gas.

In 1948, the United States became a net fuels importer, and there was considerable interest in transferring the German technology. Between 1944 and 1955, the Bureau of Mines conducted extensive investigations of the German technology under the Synthetic Fuels Act. During this period, $60 million was spent on coal conversion and $25 million on production of a satisfactory liquid fuel oil shale. But in 1955, the program was halted because of the discovery of large deposits of Middle Eastern oil, with which a coal-to-oil process could never hope to compete.

As part of an effort to reinvigorate the coal industry in the 1950s, Congress created the Office of Coal Research, which once more began to explore synthetic gas as a means of reinvigorating the depressed industry. The funding for the Office of Coal Research is relatively small ($17 million in 1971), but it provides money for research along several different lines, including processes for changing coal into natural gas, and coal into gasoline. In addition, it finances projects aimed at finding more efficient ways to burn coal. Major research projects aimed at creating synthetic pipeline gas from coal include:

Institute of Gas Technology, $11.6 million U.S. funds; $2.3 million American Gas Association. The Hygas process has been under development for 25 years, and a large-scale pilot plant was finished in 1971. This process involves first grinding up the coal, blowing hot air through it. Then the coal is mixed with an oil, pressurized and heated. The coal falls down through a rising stream of hydrogen, creating methane. The product gas is scrubbed at successive stages.

Consolidation Coal Co., $16.6 million. This experiment also involves building a pilot plant at Rapid City, South Dakota, where lignite is mixed with dolomite (a form of limestone), pressurized, and gas created.

Bituminous Coal Research, Inc., $3.4 million. The project, in an early stage of development, involves an oxygen blown system.

Iowa State University, $276,200. In this experiment coal char is heated by passage of electrical current through a fluidized bed of the conductive char particles. The resulting gas may also be used in manufacture of various chemicals.

Avco Corp., $1.8 million. This project involves converting coal to acetylene.

University of Wyoming Natural Resources Research Institute, $613,000. The project entails experiments in determining proper pressures and temperatures and catalyst characteristics that will result in commercially successful processes.

West Virginia University, $200,959. This project builds computer models for developing gasification processes.

In addition, the Office of Coal Research sponsored Consolidation Coal Co.'s Project Gasoline, $17.8 million, a pilot plant which aimed at producing gasoline from coal. The plant did not operate properly, and was shut down.

In their study of the industry, *Coal: the Captive Giant*, in 1971, Beck and Rawlings say, "Two things are noteworthy here. First the oil companies—particularly Continental Oil and Atlantic

Richfield—have substantial interests in the development (or non-development) of these processes. Secondly, the actual commercial use of this process has been postponed. Mr. Neil Cochran of the Office of Coal Research believes that such a commercial process could have been developed by now, and he says that there is no question but that it could be developed by 1975. However, he acknowledges that no company has done this yet because of the risk of doing it first and failing."

Charles Ertel and Carl Sopcisak—two engineers of the Sterns-Rogers Corporation—have said that the Hygas process of converting coal into pipeline quality gas could be developed commercially by mid-1974. However, they, like Mr. Cochran, foresee the coal producers postponing this development until 1978 or 1980 due to the "considerable risk."

Because of the energy crisis, interest in changing coal to gas has picked up. In 1971, the American Gas Association had made a secret study that pinpointed 170 different locations for gasification plants, most of them in the Rocky Mountain states. In August 1971 the Interior Department signed an agreement with the gas industry that will add $80 million in federal funds to $40 million in industry money for a four-year acceleration of existing work on small-scale but workable pilot coal gasification plants. El Paso Natural Gas announced plans to build the world's first coal-to-gas commercial plant, involving $250 million. The plant, which will produce 250,000 million cubic feet of gas per day, is to be constructed in New Mexico, where the company has 900 million tons of coal reserves, and nearby the existing pipeline.

Senator Henry Jackson of Washington proposed legislation establishing a joint government-industry corporation to promote and develop coal gasification, but the administration seemed reluctant to support the measure. Instead the administration wants to speed up research.

Gasification projects will involve large amounts of water, which will be consumed and not returned after use. Water is scarce in the mountain states, and the proposed projects will necessitate large-scale aqueduct systems. Opposition to gasification began to form among westerners who worried lest their water supplies be exhausted in producing fuels for other parts of the country.

CANADA: Coal deposits in western Canada are estimated at 118.7 billion tons, with half the resources located in British Columbia, the scene of a current coal boom.

In 1969, Canada imported more coal than it produced, but the situation is changing as new mines in the west are developed to supply the Japanese steel industry. In 1969, Canada produced 10.6 million tons and imported 17.3 million tons, 95 percent of its bituminous coal from the United States for electric power generation in Ontario province. About half of all coal produced in Canada is for electricity.

Canada is fast becoming a major world supplier of metallurgical coal. Led by Kaiser Resources Ltd., an arm of Kaiser Industries, the U.S. company, five mining firms have signed contracts to provide the Japanese steel industry with 180 million tons of coking coal worth $2.5 billion over 15 years. Kaiser is to provide 75 million tons for $1 billion, and it is developing Canada's biggest mining complex, a coal processing plant and elaborate shipping terminal at Roberts Bank, the superport near Vancouver. While this is an immense contract, Kaiser has had troubles, and in 1971 revised the contract rates upward to reduce losses. Even so, losses are expected to continue for some time. Kaiser's intervention started the coal boom. In the mid-1960s the Japanese steel makers, who also buy coal from the United States and Australia, were put out with the Canadians because the Canadian Pacific Railway refused to reduce rates necessary to make coal purchases economical. Kaiser became interested, purchased coal lands, and threatened to ship the coal via the U.S. Great Northern Railway. At that point, Canadian Pacific cut the freight rate 35 percent and plunged into the coal business itself through Fording Coal Ltd. and now holds the second largest Japanese contracts, 45 million tons worth $650 million. Canpac Minerals, Canadian Pacific's exploration subsidiary, has extensive coal holdings through the west, and Cascade Pipe Ltd., another subsidiary, wants to build a pipeline to run coal from mines in southeastern British Columbia to the Roberts Bank superport. The Japanese also have a 15-million-ton contract for $200 million with Cardinal River Coals, a joint venture of Luscar Ltd., and Consolidation Coal, the U.S. coal company which is owned in turn by Continental Oil.

The growing coal business in western Canada depends on two main factors: inexpensive rail rates, making it possible to haul coal from the mines through the mountains to Vancouver; and the modern Roberts Bank superport, managed by the Canadian National Harbors Board. Roberts Bank is designed for supertankers of 200,000 tons and is meant to service the Orient, loading coal for Japan and wheat for China. Kaiser is considering the possibility of hauling coal into the United States for its steel operations in California, and shipping it to Canadian steel makers in Ontario. They also are considering the feasibility of European markets. By 1975, when coal shipments to Japan are in full swing, Canada is expected to rate as a fairly close third behind the United States and Australia as a supplier of coking coal to Japan.

AUSTRALIA: The coal industry, while relatively small, is booming. It is dominated by U.S. and British companies which sell coal to Japanese steel, gas, and chemical concerns. Small sales also have been made to European markets. Black coal production is centered in New South Wales and Queensland.

In 1969, Australia produced 47.5 million tons of black coal, almost all of it from New South Wales and Queensland. Exports totaled 17.7 million tons. (Shipments to Japanese customers during the period totaled 16.3 million tons.) Domestic power stations used 12.7 million tons of the coal, with Australian iron and steel industry buying 7.8 million tons.

A major expansion of coal mining is under way in the Bowen Basin of Queensland, where companies expect to develop 150 million tons by 1985. Two new superports are being built, one at Gladstone Harbor, another at Hay Point.

Mining operations include a joint venture by Theiss Brothers, a Queensland firm, with Peabody Coal of the United States and Mitsui & Co., Ltd., of Japan. Peabody expertise brought to life a sagging strip mine operation. Contract negotiations are in progress for 49.7 million tons of coal by 1978, worth $500 million. The state financed a railroad to haul the coal to port.

Utah Development Co. has a contract to supply 21.4 million tons of coking coal to Japanese steel and chemical companies over ten years to 1978. The coal is first to be stripped, then mined underground.

Blair Athol Coal Pty., Ltd., owned 57 percent by Conzinc Riotinto of Australia, supplies 70,000 tons of steaming coal for a power station and cement works. The company is involved in further prospecting, with reports of extensive finds of coking coal.

Central Queensland Coal Associates, 85 percent owned by Utah Development Co. and 15 percent by Mitsubishi of Japan, is undertaking most spectacular coal development in the Goon-yella-Peak Downs area to supply 14 Japanese steel, gas, and chemical companies with 85 million tons of coal from 1971 to 1984. The contract is worth $893 million.

The companies pay standard Queensland royalty of 5 cents a ton and yearly rental of $1 an acre. They are limited to a total of 300 million tons of coking coal. The combine built a new railroad, a new town, and a harbor at Hay Point. Output is expected to reach five million tons annually by 1974.

Cluthe Development (controlled by Daniel K. Ludwig, the U.S. shipping magnate) has a 38 percent interest in the Blair Athol operation, and is prospecting a 24-square-mile area at Siruius Creek where resources are estimated at 200 million tons of coking coal. Speculation is that Ludwig will make money two ways—both in mining and shipping the coal to Japan.

The export of coking coal to Japan and elsewhere came under sharp attack in Parliament in 1971. The argument was made that foreign interests were draining the south coastal coal fields of coking coal for export, and as a result there would be no coal remaining to support growth of Australia's own iron and steel industry. It was pointed out that the Japanese buy Australian coal at rates much cheaper than they do from the United States or Canada.

SOVIET UNION: With reserves of 6,800 billion tons, the Soviet Union has the largest coal reserves in the world. Of that total, 179 billion tons are thought to be exploitable at current levels of technology. Of the minable coal, the Donets Basin has 25 percent of the total reserves; more than 60 percent are spread around the eastern part of the country, with major deposits in the Kuznetsk. Major coal deposits are far from the industrial Urals, and that section relies on natural gas for fuel.

In 1969, the Soviet Union produced 608 million tons of run of the mine coal, or an estimated 348 million tons of clean coal. Production breaks down as follows: 390 million tons of bituminous, 78 million tons anthracite, and 140 million tons lignite.

About one-third of all coal produced is used to produce electricity. Consumption of coal instead of oil is widely urged in order to increase the availability of oil for export. The demand for coal exceeds the Soviet Union's capacity to produce it: 44 percent of coal mines did not meet production quotas in 1969. About a quarter of all coal mined came from stripping operations.

Exports of coal and coke totaled 27.3 million tons, with about 11 million tons going to non-Communist countries. The Soviets and Japanese steel makers negotiated for possible development of the Yakutsk coal fields in Siberia. Russians are offering a long-term contract in exchange for Japanese capital investment. The Yakutsk area has an estimated 20.5 million tons of high-grade coking coal, which could be hauled by the Trans Siberian Railroad to Nekhodka port and then to Japan by ship. In 1969, the Soviet Union supplied Japan with nearly three million metric tons of coking coal. The Soviet Union is the third ranking supplier of coking coal to Japan, after the United States and Australia.

5: TRANSPORTATION

Pipelines and tankers provide the major means of transporting oil and natural gas from the wellhead to refineries and consumers. The large oil companies operate navies which account for two-thirds of all ocean-going commerce. With the exception of natural gas pipelines in the United States, which are regulated as public utilities, the large oil companies control oil pipelines throughout the world, and in Europe where a natural gas market is growing up, they are a major factor in the natural gas pipeline business.

PIPELINES

UNITED STATES: Natural gas and oil are generally moved about the United States through pipelines, and the continent is interlaced with them. There are nearly a quarter of a million miles of oil pipelines, more pipelines than miles of railroad tracks. Pipelines not only transport liquids and gases, but also solids and slurries.

Pipelines are cheaper than other forms of transport. Costs range from $0.02 to $0.08 per hundred barrel miles. That compares with rail rates of from $0.05 to $0.40 and truck rates of from $0.30 to $0.60. Some pipelines can even match tanker rates of from $0.015 to $0.04 a barrel per hundred miles.

In the early years after the discovery of oil in 1859, oil was carried to the nearest rail depot by mule-drawn wagon. In 1865 Samuel Van Syckel laid the first pipeline—a two-inch diameter, six-mile line in Pennsylvania. To ward off marauders he posted guards along the line. He was able to offer transportation for $1 a barrel, 50 cents less than the wagon rate. The actual cost was about 5 cents a barrel. Railroads and water carriers then promoted pipelines, believing that pipes which terminated at their facilities would guarantee long-term business. But their attitude began to change as the long-haul pipelines went into operation in 1879, and they observed pipelines as a competitive threat. The first continental pipeline was built in 1931 from the Texas panhandle to Chicago. The pipelines underwent their greatest expansion during World War II. In 1940, about 95 percent of the crude oil products delivered to the eastern seaboard were still transported by tank ship and barge. The war effort diverted ships and the German submarines sank intercoastal tankers. As an interim solution, oil was shipped by rail. The government then helped build large pipelines including the Big Inch and Little Big Inch lines from Texas to New York.

The current system delivers 75 percent of total crude input to refineries. Greatest concentration of crude oil pipelines is from New Mexico, Texas, and the mid-continent to the Texas Gulf coast.

Twenty pipelines between these areas have a total capacity of two million b/d. Nine pipelines with a capacity of 1.8 million b/d connect the Southwest to the Midwest, and three pipelines with a capacity of 500,000 b/d connect the Midwest with the Rocky Mountains.

Natural Gas Pipelines: There are 65 natural gas pipelines in interstate commerce, but 24 of them control 97 percent of all natural gas reserves and production. And of that total, five or six are of particular importance. El Paso Natural Gas is one of the largest. Historically it has been the major supplier to the California gas market. The Supreme Court has ordered El Paso

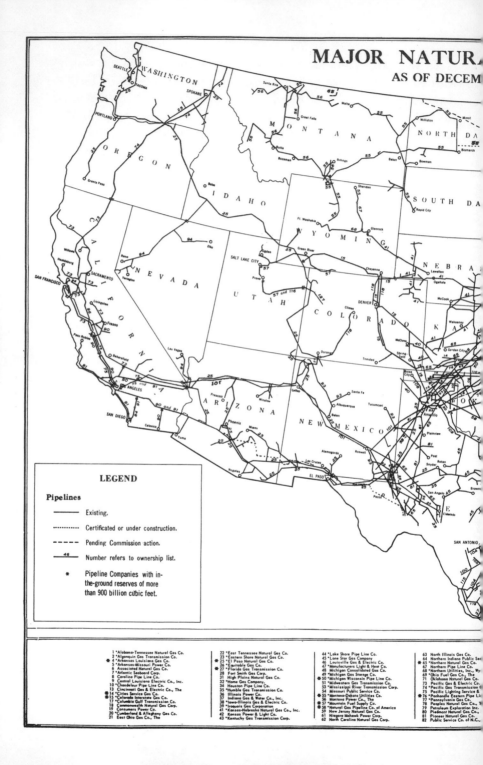

MAJOR NATURA

AS OF DECEM

LEGEND

Pipelines

——— Existing.

············ Certificated or under construction.

- - - - Pending Commission action.

——46—— Number refers to ownership list.

* Pipeline Companies with in-the-ground reserves of more than 900 billion cubic feet.

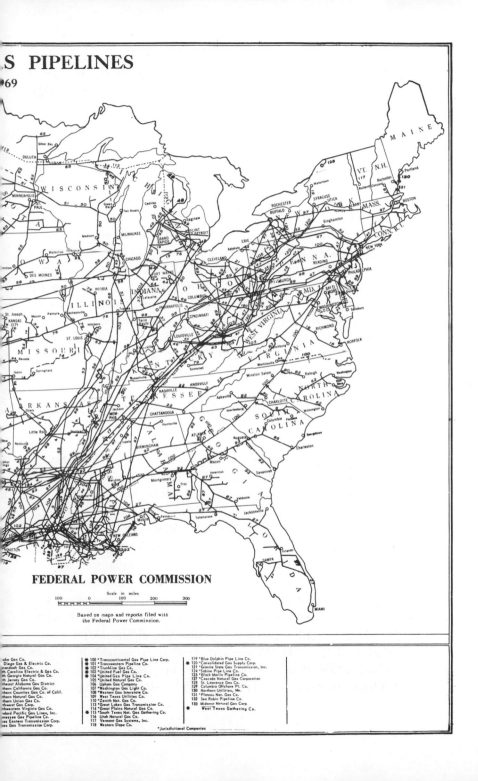

S PIPELINES

'69

MAINE

FEDERAL POWER COMMISSION

Scale in miles
100   0   100   200   300

Based on maps and reports filed with
the Federal Power Commission.

...oke Gas Co.
...Diego Gas & Electric Co.
...nandoah Gas Co.
...th Carolina Electric & Gas Co.
...th Carolina Natural Gas Co.
...th Jersey Gas Co.
...theast Alabama Gas District
...thern California Gas Co.
...thern Counties Gas Co. of Calif.
...thern Natural Gas Co.
...thern Union Gas Co.
...thwest Gas Corp.
...thwestern Virginia Gas Co.
...dard Pacific Gas Lines, Inc.
...nessee Gas Pipeline Co.
...nessee Eastern Transmission Corp.
...as Gas Transmission Corp.

100 *Transcontinental Gas Pipe Line Corp.
101 *Transwestern Pipeline Co.
102 *Trunkline Gas Co.
103 *United Fuel Gas Co.
104 *United Gas Pipe Line Co.
105 *United Natural Gas Co.
106 Upham Gas Company
107 *Washington Gas Light Co.
108 *Western Gas Interstate Co.
109 West Texas Utilities Co.
110 *Zenith Nat. Gas Co.
113 *Great Lakes Gas Transmission Co.
114 *Great Plains Natural Gas Co.
115 *South Texas Nat. Gas Gathering Co.
116 Utah Natural Gas Co.
117 Vermont Gas Systems, Inc.
118 Western Slope Co.

119 *Blue Dolphin Pipe Line Co.
120 *Consolidated Gas Supply Corp.
121 *Granite State Gas Transmission, Inc.
124 *Sabine Pipe Line Co.
125 *Black Marlin Pipeline Co.
127 *Cascade Natural Gas Corporation
128 St. Lawrence Gas Co.
129 Columbia Offshore Pl. Co.
130 Northern Utilities, Me.
131 *Plateau Nat. Gas Co.
132 Sea Robin Pipeline Co.
133 Midwest Natural Gas Corp.
     West Texas Gathering Co.

*Jurisdictional Companies

to divest itself of another pipeline running from the Canadian border down through the mountain states to gas fields in Colorado. The company still fights this decision. Another large system is managed by Tenneco, a conglomerate, which originally began business as Tennessee Gas Transmission Co., a pipeline. The pipeline is now a relatively small subsidiary in Tenneco's sprawling operations, but in terms of the pipeline business it plays an important role, with the main line running from producing fields in Texas and Louisiana into the East. A branch line goes to Chicago. Texas Eastern and Transcontinental both run long pipelines from the Gulf producing areas to New York and the populated eastern megalopolis. United Gas Pipe Line, a subsidiary of Pennzoil, carries gas from the Gulf to expanding markets in Florida. Other major companies include Panhandle Eastern, which runs from the Southwest up to Chicago and other industrial middle western markets, and Columbia Gas Transmission System, which through a clutch of subsidiaries supplies gas up and down the East Coast.

Oil Pipelines: In general oil companies own most of the pipelines that carry liquid crude oil or oil products. In terms of miles of pipe, the top three interstate liquid systems are Jersey Standard, 12,692 miles; Mobil, 12,257 miles; and Indiana Standard, 11,045 miles. In terms of traffic, Jersey Standard is by far the largest, delivering 633 million barrels. Other leaders are Texaco, 485 million barrels; Indiana Standard, 463 million; Gulf, 450 million; Colonial, 418 million; and Shell, 400 million.

The main pipelines carrying oil products from the Gulf coast to the East are the Colonial and Plantation systems.

Colonial Pipeline Co. is owned by a consortium of oil companies including Arco, 3,795 shares; Indiana Standard, 5,155; Cities Service, 5,033; Continental, 2,717; Mobil, 4,136; Phillips, 2,556; Texaco, 5,138; Toronto Pipeline Co., 6,040; Union Oil of California, 1,430. The Plantation System is owned by Jersey Standard, 62,260 shares; Refiners Oil Corp., 34,593; Shell, 30,647.

Williams Brothers and Texas Eastern carry oil products from

the mid-continent to the Midwest. Williams Brothers is independently owned; Texas Eastern is a natural gas pipeline company as well, operating major gas lines to the New York area. The Brown & Root engineering firm was instrumental in starting Texas Eastern and has major stockholdings in the company.

Wyco and Olympic operate in the Rocky Mountains and Pacific northwest. Wyco is owned by Indiana Standard, 14,000 shares; Texaco, 14,000 shares; and Mobil, 7,000. Olympic is owned by Shell, 10,875 shares; Mobil, 7,375 shares; and Texaco, 6,750. The Southern Pacific system operates in the Southwest. It is a subsidiary of the Southern Pacific Transportation Co. Capline, the nation's largest crude oil pipeline, made of 40-inch pipe with a planned capacity of more than one million barrels daily, extends from St. James, Louisiana, to the middle western refineries. The pipeline terminates at Patoka, Illinois. Principal owners include Clark Oil and Union Oil of California, 20 percent; Ashland Oil, 19 percent; Texaco, 18 percent; Shell, 14 percent; Marathon, 10 percent; Indiana Standard, 10 percent; Ohio Standard and Sun Oil, 9 percent. Seven oil companies are combined in a joint venture to build the Alyeska Pipeline running from the North Slope of Alaska to a deep-water port at Valdex. The owners include Ohio Standard, 28.08 percent; Arco, 28.08 percent; Jersey Standard, 25.52 percent; Mobil, 8.68 percent; Phillips, 3.32 percent; Union Oil of California, 3.32 percent; Amerada Hess, 3 percent.

CANADA: There are several major proposals for piping oil and gas from Alaska and northern Canada into the United States. The success or failure of all of these hinge on the ability of the two countries to work out some sort of an energy alliance. The pipelines are key bargaining points within the framework of ongoing discussions. For example, it is unlikely the oil companies in Alaska will produce much oil without also seeking a market for gas, which also occurs in these deposits. To market that gas they must pass through Canada to reach U.S. markets. The Canadians have stiffened resistance to sale of their own gas.

While the Canadian resources are essentially owned outright or controlled by U.S. firms, the Canadian government controls the pipeline routes, and hence is in a somewhat strengthened bargaining position when it comes to American demands for more gas.

In western Canada there is resistance to the Alaska TAPS pipeline project on grounds that ships carrying oil from Valdez, southern terminal of the proposed oil pipeline, to California will create a large oil traffic along the Vancouver coast, bringing with it the threat of spills and environmental hazards. Thus, some factions in Canada encouraged the Canadian government to allow the Americans to take everything out, both oil and gas, through the Mackenzie River delta.

Several different schemes were proposed for bringing down natural gas from Alaska through Canada's Mackenzie River valley, to various market zones within the United States. Three different routes were widely discussed:

The Northwest Group proposed the longest pipeline, a $3 billion, 2,500-mile route ending in the Great Lakes area. The group is made up of Trans Canada Pipelines Ltd, Canada's largest pipeline system; units of two major U.S. suppliers of midwest markets, American Natural Gas Co. and People's Gas Co.; and the three major holders of North Slope oil and gas leases, Atlantic Richfield Co., Standard Oil of New Jersey, and Standard Oil of Ohio.

The Mountain Pacific Group proposed a $1.8 billion, 2,050-mile pipeline to the West Coast. This group was formed by Bechtel Corp., the construction company; Westcoast Transmission Co., which operates the Canadian gas pipeline that already extends to the Northwest territories; El Paso Natural Gas Co., biggest supplier to the West Coast; and two large California utilities, Pacific Lighting Corp. and Southern California Edison Co.

Gas Arctic's 2,500-mile route would run to the U.S. Great Plains and cost $1.5 billion. It would distribute gas throughout the United States and Canada by utilizing Alberta Gas Trunk's existing pipelines. Other members of this group include the government-owned Canadian National Railway Co.; three big U.S. pipeline companies, Columbia Gas System, Inc.; Texas Eastern Transmission Corp., and Northern Natural Gas Co. Columbia serves the East; Texas Eastern the East and West, and Northern Natural the Great Plains.

Tenneco also is involved in planning a pipeline project. It is in a joint venture with Panarctic Oils, Ltd.

EUROPE: In Europe, where most of the oil comes from Africa or the Middle East, the main crude oil pipelines begin at tanker terminals, then run inland to refining centers, based around industrial and population centers. Future plans call for building extended oil pipelines from supertanker ports. And natural gas, hitherto seldom used in Europe, is now a major fuel.

It costs more to build pipelines in Europe than in the United States, partly because of the physical terrain, but also because European governments insist on stiff safety precautions, which the industry believes are too stringent.

American pipelines are regarded as common carriers and are required to ship for third parties at nondiscriminatory rates, if necessary, at the expense of the owner's requirements. But in Europe pipelines are only required to ship for third parties at a time of scarce demand.

Of the major crude oil pipelines in western Europe, Shell and Jersey Standard are the dominant owners, holding together between 35 and 50 percent interests in the two major pipelines running inland from the Mediterranean. In a third line, owned by ENI, the Italian oil agency, they have 40-year agreements which account for half the line's capacity.

Moreover, Shell and Jersey Standard together with the Netherlands government control production and distribution of natural gas from the Groningen gas fields, the only major gas field in western Europe.

The threat to their operation is from the Russians who are extending a large-scale pipeline system from Siberia into western

Europe, where Siberian gas eventually will be sold to Italian consumers.

Two pipelines from the North Sea to the lower Rhine and Ruhr areas have been in operation since the early 1960s. More important, an intricate continental system has developed beginning at Mediterranean ports, which receive oil from North Africa.

The Mediterranean system consists basically of four major lines. They are:

The South European Pipeline (SEPL) extends from Fos (near Marseilles) to Karlsruhe. Its principal owners are Jersey Standard, 28 percent; Shell, 23 percent; French interests, 15 percent. SEPL has a diameter of 34 inches and a capacity of 34.4 million metric tons a year. Plans are to expand SEPL to a capacity of 90 million tons a year. At the same time, the port of Fos will be enlarged to accommodate supertankers of more than 250,000 tons.

The Central European Line (CEL) from Genoa to Aigle and on to Ingolstadt was completed in 1966. It is owned by ENI, the Italian oil company, but Jersey Standard, Shell, and BP have a 20-year agreement, allowing them to transport four million tons of oil a year through the pipes. That accounts for half the line's total capacity of eight million tons. Diameter is 12–26 inches.

The Trans-Alpine line from Trieste to Ingolstadt was finished in 1967, is 40 inches in diameter and carries 25 million tons annually. A Rhine-Danube line, completed in the early 1960s and running between Karlsruhe and Ingolstadt, is now operated as an extension of Trans-Alpine. It has 26-inch diameter pipes and a capacity of 12 million tons annually. Jersey Standard has a 20 percent holding in these two lines; Shell, 15 percent. BP and Mobil each have 11 percent interests. Trans-Alpine proposes to expand its system to 54 million tons a year.

MIDDLE EAST: While the closing of the Suez Canal in 1967 provided a major incentive for construction of economical supertankers to haul oil the long way around, by the Cape of Good

Hope and on up to Europe, it also occasioned construction of a large, extensive pipeline system connecting the Persian Gulf to the Mediterranean.

These new pipes probably will become more important in the next decade for several reasons. For one thing, Middle Eastern oil is beginning to lose out in Europe to African oil because of the long-haul around the Cape. Thus, Middle Eastern producers may well compete more vigorously for European markets, the largest in the world. At the same time, costs of supertankers are steadily going up, which will enhance the economies of pipelines. Completion of the various pipelines now in progress or planned would make 260 million tons of oil available at terminals on the eastern Mediterranean.

The most important operating pipeline in the Middle East is the Tapline, owned by Trans Arabian Pipeline Co., a subsidiary of Aramco. Tapline extends from Saudi Arabia to the Mediterranean coast about 30 miles south of Beirut. It delivers 480,000 b/d. The line was shut down from May 3, 1970, to January 29, 1971, after a Syrian farmer drove a bulldozer into it. The Syrians refused to permit repairs, but eventually settled after Aramco agreed to an increase in transit payments from $4.5 million to $8.5 million a year. It was briefly closed again after explosions in late summer 1971.

Egypt is proposing to construct the Sumed Line, from Ain Soukhna on the Gulf of Suez to a point on the Mediterranean coast ten miles west of Alexandria. It would have 40 million tons capacity a year. Companies agreeing to use the line include: Shell, BP, and CFP for 7.5 million tons a year; Mobil, 5 million tons; the French state company, ERAP, and Gelsenberg of Germany, three million tons each; the Spanish company, Hispanoil, six million; and Amoco, an undisclosed amount. Aristotle Onassis also has been in discussions with the Egyptians. He originally proposed building a line alongside the Suez Canal.

In 1969, Israel completed the Trans-Israel pipeline, with an initial capacity of 400,000 b/d, linking Elath on the Gulf of Aqaba to Ashkelon on the Mediterranean. The pipeline will eventually have a capacity of 1.2 million b/d. Tankers haul oil to Elath, a natural deep-water port, and from there it is shipped to Ashkelon. During the time Tapline was shut down, oil from Saudi Arabia apparently was shunted through the Trans-Israel pipeline.

Plans are underway for an immense pipeline connecting Iran's Ahwaz oil field to the Turkish Mediterranean port of Iskenderun.

SOVIET UNION: The Soviet Union is building a long natural gas pipeline from Iran to gas deficient areas of its territory. At the same time, it is involved in building an immense pipeline system, the Northern Lights system, to bring natural gas from western Siberia to Moscow and from there down through Europe to Italy.

JAPAN: The Soviet Union and Japan have an agreement for importation of large amounts of Soviet natural gas by pipeline from Soviet fields on Sakhalin Island and in Yakutsk in the Soviet far east. First pipelines will have a capacity of 85 billion cubic feet of gas. A second line is to be arranged for the future.

LATIN AMERICA: Texaco and Gulf discovered oil in eastern Ecuador and are building a pipeline across the Andes to the Pacific. It will have an initial capacity of 250,000 barrels a day. In 1971 Occidental reached an agreement with Peru whereby in exchange for rights to drill for oil, the company would build a pipeline, if oil was discovered, over the Andes to the Pacific.

RAILROADS

Nearly three-quarters of all coal mined is loaded onto trains at the mine. In 1970 coal shipments accounted for 10.8 percent of all freight revenue. Two major railroads dominate the business in the Appalachian sections of the country: Norfolk & Western, which handles the greatest amount of tonnage, and the C&O/

B&O system. Both rail systems have extensive coal landholdings as well. They are actively engaged in the sale abroad.

In terms of revenue, these two railways accounted for about 22 percent each of total coal freight revenues in 1970. The Penn Central was third with 17.3 percent.

The C&O/B&O system carried 111 million tons of coal, or 17 percent of the total tonnage. The N&W and Penn Central handled between 90 and 95 million tons, for 15 percent of the total each.

In 1970 the N&W carried 90.6 million tons of coal, representing $304.5 million. During the year 33.2 million tons were loaded into vessels at the railroad's Norfolk pier for export. The railroad's total income was $748.6 million.

N&W is the largest landholder in the major coal-producing counties of West Virginia. Through Pocahontas Land Corp. it owns 341,496 acres in 14 coal-producing counties, or 7.2 percent of all land.

The C&O/B&O railroad income from coal totaled $369.1 million in 1970 out of total revenues of $1 billion.

C&O/B&O owns land through several different subsidiaries. They include New Gauley Coal Co. in southern West Virginia; the B&O in northern West Virginia. A subsidiary, Western Pocahontas Corp. owns 152,651 acres in West Virginia and Kentucky.

C&O/B&O owns one-half undivided interest in 2,929 acres in West Virginia and wholly owns the New River Co. It also owns Greenbrier Resort at White Sulphur Springs. The C&O/B&O is third largest landholder in the 14 leading coal-producing counties in West Virginia and controls 4.4 percent of the land.

(Note: The N&W and C&O/B&O had proposed to merge, but the merger was subsequently abandoned. The Penn Central Railroad, third largest coal-hauling railroad, has maintained a 17 percent investment in the N&W. However, under a current arrangement the N&W is buying back that stock from the Penn Central trustee.)

Other railroads hold coal in the western states. Chief among them is the Union Pacific which has vast coal holdings in the Rocky Mountains. The railroad is investigating possible sale to companies in both the West and Middle West.

SLURRY PIPELINES

Consolidation Coal Co., now Continental Oil's subsidiary, developed an extensive scheme for slurry pipelines in the 1950s. The September 1962 *Fortune* describes the plan: "Back in 1957, Consol first sent its slurry (a burnable mixture of coal and water) surging through a 108-mile pipeline running from its mine in Cadiz, Ohio, direct to the Eastlake station of the Cleveland Electric Illuminating Co. at a saving over rail rates of $1 a ton. Now Consol has the plans prepared and the customers on the ready for the construction of a 350-mile pipeline running from its West Virginia and western Pennsylvania fields to east-coast generating plants in the Philadelphia, New Jersey, and New York areas."

In 1961, George Love, the company's chairman, had reported, "Consol is in a position to offer to large users of fuel throughout the country a brand new means of competing with or replacing oil or natural gas. Not only will this new fuel be much more economical to transport than coal in its traditional form, but it will also eliminate the great majority of the expensive coal-handling installations required in the present day utility plant.

"We are tremendously enthusiastic over the prospects for this new fuel as a major contribution particularly to the electric utility industry, and through it to improving the living standard of the country." The company said it was hopeful of persuading various state legislatures to grant the right of eminent domain for construction of coal pipelines.

Then, suddenly Consolidation abandoned this promising project. The company magazine, *Consol News,* in 1964, explained, "Consol's Ohio pipeline, which opened in 1957, did more than deliver coal—it delivered a shot of adrenalin to the railroads and spurred them into developing the unit train. So successfully did the railroads compete that the pioneer pipeline was placed in mothballs in 1963—a victim of its own success."

Peabody Coal Co., subsidiary of Kennecott, is shipping coal from its Black Mesa mine to the Mohave power plant through a slurry pipeline that runs 275 miles underground from the mine to the plant. The coal is pulverized, then mixed with water to form slurry that is half water and half coal by weight. The water comes from five deep wells located on leased land from Indians. The slurry is pumped into an 18-inch steel pipeline which goes into the ground at the plant and remains underground until it emerges in Nevada, near Bullhead City, Arizona. Running at full capacity, the pipeline will hold 43,000 tons of coal. It takes coal slurry 2.8 days to make the trip.

The pipeline is operated by Black Mesa Pipeline, Inc., a subsidiary of Southern Pacific Pipelines, Inc.

Black Mesa is a massive highland in northeast Arizona; it lies on both the Navajo and Hopi Indian reservations. Peabody on a lease opened the mine in 1970. The mine is to be expanded to provide coal for another power plant at Page, Arizona, on the Navajo reservation. The Mohave plant is a 1,500-megawatt installation located in Nevada, near the state's southern tip, and is jointly owned by Southern California Edison Co., Los Angeles Department of Water and Power, Nevada Power Co., and Salt River Project Agricultural Improvement and Power District—all members of West Associates.

In another possible project, Bechtel Corp., Burlington Northern, and Peabody are studying a proposal to build a coal slurry pipeline more than one thousand miles long to feed low-sulphur Montana or Wyoming coal to power plants in the Midwest.

TANKERS

The shipment of oil and oil products accounts for nearly two-thirds of all ocean commerce, and the major oil companies either through outright ownership or by charter operate navies of several thousand ships. Ships are growing ever larger, with supertankers of over 200,000 tons a popular size. The mammoths ply the routes extending from the Persian Gulf to northern Europe, Japan, the United States, and the Caribbean. One supertanker is less expensive to operate than several smaller tankers, but, of course, in the case of a spill or collision in coastal waters it can have a devastating effect, unloosing thousands of barrels of oil.

At the end of 1970 there were 3,102 ships in the world tanker fleet, totaling 152 million deadweight tons. Another 432 ships, representing 70 million deadweight tons, were on order.

Although supertankers are popular, the tanker fleet in 1970 was predominantly made up of ships under 100,000 tons. But of the new ships on order, over half are 200,000 tons each. There are 131 ships over 200,000 tons in operation.

One-quarter of the world fleet is registered in Liberia. Other main registrations, in rank, are Great Britain, Norway, Japan, and the United States.

Sixty-five percent of the new ships are for independent owners, who then charter the ships to oil companies. The remainder are for oil companies. Following is a list of supertankers (over 175,-000 tons) owned or chartered by the seven large international oil companies which have the largest fleets:

Company	Chartered		Owned		Total	
	No. of vessels	Thousand dwt	No. of vessels	Thousand dwt	No. of vessels	Thousand dwt
BP	33	7,348	16	3,696	49	11,044
Esso	21	5,172	32	7,733	53	12,905
Gulf	17	4,769	9	2,543	26	7,313
Mobil	7	1,543	5	1,055	12	2,599
Shell	42	9,774	29	6,461	71	16,235
Socal	2	443	16	3,861	18	4,304
Texaco	13	2,932	14	3,322	27	6,253
Sub-total	135	31,981	121	28,671	256	60,653

SOURCE: Petroleum Press Service, December, 1969.

Nearly two-thirds of the new ships are under construction in European yards, with Sweden doing the most work. Spain has emerged as a large shipbuilder. Yards in Japan construct the remaining one-third of the fleet.

The supertankers were built because of the closing of the Suez Canal in order for the oil companies to economize on long trips from the Persian Gulf around the Cape of Good Hope. Since then, tanker costs have risen sharply with a resulting rise in rates. Insurance premiums are high and the actual construction costs have risen steeply. In addition, some tankers have had structural problems with explosions in their tanks.

The fastest growing part of the tanker business involves construction of large LNG ships, which carry frozen liquified natural gas.

At the end of 1970, nine LNG tankers were in service with 21 vessels on order. Of the tankers operating, Jersey Standard owned four, and Phillips-Marathon had two. Of those on order, Shell accounted for seven, and El Paso three.

Jersey Standard's tankers will ply from Libya gas fields to Italy and Spain. El Paso's tankers will carry gas to the U.S. east coast ports, and Shell's tanker fleet will haul gas from Brunei to Japan.

Additional routes will run from Alteria to Fos, the French Mediterranean port. Another will go to Boston from Algeria.

According to Petroleum Press Service, expectations are that 70 LNG ships will be in operation by 1980.

Algerian gas has been going to the United Kingdom and northern France since 1964. The Alaska-Japan route began operating at the end of 1969.

Shell's big gas deal with Mitsubishi will send gas from Brunei to Japan where it will be purchased by Tokyo Electric, Tokyo Gas, and Osaka Gas. Some of Shell's tankers may be used to open other aspects of the Far Eastern trade.

El Paso has ordered the first of 11 LNG tankers to bring gas to the United States. They will be the world's largest LNG ships, with a capacity to carry 120,000 cubic meters. Philadelphia Gas Works plans to import LNG from Venezuela. Three tankers will be involved. Jersey Standard also says it is interested in bringing LNG to the United States, and is negotiating an agreement with

Columbia Gas. Amoco is considering bringing gas to the United States from Trinidad. Also BP/CFP have a joint venture, discussing shipping offshore Abu Dhabi gas to Japan.

Russian gas from Yakutsk might be taken to Magadan for liquefaction and shipment to Japan and the U.S.

Other possible routes might include shipment of Shell/BP gas from Nigeria to the United States, and Phillips's shipment of African or North Sea gas to the United States.

PORTS

Most ports of the world are limited to ships of 70,000 tons, and therefore are not able to accommodate the growing fleet of super-tankers. The pressure to build deeper ports is greatest near the refining centers of Japan and western Europe, which receive 75 percent of all oil shipped from the Persian Gulf.

The most serious limitation is water depth. A fully loaded 100,000-ton tanker draws about 47 feet and that rises to 61 feet for a 200,000 tonner. A 367,000-ton tanker will require 90 feet.

Heretofore, tankers of 200,000 tons can only call at nine ports. They include Gothenburg and Slagentangen in Scandinavia; Rotterdam, Le Havre, and Fos on the European continent; Bantry Bay, Ireland; Milford Haven and Finnart in Great Britain; and Tokyo Bay in Japan. In order to use the large ships, oil companies must transship or employ some sort of lightening method at sea. Gulf, for instance, which has a net of deep-water ports in Ireland, Canada, Okinawa, ships from the Persian Gulf to one or another of these ports, then transships the cargo to final destination. Shell, on the other hand, partly unloads big ships into smaller vessels offshore.

There are several types of port schemes for large tankers. Until recently one popular method has been the mooring buoy, which enables a tanker to tie up and attach a hose to a buoy that holds a pipeline that connects with shore. There are 65 of these around the world. The problem is that hoses are fairly small in diameter and a good deal of time is consumed in unloading. Another

method involves building artificial floating island ports in deep
water. Tankers can circle around and edge up to these long
docks.

In Europe, Bremen and Hamburg, both river ports well inland, are considering plans for an artificial island at the mouth of
the Elbe to accommodate tankers of 500,000 tons. It may be
linked to the mainland by underwater pipeline. Rotterdam is engaged in a dredging program to gash out a harbor so that 250,-
000-ton ships can sail in from the North Sea.

Offshore facilities for 500,000-ton tankers are under study for
Le Havre, Cherbourg, and Brest. Another terminal for 500,000-
ton ships has been discussed for Bilbao on the Bay of Biscay.
Spain plans a mooring buoy for 300,000-ton ships of Tarragona.

Four Italian ports are being expanded. A steel mooring island
is under construction in Genoa. Other projects include an artificial island off Sardinia's Porto Torres, new facilities at Milazzo,
Sicily, and Sibari in southern Italy. Access to Trieste, terminal
for the Trans-Alpine pipeline, is limited to 160,000-ton ships because of shallow waters in the northern Adriatic.

Large-scale port development in Europe could turn out to be
unnecessary. Tanker costs are rising, and construction of the
European and Middle Eastern pipeline systems might result in
making pipelines a more efficient, less expensive way of shipping
petroleum.

Outside Europe, port developments include: Two mooring
buoys off Durban and Johannesburg, South Africa. Jersey Standard and Shell are each building mooring buoys off Singapore,
which has become a major refining center. Japan, whose entire
economy is based on imported oil, has two offshore berths for
200,000-ton tankers in Tokyo Bay. A staging terminal for 500,000-
ton ships is planned for Shikoku Island. Gulf has a transshipment
terminal at Okinawa. Iran is expanding deep-water facilities at
Kharg Island.

There are few deep water ports in the Western Hemisphere.
The Canadian government is constructing a deep water port on
the straits of Canso, off Nova Scotia. It will be leased to Gulf. In

addition, the Canadians are building a deep water harbor in Newfoundland nearby Come-by-Chance refinery. Another is scheduled for St. John, New Brunswick, and it will have an off-shore buoy.

With possible exception of Long Beach, California, no U.S. port has facilities for large tankers. The Trans-Alaskan pipeline terminal at Valdez, Alaska, will have facilities for loading 500,-000-ton ships. Atlantic-Richfield proposed to build a 300,000-ton port at Machiasport, Maine, but those plans have been stalled for several years partly because of conservationist protests and be-cause the government won't agree to establishment of a free trade zone there.

Other proposals by both oil and coal men to widen and dredge deep water ports along the U.S. east and Gulf coasts have met with staunch opposition by conservationists. In Delaware, citi-zens groups persuaded the governor to reject an oil company plan, put forward by Shell and 12 others, for an artificial island port off the mouth of the Delaware Bay for unloading oil and transshipment of coal to Japan from Chesapeake Bay barge ter-minals. The Delaware legislature banned both the port and heavy industry along the bay as well. The legislation was passed and signed by the governor over the objections of Maurice Stans, the secretary of Commerce, who was quoted by the *Washington Post* as commenting, "You are interfering with the prosperity and security of America." However, by late 1972 the government had revived plans for an offshore, transshipment port in the Atlantic, off Delaware.

In a study financed by the oil industry, Texas A&M proposed building an immense offshore floating island port off the Texas coast in the Gulf of Mexico. The U.S. Department of Commerce insists deep water ports must be constructed so that the expected increases in foreign oil shipments can be accommodated. The most discussed port projects are Machiasport, Maine; Montauk Point, Long Island; and the mouth of the Delaware Bay. There are also studies of sites south of Delaware along the Atlantic.

6: U.S. ELECTRICITY

There is surprisingly little comprehensive information on either current electricity production or plans for future electrical production within the United States. In 1964, the Federal Power Commission published its first National Power Survey, which by breaking the country down into different regions attempted to assess both the then-current production and demand as well as make some future predictions. At the time, the survey was criticized as another industry-document, and in a way it was. Data and predictions for each region were produced by committees, dominated by private power representatives, but also containing FPC and some public power people. At any rate that survey summarized the industry's assessment of power resources and represented an effort to develop some planning.

Since then, in 1966 the FPC established six regional advisory committees, again mostly made up of private industry representatives, to update the National Power Survey. Supplements appeared in 1968–1970 which provide a wealth of basic information on systems, fuels, and electric transmission lines and also attempt to forecast industry growth to 1990.

The following material is extracted from those reports:

Northeast (Region I): This region comprises the 11 northeastern states of Connecticut, Delaware, Maine, Maryland, Massachusetts, New Hampshire, New Jersey, New York, Pennsylvania, Rhode Island, Vermont, and the District of Columbia.

While the region has only 6 percent of the nation's land, it contains 27 percent of the population, and produces more than one-quarter of its electricity.

Region I consists of several electrical combinations, or pools, whereby companies are intertied with one another so that in case of an emergency or shortage they can tap into one another's sources of supply. The major pools include NEPOOL (New England Power Pool); NYPP (New York Power Pool); and PJM (Pennsylvania-New Jersey-Maryland Interconnection). These pools, in turn, are meant to be interconnected with one another, but in practice this doesn't always work the way it should. In the late 1960s, for instance, there was constant criticism of PJM pool for failure to install large enough switches to accommodate large blocks of electricity that were available to power-hungry New York from the Tennessee Valley Authority or western power systems. Electric industry officials complained that while power lines were big enough in the West and Southeast to handle large blocks of electricity, when the power came to PJM interconnections it was like switching from a four-lane turnpike to a one-way bridle path. Since then, however, there have been efforts to improve the interconnections in Region I.

According to the FPC projections, electricity requirements will increase by as much as 7 percent from 1970 to 1990. The area for the greatest growth will be in New England (6.6 percent); upstate New York (5 percent per annum); New York City (6.6 percent); PJM (5.8–7.7 percent per annum).

Industry uses most of the electricity consumed in the region, about 38 percent of the 204 kilowatts produced in 1965. This is expected to decline to 34 percent in 1990. Residential uses accounted for about one-quarter of all electricity. In metropolitan New York, industrial sales ranked behind commercial, rural, and residential. In Washington they were second to commercial sales.

Fossil fuels, which now create most of the electricity, are expected to decline in importance over the next 20 years. Natural gas will show an increase from 100 billion cubic feet in 1967 to 117 billion cubic feet in 1990. The use of coal in the region is expected to decline from 60 million tons in 1966 to 4 million tons in 1990, or from 67 percent used in generation in 1966 to 11 percent in 1990. The use of fuel oil will decrease from 76 million to 37 million barrels.

The region is expected largely to change over to nuclear fuels. The 1964 power survey indicated that by 1980 nuclear capability would be supplying 10 percent of the nation's generation. The supplementary survey indicated that this 10 percent point was reached in Region I in 1969, and that nuclear power will account for 60 percent of the total generation by 1980, and 82 percent by 1990.

A major problem in the continued use of fossil fuel in the region is the cost of transportation from mine to the utilities, and the stringent air pollution standards. It is not clear how development of synthetic gas or importation of LNG will affect the region except that these gas supplies in all likelihood will be used for peaking or shaving purposes, that is, put into the system when there is an especially acute need for electricity, i.e. in the winter for heating in early evening or in the summer for air conditioning around five in the evening.

All predictions for nuclear energy must be regarded warily. Plans for nuclear development have been forestalled in part because of unforeseen costs by manufacturers, and because of costs due to delays created by environmental opposition. In addition, environmental groups have raised substantial challenges on safety and environmental grounds that could well delay indefinitely introduction of nuclear power plants.

In the interim, the utilities in heavily populated northeastern cities may find themselves increasingly dependent on wholesale purchase of power from other regions, i.e. mine mouth power from TVA and American Electric Power regions, or through widened import of oil, both from the Middle East and Africa, but also perhaps from the eastern arctic islands of Canada.

East Central (Region II): This region extends over an area including all or portions of nine states. It includes all of Ohio and Indiana, Michigan's lower peninsula, all but a small portion of the states of West Virginia and Kentucky, significant parts of Pennsylvania, Maryland, and Virginia, and a small area in and around Kingsport, Tennessee.

More than two-thirds of the 32 million people who live in this region are located in cities. The population accounts for 15 percent of the total in the nation, encompasses about 7 percent of the land area of the United States, and utilizes about 17 percent of the nation's electric energy.

According to the report, "The non-coincident peak load of the East Central Region for 1965 was 31,000 megawatts (Mw) and the electric energy requirements were 180 billion kilowatt-hours. The expected non-coincident peak demand will reach about 44,000 Mw by 1970 with total energy requirements of approximately 252 billion kilowatt-hours. By the year 1990 the projected values of demand and energy requirements are expected to be approximately 146,000 Mw and 857 kilowatt-hours respectively. This represents an average annual compound growth rate of 6.3 percent."

Current breakdown of usage by groups is 26 percent for rural and residential; 16 percent for commercial; 54 percent for industrial; and 4 percent for other usages. The report anticipates no marked change in this usage pattern.

The region encompasses a major portion of the Appalachian coal fields, and historically coal provided most of the fuel for electricity. In 1970 coal supplied 97 percent of all electric energy requirements. Even though nuclear power is expected to grow substantially out to 1990, approximately 50 percent of all electric energy requirements within the region are projected to be supplied by coal-fired plants in 1990.

"Since less than 25 percent of the coal reserves in the East

Central Region are of low sulphur type (one percent or less), since these reserves are relatively concentrated geographically in southeastern Virginia, southern West Virginia, and eastern Kentucky, and since they are and will continue to be in high demand by the metallurgical industry, the bulk of the fuel for future coal-fired plants in the region will be higher sulphur content. With this in mind, the use of tall stacks of 800 to 1,200 feet in height to give better flue gas dispersal has been projected in many instances. Also since there are, at present, no effective methods of sulphur dioxide removal, tall stacks will continued to provide an interim solution to the achievement of low ground-level sulphur dioxide concentrations."

The region is heavily interconnected through a transmission grid and it includes ties to Illinois, Tennessee, North Carolina, and Ontario as well as to other systems in Virginia, Kentucky, Maryland, and Pennsylvania.

The report anticipates utilities will use 24 percent nuclear energy by 1990.

Natural gas used in burning electricity is minor, about 0.1 percent of the total electric generation in 1966. Oil as a fuel for electric generation is insignificant.

Southeast (Region III): This area includes all of North Carolina, South Carolina, Georgia, Florida, Alabama, and Tennessee along with parts of Virginia, Kentucky, Mississippi, and West Virginia. It has a population in excess of 30 million, and covers 355,000 square miles.

While there are over 550 different electric systems, the region is clearly dominated by a handful of giant operations, including TVA; the Southern Company, a holding company which controls utilities in Georgia, Mississippi, and Alabama; the Florida group, comprising Florida Power & Light and Florida Power Co.; Duke and North Carolina Power & Light.

Fossil fuels accounted for about 89 percent of the total electric generation in the region during 1966. Large amounts of coal originating at mines in West Virginia, western Kentucky, and Alabama, and smaller shipments from Illinois and Tennessee, accounted for 74 percent of the generation by fossil fuels. Residual fuel oil was used extensively in Florida and accounted for about 8 percent of the electric generation in 1966. Gas delivered by pipeline from Louisiana and Texas accounted for about 7 percent of the generation in 1966.

In 1966, over 63 million tons of coal were used at generating plants in the region along with 28 million barrels of oil and about 141 billion cubic feet of gas.

Estimates of fossil fuel requirements for 1990 show a need for 121.5 million tons of coal, 18.7 million barrels of oil, and over 422 billion cubic feet of gas.

At the writing of this report, Region III did not have nuclear units on line. However, 23 units were scheduled for service by 1975.

An addendum to the fuels report prepared June 2, 1969, shows that, at least for the short run, fuel oil and natural gas consumption in the Southeast region has taken a decided upward trend from that forecast in the report. This upward trend is due to greater use of electric power, delayed nuclear plants, accelerated air pollution control programs, increased cost of railway freight and coal, decreased cost of fuel oil, and availability of low-sulphur oil.

Total energy requirements in the region in 1965 amounted to 203,145 gigawatt-hours with a coincidental peak load of 33.8 million kilowatts and a load factor of 68.6 percent. For 1990 these are projected at 1,204,580 gigawatt-hours, 210.4 million kilowatts, and 65.4 percent respectively. This represents an energy growth by 1990 of nearly six times over 1965, and an average annual compound rate of growth of 7.6 percent over the period.

In 1965, 29.1 percent of the load was classified as rural and residential. Of that amount 90 percent was nonfarm residential. By 1990 commercial sales are expected to increase to about 20 percent of the total load from about 14 percent in 1965. During this period the industrial load is expected to remain at about 46 percent of the total load.

West Central (Region IV):   This area encompasses the states of Illinois, Iowa, Minnesota, North Dakota, and Wisconsin in their entirety; substantial portions of Missouri, Nebraska, and South Dakota; the upper peninsula of Michigan; and small sections of Montana and Wyoming. In all the area includes one-fifth of the land of the United States, 14 percent of the population, and in 1960 utilized 11 percent of the total electric generation of the United States.

Power requirements for Region IV in 1965 amounted to 126.8 billion kilowatt-hours with an associated peak demand of 24.3 million kilowatts. For 1990 the power requirements are estimated at 698.3 billion kilowatt-hours and 131.7 million kilowatts. Projected annual growth rate is about 7 percent.

The largest share of total regional energy in 1965 was industrial with 38 percent, followed by 23 percent for residential, and 17 percent for commercial. By 1990 it is expected that these three loads as a group will require approximately the same share of the regional energy despite a decline in the industrial share. Residential requirements are expected to increase from 23 percent of the total energy in 1965 to 27 percent in 1990. The commercial share is expected to increase slightly from 17 to 18 percent during the same period. The industrial share is projected to decrease from over 38 percent to less than 36 percent.

The region has substantial fossil fuel resources. Estimates of recoverable coal are placed at 370 billion tons, with another 225 billion more tons recoverable in unmapped and unexplored areas. In fact, this region sits astride the greatest coal beds in the United States, most of the coal recoverable through stripping.

Natural gas reserves of the region comprise less than 1 percent of the total reserves in the United States. Crude oil and natural gas liquids approximate 2 percent of the total liquid hydrocarbon reserves in the United States.

Investor-owned power plants supply most of the electricity.

The five largest of the 85 investor-owned systems supply 60 percent of all the electricity. Commonwealth Edison Co. accounts for about 27 percent of the market itself.

While about 90 percent of the electric energy produced in the region now is supplied by fossil fuel generation, by 1990 nuclear generating capacity is anticipated to comprise 57 percent of the region's capacity. Nuclear generation is expected to supply nearly 70 percent of the region's energy requirements by that time. While the quantity of coal burned annually is expected to increase from 51 million tons in 1966 to 69 million tons in 1975, the regional use of coal apparently will remain relatively constant at about 65 million tons for the remainder of the period.

In 1965 the peak load for the region was 24,290 megawatts and projections are for 35,930 megawatts for 1970, 70,610 megawatts for 1980, and 131,680 megawatts for 1990. According to the advisory report, "Generating capacity of 79,832 megawatts is projected by 1980 to supply a non-coincident summer peak of 69,780 Mw with a reserve of 15.6 percent. By 1990, generating capacity of 151,041 megawatts is projected to cover a non-coincident summer peak of 130,240 megawatts reflecting a reserve of 16.6 percent. An importation of 800 Mw of hydro power from Canada is included in each of these reserve calculations. Additional reserve of an undertermined amount exists because of the diversity of load between utilities within the season. About half of the 1990 capacity is shown to be in units of 800 megawatts or larger. Generator unit size up to 2,000 megawatts and total plant size up to 4,000 megawatts are included."

There are six power pools within the region, and three major regional coordinating groups.

South Central (Region V):   Population of the region was 23.2 million in 1966, and expected to reach 33 million by 1990. The average growth rate between 1965 and 1970 was projected at 10.3 percent, and gradually expected to decline to 6.9 percent between 1985 and 1990. States in this region include Kansas, western Missouri, Arkansas, Oklahoma, westernmost portions of Mississippi, and Louisiana and Texas.

Energy requirements in 1965 and 1966 were 118,641 million kilowatt-hours and 131,565 kilowatt-hours respectively. The projected energy requirements in 1990 are estimated at 900,380 million kilowatt-hours. Nonfarm residential usage per customer for Region V averaged 5,310 kilowatt-hours per customer in 1966 and is predicted to reach 18,510 kilowatt-hours per customer in 1990. Commercial energy usage per customer during the same period is expected to increase from 30,063 kilowatt-hours to 99,630 kilowatt-hours. Industrial energy use is by far the largest category of classified sales and in 1966 represented 51,039 million kilowatt-hours energy requirements and is predicted to reach 418,963 million kilowatt-hours in 1990 or 46.5 percent of the total regional requirements.

Over 90 percent of all known gas reserves in the contiguous United States lie in the region and utilization of relatively short pipelines with low operating costs has always given natural gas a substantial competitive edge over other fuels for thermal generating plants in the area.

According to the advisory committee report, "Only three systems in this region utilized coal in any substantial quantity in 1966, and there are no nuclear fueled plants in operation at this time. While natural gas reserves continue to increase, the present drilling activities and discoveries of new reserves show little promise of increasing at the same rate as the fuel requirements of electric utility companies during the next 25 years. All systems thus indicate plans for increased usage of coal or nuclear fuels in the period to 1990."

In 1966, about 95 percent of electricity came from natural gas, 5 percent from coal. By 1990, fuel forecast is 46 percent from gas, 43 percent from nuclear, and 10 percent from coal. "The ultimate development will depend on the competitive race between suppliers of nuclear fuels and coal. As the prices of gas increase to a point where conversion to coal is considered, oil usage for fuel may show development due to the inexpensive conversion factor from gas to oil."

As more coal is used transportation will become a problem. Plants located nearby big cities probably can use unit trains. Others plan to barge coal from western Kentucky down the Mississippi, and along the Gulf coast. The navigation system on the Arkansas River also will be utilized.

In 1966, the region had estimated coal reserves of 112 billion tons located mainly in Missouri, eastern Kansas, eastern Oklahoma, and western Arkansas. There are extensive lignite deposits in Texas.

The South Central region produced about 14.5 trillion cubic feet of gas in 1966. Of that total, 6.9 trillion cubic feet were consumed in the area. Generation of electricity accounted for 1.2 trillion cubic feet or 17 percent of that. By 1990 requirements for electric generation are expected to represent 26 percent of the total requirements for gas.

West (Region VI): This region encompasses the states of Washington, Montana, Oregon, Idaho, Wyoming, California, Nevada, Utah, Colorado, Arizona, and New Mexico as well as the western portion of Texas. One-third of the United States lies within this section, and the energy requirements in 1965 amounted to about 20 percent of the nation's total. In 1990 the energy requirements are expected to represent 21 percent of the nation's.

About 70 percent of the electricity goes to load centers along the Pacific Coast. Those load centers will take 72 percent by 1990.

Estimated loads for 1970 were 54,035 megawatts and 307,759 gigawatt-hours. By 1990, they will quadruple to 216,420 megawatts and 1,232,800 gigawatt-hours.

Region VI is interconnected through a loop of extra high voltage lines that run along the coast, then back and around the mountain states.

By 1990, industrial use of electricity will be the largest single category, accounting for 34 percent of the total use in the region. Residential and rural will decline from 30.3 percent to 28.2 percent. The commercial class will decline from 20.3 percent to 18.9 percent.

In fuels, major developments will involve nuclear energy. In 1970 nuclear fuel capacity represented less than 2 percent of the region's total capacity. By 1990, it will represent 40 percent of the total capacity.

Oil and gas have been the primary fuels used for electrical thermal production. Coal and nuclear are expected to supply the bulk of the increase in generation after 1970. Most of the nuclear plants are planned for California and in the northwest. Coal-fired plants will be constructed outside California, but half of the increase in use of coal in the Rocky Mountain states will go to serve California.

Supply cannot keep pace with the demand for gas, and its use for electric generation will begin to decline. Requirements for fuel oil for electric generation are expected to double to about 50 million barrels by 1975, and even though gas and oil are scheduled to decline after that, oil should remain pretty constant because of the declining use of gas. Electric utilities, which must burn clean fuels, have backed up their gas supplies with low-sulphur fuel oil. It is not believed likely that western domestic suppliers, including those in Alaska, can supply low-sulphur fuel oil in sufficient quantities, and thus some of it must come from abroad. In addition, it is expected that synthetic fuels, coal gas, etc., will be introduced into the electric generation business.

Overall, coal will greatly improve its position, especially if after 1975 it can be changed into gas. There are, of course, immense untapped reserves of coal that can be strip mined in the mountain states.

7: FUTURE FUELS

POLLUTION-FREE ENERGY SOURCES

In April 1971 a group of faculty and students in the engineering, business, administration, and physics departments at the University of Massachusetts at Amherst submitted a detailed proposal to the National Science Foundation for investigation of a national network of pollution-free energy sources.

Portions of the proposal were published in the *Congressional Record,* December 7, 1971, by Senator Gravel and are set forth below:

Solar Energy: Members of the UMass team are convinced that there is a reasonable probability of satisfying an important fraction of the U.S. demand for electricity and fuel in the year 2,000 without pollution. This technological turnabout could be accomplished by utilizing solar energy stored in the oceans and the winds to generate electricity and direct solar radiation to dissociate water into hydrogen fuel. These new pollution-free sources are located geographically along parts of the East and West Coasts, along the Alabama-Florida Gulf coast, in the Great Plains, and in the Southwest.

The fact that some of these locations are removed from population and industrial centers and from major electrical transmission networks, need not cause concern for two reasons. Available technology with reasonable extensions should permit economical transmission to existing networks or population centers. On the other hand, the availability of ample power and fuel in environmentally attractive open country should encourage the migration of industry and population away from our increasingly polluted metropolitan areas.

But these desirable developments and the general turnabout suggested earlier will occur only as the result of a series of actions and accomplishments. Pollution-free electrical power of the order of 3×10^5 Mw must be generated to satisfy a major part of the demand anticipated in the year 2,000. Pollution-free sources of energy flux of many times this amount must be tapped on the assumption that only a small fraction of the potentially available energy will actually be harnessed. The technology of power generation and transmission based on these sources must be developed. Power plants and distribution systems must be designated and built. Hydrogen fuel must be generated in enormous quantities to replace natural gas as our reserves are depleted and, in addition, substitute for an important fraction of the projected growth in fossil fuels. In general, a gradual transition must be made from our current pollution-rich technology to a new pollution-free technology.

This conversion in technology would bring with it a series of political, economic, and social problems. There would be problems of capitalization, management, and land use, and of ameliorating wide-spread economic hardship caused by the transition. There would be the question of public versus private enterprise. There would be new bookkeeping, recognizing perhaps larger capital and operating costs, but no pollution costs and no fuel costs. This latter feature would have an important bearing on geopolitics. These political, social, and economic problems would have to be analyzed even as the new technology was being developed.

A preliminary exploration has brought to light a great number of pollution-free energy sources. These sources vary greatly as to their nature, their geographical distribution, their potential for making a significant contribution, and the technology needed to harness the energy. In a series of appendices, scientific and technical justification is presented for investigating several of these pollution-free energy sources.

Ocean Thermal Gradients: The concept of an ocean thermal gradient heat engine has been with us for decades, was first demonstrated in 1929, and still has enthusiastic supporters. Thermal gradients in the Gulf Stream offer considerable promise, especially with a Mass concept for capitalizing on the velocity of the Gulf Stream to improve plant design and performance. . . . If it can be extracted economically, this source alone would supply the entire U.S. requirement for electricity in the year 2,000.

Tethered Kinetic Energy, Ocean: The Florida Current and Gulf Stream offer a particularly promising locale for tethered kinetic energy machines, machines which will extract momentum from the current. Within a core of water 10 miles wide by 450 feet deep by several hundred miles long, there appear to be velocities strong enough to turn either rotor type machines or free-stream propeller-type machines. . . . Conceptual designs are worked out for several of these machines and used for detailed calculations. These calculations show that a 240-foot diameter, 4-disc, propeller-type machine operating in a free-stream velocity of 7 feet per second might be expected to generate 24 megawatts of electrical power. Twelve of these machines might be submerged abreast across the core of the stream, and this assembly could be repeated once a mile along the stream for some 350 miles. Tapping this 100,000 megawatts of pollution-free power may not be economically feasible, but it certainly deserves serious investigation.

Tidal River Kinetic Energy: Tidal river kinetic energy machines have been used in the past in Europe and in this country.

Today, France gets 340 megawatts of electrical power from the Rance River using a combination of potential and kinetic energy and requiring the damming of an estuary.

A number of sizable tidal rivers in New Hampshire and Maine could contribute a significant amount of power without damming or embayment, and at no appreciable cost to navigation, marine ecology, or recreation. Detailed calculations . . . show that from two of five promising sites on the Piscataqua River, an annual average of 39 megawatts might be extracted.

Nuclear Fission: As has been pointed out earlier, planned nuclear fission power plants will tax the cooling capacity of our rivers and lakes. In the process, these plants will inflict serious if unknown ecological damage on our fresh water environment. To the extent that these plants could be built into submarine hulls and moored submerged in shallow off-shore waters, especially off New England and the Middle Atlantic coast, thermal pollution problems could be eliminated. . . .

Wind Power: During the latter part of the last century, windmills in northern Europe extracted power from the winds at an average level equivalent to at least 100 megawatts. More recently, in 1945, fatigue failure in the windmill blade shut down a 1.2 megawatt generator that had been feeding into a power system in Vermont. The concept faded with post WWII retrenchment. More recently, the World Meteorological Organization has concluded that wind power available for turbines at favorable sites throughout the world totals 20 million megawatts. Great Britain still hopes to build individual aerogenerators of 6 megawatt capacity.

In the United States, regions of moderately high average wind velocities are found along portions of both coasts but especially over a large area of the Great Plains. . . . The economic and engineering feasibility of a large number of 2 to 6 megawatt aerogenerators is considered for the Great Plains area, and recommendations are made for a detailed investigation of tower and

blade design and a cost comparison with other means of generation.

Transmission Nets: The ocean-based thermal gradient engines
and kinetic energy machines, discussed above, will each require
a combination mooring line and electrical tether. Its design pre-
sents a complex of mechanical, hydrodynamic, and electrical engineering problems. Power from the multiple sources must be
combined in a compatible way and transmitted to shore. An even
more complex (but perhaps not so difficult) network will be
needed to tie together the multiplicity of disparate sources on
land into regional networks. . . . For both underwater and land
use, emphasis will be given to coaxial cable and high voltage direct current for transmission.

Electrostatic Generators: Most of the pollution-free energy
sources discussed above are variable and in some cases, unpredictable in strength. Furthermore, there are a very large number
of relatively small sources. Combining these into a conventional
three-phase A.C. network would pose very serious problems of
controlling frequency, phase, and voltage. These network problems would be largely eliminated if D.C. transmission and current-limited, rather than voltage-limited were generators were
employed.

. . . Belt electrostatic generators have been employed since the
turn of the century, but always for the development of voltage
rather than the generation of power. And belt electrostatic generators are current-limited devices which convert from a mechanical shaft rotation to high voltage D.C. power with a single
moving element, the electrostatically-charged belt. Surprising as
it may seem, these generators have the potential for significant
power generation at reasonable efficiencies. . . . It is of particular
interest that the use of high voltage D.C. in coaxial transmission
lines is especially attractive in terms of low transmission line
losses.

Mooring mammoth generating plants in the world's strongest

ocean current poses a new level of tethering problems. But the availability of new materials technology and submersible work vehicles allows this problem to be tackled with some confidence. The floating or submerged hulls and the deep water conduits for offshore generating plants create problems of the sort commonly encountered in ship and submarine design. . . .

Hydrogen Via Sun Power: Natural gas is the most attractive fuel today from a cost and pollution-free point of view, but U.S. natural reserves will not last into year 2,000 at the predicted expenditure rate. Hydrogen is an excellent substitute for natural gas as a fuel. It can be combined with oxygen to produce electricity in fuel cells or to operate clean internal or external combustion engines. . . . A concept is proposed for generation of molecular hydrogen by dissociation of water using solar energy. A novel concept for a low-cost optical system is proposed for study.

SOLAR ENERGY

Different schemes have been proposed and actual plants built for harnessing solar power. James H. Anderson, a well-known consulting engineer, made a detailed proposal at the May 1971 conference of the International Solar Energy Society. The entire paper, along with other technical papers by Anderson and his son, both of them experts on solar energy, were published in the *Congressional Record,* October 27, 1961, also by Gravel.

Excerpts from the conference paper follow:

The only source of power that can supply all the world's needs for the foreseeable future, and do so without polluting our atmosphere and our waters, is the sun. This has been stated many times, and is so fundamental that few people will argue the point.

Much effort has been spent for many years to convert the sun's energy into useful power. Many applications are in actual service for small-scale power usage in isolated locations. The basic problem is economic, and it stems from the fact that the sun's energy is available to a given location for a part of each day, and the density of radiation is so low that the collection of much energy is costly. A possible future approach has been proposed by Glaser. He proposes putting large collectors into orbit around the earth and beaming the power generated by photo cells back to an earth station. This scheme is theoretically sound, but admittedly requires much development of technology over a period of years.

However, one scheme for developing large amounts of power from the sun's energy that is feasible economically and technically today uses an indirect approach by taking advantage of the sun's energy collected by the ocean. The ocean covers 70 percent of the earth's surface. It stores the sun's energy in the surface waters and creates the vast major ocean currents, such as the Gulf Stream in the Atlantic and the Japan Current in the Pacific. Since these currents flow north from the Equator, the water must be replaced from the Northern Ocean. This causes currents of cold water to flow south toward the Equator deep in the ocean. As a result, we have in many parts of the ocean a layer of warm water directly over a vast reservoir of cold water at temperatures just a few degrees above freezing.

The basic requirements for generating power in any heat engine are a source of heat and a lower-temperature heat sink toward which heat can flow. The warm water at the surface provides the heat source and the cold water at depths of 2,000 feet or more provides the heat sink. Having the heat source so close to the heat sink should make a heat engine possible.

The potential of the heat available can be illustrated by noting that the heat in the Gulf Stream alone is sufficient to supply 200 times the total power requirements of the United States. This energy supply is continually being replaced by the sun, and usage for generating power could never conceivably deplete it.

The idea of using the thermal gradients in the ocean to develop power was proposed as early as 1901 by d'Arsonval. While the theory has been known for many years, no economically practical means for developing power was available. Claude developed a scheme to boil the sea water in a vacuum, expand the vaporized steam through a turbine, and condense the exhaust steam on the cold water pumped from deep in the ocean. He did actually produce power, proving the theory to be sound. However, as pointed out, this scheme was doomed to economic failure and really only served to prove the skeptics right.

A new scheme for producing power on a large scale, practically and economically, was presented by the authors. This scheme utilizes the basic Rankine cycle, similar to that in the simple steam power plant. There are, however, important differences. Instead of steam as a working fluid, this plant uses propane, a cheap petroleum fluid commonly used in portable torches, but also used as a refrigerant.

The power plant is on a floating platform located in the open sea, where warm water is available in ample quantities, and cold water is available at depths of 2,000 feet or more. A cold water pipe is suspended from the floating platform deep enough to reach cold water. The cold water is pumped to the plant from this depth. For a typical plant of 100,000 kilowatt capacity the cold water pipe might be 35 to 40 feet in diameter.

The warm water is taken from the surface through screens around the periphery of the floating plant, and is pumped through boilers, where the propane is boiled at high pressure of approximately 131 lbs. per sq. in. The heat taken from the water drops its temperature from approximately 82°F to 79°F. The heat transferred from the water to the liquid propane evaporates it into high pressure vapor at a temperature of approximately 74°F.

The propane vapor flows from the boiler to the turbine where it expands to a high velocity and lower pressure, giving up expansion energy to drive the turbine, which in turn drives an electrical generator to generate power.

From the turbine exhaust the propane vapor flows to the

condenser where it condenses into liquid at approximately 54°F. The heat of condensation flows into the cold water which is heated from 43°F to 49°F.

The condensed liquid propane is returned to the boiler by a boiler feed pump and the cycle of boiling, expansion, and condensing is repeated, using the same propane continuously circulated through the power cycle. . . .

Warm water from the surface is used to boil propane. The propane vapor expands through a turbine driving a generator. The spent vapor passes from the turbine to a condenser, where it is condensed to a liquid on surfaces cooled by cold water pumped from deep in the ocean. The liquid propane is then pumped to the boiler to repeat the cycle. . . . It is now possible to produce power in any quantities that we need at a lower price than that for any other major source of power.

There are a number of reasons why this new scheme can be practical and economically feasible, whereas Claude's original scheme could never be expected to be successful.

1. The floating plant permits sufficient movement to insure a continual supply of warm water without depletion.

2. The floating plant permits short cold water lines, thereby reducing cost of pipe and pumping losses.

3. The floating plant permits submergence of boilers and condensers, thereby equalizing the pressure of the propane inside to that of the water outside. This makes possible low-cost heat exchange surface.

4. The deeply submerged boilers and condensers, and the suspended cold water pipe make the floating plant very stable and, with proper design, impervious to storms.

5. The propane turbine is simpler, smaller, and much lower in cost than the steam turbine. As an example, a 20,000 Kw steam turbine would need to be approximately 32 feet in diameter with two stages running at 1,000 RPM. The same capacity propane turbine could be 42 inches in diameter and run at 3,600 RPM. This means that the propane turbine cost would be less than 4 percent of the steam turbine cost for the same power output.

The 3,600 RPM generator would also cost much less than the 1,000 RPM generator.

6. Propane is a cheap fluid, readily available, non-corrosive, and almost insoluble in water.

Fresh Water Production: Since power is generated by bringing cold and warm sea water together in one floating plant, it becomes logical to use these same ingredients for the production of cheap fresh water from salt water. Fresh water can be produced very simply. Warm salt water is deaerated and put into a large vacuum chamber of low enough pressure so that it boils. The steam that boils off is conducted to a condenser, cooled by the cold water from the power plant outlet. Here it simply condenses to fresh water. The remaining salt brine drains back to the sea. While this is basically a very simple process, up until recently there were serious problems that appeared to prevent economical development of this process. . . . It takes 1,000 BTUs of heat to evaporate one pound of water through 10°F. Therefore in very rough approximation, you can get only one or two pounds of fresh water from each 100 pounds of warm water furnished to the evaporator. This means that a lot of water must be pumped and deaerated to produce one pound of fresh water. In first analysis and attempts at such a desalting scheme, the amount of power to deaerate and pump the water appeared to be too high to make this scheme feasible. However, means have now been found to reduce the power required for deaeration and pumping to a very small amount. Since the power is cheaply generated in the floating sea thermal power plant, the combination of available water and power can produce fresh water for a cost of approximately three to four cents per thousand gallons of water. This puts a whole new dimension on the possibilities of producing fresh water for both industrial and agricultural purposes. . . .

Chemical Production: A natural by-product of water desalting is cheap oxygen. The gases dissolved in natural sea water are composed of approximately 34 percent oxygen, whereas atmospheric air contains only 23 percent oxygen. Separation of oxygen from air is basically a refrigeration process. This requires heat exchangers, refrigeration compressors, a heat sink and power to run the compressors. With a higher percentage of oxygen in the supply, less refrigeration and equipment is needed. The cold water provides a heat sink at lower than usual ambient temperatures. This reduces required power input as well as cost of compressors and heat exchangers. The condensed propane from the power plant condensers can be used as the refrigerant to cool the air to the oxygen plant. The propane from the boilers can also be used to energize propane turbines to drive the refrigerant compressors. This eliminates the conversion to electric power for refrigeration. These combined factors can reduce the cost of oxygen to less than half of what it costs today.

A typical plant of 100 Mw gross power capacity and 60,000,000 gallons per day fresh water capacity could also produce 115 tons of oxygen daily from the gases that must be removed from the water. This can be an extremely valuable by-product with many uses.

A side benefit of removing oxygen from the water occurs because oxygen is the primary cause of the corrosive action of sea water on metals. Removing the oxygen before passing the water through the boilers should virtually eliminate corrosion. It should also eliminate fouling by marine organisms, because most of them require oxygen to live.

With cheap power, fresh water, cheap oxygen, and location on the ocean, we have the basic ingredients for many kinds of chemical or metallurgical plants. For example, fresh water and oxygen are important ingredients to make low-cost steel manufacturing possible. It is also important to have a steel plant located where cheap transportation for iron ore, coke, and limestone is possible. Many steel plants are already located close to the ocean to reduce transportation costs. It becomes reasonably obvious that the sea thermal plant could be an ideal base for a steel plant.

The steel plant can be located on shore close to the sea thermal plant, which could provide cheap electric power, fresh water, and oxygen. Ocean transport could furnish ore, coke, and limestone.

A little more advanced, but even more logical plan would be to locate the blast furnace on the floating sea plant. The power for the blast furnaces could be provided directly by propane turbines. Fresh water and oxygen would be available on the floating plant. Deep water docking would be available. An extra benefit would be that slag could be dumped directly into the deep water. Waste heat from the blast furnaces could also be used to generate power by boiling propane, expanding it through turbines, and condensing it in condensers cooled by cold water from the depths. It may seem far-fetched to build a floating power plant, yet no more so than present plans to build a floating airport or a floating city.

Another example would be the aluminum reduction plant. The major costs in reduction of bauxite to aluminum are for electric power and transportation costs. Fortunately, much aluminum ore is available in the tropics where sea thermal plants can easily be placed, and the bauxite could be reduced directly to aluminum locally, thereby saving on shipping costs as well as power costs. Jamaica provides vast amounts of bauxite. This must now be mined and much of it shipped to Canada where cheap power is available to convert it to aluminum. Yet Jamaica provides a perfect location for a sea thermal plant. On the northeast tip of Australia are some of the world's largest deposits of bauxite. Conventional power is not easily available there. Yet just off the northeastern coast is plenty of warm water where sea thermal plants could be built for aluminum conversion.

Possibly the most attractive potential use for a sea thermal plant is to convert the chemicals in sea water directly into commercial chemicals and fertilizers. This opens up all kinds of attractive possibilities. Bromine and magnesium are already being produced commercially from sea water. Concentration of the sea water into brine while making fresh water and power should make bromine and magnesium production considerably cheaper than it now is.

Research has already shown that chemical fertilizers can be produced in the form of magnesium ammonium phosphate directly from sea water. If the sea water is concentrated into a brine by the desalting process, then the fertilizer manufacturing process should be lower in cost.

Another process is under development that produces potash using sea water, limestone, and electrical power as raw materials. Sea thermal power and brine concentrated by desalting can furnish the cheap ingredients necessary to make this development economic. Many tropical islands are built from coral, which is practically pure limestone. In these tropical islands all the ingredients would be present for potash fertilizer production. All that is needed is the sea thermal plant to provide the energy.

It should be pointed out that in the case where chemicals from the sea water are the important consideration, then it would probably be preferable to use a freezing process to desalt the water. This process merely uses electric or turbine power, and concentrates the brine by yielding 50 percent or more of fresh water. With 50 percent of the fresh water removed from the sea water the concentration of chemicals in the sea water is doubled. This means that chemicals are more readily available than they would be from the raw sea water. A number of useful products could be commercially obtainable from this brine.

With economic production of common bulk chemicals made possible by sea thermal power, it is also quite conceivable that we can produce more exotic ones such as gold, from sea water. Salutsky has pointed out that there are many needed chemicals in sea water well worth the effort to produce.

Fish Production Possibilities: It has been proposed many times that fish production could be increased by pumping cold nutrient-rich water from the ocean depths up to the upper levels, where sunlight can promote photosynthesis. As Isaacs has pointed out, this involves not only getting the cold water to the surface, but also warming it sufficiently so that it will stay in the 75 meter top layer, where photosynthesis and food production can occur.

Fortunately, the sea thermal plant brings the cold water to a level near the surface as a by-product. When fresh water production is combined with power production, the cold water is also warmed by condensation of the fresh water vapor. The temperature is then high enough so that this rich naturally fertilized water will stay in the intermediate upper layers, where it can serve as food supply for plankton and the entire marine organic life structure. . . .

A careful survey of the ocean temperatures and depths throughout the world shows that sea thermal power can be generated almost anywhere in the tropics or semitropics. There are at least 18,000 miles of tropical coastline in the world that are relatively useless because they are arid. Sea plants could provide the power and water to make them useful to man.

The Gulf Stream could provide power for the entire eastern half of the United States. The development of cryogenic high voltage power transmission is almost certain to come in the near future.

This, in conjunction with high voltage D.C. lines, will make it economically possible to transmit electric power for distances of over 1,000 miles. The Soviet Union is already planning an 1,800-mile line.

Water conditions and depth conditions are suitable for sea thermal plants in the Gulf of Mexico from Tampico south. Transmission lines to Texas would be quite feasible.

Power for California could be furnished by sea plants off the tip of Baja California. These plants could also furnish irrigation water for Baja California and the entire west coast of Mexico.

Conditions for sea plants are good on the entire west coast and east coast of Central America, also on the east coast of South America as far south as Recife, Brazil. The entire Caribbean area is most suitable for sea thermal power.

Both the east and west coasts of tropical Africa are well suited for sea thermal power. Water could be shipped along the entire length of the arid west coast.

The eastern end of the Mediterranean just off Israel has both deep cold water and warm surface water. This could provide power and the vital water to this entire region, where water is already in such short supply.

Almost the entire western and northern shores of the Indian Ocean are suitable for sea thermal power. This could do more than any other one thing to feed these crowded impoverished lands.

Australia could develop all the power it ever needed off the northeast shore, beyond the Great Barrier Reef.

The greatest storehouse of thermal energy in the world is in the tropical western Pacific, covering more than 5 million square miles, extending over most of the Pacific Islands, to the Philippines and north to Taiwan.

It is fortunate that the conditions are good for sea thermal power in many areas of the world where it is most needed. It can provide power, water, food, and industry to the impoverished tropic lands, and at the same time provide air conditioning to make these areas more comfortable and attractive places to live.

When we consider all of the benefits to mankind that can be obtained from sea thermal power and its by-products, it is difficult to find any other technical and economic development that can compare to it in importance. It is truly the key that can unlock the ocean's wealth for the good of man.

GEOTHERMAL POWER

Senator Gravel inserted this statement in the *Congressional Record*, December 11, 1971:

The importance of our geothermal hot water as a source of clean, safe energy could be immense.

The potential electrical power of the steam and hot water under the Imperial Valley alone may be as large as 30 to 90 percent of the entire country's 1970 electrical production, which was 1,540 billion kilowatt-hours.

An additional 1,500 megawatts of geothermal steam are available at the Geysers, 75 miles north of San Francisco. That is three times the power of the Hoover Dam. The potential of geothermal energy in Oregon is estimated by a member of the state geological staff at an additional 20,000 megawatts.

At least 1,000 hot springs have already been located in the western states, including Washington, Oregon, California, Idaho, Montana, Wyoming, Utah, Colorado, Arizona, and New Mexico. Hawaii and possibly Alaska also have promising geothermal areas. Large reservoirs of hot water exist along the Gulf coast, too. Famous hot springs in Arkansas, Virginia, and New York may hint at geothermal hot water resources in the East, also.

With advances in deep-drilling techniques, man might be able to tap geothermal energy anywhere on earth, according to engineering professor Robert L. Whitelaw at the Virginia Polytechnic Institute in Blacksburg.

The production of electricity from geothermal steam and hot water is a proved capability. It is being done today in the United States (California), Russia, Japan, New Zealand, Mexico, Italy, and Iceland.

Good articles on geothermal energy have appeared in *Fortune* magazine, June 1969, and in the *Saturday Review*, December 5, 1970.

To facilitate the leasing of geothermal areas, the Congress passed S.368, a bill introduced by Senator Alan Bible of Nevada, authorizing the Secretary of the Interior to make disposition of geothermal steam and associated geothermal resources. The Senate report on that bill is No. 1160, dated September 4, 1970. In December 1970 the act was signed by the president into law—Public Law 91-581.

Experience to date indicates that far more hot water than steam will be found in geothermal exploration. Perhaps the ratio will be 20 to 1.

A discovery of superheated dry steam is the ideal, thermodynamically and economically. Dry geothermal steam is what the Pacific Gas & Electric Co. has at the geysers.

Last year, that steam made the cheapest electricity in the utility's whole system. According to PG&E's form No. 1, on public file with the Federal Power Commission, the 1970 operating cost for the Geyser geothermal plants was 3.05 mills per kilowatt-hour. Nuclear electricity out of the Humboldt plant cost 5.63 mills and a steam plant at Humboldt cost 8.56 mills.

The likelihood of finding superheated dry steam elsewhere is low. So far, it has been found only at the Geysers and at Larderello, Italy.

Therefore, what is usually meant by geothermal electricity is electricity made by flashing hot water into wet steam, which drives a turbine. This is done successfully. However, it can have certain disadvantages, one of which is corrosion of valves and turbines if there are substantial salt or minerals in the steam. The well itself may become plugged with deposits.

A new geothermal design called Magmamax is likely to eliminate those disadvantages. Instead of flashing the geothermal hot water into steam, the design uses a vapor-turbine driven by isobutane, which is heated by the geothermal hot water via heat exchangers.

If mineral deposits can foul up valves and turbines, why will they not foul up the tubes of the heat exchanger?

The big difference is that the water never flashes to steam in the Magmamax process. Therefore the dissolved gases in the water, which help keep the minerals in solution, do not escape. In the Magmamax process, the geothermal hot water stays water, and is pumped under pressure through the heat exchanger.

Although silica and perhaps some other minerals will tend to solidify out as the temperature of the water goes down in the heat exchanger, there seems to be no insurmountable problem.

A test run on a geothermal well at Brady, Nevada, has been extremely successful. The well was pumped at a pressure in excess of the pressure corresponding to the flash point temperature, and the water circulated through a small heat exchanger. Upon discharge, it was then cooled and circulated back through the tubes of the heat exchanger before discharging at a pressure approximately equal to the inlet pressure. There was virtually no corrosion or other trouble.

James H. Anderson, who is the principal designer, points out that the geothermal water is not the same in Nevada and California. The California water is saltier, more like sea water at 3 percent salt. Mr. Anderson says that additional measures can deal with the difference.

North of the Imperial Valley, in the Salton Sea region, the salinity of the geothermal water is nearer 30 percent. Mr. Anderson said: "We don't pretend to be able to use that water economically. But we don't need to. There is so much good water under the Imperial Valley, that we wouldn't bother with 30 percent salt. Even if the estimates for the Imperial Valley supply were only 10 percent correct, that's a huge amount of power."

One reason for the wide range in those estimates is the uncertainty about the distribution of salinity in the wells.

Another reason is that different power estimates postulate different methods of recovering the energy. For instance, Dr. Robert Rex at the University of California in Riverside bases his estimate of electrical power potential on use of the flashing wet-steam method, which is a less efficient use of the water's heat than the Magmamax method; Dr. Rex also postulates the use of geothermal water, desalted, for agricultural and other uses, whereas the water can be recycled underground in the Magmamax process.

WIND

Senator Gravel, *Congressional Record,* December 7, 1971:

Windpower, which is a variant of solar energy, is a nonpolluting form of energy available in great quantity.

The World Meteorological Organization has estimated that windpower available for turbines at favorable sites throughout the world is approximately 20 million megawatts. In comparison, the entire present installed electrical generating capacity in the United States is 350,000 megawatts.

Alaska, Hawaii, great areas of both continental coasts, and an extensive area stretching from the middle of Texas through Oklahoma, Kansas, Nebraska, South and North Dakota, plus parts of Colorado, Montana, Minnesota, Michigan, New York, and New England, experience winds which average 12 miles per hour or more. That speed may turn out to be sufficient for producing nonpolluting electricity at reasonable cost. Wind-velocity maps of the United States are available from the U.S. Department of Commerce Weather Bureau, and from the Federal Power Commission.

The capability to generate electricity from windpower was demonstrated decades ago, but development was ignored in light of claims that nuclear electricity would be "too cheap to meter."

However, at the time of the report to the Senate Interior Committee by the National Fuels and Energy Study Group in 1962, electric generators run by windmills were operating in Germany, South Africa, Russia, the United States, Britain, and elsewhere. Thousands of small 3- or 4-kilowatt generators were in use throughout the world. A 100-kilowatt wind-driven generator had been operating successfully in Denmark for several years; one that size had been installed also on the Isle of Man; and a 640-kilowatt wind generator had been tested in France.

Another government-sponsored study group, under Ali B. Cambel, concluded in 1964 as follows:

"There is sufficient knowledge for construction of a 5,000- to 10,000-kilowatt prototype installation that would allow a realistic appraisal of the use of wind energy. A design study of the apparatus and a meteorologic survey of possible sites would need to precede construction. Such a program would provide important information about the economic feasibility of aerogenerators, including their integration into electric grids. . . . On a long-term basis, wind-power is a reliable energy source . . . the supply is inexhaustible, and its use has no detrimental effect on the surrounding area since there are no harmful or disagreeable by-products."

New respect was paid to windpower recently in the September 1971 issue of *The Conversion of Energy*. Engineering Professor Claude Summers, of Rensselaer Polytechnic Institute, says:

"What about the wind? . . . A propeller-driven turbine could convert the wind's energy into electricity at an efficiency somewhere between 60 and 80 percent. . . . Wind-power would have the great advantage of not introducing waste heat into the biosphere.

"The difficulty of harnessing the wind's energy comes down to a problem of energy storage. Of all natural energy sources, the wind is the most variable. One must extract the energy from the wind as it becomes available and store it, if one is to have a power plant with a reasonably steady output. . . .

"One scheme that seems to offer promise is to use the variable power output of a wind generator to decompose water into hydrogen and oxygen. These would be stored under pressure, and recombined in a fuel cell to generate electricity on a steady basis. Alternatively, the hydrogen could be burned in a gas turbine which would turn a conventional generator."

A similar solution to the storage question was suggested in a paper entitled, "Outline of Windpower Application Data," October 18, 1963, by engineer Hellmut R. Voigt of Sun Valley, California.

In fact, Mr. Voigt has worked extensively on windpower designs, and has written a book-length manuscript in German which includes extensive figures and drawings for his proposed "Cyclone D-30" windpower plant.

Mr. Voigt and another engineer, Joseph Tompkin of Salem, Oregon, would like to see the construction of a prototype "Cyclone D-30" windpower plant with a 750-kilowatt capacity completed within three years and within a budget of $1 million.

OIL AND GAS FROM ORGANIC MATTER

Senator Gravel, *Congressional Record,* December 11, 1971:

Every year the domestic animals in this country produce enough waste to make about two billion barrels of oil, or nearly 40 percent of our present oil consumption, which is over five billion barrels. In addition, our cities generate 400 million tons of presently troublesome organic waste per year. That amount of garbage could be converted into about 400 million barrels of oil. This source alone could permit nearly an 8 percent reduction in the amount of oil we would otherwise drain out of the earth for domestic consumption.

Organic waste should be returned to the land to replenish the soil from which it all originates. I was pleased to see in the December 6 issue of *Time* magazine that a plant in Brooklyn is producing and selling fertilizer made out of 150 tons of New York garbage per day. Undoubtedly, that is the kind of thing we need to do on a grand scale, if we want healthy soil and food.

Instead, we are spending billions to incinerate and dump our urban waste; and animal waste on feed lots is regarded as "a pollution problem."

Meanwhile, the Bureau of Mines in the Department of the Interior has already succeeded in making low-sulfur oil out of both urban wastes and animal wastes.

One of the ecological advantages of using man-made oil is that it does not add to the worrisome carbon dioxide build-up in the planet's atmosphere. Burning man-made oil, in contrast to fossil fuel, only recirculates carbon dioxide which is already in the biosphere.

The ecological and international implications of clean, man-made oil are enormous.

What are we spending on this extremely promising energy technology? Which industries have expressed support?

In response to my questions, Elburt F. Osborn, Director of the Bureau of Mines, replied as follows:

"We are spending $255,000 this fiscal year on an accelerated program of bench-scale research on converting organic solid wastes that will give us enough information to make a preliminary engineering design and cost estimate of the process. If this appraisal shows the concept and process continues to have promise, we will request funds for a Development Plan that would take several years and cost $15 to $20 million.

"Substantial interest in our proposed process has been expressed by oil companies, the chicken industry, cattle feed lot operators, and public officials. Prompt construction of a full-scale plant has even been suggested. We believe, however, that attempts at commercial application would be premature until the steps optimal to the process have been determined and definitive cost estimates have been prepared."

A report entitled "Conversion of Urban Refuse to Oil," by Drs. Herbert R. Appell, Irving Wender, and Ronald D. Miller, was issued in May 1970 by the Bureau of Mines. The summary states four points, as follows:

"1. Cellulosic wastes, including materials such as urban refuse, wood industry wastes, and sewage sludge, have been converted to a heavy oil by heating in the presence of carbon monoxide and steam under pressure.

2. A high-temperature version, conducted at 380 degree C, and a low-temperature version, conducted at 250 degree C, have been developed on a laboratory scale.

3. The oil from cellulosic wastes, exclusive of sewage sludge, is characterized by a high oxygen content and a low-sulfur content.

4. Additional studies in the laboratory and on a pilot plant scale are underway for cost estimates and a thorough evaluation of the process."

A 1971 report entitled "Converting Organic Wastes to Oil, A Replenishable Energy Source," by Drs. Appell, Fu, Friedman, Yavorsky, and Wender concludes:

"A significant part of the energy demand of the Nation can be obtained on a renewable basis by converting nearly every kind of organic solid waste to a low-sulfur oil by treatment under pressure with carbon monoxide and water.

"Methods for lowering carbon monoxide consumption and for operating at lower pressures have been found; these offer the potential of low processing-costs for converting cellulosic wastes to oil.

"While the effects of temperature, pressure, and water on this process have been explored, more work is required to find optimum conditions for the conversion.

"A continuous unit has operated successfully, and preliminary results have been obtained on the conversion of sucrose to oil."

The work of this research team is being performed in Pennsylvania at the Pittsburgh Energy Research Center, U.S. Bureau of Mines.

At the University of Wyoming College of Engineering in Laramie, Prof. Ed J. Hoffman and his research team have been performing similar feats by making high-B.T.U. gas out of waste paper, polyethylene plastic bottles, shredded tire rubber, manure, and sewer sludge.

Their specialty is the gasification of coal in cooperation with the Office of Coal Research: the conversion of organic waste to gas was performed more or less for the sake of knowing.

Referring to organic waste, Professor Hoffman says:

"Whenever feasible, organic wastes are best returned to the soil. In instances, however, in which this may not be possible, production of a desirable product would be a reasonable alternative."

Pointing out that organic materials are just stored sun power, Professor Hoffman concludes that solar energy is the ultimate source of future fuel:

"All other energy sources can be exhausted, are being exhausted. That leaves only solar energy, which is the source of all our carbonaceous materials."

8: CHINA

In general, coal reserves and hydroelectric potential in China compare favorably with the United States and the Soviet Union. Petroleum reserves appear adequate to support substantial increases in production over the next ten years.

Coal: In 1970 coal accounted for 90 percent of all primary energy available in China. Total reserves are estimated to range from 1 to 1.5 trillion tons. Proved reserves probably run from 70 to 80 billion tons, placing China third in the world after the United States and Soviet Union. Most of the reserves are in Shensi and Szechwan. While there are deposits of lignite and anthracite, bituminous coal predominates. Many of the deposits are poor and must be improved by cleaning and preparation before use. There are ample reserves of good coking coals, but they are located far from coking plants.

Coal production which ranged from 25 to 30 million tons annually during the 1930s increased to 200 to 300 million tons annually in the last decade. Production suffered a bit because of the cultural revolution and economic downturns. Over half of the coal is produced in the north and northeast.

China exports about 1 percent of total production to markets

CHINA FUELS AND POWER

Source: *People's Republic of China Atlas*,
Central Intelligence Agency, November 1971.

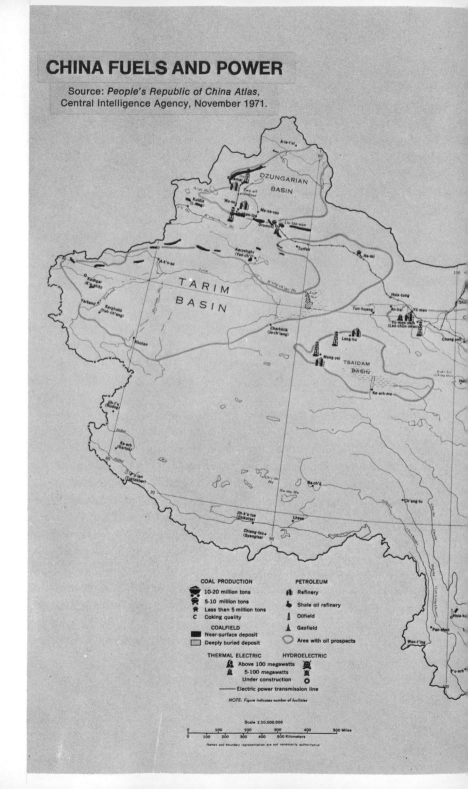

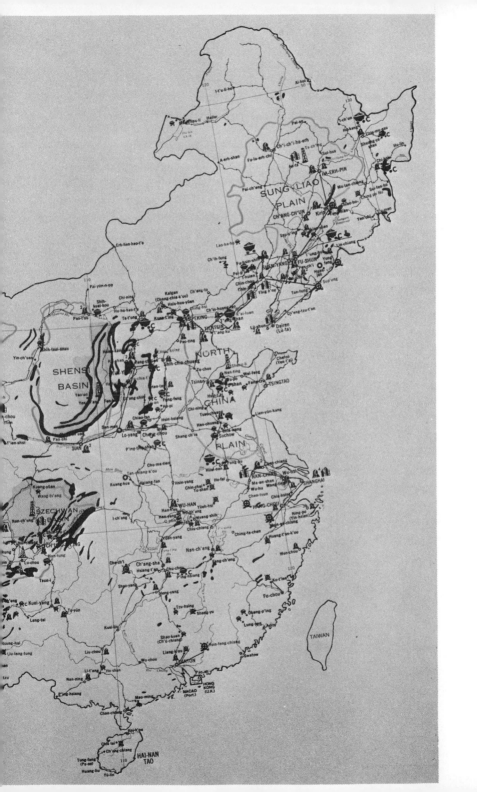

in Japan, Hong Kong, and other Asian countries. It imports a little anthracite from North Vietnam. In early 1972 China made inquiries about buying coking coal from the Appalachian area of the United States.

Oil: By U.S. standards China does not produce or consume much oil. According to the Central Intelligence Agency estimates, China produced 18 million tons of oil in 1970. That's equivalent to 14 days' output in the United States. Recently China reported a 27 percent production increase for 1971, putting the total output at 26 million tons. China achieved self-sufficiency in oil in 1966, but still imports some. Most of the oil-producing regions are far from principal areas of consumption, and considered vulnerable because they are near the Soviet border. Main producing areas are in the Karamai field at Sinkiang and the fields in the western portion of the Tsaidam Basin. These fields along with the older Yümen field in western Kansu provide the bulk of China's crude oil.

This helps to explain why development of oil on the wide continental shelf would be important. If developed it would be far less vulnerable and closer to consuming centers. Also China wants to export oil, probably to Japan.

The China shelf is the center of considerable controversy, with all the major international oil companies, the governments of South Korea, Taiwan, and Japan maneuvering for control.

The U.S. Navy's Oceanographic office believes the continental shelf off China, Korea, and Japan is "potentially one of the most prolific oil reserves in the world." According to Economic Commission for Asia and the Far East (ECAFE), one shallow stretch of sea between Japan and Taiwan "may contain substantial resources of petroleum, perhaps comparable to the Persian Gulf."

So far three sets of conflicting concessions have been made by the governments of South Korea, Taiwan, and Japan without any consultation with China.

In the Yellow Sea, South Korea granted concessions to Shell, Gulf Oil, and a Texaco/Chevron group. Another concession went to Wendell Phillips Oil Co., an independent based in Honolulu.

Six separate groups are exploring for oil on concessions granted by Japan. Of those, four involve foreign oil interests. Mitsui and Continental are exploring off the northern Japanese island of Hokkaido. West Japan Oil Exploration, owned by Shell and Mitsubishi, is exploring in the Sea of Japan and the Korean strait. Nippon Oil and Texaco/Chevron are in the East China Sea. Gulf and Teikoku also are in the East China Sea off the west coast of Kyushu.

The Taiwan government has granted concessions to four U.S. oil companies, all of them jointly held with the government-controlled Chinese Petroleum Corp. One concession off northwest Taiwan went to Indiana Standard; two concessions in the East China Sea were let to small independents, Clinton Oil Co., Wichita, Kansas; and Oceanic Exploration Co., Denver, Colorado. Both these tracts are within 100 miles of mainland China. The largest, most controversial tract is under lease to Gulf in an area between Japan and Taiwan, and it is thought to be the most valuable. In the middle of Gulf's concession is the contested chain of islands, called the Taioyutai, known in Japan as Senkaku Gunto.

China is believed to have made oil finds off the Yellow River and in 1971 had approached U.S. drilling companies in Singapore with a view to buying rigs for drilling in fairly shallow water.

Electric Power: Coal-fired, thermal electric plants account for 70 percent of all electricity. Despite great potential, development of hydroelectric power remains slow. Installed electric generating capacity in China has increased from a low of 1.8 million kilowatts in 1949 to about 18.1 million kilowatts in 1970. Many of China's electric power facilities were developed by Russian, Czechoslovakian, and East German technicians, working on a base left by the Japanese.

Most of China's power stations are concentrated in the industrialized northeast, in the Peking area, and in the Shanghai-Nanching region. Major power plants and transmission systems serve these areas.

9: MAJOR ENERGY CORPORATIONS

This section includes brief profiles of major energy companies. They are drawn largely from public sources, including annual reports, proxy statements, and prospectus filings.

Company profiles include: the seven largest international oil companies; the five leading U.S. coal producers; the five leading U.S. uranium producers; five large U.S. natural gas pipelines; and ten major electric utilities. In addition, there are profiles of several companies prominent in the international energy trade.

Sources of Information:

Basic Company Data

1970 annual reports, proxy statements, prospectus filings, reports to regulatory commissions.

Interlocks

1970 annual reports, cross checked against Standard & Poor's Register of Corporations, Directors & Executives, 1971 ed.

Taxes

Congressional Record reprint from *U.S. Oil Week*, August 17, 1970.

Ownership Information

Banks: All data is from *Commercial Banks and Their Trust Ac-*

tivities: Emerging Influence on the American Economy: Vols. I & II. Staff Report for the Subcommittee on Domestic Finance, Committee on Banking & Currency, House of Representatives, 90th Congress, 2nd Session, July 8, 1968. Referred to as "Patman."

Insurance: Industry-wide common stockholdings are from Best's insurance guide, 1969. Other 1969 common stockholdings are from this volume. The 1970 figures were compiled from 1970 annual statements of the ten largest life insurance companies, on file with the D.C. Department of Insurance.

Mutual Funds: Facts on Funds, first quarter, 1971, Weisenberger Financial Services, Five Hanover Square, New York, N.Y., 10004.

Foundations: Nine of the 12 largest foundations from reports on file at the Foundation Library Center, Washington, D.C. Listed below are the foundations surveyed, date of the report on file, and the assets: Ford Foundation, 1970, $2.9 billion; Rockefeller Foundation, 1970, $890 million; Duke Endowment, 1970, $629 million; Lilly Endowment, no report filed; Pew Memorial Trust, no report filed; Chas. Stewart Mott Foundation, no report filed; W. K. Kellogg Foundation, 1969, $409 million; Kresge Foundation, 1969, $353 million; John A. Hartford Foundation, 1970, $352 million; Carnegie Corp. New York, 1970, $335 million; Alfred P. Sloan Foundation, 1970, $329 million; Andrew W. Mellon Foundation, 1970, $272 million.

Universities: "University and the Corporation" introduced into the *Congressional Record,* December 28, 1970, by Senator Lee Metcalf, Montana. Portfolios of 53 colleges and universities were surveyed in respect to their energy company holdings.

Ten Largest Securities Holders: Natural gas pipelines and electric utilities must furnish the Federal Power Commission with a listing of 10 largest securities holders. Under this heading the significant holders are reported from FPC files.

STANDARD OIL CO. (NEW JERSEY)

30 Rockefeller Plaza, New York, N.Y. 10020.

Basic Company Data

J.K. Jamieson, Chairman; M.M. Brisco, President. Directors: Nicholas J. Campbell, Jr., Emilio G. Collado, Bert S. Cross, William H. Franklin, Clifton C. Garvin, Jr., T. Vincent Learson, Franklin A. Long, Donald S. MacNaughton, Robert H. Milbrath, George T. Piercy, Siro Vazquez, J.R. White.

Total revenues, 1970, $18.6 billion; net income, $1.3 billion; average common stock outstanding, 1970: 221.7 million shares.

Taxes

Jersey Standard paid $265,789,000 in federal income taxes in 1969 or 12.84 percent of net income. (In 1968 the company paid 10.1 percent. In 1970, 10.8 percent.)

Interlocks

1 ea w/ Chase Manhattan Bank; Chemical Bank NY Trust Co.; 2 ea w/ Morgan Guaranty Trust; Intl. Nickel Co. (Canada); 3M Co.; First Natl. Bank (St. Paul); Business Products Sales; Ferrania SPA (Italy); 3M Research Ltd.; St. Paul Companies; Intl. Chamber of Commerce; Northwestern Bell Tel.; Dow Jones; Natl. Industrial Pollution Control Council; IBM; Carborundum Co.; Harvard; Cornell; The Prudential Life Insurance Co.; Caterpillar Tractor; Carson Pirie Scott; Federal Reserve Bank (Chicago); Toledo, Peoria & Western RR; Discount Corp. of NY; Channing Shares Inc.; J.P. Morgan & Co.; Royal Bank of Canada; Manhattan Life Ins. Co.; Natl. Foreign Trade Council, Inc.; Aramco; Trans-Arabian Pipeline Co.; Near East Foundation; Educational Broadcasting Corp.; American Petroleum Institute; Foreign Policy Assn.; Chemical NY Corp.; Council on Foreign Relations Inc.; Amer. Inst. of Chem. Engineers.

Ownership Information

Bank: Patman: 2 interlocks w/ Chase Manhattan; 1 w/ First Natl. City Bank NY. Each of these banks manages one fund with investments in Jersey Standard. Morgan Guaranty manages two funds with investments in Jersey Bankers Trust, First Natl. Bank of Chicago, Old Colony Trust Co., and Continental Illinois Bank each manage one fund with investments in Jersey Standard.

Insurance: Insurance companies owned 6.2 million shares. Major holdings 1969, INA, 803,153; Continental Ins., 393,220; Great American Ins., 142,260; John Hancock, 227,000. 1970, Prudential (one interlock), 410,000, $5.3 m debentures; Metropolitan, 41,-600, $21.2 m notes and debs.

Mutual Funds: Seventy-four funds held 8.3 million shares or 3.7 percent of the outstanding stock. Major holdings: Wellington Fund, 605,800; Oppenheimer Fund, 484,000; Mass Investors Trust, 669,568; Dreyfus Fund, 313,258; Hamilton Funds, 364,000.

Foundations: Rockefeller Foundation, 3 million shares. (Patman's 1966 foundation study showed nine Rockefeller controlled foundations held 5.7 million shares.) Ford Foundation, 400,000; Carnegie Corp., 68,600; Alfred P. Sloan Foundation, 53,967, and $5 million debentures; Kresge Foundation, 7,000, and $2.5 million debentures; Duke Endowment, 4,000 shares.

Universities: Universities owned 1.7 million shares. Major holdings: Rockefeller University (June 30, 1969), 425,000; Harvard (June 30, 1970), 245,914; Yale (November 1, 1969), 148,409; MIT (June 30, 1969), 143,592; Princeton (June 30, 1969), 107,584.

Oil and Gas Reserves: Crude oil reserves gross worldwide in 1970 were 50.5 billion barrels, including US, 6.2 billion; Canada, 1.5 billion; Latin America, 7.4 billion; Europe, 186 million; Middle East and Africa, 34.3 billion; Australia and Far East, 833 million.

Worldwide net oil production in 1970 was 4.6 million b/d, including United States, 946 million b/d (600 million b/d came from Texas); Canada, 170 million b/d; Venezuela, 140 million b/d; Libya, 552 million b/d; Saudi Arabia, 946 million b/d; Iraq, Qatar, Abu Dhabi, 216 million b/d; Iran 214 million b/d; Australia and Far East, 92 million b/d.

Natural gas reserves gross worldwide in 1970 were 126.3 trillion cubic feet, including United States, 39.5 trillion; Canada, 3.3 trillion; Latin America, 15 trillion; Europe, 24.6 trillion; Middle East and Africa, 39.3 trillion; Australia, 4.3 trillion.

Natural gas sales worldwide, 1970, 7.4 trillion cubic feet daily, including United States, 5.4 billon cubic feet; Canada,, 386 million; Latin America, 57 million; Europe, 1.5 billion; other Eastern Hemisphere, 57 million.

The company is the descendant of the Standard Oil Co., organized in Cleveland in 1870 by John D. Rockefeller. Rockefeller built an oil monopoly by obtaining lower freight rates than were available to his competitors. Standard Oil was broken up by the Supreme Court, which held it in violation of the antitrust laws. Standard Oil distributed its holdings to 33 subsidiary companies during 1911–1912, but still controls various corporations which provide it with considerable income. At any rate, the company now is many times greater than the famed trust of the turn of the century.

Jersey Standard's regional and operating organizations include: (United States) Humble Oil & Refining Co. (100 percent); (Canada) Imperial Oil Ltd. (70 percent); (Latin America) Creole Petroleum Corp. (95 percent); Esso-Inter-America, Inc. (100 percent); (Europe and Africa) Esso Europe Inc. (100 percent); (Middle East and Libya) Esso Middle East coordinates Jersey's interests in Arabian American Oil Co. in which it has a 30 percent interest; Esso Standard Libya Inc. (100 percent);

Iranian Oil Participants Ltd. (7 percent); and Iraq Petroleum Co. and associated companies (12 percent) in Iraq, Qatar, Abu Dhabi, Syria, and Lebanon. (Australia and Far East) Esso Eastern, Inc. (100 percent); (Interregional) Esso Exploration Inc. (100 percent); Esso International (100 percent); Esso Research & Engineering Co. (100 percent); Esso Chemical Co. Inc. (100 percent); Jersey Enterprises, Inc. (100 percent).

The company receives about 16 percent of its income from Creole, its Venezuelan subsidiary which accounts for about one-half of all production in that country. In 1971 the stock of the company declined due to reaction to pending legislation in the Venezuelan legislature to impose added controls on oil companies in the 12 years before the oil concessions revert to the state. Creole insisted the laws would not restrict repatriation of profits or make dividends subject to approval by Venezuela's central bank.

In Australia, Jersey Standard is involved in a major undertaking in the Bass Straits, offshore of Australia's southeast tip, between Melbourne and Tasmania. The venture is equally owned by Esso Exploration and Broken Hill Proprietary Co., Inc. (Broken Hill, in turn, is owned in part by American Metal Climax.) Production in several fields rose to 100,000 barrels a day and 30 million cubic feet of gas a day by the end of 1970. Prior to the Bass Straits find, Australia imported nearly all its oil. Elsewhere in the Pacific, Jersey expanded its refinery at Singapore which now produces 81,000 barrels a day. It is constructing another refinery (72,000 barrels a day) in Okinawa. In Indonesia it owns with Mobil PT Stanvac Indonesia. Affiliates are exploring for oil and gas in Indonesia. Wells drilled offshore Malaysia showed some gas. The company is building a special ship to haul liquified petroleum to Japanese markets from Australia.

In Europe Jersey Standard has an important position in controlling the large Groningen gas fields in the Netherlands. Discovery of these fields, controlled by Jersey Standard and Shell, make it possible for the Netherlands to be a central supplier of gas to Europe. Jersey and Shell together with the Dutch government also control the distribution system. In Libya Jersey built an LNG plant and arranged for purchase of LNG tankers to carry gas to Italy and Spain.

Imperial Oil, Jersey's subsidiary and Canada's largest oil company, discovered a significant oil field at Atkinson Point in the arctic Mackenzie River delta area.

While two thirds of Jersey's U.S. production comes from Texas, the company is developing potentially rich oil resources at the Jay oilfield in the Florida panhandle. Together with Columbia Gas Transmission Corp., Jersey in 1972 began exploring for gas in central West Virginia. The company also leads a consortium of oil firms which undertook preliminary investigation of the offshore areas of the East Coast in the Atlantic Ocean, reporting signs were favorable for oil and gas.

In a joint project Jersey and General Electric undertook research aimed at developing hydrogen fusion.

At the end of 1969, Jersey had a financial interest in 70 refineries in 37 countries, with a total refinery run of 4.8 million barrels a day.

At the end of 1969, Jersey owned 184 tankers, with a deadweight tonnage of 7.3 million tons. In addition, it has under longterm charter 142 ocean tankers. Eighteen tankers were on order, including 12 supertankers of 250,000 tons each.

Jersey has a 25 percent interest in the Trans-Alaskan pipeline, and it has a major interest in the main European oil pipelines, as well as in U.S. pipelines.

Foundation of Jersey's future in fuels other than oil and gas are its enormous coal reserves, estimated at more than six million tons. The company says they were purchased with an eye to making synthetic fuels, but now the company is also interested in the primary mining enterprise as well. Jersey operates Monterey Coal Co., as a subsidiary of its wholly owned Carter Oil Co. Monterey produces three million tons a year from the Carlinville, Illinois, mine.

The company owns uranium properties at Live Oak, Texas, which are mined by Susquehanna Corp. In addition, it is building a 2,000-ton-a-day ore processing mill at a new uranium mine

at Converse County, Wyoming. It is scheduled to begin operations in 1972. Jersey Nuclear Co. has two contracts for $70 mil-
lion for fabrication of nuclear fuel, one with General Public Utilities Corp., and the other with Consumers Power Co.

Jersey is involved in a variety of realty projects, some of them
in conjunction with the King Ranch. Friendswood Development
Co., a subsidiary, is developing Rollingbrook at Baytown, Texas,
and Woodlake, in Houston. It also is developing a "total" community at Kingwood development, north of Houston. Friendswood also bought a residential development called Cypresswood,
north of Houston, and in all has 80,000 acres under development.

The company has a chain of 37 hotels, Esso Motor Hotels, in
Europe.

ROYAL DUTCH/SHELL GROUP
ROYAL DUTCH PETROLEUM COMPANY

30 Carel van Bylandtlaan, The Hague, the Netherlands.

Basic Company Data

Jonkheer J.H. Loudon, Chairman; L.E.J. Brouwer, President. Directors: P.M. van Doormaal, A. Hofland, M.W. Holtrop, R.E.
Marjolin, Wm. McC. Martin, Jr.; L. Schepers, M.E. Spaght,
W.F.G.L. Starrenburg, C.R.C. Wijckerheld Bisdom, G.A. Wagner, E.G.G.G. Werner, K. Swart.

THE "SHELL" TRANSPORT AND TRADING COMPANY, LTD.

Shell Center, London, SE 1, England.

Basic Company Data

Sir David Barran, Chairman; Managing Directors: Sir David
Barran, Sir Harold Wilkinson, F.S. McFadzean. Directors: J.P.
Berkin, Sir Archibald F. Forbes, Sir Reay Geddes, Rt. Hon. Lord

Inchyra, C.C.P. Pocock, Hon. Peter Samuel, Rt. Hon. Lord Shaw-cross.

In 1970 the Royal Dutch/Shell Group had total sales of $10.5 billion; net income, $882 million. Royal Dutch Petroleum Company, with a 60 percent equity in the group's income, showed a net income of $528 million. Royal Dutch had 134 million ordinary shares outstanding. Shell Transport and Trading, with a 40 percent interest in the group's income, had a net income of $378 million, with 552 million ordinary shares outstanding.

Interlocks

Royal Dutch Petroleum Company (Netherlands): 1 ea w/ Chase Manhattan Bank; Ford Foundation; Univ. Paris, US Steel; Caterpillar Tractor; Yale; Johns Hopkins, Amer. Pet Inst.; Stanford; Iranian oil consortium.

"Shell" Transport and Trading Company, Ltd. (U.K.): 2 w/ Midland Bank Ltd.; 1 ea w/ Midland & Intl. Banks Ltd.; National & Grindlays Bank; Spillers Ltd.; Dunlop Co. Ltd.; Gen. Accident Fire & Life Assurance Corp.; Stockholders Investment Trust; Grampion Holdings Ltd.; Rootes Motors; British Linen Managers Ltd.; EMI Ltd.; Rank-Hovis-McDougall & Caffyns Motors Ltd.; London University; Rainier Foundation; Morgan & CIE Intl.; Upjohn & Co. Ltd.; Times Newspapers Ltd.; Morgan Guaranty Trust Company; Dominion-Lincoln Assurance Co.

Ownership Information

Insurance: Insurance companies owned 691,137 shares. Major holdings: Prudential, 245,850.

Mutual Funds: Thirty-two funds held 5.6 million shares or 4.2 percent of the outstanding stock. Major holdings: Wellington Fund, 1,077,099; Investors Group, 1,022,744 (Investors Mutual, 627,400; Investors Stock Fund, 395,344).

Foundations: Alfred P. Sloan Foundation, 102,300 shares (one director interlock).

Universities: Universities held 297,827 shares. Major holdings: Harvard (June 30, 1970), 113,217.

The Royal Dutch/Shell Group of companies resulted from a merger in 1907 of the interests of Henri Dterding, a Dutch financier, and Marcus Samuel, an English trader, who began by importing sea shells from the Far East. The annual report explains the current organization, "The Royal Dutch/Shell Group of companies grew out of an alliance made in 1907 between two companies, Royal Dutch Petroleum Company, and the 'Shell' Transport and Trading Company, Ltd; by which they agreed to merge their interests on a 60–40 basis respectively while keeping their separate identities. The parent companies are public companies, one domiciled in the Netherlands, the other in Great Britain. They do not themselves directly engage in operational activities, and are mainly vehicles for investment. Their merging of interests is expressed in joint ownership of two holding companies, Shell Petroleum NV, a Netherlands company, and the Shell Petroleum Company, Ltd, a United Kingdom company. These two companies directly or indirectly hold the shares for the entire group. The holding companies own or control various operating companies in different countries. They also own four service companies, two for oil and two for chemicals (one of each in The Hague and London). The service companies coordinate the activities of the group operations, keeping the budgets straight, arranging for capital, and handling shipping of products and crude."

The table on pp. 284–288 shows the group's interests in various operating companies.

While the British have but a 40 percent interest, the group's financial headquarters are in London. British investors own 39 percent of the stock; Americans hold 21 percent and the Dutch 19 percent.

Shell is second only to Jersey Standard among oil companies. Over the years the giants have warred around the world. Shell provides 14 percent of the world's oil, has the largest fleet of ships in the world, and invests more abroad than the entire United Kingdom.

In 1938 the Mexican government expropriated oil wells of the Shell subsidiary, El Aquila, thereby forcing the company to face up to the problems of racism and nationalism much earlier than other international companies. Shell deliberately downgraded its Oxbridge managers, and actively recruited and promoted Asians, Africans, and South Americans up through the ranks. Key political figures in certain countries were employed. The company pointedly plays down the Royal Dutch/Shell Group, and instead promotes the image of the local Shell company, in which the parent company holds a percentage of the stock, but which is managed by local people. In this way Shell has met with some success in promoting at the least the appearance of local control.

The Royal Dutch/Shell Group does not publish reserves. 1970 gross crude production totaled 4.1 million barrels a day, including, U.S. 678,000 b/d; Canada, 78,000 b/d; Venezuela, 1 million b/d; Trinidad, 30,000 b/d; Colombia, 20,000 b/d; Argentina, 2,000 b/d; Europe: West Germany, 21,000 b/d, Netherlands, 18,000 b/d; Austria, 4,000 b/d; Africa: Nigeria, 396,000 b/d; Libya, 141,000 b/d; Algeria, 44,000 b/d; Gabon, 25,000 b/d; Middle East: Iran, 492,000 b/d; Iraq, 349,000 b/d; Oman, 332,-000 b/d; Qatar, 217,000 b/d; Abu Dhabi, 101,000 b/d; Turkey, 39,000 b/d; Far East and Australasia: Brunei, 139,000 b/d; Australia, 13,000 b/d; Malaysia, 18,000 b/d.

Shell and Jersey Standard together control between 35 and 50 percent interests in the major European pipeline systems carrying crude oil from Mediterranean ports to inland refineries. Major holdings are Southern European, 23.2 percent; Trans-Alpine, 15 percent; Central European owned by ENI has a 20-year throughput agreement with Shell, BP, and Jersey. Jersey Standard and Shell control production of natural gas in the Netherlands Groningen field, and participate in distribution with the Dutch government.

Shell owns or manages 415 tankers, totaling 23.6 million tons.

Shell is the largest owner of LNG tankers with seven on order. The company, has 35,000 miles of crude and product pipelines and 11,650 miles of natural gas pipelines.

Shell refineries process 252 million metric tons of crude a year as follows: U.S., 44 million tons; Canada, 11; Latin America, 44; Europe, 112; Africa, 4; Middle East, 4; Far East and Australasia, 33.

THE WORLD OF SHELL

The main operations of the following companies are indicated by the letters against their names, the key to these letters appearing below.

Subsidiaries of these companies are, in general, not shown and some small operating companies have been omitted. The ownership percentages shown below include both direct and indirect holdings of ordinary shares in the companies named, in some cases rounded off to the nearest whole figure.

C	Chemicals	M	Manufacturing
E	Exploration	Mk	Marketing
Es	Engineering services for off-shore operations	MM	Mining and Metals
		N	Natural gas
G	Geological studies	O	All main oil functions
I	Industrial gas manufacturing and marketing	P	Production
		R	Research
L	Liquified petroleum gas marketing	T	Transportation

	%			%	
USA			*(Bahamas)*	40	N
Shell Oil Company	69	O, N, C	Shell Bahamas	100	Mk
Asiatic Petroleum	100	Mk	Shell Bermuda	100	Mk
			Shell Antilles and Guianas	100	Mk
CANADA			Refinería Dominicana	50	M
Shell Canada	87	O, N, C	Shell (W.I.)		
Canadian Fuel Marketers	100	Mk	*(Dominican Republic, Haiti, Jamaica, and Panama)*	100	Mk
REST OF WESTERN HEMISPHERE			Shell des Antilles et de la Guyane Françaises	100	Mk
Caribbean			Antillaise d'Enteposage		
Conch International Methane					

	%	
(Martinique)	25	Mk
Raffinerie des Antilles		
(Martinique)	24	M
Shell Curaçao	100	M
Shell Nederlandse Antillen	100	Mk
Pipelines of Puerto Rico	40	T
Shell (Puerto Rico)	100	Mk
Shell and Commonwealth		
Chemicals (Puerto Rico)	50	C
Shell Trinidad	100	P, M, Mk, N

Central America

	%	
Shell British Honduras	100	Mk
Shell Costa Rica	100	Mk
Refinería Acajutla		
(El Salvador)	35	M
Shell El Salvador	100	Mk
Refinería Petrolera de		
Guatemala-California	40	M
Guatemalteca Shell	100	Mk
Shell de Exploración		
Honduras	100	E
Shell Honduras	100	Mk
Distribuidora Shell de		
México	100	C
Shell de Exploración		
Nicaragua	100	E
Shell Nicaragua	100	Mk

South America

	%	
Shell Argentina de Petróleo	100	P, M, Mk
"Estrella Marítima"		
(Argentina)	100	T
Shell Brasil	100	Mk
Shell Chile	100	Mk
Shell Cóndor (Colombia)	100	P
Shell Colombia	100	Mk
Ecuatoriana de Lubricantes	70	Mk
Shellgas (Ecuador)	50	L
Shell de Recherches et		
d'Exploitation de Guyane		
(Fr. Guiana)	100	E
Guyana Shell	100	E
Shell Paraguay	100	Mk
Shell del Perú	100	Mk
Shell Suriname N.V.	100	E
Shell Suriname Verkoop	100	Mk
Shell Uruguay	100	Mk
Shell Sur del Lago		
(Venezuela)	100	E
Shell de Venezuela	100	O, N
Shell Química de Venezuela	100	C

EUROPE

Austria

	%	
Rohoel-Gewinnungs	50	P
Adria-Wien Pipeline	14½	T
Transalpine Oelleitung in		
Oesterreich	15	T
Shell Austria	100	M, Mk

Belgium

	%	
Belgian Shell	100	M, Mk
Distrigaz	16⅔	N
Bayer-Shell Isocyanates	50	C

Denmark

	%	
Shell Denmark	100	E
Dansk Shell	100	M, Mk

Finland

	%	
oy Shell ab	100	Mk

France

	%	
Shell Française:	82	
Maritime Shell	82	T
Raffinage Shell Berre	49¼	M
Pétroles Shell Berre	57	Mk
Française de Stockage		
12		G, RGéologique
Shell-Gascogne	94	E
Pétroles de Sud-Est Parisien	91	P
Pipe-Line du Jura	96	T
Pipe-Line Sud-Européen	15	T
Rhénane de Raffinage	66	M
Produits de l'Air	50	I
Utilisation Rationnelle		
des Gaz	100	L
Shell Chimie	100	C
Chimique de la Méditerranée	50	C

Gibraltar

	%	
Shell Gibraltar	100	Mk

Greece

	%	
Shell (Hellas)	100	Mk

Irish Republic

	%	
Irish Refining	24	M
Irish Shell and BP	60	Mk

Italy

	%	
Italiana per l'Oleodotto		
Transalpino	15	T
Shell Italiana	100	E, M, Mk
Sub-Sea Oil Services	60	Es

	%	
Luxembourg		
Shell Luxembourgeoise	100	Mk
Malta		
Shell (Malta)	100	Mk
Netherlands		
Shell Delfstoffen	100	E
Nederlandse Aardolie	50	P, N
Internationale		
Riviertankscheepvaart	50	T
Rotterdam-Rijn Pijpleiding	40	T
Shell Tankers N.V.	100	T
Shell Nederland Raffinaderij	100	M
Shell Nederland Verkoop	100	Mk
Nederlandse Gasunie	25	N
Internationale Gas Transport	50	N
Rotterdamse Polyolefinen	60	C
Shell Nederland Chemie	100	C
Verenigde		
Kunstmestfabrieken	40	C
Wavin	50	C
Shell Research N.V.	100	R
Billiton	99	MM
Norway		
Norske Shell	100	E, M, Mk
Portugal		
Shell Portuguesa	100	Mk
Spain		
Shell Spanje	100	E
Española Shell	100	Mk
Industrias Químicas Asociadas	25	C
Sweden		
Koppartrans	100	M, Mk
Svenska Shell	100	Mk
Switzerland		
Oléoduc du Jura		
Neuchâtelois	49	T
Raffinerie de Cressier	75	M
Shell (Switzerland)	100	Mk
United Kingdom		
Shell U.K. Exploration		
and Production	100	P
Shell International Marine	100	T
Shell Tankers (U.K.)	100	T
United Kingdom Oil Pipelines	36	T
Shell U.K.	100	M, N
I.B.E. Ltd.	100	M, Mk
Shell Composites	100	M, Mk
Shell-Mex and B.P.	60	Mk

	%	
Lubricants Producers	80	Mk
Shell Chemicals U.K.	100	C
Shellstar	100	C
Associated Octel	36⅔	M, Mk
Shell Research Ltd.	100	R
West Germany		
Gewerkschaft Brigitta	50	P, N
Gewerkschaft Elwerath	50	P, M, N
Deutsche Shell Tanker	100	T
Deutsche Transalpine		
Oelleitung	15	T
Rhein-Donau Oelleitung	15	T
Rhein-Main		
Rohrleitungstransport	41	T
Deutsche Shell	100	M, Mk
Gewerkschaft Deurag-Nerag	50	M
Ruhrgas	15	N
Thyssengas	25	N
Deutsche Shell Chemie	100	C
Rheinische Olefinwerke	50	C
AFRICA		
North Africa		
Algérienne du		
Méthane Liquide	16	N
Sirtica Shell *(Libya)*	100	E
Shell Exploratie en		
Productie (Libya)	100	P
Shell du Maroc	100	Mk
Shell de Tunisie	100	Mk
West and Equatorial Africa		
Shell West Africa		
(Angola and Gambia)	100	Mk
Shell Camerounaise	100	E
Shell du Cameroun	100	Mk
Shell de l'Afrique Équatoriale	100	Mk
Shell Congo Kinshasa	100	E
Congolaise des		
Pétroles Shell *(Kinshasa)*	100	Mk
Shell Gabon	100	P
Equatoriale de Raffinage		
(Gabon)	11	M
Shell Ghana	100	Mk
Shell Guinée	100	Mk
Shell Ivoirienne	100	E
Ivoirienne de Raffinage	15	M
Shell de l'Afrique		
Occidentale	100	Mk
Shell-BP Nigeria	50	P, N
Nigerian Petroleum Refining	25	M
Shell Nigeria	100	Mk
Africaine de Raffinage		
(Senegal)	12	M
Shell Sénégal	100	Mk

	%	
Sierra Leone Petroleum Refining	18	M
Shell Sierra Leone	100	Mk

East Africa

Pétroles des Djibouti	50	Mk
Shell Ethiopia	50	Mk
BP-Shell Kenya	50	E
East African Oil Refineries	25½	M
Kenya Shell	50	Mk
Shell Chemical Eastern Africa	100	C
Maritime de Madagascar	30	T
Malgache de Raffinage (Malagasy Republic)	6½	M
Shell de Madagascar et des Comores	50	Mk
Shell Co. of the Islands (Mauritius and Seychelles)	50	Mk
Shell Moçambique	50	Mk
Shell Red Sea (Hedjaz)	50	Mk
Shell de la Réunion	50	Mk
Shell and BP (Sudan)	50	M
Shell Sudan	50	Mk
Shell and BP Tanzania	25	Mk
Shell and BP Uganda	25	Mk
Shell and BP Zambia	25	Mk

Central and Southern Africa

Shell Botswana	50	Mk
Shell Lesotho	50	Mk
Shell (Malawi)	50	Mk
Shell Chemical Central Africa	100	C
Central African Refineries (Rhodesia)	20¾	M
Shell Rhodesia	50	Mk
Shell Eksplorasie Suid-Afrika	100	E
Shell and BP South African Refineries	50	M
Shell South Africa	50	Mk
Shell Chemical South Africa	100	C
Shell Eksplorasie Suidwes-Afrika	100	E
Shell South West Africa	50	Mk
Shell Swaziland	50	Mk

MIDDLE EAST

Abu Dhabi

Abu Dhabi Petroleum	23¾	P

Cyprus

Cyprus Petroleum Refinery	25½	M
Shell Cyprus	50	Mk

Iran

	%	
Iranian Oil Exploration and Producing	14	P
Iranian Oil Refining	14	M
Naft Pars	33⅓	M, Mk
Shell Chemical Iran	42½	C

Iraq

Basrah Petroleum	23¾	P
Iraq Petroleum	23¾	P, T, M
Mosul Petroleum	23¾	P

Kuwait

Kuwait Shell Petroleum Development	100	E

Lebanon

Shell Lebanon	50	Mk

Oman

Oman Shell	100	E
Petroleum Development (Oman)	85	P

Qatar

Qatar Petroleum	23¾	P
Shell Qatar	100	P
Shell Markets (Middle East)	100	Mk

Trucial States

Shell Hydrocarbons	100	E
Shell Minerals	100	E

Turkey

Turkse Shell	100	P
Anadolu Tasfiyehanesi	27	M
Shell Turkey	100	Mk

FAR EAST AND AUSTRALASIA

Brunei

Brunei Shell	100	P, N
Brunei LNG	45	N

Cambodia

Shell du Cambodge	100	Mk

Ceylon

Shell Ceylon	50	Mk

Hong Kong

Shell Hong Kong	100	Mk

India

Burmah-Shell Refineries	50	M

	%	
Burmah-Shell India	50	Mk
National Organic Chemical		
Industries	33⅓	C

Indonesia

Djawa Shell	100	E
Shell Indonesia	100	E

Japan

Nishi Nihon	50	E
Shell Sempaku	100	T
Seibu Sekiyu	20	M
Showa Sekiyu	50	M, Mk
Showa Yokkaichi	50	M
Shell Sekiyu	100	Mk
Mitsubishi Yuka	27½	C
Shell Kagaku	100	C

Korea

Korea Shell	100	E
Kukdong Shell Oil	50	M, Mk
Kukdong Shell Petroleum	50	M, Mk

Laos

Shell du Laos	100	Mk

Malaysia

Sabah Shell	100	E
Sarawak Shell	100	P, M
Shell Refining (F.O.M.)	75	M
Shell Malaysia	100	Mk
Shell Malaysia Trading	100	Mk
Shell Marketing Borneo	100	Mk

Pakistan

Pakistan Shell Oil	75	E, N
Pakistan Refinery	15	M
Pakistan Burmah Shell	24½	Mk
Titas Gas (	10	N
Burshane (Pakistan)	41	L

Philippines

	%	
Shell Philippines	75	M, Mk
Shell Chemical (Philippines)	40	C

Singapore

Shell Eastern Petroleum	100	M
Shell Singapore	100	Mk

Thailand

Shell Thailand	100	Mk

Vietnam

Shell Viet-Nam	100	Mk

Australia

Shell Development		
(Australia)	100	P
W.A.G. Pipeline	33⅓	T
Shell Refining (Australia)	100	M
Shell Australia	100	T, Mk
Shell Chemical (Australia)	100	C

New Zealand

BP Shell Aquitaine and Todd	25	E
BP Shell Todd (Canterbury)		
Services	25	E
Shell BP and Todd	37½	E, N
Shell and BP Pipeline		
Services	50	T
New Zealand Refining	17	M
Shell Oil New Zealand	100	Mk

Pacific Islands

Shell (Pacific Islands)	100	Mk
Shell des Iles Françaises		
du Pacifique	100	Mk

Tonga

Tonga Shell N.V.	100	E

Source: Annual Report, Shell Transport & Trading Co., 1970.

MOBIL OIL CORP.

150 East 42 Street, New York, N.Y. 10017.

Basic Company Data

Rawleigh Warner, Jr., Chairman; William P. Tavoulareas, President. Directors: Grayson L. Kirk, Lewis A. Lapham, George C. McGhee, Theodore W. Nelson, Albert L. Nickerson, James Q.

Riordan, Herman J. Schmidt, Charles E. Solomon, Richard F. Tucker, Albert L. Williams.

Total revenues, 1970, $8.3 billion; net income, $482.7 million; stock outstanding, 1970: 101,313,000 shares.

Taxes

In 1969 Mobil paid $41.8 million in federal income taxes or 5.73 percent of the net income. In 1968, the company paid 3.3 percent in taxes; in 1970, 10.9 percent.

Interlocks

2 ea w/ IBM; 1 ea w/ Amer. Pet Inst.; Council for Latin America; Industrial Relations Counselors; Time, Inc.; Princeton; Center for Inter-American Relations; Caterpillar Tractor; Bankers Trust; H.J. Heinz Co.; North Amer. Phillips Corp.; Federal Insurance; Tri-Continental Corp.; Bankers Trust NY Corp.; ET Barwick Industries; Intermodal Transportation Systems; Consolidated Edison; Dividend Shares; Nationwide Securities Co.; Greenwich Savings Bank; Asia Foundation; Inst. Intl. Education; Japan Society; First National City Bank; General Foods; Eli Lilly & Co., Alfred P. Sloan Foundation; Metropolitan Life Ins.; Federal Reserve Bank, N.Y.; State Street Investment Co.; Brooklyn Savings Bank; Dow Jones & Co.; Chemical Bank N.Y. Trust Co.; Aramco.

Ownership Information

Banks: Patman: 2 director interlocks w/ Citibank; 1 ea w/ First Natl. Bank of Boston; Cleveland Trust Co.; Bankers Trust Co. Bankers Trust manages two funds with investments in Mobil. Chase Manhattan and Morgan Guaranty each manage one fund with investments in Mobil.

Insurance: Insurance companies owned a total of 4,268,236 shares. Major holdings, 1969: INA, 280,500; John Hancock, 270,-000; Metropolitan Life, 60,000 (one interlock); Federal Insurance, 31,026 (one interlock); 1970, Prudential, 350,000; NY Life, 201,850.

Mutual Funds: Forty-five funds held 4.5 million shares or 4.4 percent of the outstanding stock. Major holdings: Investors Group, 1,153,500 (Inv. Mutual, 553,500; Inv. Stock Fund, 400,-000; Inv. Variable Payment, 200,000); Investment Co. of America, 374,00; Fundamental Investors, 310,000.

Foundations: Rockefeller Foundation, 600,000 shares. (The Patman foundation study of 1966 showed seven Rockefeller controlled foundations held a total of 1,202,523 shares; Alfred P. Sloan Foundation, 74,000 shares; Carnegie Corp., 68,000 shares; Ford Foundation, 139,000 shares.

Universities: Universities owned 773,060 shares worth $44.5 million. Major holdings: Harvard (June 30, 1970), 242,010; Columbia (March 31, 1970), 83,633.

Mobil does not publish either petroleum or natural gas reserves.

In 1970 net worldwide crude oil production was 1.5 million barrels a day as follows: U.S. 385,000 b/d; Canada, 96,000 b/d; Latin America, 104,000 b/d; Middle East, 747,000 b/d; other Eastern Hemisphere, 241,000 b/d.

Natural gas production in the United States and Canada in 1970 averaged three billion cubic feet daily, and accounted for 89 percent of the company's natural gas production during the year. In Germany the company has a natural gas production of 302 million cubic feet per day. Mobil participates in North Sea gas production.

In the United States, crude oil production is obtained principally from Texas, California, Louisiana, and Oklahoma and from western Canada, and amounts to 27 percent of the company's worldwide gross production. Holdings in Latin America are principally in Venezuela. The company has interests in Saudi Arabia, Iran, Iraq, Abu Dhabi, and Qatar. These include a 10 percent holding in Arabian American Oil Co. (Aramco); an 11.875 percent interest in Iraq Petroleum Co., Ltd., and its associated companies held through Near East Development Corp., which produce oil in Iraq, Abu Dhabi, and Qatar; a 7 percent interest in the Iranian oil consortium. There are long-term contracts for purchases of other Iranian and Kuwait crudes. All told, Mobil's share in these production facilities averaged 54 percent of the corporation's worldwide gross production.

In February 1970 Mobil began full-scale production from its acreage offshore Nigeria, and production was 91,000 b/d. In Libya, where the company has a 65 percent interest in producing properties, its share in production averaged 180,000 b/d. Other interests include a 50 percent holding in PT Stanvac Indonesia, various interests in Germany and Turkey, and a 50 percent interest in an Austrian producing company.

Mobil is exploring for oil onshore and offshore Indonesia, in the Straits of Malacca offshore Malaysia, in the North Sea off the Bahamas, in the arctic islands of Canada, offshore Canada in the Atlantic, in the Northwest-Mackenzie delta, in various offshore Caribbean areas—Honduras, Nicaragua, Guatemala, and Panama. There are explorations offshore Africa—Cameroons, Ghana, South Africa, and the Congo. The company has onshore interests in Australia and offshore rights in New Zealand. In 1971 Mobil and Texas Eastern discovered significant amounts of oil and gas off Nova Scotia in the Atlantic.

Mobil owns or has interests in 40 refineries in 22 countries; 40 percent of capacity is in the United States (829,000 b/d). The company owns 31 domestic chemical facilities, and owns or has interests in 13 foreign facilities. Mobil is in the midst of a program to expand refining capacity in Asia. A refinery at Singapore is being expanded to 100,000 b/d in order to supply Japan and other parts of Southeast Asia. A new refinery at Altona, Australia, in which Mobil has a 65 percent interest, was expanded to handle 93,000 barrels a day.

In 1970 the company owned 34 tankers, of which eight were registered in the United States and the remainder with foreign countries. An additional 74 tankers are under charter. In 1970 the company had under construction or on order ten ocean-going tankers, two of them supertankers in the 200,000-ton range.

The company's U.S. pipeline system includes 13,400 miles of crude and natural gas trunk lines, and 8,500 miles of product lines. Mobil has an 8.68 percent interest in the proposed 800-mile Trans-Alaskan pipeline system, 11 percent interest in the Trans-Alpine pipeline in Europe, and pipeline interests in Japan and Australia.

Mobil's oil and gas properties in the United States total 7.5 million net acres; in Canada, 51.5 million acres. The company has a Canadian-based real estate subsidiary.

TEXACO, INC.

135 East 42 Street, New York, N.Y. 10017.

Basic Company Data

Augustus C. Long, Chairman executive committee, chief executive officer; Marion J. Epley, Jr., Chairman; Maurice F. Granville, President. Directors: Arleigh Burke, Laurie W. Folmar, Donald M. Graham, Henry U. Harris, Gilbert W. Humphrey, Lester J. Norris, George Parker, Jr., Ogden Phipps, Dwight P. Robinson, Jr., Robert V. Roosa, Langbourne M. Williams.

Total revenues, 1970: $6.7 billion; net income, $822 million; average shares outstanding, 1970: 272,344,000.

Taxes

In 1969 Texaco paid $7.2 million in taxes or .76 percent of net income. That was the second lowest amount paid by oil companies. Texaco paid $23 million in federal income taxes in 1968, or 2.36 percent of net; in 1970, 6.4 percent.

Interlocks

2 ea w/ Freeport Sulphur Co.; Marineland of Pacific. 1 ea
w/ Amer. Pet Instit; Jefferson Chemical Corp.; Harris, Upham &
Co.; Chemical Bank NY Trust Co.; Chemical NY Corp.; Stone &
Webster, Inc.; Southern Pacific Co.; State Bank, St. Charles, Ill.;
Key Island, Inc.; Norbak Corp.; Moose Mountain Ltd.; Brown
Brothers Harriman Co.; American Express Co.; American Ex-
press Intl. Banking Corp.; Anaconda Co.; Rockefeller Foundation;
Council on Foreign Relations; Natl. Bureau of Econ. Research;
Fleming, Suez, Brown Brothers (London); Owens-Corning Fi-
berglass Corp.; Central & Southwest Corp.; Exchange Fund of
Boston; Depositors Fund; Fiduciary Exchange Fund; Second
Fiduciary Exchange Fund; Leverage Fund, Inc.; Northeastern
University; Diversification Fund Inc.; Boston 5¢ Savings Bank;
Suffolk Franklin Savings Bank; Amer. R&D Corp.; Capital Ex-
change Fund; Massachusetts Financial Services; Nat. Bank of
Detroit; Hanna Mining Co.; General Electric; Natl. City Bank
of Cleveland; St. John d'el Rey Mining Co.; Natl. Steel Corp.;
Massey Ferguson Ltd.; Algoma Steel Corp.; Sun Life Assurance
Co., Canada; Southwire Co.; General Reinsurance Corp.; Center
for Strategic & Intl. Studies; Thiokol Chemical Corp.; First Natl.
Bank of Washington D.C.; Dukane Corp.; Foster Wheeler Corp.;
Financial General Bank Shares Inc.; NUS Corp.; Bessemer Se-
curities Corp.; Continental Illinois Bank & Trust; Illinois Power
Co.; Clow Corp.; Abbott Laboratories; American Airlines; Mar-
cor Inc.; U.S. Gypsum; Chicago Clearing House; Conill Corp.;
Notre Dame University.

Ownership Information

Banks: Patman: Manufacturers Hanover and Chemical Bank
NY Trust each manage two trust funds with investments in
Texaco. Continental Illinois Bank manages one fund. At the
time of the Patman study, the company had two director inter-
locks with Chemical Bank, and one each with Natl. City Bank,
Cleveland, and Union Natl. Bank, Pittsburgh.

Insurance: Insurance companies owned 7.1 million shares. Major holdings: Prudential, 480,000; John Hancock, 300,000; NY Life, 247,978; Travelers, $28.3 m notes.

Mutual Funds: Fifty-one funds held 9.7 million shares or 3.6 percent of the outstanding stock. Major holdings: Affiliated Fund, 1,000,420; Investors Group, 1,915,900 (Inv. Stock Fund, one million shares; Inv. Mutual, 915,900); Mass Investors Fund, 755,000; Wellington Fund, 589,600.

Foundations: Ford Foundation, 252,000 shares; Alfred P. Sloan Foundation, 118,652; Andrew W. Mellon Foundation, $1 million notes and bonds; Kellogg Foundation, 14,182 shares and $500,000 in notes; Duke Endowment, 20,000 shares; Kresge Foundation, 6,500 shares.

Universities: Universities owned two million shares. Major holdings: Harvard (June 30, 1970), 770,259; Princeton (June 30, 1969), 170,910; Northwestern (May 31, 1970), 126,754; Univ. Texas (August 31, 1969), 120,572; Univ. California (June 30, 1969), 92,303; Columbia (March 31, 1970), 88,846; California Institute of Technology, 71,322.

At the end of 1969 Texaco's crude oil reserves amounted to 35.3 billion barrels. Of that total 26 billion were in the Middle East, with only 3.3 billion in the United States. Net crude oil production in 1969 was a little more than one billion barrels. Major production in millions of barrels: U.S. 269.4; Venezuela, 56.2; Libya, 59.1; Iran, 56.3; Canada, 28; Trinidad, 26.4; Colombia, 17.4; West Germany, 12.2; Australia, 3.5. Affiliated companies: Saudi Arabia, 346.4; Indonesia, 109.7; Bahrain, 13.8; Colombia, 3.4; United States, 2.1; Venezuela, 551,000.

Total U.S. natural gas production in 1969 was 1.43 trillion cubic feet. Total domestic gas reserves were then estimated at 23.9 trillion cubic feet. The company also had gas reserves of 2 trillion cubic feet in Canada. In Latin America, gas reserves were 1.7 trillion cubic feet.

Texaco's interests in oil abroad include a 30 percent holding in Arabian American Oil Co. (Aramco) in Saudi Arabia; a 7 percent interest in the Iranian consortium; a 50 percent interest in producing properties in Libya; a 50 percent interest in the Caltex group which produces in Indonesia and Bahrain; a two-sevenths interest in production of the West Australian Petroleum Pty. Ltd.; and a 96.8 percent interest in Deutsche Erdol A. G. (DEA). In addition, there is a 25 percent interest in producing properties in Spain. Production of DEA is located mainly in Germany, with exploration conducted jointly in West Germany, Italy, Libya, Somalia, and Dubai.

In addition, Texaco is exploring wholly-owned or jointly-owned holdings in Spain, Libya, Australia, Papua, Philippines, Norway, United Kingdom, Denmark, Netherlands, Nigeria, Indonesia, South Africa, Angola, Greece, Gabon, Ghana, South Korea, Southwest Africa, and Indonesia.

In the United States Texaco owns 12 refineries with a total rated crude daily capacity of 960,000 barrels. They include refineries at Port Arthur, Texas; Westville, N.J.; Lockport and Lawrenceville, Ill.; Los Angeles; Anacortes, Washington; Tulsa and Convent, La. Texaco owns four refineries in Canada, owns or has interests in nine refineries in Latin America, the largest of which is at Pointe-a-Pierre, Trinidad. In West Africa, Texaco has interests in refineries in Ivory Coast, Senegal, and Gabon. Texaco has interests in 15 European refineries with a total capacity of 577,000 barrels a day, including a wholly-owned 115,000 barrel a day refinery at Ghent, Belgium; and a 120,000 barrel a day refinery at Pembroke, Wales. Elsewhere in the Eastern Hemisphere Texaco has interests in 21 refineries including three Persian Gulf refineries with a capacity for Texaco of 240,000 barrels a day.

The company owns or operates 146 ocean-going tankers, aggregating 7.2 million tons, and including four supertankers of over 200,000 tons each. By the end of 1973, Texaco plans to have in service 22 vessels in the 200,000–250,000-ton range.

Texaco owns nearly 33,000 miles of pipelines in various parts of the world, including 6,062 miles of crude lines and 1,033 miles of product lines. In the United States and Canada, the company has a 16 percent interest in the Colonial product pipeline system. It also owns 18 percent of Capline, the largest diameter crude line in the United States. The company owns or has an interest in seven crude lines and eight product lines in the United Kingdom and in western Europe. Crude lines serve refineries owned by Texaco in Belgium, Italy, France, Netherlands, and West Germany. It also owns a 9 percent interest in Trans-Alpine, a major crude pipeline in western Europe. Together with Gulf, Texaco has holdings in the Amazon Basin of Ecuador.

GULF OIL CORPORATION

Gulf Building, Pittsburgh, Pa. 15230.

Basic Company Data

E. D. Brockett, Chairman; B. R. Dorsey, President; Directors: Charles M. Beeghly, I. G. Davis, R. Hal Dean, F. R. Denton, James H. Higgins, E. D. Loughney, Beverley Matthews, Nathan W. Pearson, Edwin Singer, James M. Walton.

Total revenues, 1970, $6.7 billion; net income, $550 million; common stock outstanding, 1970: 207,596,392 shares.

Taxes

Gulf paid $4,264,000 in federal income taxes in 1969, which was .43 percent of net income. This was the least amount paid by any oil company that year. In 1968 Gulf paid $8,005,000 or 0.81 percent of net income; in 1970, 1.2 percent.

Interlocks

4 w/ Mellon Natl. Bank & Trust Co. 2 w/ PPG Industries. 1

ea w/ Carnegie-Mellon Univ.; ALCOA; Univ. Pittsburgh; Mellon Bank Intl.; Westinghouse, McCarthy & McCarthy (Toronto); Bank of Nova Scotia; Amer. Pet Inst.; Federal Reserve, Cleveland; General Foods; Southwest Research Institute; Joy Mfg.; White Cons. Industries; Jay F. Look, Inc.; Pullman, Inc.; Pittsburgh Athletic Co.; Trailmobile Fin. Co.; British Canadian Lithium Mines, Ltd.; St. Lawrence Diversified Lands, Ltd.; Intl. Bronze Powders, Ltd.; Jones & Laughlin Steel; Brascan Ltd.; Toronto Dominion Bank; Trans-Canada Pipelines; Canadian Gypsum; Canadian Niagara Power Co.; Canadian Westinghouse; Rheem Canada; Minnesota Mining & Mfg.; Transamerica Coml Corp.; W. H. Smith & Son (Can.); Canada Life Assurance Co.; Univ. Toronto; Mr. Wiggs Dept. Stores Inc.; Sandusky Properties.

Ownership Information

Banks: Patman: 4 interlocks w/ Mellon Bank & Trust. Ten trust funds managed by this bank had investments in Gulf. Mellon Bank holds 17.1 percent of the outstanding common stock of Gulf, which gives the bank a 1.9 percent sole voting right and a 10.8 percent partial voting right. One trust fund managed by First Natl. Bank of Chicago had investments in Gulf.

Insurance: Insurance companies owned 9.8 million shares. Major holdings: 1969, INA, 868,304; Continental Ins., 717,927; Gen. Reins. Corp., 365,587; Aetna Cas. & Surety, 265,626; Canada Life Assurance, 35,082 (one director interlock); 1970, Prudential, 560,000, $21 m notes; NY Life, 370,796; Equitable, 230,000, $22 m notes; Metropolitan, 50,000, $176.9 m notes.

Mutual Funds: Thirty-nine funds held 6,578,562 shares or 3.2 percent of outstanding stock. Major holdings: Investors Group, 1,685,900 (Inv. Mutual, 766,600; Inv. Stock Fund, 578,300; Inv. Variable Payment, 341,000); United Group, 743,900 (United Science, 189,000; United Income, 300,000; United Accumulative, 254,900); Mass Investors Trust, 765,848; Fidelity Group, 623,200

(Fidelity Fund, 271,000; Fidelity Trend Fund, 352,000); Dreyfus Fund, 360,574.

Foundations: Andrew W. Mellon Foundation, 10,213,709 shares; Ford Foundation, 250,000; Alfred P. Sloan Foundation, 56,768; Kresge Foundation, 5,000 shares and $1 million debentures; Kellogg Foundation, 19,934 shares.

Universities: Universities owned 2.3 million shares. Major holdings: Harvard (June 30, 1970), 671,187; Univ. Pittsburgh (June 30, 1970), 279,116; Princeton (June 30, 1969), 271,856; Univ. Texas (August 31, 1969); 118,436; Northwestern (May 31, 1970), 107,567.

Gulf's total crude reserves (1969) were 26.3 billion barrels and included, U.S., 1.6 billion barrels; Canada, 481 million; Latin America, 680 million; Kuwait, 20.7 billion; other Eastern Hemisphere, 2.7 billion.

Total net crude oil production, 1969, was 2.6 million b/d. Production included, U.S., 523,670 b/d; Canada, 74,919 b/d; Latin America, 205,535 b/d; Kuwait, 1.4 million b/d; other Eastern Hemisphere, 384,833 b/d.

Gulf's total natural gas reserves in 1969 consisted of 23.8 trillion cubic feet, and included, U.S., 12.4 trillion cubic feet; Canada, 3.5 trillion cubic feet; Latin America, 2.9 trillion cubic feet; other Eastern Hemisphere, 5 trillion cubic feet. Natural gas production, 1969, amounted to 3.1 billion cubic feet per day, including, U.S. 2.5 billion cubic feet; Canada, 354.9 million; Latin America, 78.5 million. In addition, there is 245 million cubic feet a day in Kuwait for which there is no market.

Gulf holds and operates oil- and gas-producing properties in 19 states and in federally-owned areas of the Gulf of Mexico and offshore California. Louisiana accounts for about 43 percent and Texas 41 percent of production. In 1969 and 1970 Gulf acquired interests in the North Slope of Alaska.

Gulf Oil Canada, Ltd., a wholly-owned subsidiary, has oil-

and gas-producing properties in Manitoba, Saskatchewan, Alberta, and British Columbia. It explores in these provinces as well as in the Northwest Territories, Quebec and offshore areas of the Atlantic, Pacific and Arctic oceans. In Venezuela, Mene Grande Oil Co., a subsidiary, holds and operates various oil properties. The corporation completed and tested wells in Colombia and Ecuador. In September 1966 Gulf commenced production of crude oil from concessions in Bolivia, but in October 1969 the Bolivian government seized the business. In Kuwait a wholly-owned subsidiary, Gulf Kuwait Co., owns a 50 percent interest in a concession which contains one of the largest oil fields in the world. (Gulf Kuwait sells substantial amounts of oil to the local Shell subsidiary.)

In Nigeria a subsidiary is exploring for oil. Gulf has a 7 percent interest in the Iranian oil consortium. Cabinda Gulf Oil, a wholly-owned subsidiary, is producing in Angola. In 1970 Gulf discovered oil offshore the Congo on concessions it has there. In Europe, Gulf's major exploration efforts are in the North Sea, where it has licenses from the United Kingdom to explore in joint ventures. It has exploring permits in the Irish Sea. The company also is exploring in Italy and Turkey.

Gulf has an ambitious program in Asia. According to the 1970 annual report, "Drilling began in a 67,000 square mile contract area in the South China Sea late in 1970. During the year Gulf acquired two additional production-sharing contract areas in and around the Island of Sulawesi. Gulf now has exploration agreements covering 117,000 square miles of Indonesia territory. In Thailand, Gulf has exploration rights to one onshore and three offshore blocks. . . . Investigations began in Tonga on a 6,000 square mile block in which Gulf holds a minority interest.

"Gulf Oil Co. of China began oil exploration in December over the continental shelf near the city of Keelung in the Republic of China. In Japan, Teikoku Oil Co., Ltd. and Gulf agreed to a joint offshore oil exploration venture in an area extending southwest from Kyushu Island and in August geophysical work began. In Korea, surveys were completed on two offshore blocks covered by an agreement made with the Korean government in 1969. Drilling in this area, which totals 31,800 square miles, is expected to begin late in 1971 or early in 1972. In partnership with an Australian firm, Gulf also applied for exploration areas in the New Guinea Territory of Papua. At year end, Gulf held license or agreement interests in more than 100 million acres of Asian waters, constituting a total area roughly the size of California."

Gulf owns and operates seven refineries in the United States. The largest are at Port Arthur, Texas (329,300 b/d); Philadelphia (158,300 b/d); and Alliance, Louisiana (155,000 b/d). The company also owns outright or has substantial interests in refineries in Kuwait, Denmark, Holland, South Korea, Spain, United Kingdom, Switzerland, Ecuador, Venezuela, Italy, Taiwan, and Okinawa.

The company has an extensive spread of crude and product pipelines in the United States. There are 8,900 miles of pipeline owned outright, and 11,000 miles in which a percentage is held. Gulf has a 16.78 percent holding in the Colonial pipeline, which runs from Houston to New York, and a 20 percent interest in Four Corners Pipeline Co., which deliveres crude from the Four Corners area of the mountain states to Los Angeles.

In 1969 the company had 77 vessels. Forty-eight were owned outright; the rest were under charter. Total tonnage was 4,933,-000. Gulf built major deep water terminals to accommodate supertankers at Bantry Bay, Ireland; Okinawa and in Kuwait.

Gulf became increasingly involved in all sectors of the nuclear industry. The company has large-scale uranium deposits under lease along with plans to mine and mill the ore by mid-1970s when the current uranium glut is expected to disappear. In addition, the company will fabricate fuel, make nuclear reactors for electric power production, and reprocess fuel. It recently formed a joint corporation with United Nuclear to make fuel assemblies.

Gulf has uranium deposits at Mariano, New Mexico, and in

1970 found more uranium in the Ambrosia Lake district of New Mexico. In Canada Gulf holds two million acres of mining claims and exploration permits, and made a major uranium find at Rabbit Lake, Saskatchewan. A joint venture of Gulf Minerals Co., Gulf Oil Canada Ltd., and a West German firm, Uranerzbergbau GmbH&co. KG (Uranerz-Bonn), was formed to develop a Rabbit Lake property. The companies are making engineering studies, leading up to construction of mine and mill. Production should begin by 1974. In the United States two Gulf subsidiaries combined to supply nuclear fuels, power reactors, research reactors, and electronic systems for reactors. They are Gulf Mineral Resources Co., and Gulf Energy & Environmental Systems Co. In 1970 Gulf entered into a partnership with Allied Chemical Corporation to build a nuclear fuel reprocessing plant near Barnwell, South Carolina.

Gulf owns Pittsburgh & Midway Coal Mining Co., which in 1970 embarked on an active program of exploration in the western states. The company mines 21,500 tons of coal a day.

The company also is developing real estate properties, and owns controlling interests in Reston, Virginia, a new town outside Washington.

BRITISH PETROLEUM COMPANY, LTD.

Britannic House, Moor Lane, London, EC2, England.

Basic Company Data

Sir Eric Drake, Chairman; R. B. Dummett, Deputy Chairman.

Gross income, 1970, $6.3 billion; net income, $218 million. Ordinary shares outstanding, 358.9 million shares.

Interlocks

2 ea w/ Guardian Royal Exchange Assurance; Hudson's Bay Co.; Burmah Oil Co.; Matheson & Co., Ltd.; Bank of England;

British Bank of the Middle East. 1 ea w/ Chamber of Shipping; Lloyds Register of Shipping; Britannic Estates, Ltd.; Gordon Woodroffe & Co.; Ionian Bank; Leda Inv. Trust Ltd.; Hellenic & General Trust, Ltd.; Dimplex, Ltd.; P&O Steam Navigation Co.; The Chartered Bank; Commonweath Development Finance Co.; Kuwait Oil Co.; Suez Finance Co.; Investment Trust Corp.; Metropolitan Trust Co.; Merchants Trust Ltd.; GE Ltd.; English Electric Co., Ltd.

Ownership Information

Insurance: U.S. insurance companies owned 45,000 shares of BP. Leading investor was Manufacturers Life, Toronto, 25,000 shares.

Mutual Funds: Five funds held 0.2 percent of the outstanding ordinary stock or 775,000 shares. Leading investors were Intl. Holdings Corp., 270,000 shares; United Income Fund, 200,000 shares.

BP owes $286.2 million to Atlantic Richfield in respect to marketing and refining assets purchased initially for $400 million.

Of the 358.9 million ordinary stock units issued as of December 31, 1970, the British government owned 174.5 million (48.62 percent). The Burmah Oil Co. owned 82.9 million (23.09 percent). The remaining 101.5 million shares (28.29 percent) were held by approximately 102,000 stockholders; 11.4 million of these units were held by approximately 35,000 American depository receipt holders. As of December 31, 1970, Rio Tinto Zinc owned 3,876,923 shares of BP worth $17.8 million.

The British Petroleum Company, Ltd., the parent company of the group, was incorporated as Anglo-Persian Oil Company in 1909 following the discovery of oil in commercial quantities in Iran. One of the original stockholders was the Burmah Oil Co., which owns about 23 percent of the ordinary capital. In 1914 the British government acquired a controlling interest in the company but now holds only 48.6 percent of the ordinary stock. The company's articles of association were amended to give the government the right to nominate two members of the board with power to veto any resolution. The government, however, pledged itself not to interfere in the company's commercial affairs, and undertook not to exercise the right of veto except in regard to certain specific matters of general policy. The right of veto has in fact never been exercised.

Most of the BP group's oil comes from Iran, Iraq and Kuwait. The company has a 40 percent interest in the Iranian consortium and it maintains a 50 percent interest in Kuwait Oil Co. through BP (Kuwait), Ltd. It has a 25.75 percent interest in Iraq Petroleum Co., Ltd., and a similar interest in other companies of that group, including Basrah Petroleum Co., Ltd., Qatar Petroleum Co., Ltd., Mosul Petroleum Co., Ltd., Abu Dhabi Petroleum Co., Ltd., and a two-thirds interest in Abu Dhabi Marine Areas Ltd.

The group's major U.S. subsidiary, BP Oil Corporation, discovered oil at Prudhoe Bay on its holdings of 96,000 acres. It is a partner with Standard Oil Co. of New Jersey and Atlantic Richfield in the Alaskan pipeline. In 1969 the BP group purchased the old Sinclair division from Atlantic Richfield. The assets included 9,700 retail units in the eastern United States, and two refineries, etc. In June 1969 the company announced there was agreement on a merger in principle with Standard Oil Co. of Ohio (SOHIO). BP acquired a 25 percent holding, with the understanding that it gradually become a majority holding.

Production: In 1970, the BP group took 3.7 million b/d from all oil resources, of which 3.1 million b/d came from Middle Eastern holdings. Production in Iran was 3.2 million b/d; from Kuwait (including sales to the Kuwait National Petroleum Co.), 2.7 million b/d; from Iraq 1.4 million b/d; from Qatar, 180,000 b/d; from Abu Dhabi, 400,000 b/d on shore and 252,000 b/d offshore; from Libya, before expropriation, 394,000 b/d; from Nigeria, 808,000 b/d; from Colombia, 6,000 b/d; from Canada, 18,000 b/d. Major gas production: 42,200 million cubic feet of gas was delivered to Britain from the North Sea; about 4,336 million cubic feet of gas was produced in Saxony in Germany. There were limited sales of gas in New Zealand.

Exploration: BP was in the midst of exploration or development in the following countries: Abu Dhabi, Australia, and Papua, Canada, Colombia, Germany, Indonesia, Iran, Italy, Kenya, Kuwait, Libya, New Zealand, Nigeria, Qatar, South Africa, Thailand, United Kingdom, United States, South West Africa, Gambia, France, Holland, Turkey, Tonga.

Transportation: At the end of 1970, BP's fleet and those of its subsidiary and associated companies totaled 127 ships of 4.4 million tons. In addition, 11.8 million tons of shipping were under long-term contract. The company expects to have 50 supertankers in service by 1974.

STANDARD OIL CO. OF CALIFORNIA

225 Bush Street, San Francisco, Calif., 94120.

Basic Company Data

O. N. Miller, Chairman; H. J. Haynes, President. Directors: J. E. Gosline, William M. Allen, D. L. Bower, J. R. Grey, J. T. Higgins, G. M. Keller, John A. McCone, James E. O'Brien, G. L. Parkhurst, Rudolph A. Peterson, E. Hornsby Wasson.

Total revenues, 1970, $5 billion; net income, $454.8 million; common stock outstanding, 1970: 84,837,251.

Taxes

In 1969 Socal paid $10.9 million in federal income taxes or 1.84 percent of net income. In 1968 the company paid 2.9 percent of net income; in 1970, 5 percent.

Interlocks

2 ea w/ Bank of America; Bancamerica Corp. 1 ea w/ Amer.

Pet Inst.; Business Council; Natl. Pet Council; Boeing Co.; Weyerhauser Co.; Pacific Natl. Bank (Seattle); Boeing of Canada; Fireman's Fund; Calif. State Chamber of Commerce; Calif. Inst. Technology; Intl. Chamber Commerce; Intl. Executives Services Corp.; Kaiser Industries; Time, Inc.; DiGiorgio Corp.; Alza Corp.; American Potato Co.; Pacific Tel. & Tel.; Prudential Insurance Co.; Bekins Co.; Stanford Research Inst.; Allied Equities Corp.; Basic Vegetable Products Inc.; Physics International Co.; Arabian American Oil Co.; Trans-Arabian Pipeline Co.; Iran California Oil; Atlas Supply Co.

Ownership Information

Insurance: Insurance companies owned 2.2 million shares. Major holdings: Continental Insurance, 250,999; Prudential, 191,464 (one director interlock); INA, 165,375; Home Ins., 107,210; Aetna Casualty & Surety, 102,893; Fireman's Fund, 57,594 (one director interlock).

Mutual Funds: Thirty funds held 2.5 million shares or 3 percent of outstanding stock. Major holdings: Investors Group, 416,-600 (Inv. Mutual, 340,900; Inv. Variable Payment, 75,700); Hamilton Funds, 315,000; Fidelity Trend Fund, 259,200.

Foundations: Andrew W. Mellon Foundation, $2 million, bonds and notes; Ford Foundation, 15,000 shares.

Universities: Universities held 705,244 shares. Major holdings: Harvard (June 30, 1970), 190,380; Rockefeller Univ. (June 30, 1969); 140,001; Univ. California (June 30, 1969), 75,918; Princeton (June 30, 1969), 66,369.

Total petroleum reserves in 1970 were 33 billion barrels, including, U.S., 2.2 billion barrels; Iran, 1.9 billion barrels; Libya, 477 million. Reserves through affiliates: Saudi Arabia, 26.4 billion barrels; Sumatra, 1 billion barrels; Bahrain, 169 million.

Total gross oil production 1970 was 2/5 million barrels a day, including, U.S., 546,825 b/d; Canada, 73,647 b/d; South America, 86,148 b/d, Iran, 218,889 b/d; Libya, 161,612 b/d; Nigeria, Spain, and western Australia, 15,054 b/d. Production through interest in affiliates: Saudi Arabia, one million b/d; Sumatra, 353,257 b/d; Bahrain, 38,319 b/d.

The company does not publish its total natural gas reserves. Gross natural gas production in 1970 was 1.9 billion cubic feet a day: United States, 1.7 billion cubic feet; Canada, 209,814 million; South America, 10 million.

In 1970, 75 percent of the company's crude oil production came from the Eastern Hemisphere and 25 percent from the Western Hemisphere. Forty-five percent of its net income came from activities in the Eastern Hemisphere and 43 percent from the United States. Over 90 percent of the company's 1970 production in the Eastern Hemisphere was from two affiliated companies, Arabian American Oil (Aramco) and Caltex. Some production also comes from the Iranian consortium. Socal owns 30 percent of Aramco (other owners Texaco, 30 percent; Jersey Standard, 30 percent; Mobil, 10 percent); Caltex is owned equally by Texaco and Socal. Socal has a 7 percent interest in the Iranian consortium.

Socal also owns Irving Oil Co., Ltd., which markets petroleum products in Canada. It has a 45 percent interest in Nippon Petroleum Detergent Co., Ltd. and Karonite Chemical Co., Japan; a 35 percent interest in Petrosynthese SA (France); a 50 percent interest in Société-Californie-Atlantique (France); and 50 percent in BP-California Ltd. (U.K.).

Socal owns outright or controls through affiliates 20 refineries in the United States. Refineries in the Western Hemisphere processed 848,926 barrels a day in 1969. Major refineries were at Richmond (190,000 b/d) and El Segundo (220,000 b/d). In addition, the company owns or has interests in refineries in Venezuela, Guatemala, Belgium, Netherlands, Peru, Canada (New Brunswick). Through Caltex, the company participates in operations of 20 refineries in 13 countries of the Eastern Hemisphere; they process 1.7 million b/d.

The company owns or charters 26 tankers under U.S. registry for intercoastal trade. (They transport crude oil from Alaska and California fields to Pacific Coast refineries, and make runs from the refineries to Alaska and Hawaii.) In addition, Socal owns 33 other ships under foreign flag; it has 37 foreign ships under charter. The company has 15 tankers on order, 12 of them in the supertanker range. Three are to be 70,000-ton U.S. flag vessels.

Socal owns and operates 4,769 miles of crude and product pipelines in the United States, Canada, western Europe and in the Middle East, including an interest in Trans Arabian Pipeline Co.

LEADING U.S. COAL PRODUCERS

CONTINENTAL OIL CO.

30 Rockefeller Plaza, New York, N.Y., 10020.

Basic Company Data

John G. McLean, Chairman. Directors: A.W. Tarkington, John G. McLean, Charles A. Anderson, J. Paul Austin, Howard W. Blauvelt, John Corcoran, Wayne E. Glenn, William A. Hewitt, Gilbert E. Jones, John E. Kircher, P.C. Lauinger, Arthur B. Lawrence, George H. Love, P. Malozemoff, Neil J. McKinnon, Eugene J. McNeely, Lauris Norstad, Frank Pace, Jr., J.S. Royds, Franz Schneider.

Total revenues, 1970, $2.9 billion; net income, $160.4 million; outstanding stock, 1970: 52,638,213 shares.

Taxes

In 1969 Conoco paid $3,294,000 in federal income taxes, which was 1.36 percent of net income. In 1968 the company paid $9.7 million or 3.3 percent; in 1970, 6.4 percent.

Interlocks

3 w/ Bankers Trust Co. 2 ea w/ Morgan Guaranty Trust Co.;

J.P. Morgan Co.; General Electric; North American Phillips; Honeywell; Hudson's Bay Oil & Gas. 1 ea w/ Tri-Continental; Stanford; IBM World Trade Corp.; Amer. Pet Institute; Petroleum Publishing Co.; Mellon Natl. Bank & Trust Co.; St. Joseph Lead Co.; Capital Natl. Bank; Lincoln Consolidated Inc; International Executive Service Corp.; Carrier & General Corp.; Colgate-Palmolive; Bullock Fund; Putnam Trust Co. (Greenwich, Conn.); Dividend Shares; Nation-Wide Securities; Time, Inc.; Amer. Fidelity Life Ins. Co. (Pensacola, Fla); Corporation for Public Broadcasting; Canadian Imperial Bank of Commerce; Canada Life Assurance Co.; Brascom, Ltd.; Allied Chemical Canada Ltd.; Trans Canada Pipelines; Campbell Soup Co.; Ford Motor Co. (Canada); Falconbridge Nickel Mines, Ltd.; East River Savings Bank; Dun & Bradstreet; Phelps-Dodge; El Paso Natural Gas; Transcontinental Gas Pipe Line Co.; Boston Co., Inc; General Reinsurance Corp.; Coca Cola; Trust Co. of Georgia; Deere & Co.; Continental Illinois Natl. Bank & Trust Co.; AT&T; Chase Manhattan Bank; Conill Corp.; Hanna Mining; Union Carbide; Univ. Pittsburgh; Princeton; F.S. Smithers & Co.; Newmont Mining Corp.; Southern Peru Copper Corp.; Canadian Export Gas & Oil Ltd.; O'okiep Copper Co., Ltd.; Sherritt Gordon Mines Ltd.; Resurrection Mining Co.; Dawn Mining Co.; Idarado Mining Co.; Tsumeb Corp.; Cassiar Asbestos Corp.; Palabora Mining Co.; Magma Copper Co.; St. Joe Mineral Corp.; Atlantic Cement Co.; Carlin Gold Mining Co.; Granduc Operating Co.; Foote Mineral Co.; Owens-Corning Fiberglass Corp.; United Airlines; Rand Corp.; Abitibi Paper Co., Ltd.; VAL, Inc.

Ownership Information

Banks: Patman: 2 interlocks each with Morgan Guaranty Trust and Bankers Trust; one with Continental Illinois Natl. Bank. Morgan Guaranty manages one fund with investments in Conoco.

Consolidation Coal Co., which was independent at the time of the Patman study, had three interlocks with Mellon Natl. Bank & Trust, and one interlock with Continental Illinois Natl. Bank.

The Mellon bank managed four funds with investments in Consolidation.

Insurance: Insurance companies owned 1,391,558 shares. Major holdings, 1969: John Hancock, 120,000; Aetna Casualty & Surety, 64,445; Equitable, 60,000.

Mutual Funds: Thirty-two funds held 4,236,809 shares or 8.5 percent of the outstanding stock. Major holdings: Investors Group, 951,100 (Inv. Mutual, 309,000; Inv. Stock Fund, 642,100); Affiliated Fund, 340,000; Tri-Continental (one interlock), 340,-000; Oppenheimer Fund, 311,300.

Foundations: Ford Foundation, 115,000 shares; Carnegie Corp.; $1.4 million in bonds and notes; Kresge Foundation, 6,000 shares.

Universities: Universities held 456,093 shares. Major holdings: Harvard (June 30, 1970), 220,356; Princeton (June 30, 1969) (one interlock), 46,822; Univ. Pittsburgh (June 30, 1970) (one interlock), 14,410.

Oil and Gas: Conoco's worldwide crude reserves totaled 3.1 billion barrels. About one-third of the reserves are in the Western Hemisphere, almost all of that in the United States or Canada. Crude oil production in 1970 worldwide was 543,000 b/d, including, U.S., 176,000 b/d (including Texas, 55,000; Wyoming, 28,000; Oklahoma, 12,000; California, 11,000; New Mexico, 8,000); Canada, 46,000 (Alberta, 34,000; British Columbia, 7,000; Saskatchewan, 5,000); Libya, 315,000; Iran, 13,000; Dubai, 30,000.

Estimated natural gas reserves in the United States and Canada amounted to 7.3 trillion cubic feet; Eastern Hemisphere natural reserves, 2.4 trillion cubic feet. Deliveries of natural gas in the United States averaged 844.1 million cubic feet per day; in Canada, 317 million cubic feet a day.

Conoco has extensive oil and gas holdings in the North Sea, Southeast Asia, and Australia, but most of the property has not been developed. In Canada Conoco operates through Hudson's Bay Oil & Gas Co., Ltd., in which it has a 54.9 percent holding. The company is a participant in the Iranian consortium.

The company operates seven refineries in the United States with a daily capacity of about 300,000 barrels. The company also runs an 80,000 barrel a day refinery on the east coast, United Kingdom, and has a 10 percent interest in a 110,000 barrel a day refinery at Karlsruhe, West Germany. The company is building a pipeline to carry gas from the North Sea Viking field to markets in England.

Coal: Conoco's coal operations are carried out through its wholly-owned subsidiary, Consolidation Coal Co. In 1970 Consolidation produced 57.4 million tons of bituminous coal; about 41.8 million tons of that total was used for steam by electric utilities. Production of metallurgical coal totaled 8.9 million tons. Consolidation is a major exporter of steam and metallurgical coal to Canada, and of metallurgical coal to Japan and other foreign steel producers. In 1971 the company had 505 violations of the federal coal mine safety laws and was assessed $95,720 in fines.

Uranium: Conoco holds 648,000 acres of prospective uranium lands. Holdings are primarily in south Texas, Wyoming, New Mexico, and Utah. Conoco's uranium acreage is in the evaluation and construction stage. A mining-milling complex is scheduled for completion in 1972 in south Texas. A copper deposit was discovered in Arizona. The company has a 37.5 percent interest in CER Geonuclear Corp., which conducts research into methods of using nuclear explosives in such fields as mining and excavation and petroleum production.

Transportation: Continental operates four tankers and has two 115,000-ton tankers under construction. Its pipelines carry 338,-638 barrels a day of crude oil and refined products. In addition, the company has a 3 percent interest in the Trans-Alpine pipeline in Europe.

KENNECOTT COPPER CORPORATION

161 East 42nd Street, New York, N.Y., 10017.

Basic Company Data

Frank R. Milliken, President. Directors: Glenn P. Bakken, Russell DeYoung, J. Peter Grace, M. M. Hardin, Ellison L. Hazard, John Jeppson, Peter O. Lawson-Johnston, Gavin K. MacBain, Arthur F. Mayne, C.D. Michaelson, T.C. Mullins, Walter H. Page, Clifton W. Phalen, George Russell, John M. Schiff, Roy W. Simmons, Edward L. Steiniger, Wm. Thayer Tutt.

Total revenues, 1970, $1.1 billion; net income, $150.8 million; stock outstanding, 1970: 33,159,153 shares.

Interlocks

4 w/ Braden Copper. 3 w/ Morgan Guaranty. 2 w/ Peabody Coal. 1 ea w/ Southwestern Illinois Coal Corp.; Jet Oil Co.; Miller & Co.; Zions Utah Bank Corporation; Keystone Insurance & Investment Corp.; Hotel Utah; Zions First Natl. Bank; Utah-Portland Cement; Heber S. Grant Co.; Beneficial Life Ins. Co.; Denver & Rio Grande RR; Mountain Fuel Supply Co.; Utah Business Development Corp.; Rio Grande Industries; Kuhn, Loeb & Co.; Los Angeles & Salt Lake RR; Westinghouse; CIT Financial; Madison Fund; Uniroyal; A&P; Getty Oil; Marine Midland Bank; Chubb Corp.; Eastern Airlines; Marine Midland Grace Trust Co.; Amer. Pet Inst.; Emigrant Ind. Savings Bank; Chemical Bank NY Trust; Pace College; Fordham Univ; CIP, Inc.; Continental Can Co.; Charter NY Corp; Guggenheim Brothers; Pacific Tin Consolidated Corp.; Feldspar Corp; Elqerbar Corp.; Minerec Corp.; Anglo Lautaro Nitrate Corp.; Chilean Nitrate Sales; W.R. Grace & Co.; Atlantic Mutual Ins. Co.; In-

gersoll-Rand Co.; First Natl. City Bank NY; Stone & Webster; Deering Milliken; Magnavox; First Natl. City Corp.; Centennial Ins. Co. NYC; Omega Fund; Brascan Ltd.; A.F. Mayne & Assocs.; Royal Bank of Canada; Trust Corp. of Bahamas; British Columbia Molybdenum; Air Liquide Can; Can. Interurban Properties; West Coast Transmission; Woodward Shoes; Dominion Bridge; Ile Reaux; Loram Ltd.; Roman Corp. Ltd.; Tex-Park Ltd; Warnock Hersey Intl. Ltd.; Chantecler Hotel Co. Ltd; Pacific Petroleums Co.; Export Develop Corp.; Campeau Corp. Ltd.; United Cooperations, Ltd.; Royerest Banking Corp. Ltd.; Bristol-Myers Co.; United Mutual Savings Bank; Simplicity Pattern Co.; First Federal Savings & Loan Assoc.; U.S. Trust Co.; Arcata Natl. Corp.; Merck & Co.; J.P. Morgan & Co., Inc.; General Motors; SS Kresge Co.; Norton Co.; New England High Carbon Wire Corp.; Guaranty Bank & Trust Co.; Foxboro Co.; Crompton & Knowles Corp.; New England Merchants Natl. Bank; Goodyear Tire & Rubber; Youngstown Corp.; Broadmoor Hotel, Inc.; Ozark Lead Co.; Church of the Latter Day Saints, Procter & Gamble.

Ownership Information

Banks: Patman: 2 interlocks w/ First Natl. City Bank of NY. Morgan Guaranty manages three funds that own 17.5 percent of the outstanding stock with a 10.5 percent sole voting right and a 2.6 percent partial voting right.

Insurance: Insurance companies owned 942,435 shares. Major holdings, 1970: NY Life, 169,000; 1969: Northwestern Mutual Life, 92,500; INA, 78,800; Continental Ins. NYC, 58,200.

Mutual Funds: Thirty funds held 2.8 million shares or 8.6 percent of the outstanding stock. Major holdings: Wellington Fund, 341,400; Windsor Fund, 386,100; Putnam Group, 299,000 (Putnam Growth, 249,000; Putnam Income, 50,000); United Group, 307,100 (United Accumulative Fund, 80,000; United Income Fund, 227,100).

Foundations: Carnegie Corp., 114,500 shares; Alfred P. Sloan Foundation, 60,000 shares; Kresge Foundation, 9,200 shares.

Universities: Universities held 298,637 shares. Major holdings: Harvard (June 30, 1970), 71,082; Smith (June 30, 1970), 42,905; Rockefeller Univ. (June 30, 1969), 30,000.

Kennecott is the largest producer of nonferrous metals. Two-thirds of the company's revenues are derived from the sale of copper; most of the rest comes from coal.

Copper: Kennecott owns and operates four large open pit copper mines in the western part of the United States, the largest of which is at Bingham, Utah. The others include Ray Mine, at Kearney, Arizona; Chino Mine at Santa Rita in the south central part of New Mexico; and a mine at Ruth, Nevada. The company's estimated recoverable copper ore reserves at the end of 1970 were three billion tons of ore, containing an estimated 18.5 million tons of recoverable copper. Molybdenum, gold, and silver are produced as by-products.

Kennecott owns Chase Brass & Copper Co., a leading fabricator of copper and brass mill products. The company holds a 66⅔ percent interest in the common stock of Quebec Iron & Titanium Corp., which owns and operates an open pit titanium mine at Allard Lake, Quebec. Kennecott owns Ozark Lead Co., which operates two underground lead-zinc mines, one near Ellington, Missouri, and the other at Eureka, Utah. Silver and cadmium are produced as by-products at these sites. The company's $140 million copper mine in Chile was nationalized in 1971.

Coal: Kennecott is the second largest coal producer in the United States through its ownership of Peabody Coal Co. Peabody operates 40 coal mines in the United States. Thirty-one are strip mines; nine are underground. For the most part these mines are in the Midwest, Illinois, Indiana, and western Kentucky.

In 1970 the company produced 62.7 million tons of coal in the

United States. Of that total, 48.8 million tons came from strip mining. In 1970, 81 percent of all domestic coal produced ,was sold to electric utilities.

In addition, Peabody produced 3.4 million tons of coal in Australia, where it has a strip mine and underground mine at Queensland. The Australian mines provide metallurgical coal for Australian customers. The mines are operated through an Australian subsidiary in which Peabody has a 50 percent interest.

Peabody's total coal reserves are listed at 8.4 billion tons. That includes an estimated 80 million ton reserve in Australia. The company is reported to hold three billion tons of coal reserves in Montana and Wyoming and it has extensive water rights adjacent to these coal lands. Water is necessary in large quantities, both for operating mine mouth electricity plants and for plants which change coal into natural gas.

The company has close ties to Morgan Guaranty. There are three interlocks between the two companies' boards, and Morgan Guaranty manages trust funds which control 17.5 percent of Kennecott's stock. Morgan Guaranty is a transfer agent, and Morgan Stanley, an affiliate, is an important Kennecott underwriter.

Through its interlocks with Zions Utah Bank Corporation, Kennecott is intertied to the extensive industrial holdings of the Mormon Church.

In 1971 Kennecott was involved in a long-drawn court dispute over its ownership of Peabody Coal. In March 1970 a Federal Trade Commission examiner had approved the merger of the two firms. After deliberating more than a year, the full commission reversed the decision. The company failed in its attempts to reopen the case at the commission, and in July 1971 appealed the decision in the U.S. Court of Appeals, Denver.

In its May 1971 decision the FTC said the acquisition of Peabody by Kennecott removed Kennecott "as a substantial potential competitive force" in the coal industry, and would result in lessened competition in the coal business. Frank R. Milliken, the president, promised to fight the decision in the courts.

In December 1969 residents of Maricope County, Arizona, filed suit against Kennecott and other mining companies seeking an injunction and punitive damages of $1 billion against air polluting copper smelters operated by the company. In four western states Kennecott is faced with air pollution regulations that the company claims it cannot meet. Nor can the company meet requirements of the federal air pollution act.

In 1971, Peabody mines had 1,190 federal safety violations. Fines were assessed at $198,980.

OCCIDENTAL PETROLEUM CORPORATION

10889 Wilshire Boulevard, Los Angeles, Calif., 90024.

Basic Company Data

Armand Hammer, Chairman; William Bellano, President. Directors: Thomas F. Willers, Arthur Groman, James L. Hamilton, Paul C. Hebner, Neil H. Jacoby, E.C. Reid, Charles K. Schwartz, Herman L. Vail.

Total revenues, 1970, $2.4 billion; net income, $153.8 million; average number of shares outstanding, 1970: 52,762,000.

Interlocks

3 w/ Island Creek Coal Co. 2 w/ Jefferson Lake Petrochemicals of Canada, Ltd. 1 ea w/ City Natl. Bank (Beverly Hills); Florida Natl. Bank (Jacksonville); Natl. Coal Mining Co.; Beatrice Pocahontas Co.; Natl. Coal Assn.; Sayre, Vail, Steele & Renkert; Forest City Publishing Co.; Cleveland Trust Co.; United Broadcasting Co.; Cleveland Co.; Plain Dealer Publishing Co.; Gottleib & Schwartz; Univ. of California; Hooker Chemical Corp.; Hooker Chemicals Ltd. (Canada); Hooker Mexicana SA; Hooker Parker (Canada); Minera de Sotavento SA; Puerto Rico Chemical Co.; Chemserve (Australia); NV Hooker Chemical SA; Parker Bonderite Pty.; Duranor SAIC (Argentina); Home

Life Ins. Co.; Udylite Corp.; Sel-Rex Corp.; Occidental Minerals Corp.; Instituto Electroquimico SA.

Ownership Information

Banks: Patman: In 1968 Island Creek Coal, an Occidental subsidiary, had three interlocks with Cleveland Trust Co. Cleveland Trust manages two funds with investments in Island Creek. The bank held 16.5 percent of the outstanding common stock, which gave it a 15.7 percent sole voting right.

Insurance: Insurance companies owned 115,200 shares. Major holdings: State Mutual Life, 22,950; Amer. Natl. Ins., 22,497.

Mutual Funds: Nine funds held 1.3 million shares or 2.4 percent of the outstanding stock. Major holdings: American Investors Fund, 140,900; Fidelity Group, 920,500 (Fidelity Capital Fund, 200,000; Fiduciary Trend Fund, 720,500).

About one-third of Occidental's income comes from oil and gas exploration, most of it in Libya. Crude oil reserves in Libya are estimated at 1.8 billion barrels, with natural gas reserves estimated at 1.7 trillion cubic feet. Occidental works through a subsidiary, Occidental of Libya, which has two principal concessions in the Sirte Basin. These concessions produce some 700,000 barrels a day. Elsewhere abroad, Occidental is negotiating for 736,-000 acres offshore Nigeria, and has received rights to drill for oil on 375,000 acres in the South Lake Maracaibo, Venezuela area. It has interests offshore Ghana, in Trinidad and Tobago, and both offshore and onshore in the Trucial states between Iran and Saudi Arabia. In addition, it holds 1.2 million acres offshore Sierra Leone, 2.8 million acres in northeastern Peru, and more than 1.9 million acres offshore Peru. Under a 35-year contract with the Peruvian government, Occidental agrees to build an oil pipeline over the Andes to the Pacific, if oil is produced.

In North America, Occidental owns oil and gas interests in 61,100 producing acres of California, three western Canadian provinces, and five other states. Reserves in North America total 33 million barrels of oil and 582 trillion cubic feet of natural gas. In 1970 the company produced net 4.8 million barrels of oil and net 41 trillion cubic feet of gas. Sixty-six percent of the company's oil reserves and 37 percent of its gas reserves are in California. The Lathrop Gas fields, 60 miles east of San Francisco, contain 26 percent of Occidental's North American gas reserves. About 40 percent of its gas reserves and 7 percent of its oil reserves are in Canada.

In 1970 Occidental and Putnam Oil Co., subsidiary of Putnam Management Co., Inc., which manages Putnam mutual funds, organized a limited partnership to explore for oil and gas in the United States. Oil and gas were discovered in Texas.

·Occidental has a fleet of 43 tankers, including three supertankers and 40 tankers chartered from others. It has 10 tankers scheduled for delivery through 1975.

In the United States, Occidental markets through Permian Corp., a subsidiary. Permian owns 4,949 miles of crude gathering pipelines, barge and truck operations.

In Europe Occidental has refineries at Antwerp, Essen, and Brunsbuttel. The company markets gasoline, heating oil, and asphalt in Europe.

Through its purchase of Island Creek Coal Co. in 1966, and Maust Coal & Coke Corp. in 1969, Occidental became the nation's third largest coal producer. The corporation's total coal reserves now total about 3.3 billion tons. About half of all coal is sold to electric utilities. In 1970 total production was 29.7 million tons. Most of the coal comes from deep mines in Kentucky, Ohio, Pennsylvania, Virginia, and West Virginia. The company's metallurgical coal goes mostly to the major eastern steel making states, or is exported to Canada, Japan, western Europe, and South America. The company is developing a new mine in Virginia with Japanese partners. Its output will be sold to Japanese steel makers.

Occidental owns Hooker Chemical Corp., a major chemical company engaged in metal finishings, plastics and in various mining endeavors aimed at securing necessary raw materials. Occidental is in' the international fertilizer business, owns or leases phosphate deposits and produces sulphur, and engages in real estate development in Southern California.

In 1971, there were 3,471 federal safety violations at Island Creek mines; the company was assessed $849,075 in fines.

PITTSTON CO.

250 Park Avenue, New York, N.Y., 10017

Basic Company Data

Joseph P. Routh, Chairman; Nicholas T. Camicia, President, chief executive officer.

Total revenues, 1970, $505.6 million; net income, $39.4 million; stock outstanding, 1970: 15,665,706 shares.

Interlocks

2 ea w/ Allegheny Corp.; Hotel Waldorf-Astoria Corp. 1 ea w U.S. Trucking Corp.; Pittston Clinchfield Coal Sales Corp.; Sheridan-Wyoming Coal Co.; Raleigh SS Agency; Amigo Smokeless Coal Co.; Baker & Williams; Brinks, Inc.; Silicone Paper Co. of America; Chemical Bank N.Y. Trust Co.; Manhattan Savings Bank; Carnegie Life Savings Fund; Bank of Commerce; CPA Co.; United Insurance Co. of America; Windsor Hotel; Northlawn Shopping Center; Penobscot Bldg., Inc.; McCandless Corp.; Brown Co.; Globe & Mail; Detroit Marine Terminals, Inc.; Burns Foods, Ltd.; Dillard Paper Co.; F.M. Kirby Foundation, Inc.; F.W. Woolworth Co.; Investors Diversified Services; Alpha Portland Cement; U.S. Industries; Lafayette College; Beneficial Mutual Savings Bank; Delaware & Bound Brook RR; Reading RR; Bonwit Teller & Co.; Bellevue-Stratford & Co.; St. Joseph's College; Philadelphia Life Ins.; Foote Mineral Co.; State National Bank of Conn.; Liberty Natl. Bank & Trust (Louisville); Penn, Stuart & Eskridge.

Ownership Information

Insurance: Insurance companies owned 53,418 shares. Major holdings, 1969: Aetna Casualty & Surety, 18,779.

Mutual Funds: Twenty-eight funds owned 2.4 million shares or 15.4 percent of outstanding stock. Major holdings: Affiliated Fund, 320,116; Selected American Shares, 230,000.

Universities: Universities owned a total of 76,734 shares. Major holdings: NYU (August 31, 1970), 46,000; Cornell (March 31, 1970), 30,263.

Pittston was founded in 1930, and acquired 18 coal companies over the next 40 years. Its most important ties are with the Penn Central Railroad, the biggest coal carrier, and the Allegheny Corp., which has substantial coal properties.

The coal division contributes about 70 percent of the company's overall revenues. In 1970 Pittston produced 20.5 million tons and exported 9.4 million tons of that total. Most of the coal comes from the eastern Appalachians. Pittston has reserves of over one billion tons of metallurgical coal, which puts it in a good position to serve the steel industries around the world. The company held back coal in the mid-1960s when prices were low, and then in 1970 was in a good position to bargain profitably with the Japanese for a contract to supply them with 140 million tons of metallurgical coal over the next ten years.

Pittston also has an oil division, Metropolitan Petroleum Co., which owns storage facilities, and has large trucking and barge fleets. A petrochemical division makes products to abate air and water pollution. The company, for instance, makes a boom to contain oil spills. Pittston also controls United States Trucking and has an 80 percent interest in Brinks, the armored car outfit.

One hundred twenty-five people were killed at Buffalo Creek, West Virginia, when the company's dam collapsed in February, 1972, flooding nearby communities.

UNITED STATES STEEL CORPORATION

71 Broadway, New York, N.Y. 10006.

Basic Company Data

Edwin H. Gott, Chairman; Edgar B. Speer, President. Directors: Thomas V. Jones, Roger M. Blough, Gordon M. Metcalf, George S. Moore, Harllee Beanch, Jr., Arthur A. Houghton, Jr., H.I. Romnes, John M. Meyer, Jr., Leslie B. Worthington, Robert C. Tyson, Franklin J. Lunding, William McC. Martin, Jr., Henry S. Wingate.

Total revenues, 1970, $4.8 billion; net income, $147.4 million; common stock outstanding, 1970: 54,169,462 shares.

Interlocks

2 ea w/ Mellon Bank & Trust; Reactive Metals Inc.; First Natl. City Bank NY; Chemical Bank New York Trust; Seaman's Bank for Savings; Morgan Guaranty Trust Co; J.P. Morgan & Co.; American Standard Inc. 1 ea w/ Aetna Life & Casualty; Gillette Co.; Eastman Kodak Co.; Burlington Northern Inc.; Texas Gulf Sulphur Co.; Intl. Nickel Co. Canada; Canadian Pacific Rwy.; Bank of Montreal; Greyhound Corp.; TRW Inc.; Williams Brothers Inc.; General Reinsurance Corp.; Southern Co.; General Motors; Sears Roebuck; Allstate Insurance Co.; First National Bank Chicago; Homart Development Co.; Uniroyal Inc.; Jewel Cos. Inc.; Penn Central Co.; Illinois Bell Telephone Co.; Thomas Industries Inc.; Pennsylvania Co.; Steuben Glass; NY Life Insurance; NY Trust Co.; Corning Glass Works; Northrop Corp.; Times-Mirror Co.; Stanford Univ.; Wells Fargo & Co.; Olympic Airways; Union Pacific Corp.; Oregon Short Line RR; Oregon—Washington RR & Navigation; LA & Salt Lake RR; W.R. Grace & Co.; AT&T; Cities Service; Mutual Life Insurance Co. NY; Colgate-Palmolive Co.; White & Case.

Ownership Information

Banks: Patman: two interlocks each w/ Chase; Morgan Guaranty; Chemical Bank NY Trust. 1 ea w. First Natl. City Bank NY; First Pennsylvania Bank & Trust; Mellon Natl. Bank & Trust. National City Bank Cleveland manages one fund with investments in US Steel.

Insurance: Insurance companies owned 185,037 shares. Major holdings: Government Employees Ins., 24,000; Equitable, 20,670; Travelers, 19,800; Aetna (one interlock), 8,851.

Mutual Funds: Eight funds held 1.4 million shares or 2.7 percent of the outstanding stock. Major holdings: Affiliated Fund, 600,000; Fidelity Trend Fund, 383,400.

Foundations: Ford Foundation, 45,000 shares; Kresge Foundation, $400,000 in debentures.

Universities: Universities owned 58,358 shares. Major holdings: NYU (August 31, 1970), 25,000; Cornell (March 31, 1970), 23,350.

US Steel produced 19.6 million tons of coking coal in 1970, most of it for the company's own use. Production is being expanded to increase the quantities of coal both for US Steel and for sale to others. A coal mine and preparation plant in West Virginia are being expanded. A new mine and preparation plant are being built in West Virginia. A new mine is planned for Kentucky.

US Steel has 50 years of metallurgical coal reserves in Alaska, Kentucky, West Virginia, Pennsylvania, Colorado, Illinois, Indiana, Tennessee, Utah and Virginia. The company moves much of the coal through transportation subsidiaries. The company owns three railroads, has 47 cargo vessels and 9 self-unloading steamships.

In 1970 US Steel mined 49 million tons of iron ore, three quarters of it used by the company. A little less than half of total production came from the US. Two subsidiaries, Orinoco Mining Co. in Venezuela and Quebec Cartier Mining Co. in Canada, shipped 18.3 million tons and 8.9 million tons respectively. Through a Brazilian subsidiary, Meridional, US Steel has a 49 percent interest in Amazonia Mineracao SA, a company formed in 1970 for possible development of iron ore fields in northern Brazil.

The company mines manganese in Gabon, through Comilog, and in Brazil. US Steel holds a minority interest in Acieries de Paris et d'Outreau, a large French producer of ferromanganese. The company owns 50 percent of Mina Matilde, which mines zinc in Bolivia. US Steel has interests in Zeerust Chrome Mines Ltd., producer of chrome in southern Africa, and a 43 percent interest in PT Pacific Nikkel Indonesia which mines nickel-cobalt in that country.

The company is investigating copper-bearing iron ore deposits in Lyon County, Nevada, copper in British Columbia, and various metals in the Yukon. It is evaluating copper and nickel deposits in Minnesota.

With US Plywood-Champion Papers, US Steel shares ownership of Birmingham Forest Products, which makes plywood, lumber, pulpwood chips and laminated decking. It has interests in chemicals; agri-chemicals, including fertilizers. It makes steel structures for schools, dormitories and other institutional buildings, and produces aluminum siding through Alside Inc.

It runs financing operations through US Steel Finance Corp., US Steel Leasing Co., Inc., and, through Percy Wilson Mortgage & Finance Corp., holds industrial and residential mortgages.

US Steel supplies machinery for drilling operations and pumping out deep wells to the oil and gas industry through its Oilwell division.

In recent years the company has become involved in realty development.

LEADING U.S. URANIUM PRODUCERS

KERR-McGEE CORPORATION

Kerr-McGee Building, Oklahoma City, Okla., 73102.

Basic Company Data

D.A. McGee, Chairman; F.C. Love, President. Directors: Peter Colefax, Grady D. Harris, Jr.; Earle M. Jorgensen, Edwin L. Kennedy, Breene M. Kerr, Robert S. Kerr, Jr., Guy C. Kiddoo, J.B. Saunders, A.T.F. Seale, Dean Terrill, James E. Webb.

Total revenues, 1970, $527.5 million; net income, $35.9 million; common shares outstanding, 1970: 7,382,275.

Interlocks

3 w/ Fidelity Natl. Bank & Trust Co. (Oklahoma City). 2 ea w/ Triangle Refineries, Inc.; Downtown Airpark, Inc.; Kermac Contractors, Inc.; Cato Oil & Grease Co.; Kerr-McGee Foundation; Kerr-McGee Iranian Oil Co.; Moss-American, Inc.; Transocean Drilling Corp., Ltd.; Amer. Potash & Chemical Corp. 1 ea w/ Kerr-McGee Building Corp.; Bighole Drillers; Central Plains Enterprises, Inc.; Tascosa Gas Co.; Bison Gas Co.; Oklahoma Natural Gas Co.; OKC Corp.; General Electric; Federal Reserve Bank, Kansas City; Chass C.; Oklahoma City Univ.; Hubbard Hall Chemical Co.; Cimarron TV Corp.; Kermac Nuclear Fuels Corp.; Kerr-McGee Chemical Corp.; Knox Industries; McGee Foundation; Pee-Dee Chemical Corp.; Southwest Research Institute; Amer. Pet Inst.; Natl. Pet Council; First Natl. Bank & Trust Co.; Kerr-McGee Pipeline Corp.; Kerr, Davis, Foster, Irvine & Burbage; Farmers & Merchants State Bank (Tulsa); Oklahoma Gas & Electric; Earle M. Jorgensen Co.; Rheem Mfg. Co.; Northrop Corp.; Cal. Inst. of Tech; Transamerica Corp.; Lehman Brothers; Gas Properties Inc.; Sunlite Oil Co.; Hiram

College; Ohio Univ.; Oil Shale Corp; Trans Canada Pipelines Ltd.; Ingraham Corp.; Security Pacific Natl. Bank; Diners Club; Investment Co. of America; J.M. Foster Co.; Webb's City, Inc.; Sperry-Rand; J.B. Saunders; Bell Oil Terminal; J.R. Butler & Co.; Cloverleaf Service Stations; Coast Stations & Butane Co.; Cotton Valley Solvents; First State Bank & Trust Co.; Liberty Corp.; Liberty Natl. Bank & Trust; San-Ann Service Inc.; Southwest Title Trust Co.; Triangle Realty Co.; Fidelity Bank NA; Resource Analysis & Management Group; Kermac Drilling Co. of Venezuela, CA; Transworld Drilling Co.; Franjo Inc.; Capitol Hill State Bank & Trust Co.

Ownership Information

Banks: Patman: First Natl. Bank of Chicago managed four funds with investments in Kerr-McGee. State Street Bank & Trust Co. holds 10.1 percent of the corporation's common stock.

Insurance: Insurance companies owned 295,792 shares. Major holdings, 1970: Prudential, 60,000 common, $70.5 m. notes; 1969: American Re-Insurance, 32,000; Connecticut General, 31,800.

Mutual Funds: Seventeen funds owned 1.3 million shares or 18.5 percent of the outstanding stock. Major holdings: Mass Investors Group, 575,450 (Mass Investors Growth Stock, 325,450; Mass Investors Trust, 250,000); United Income Fund, 150,000.

Kerr-McGee was begun in 1932 by the late Senator Robert Kerr of Oklahoma. When he entered politics, Kerr made Dean A. McGee president of the firm. He had hired McGee, a geologist, from Phillips Petroleum. McGee is credited with building this relatively small firm into the first of the total "energy" companies; he shrewdly took positions in uranium and western coal, and developed offshore drilling methods before other, larger firms. Kerr remained close to the company. When McGee began buying coal lands in Oklahoma, Kerr pushed a bill through the Congress which opened up the Arkansas barge canal, thereby making it possible to haul coal to steel plants on the Mississippi.

Kerr-McGee produces gas and oil in 12 states, Canada and Venezuela. Most of the oil and gas comes from Oklahoma, Texas, and Louisiana. It has oil and gas interests offshore Louisiana. Three refineries have a total crude capacity of 50,500 barrels daily. Two-thirds of Kerr-McGee income comes from oil and gas.

The company is best known as the nation's leading uranium producer. Kerr-McGee controls an estimated 25 percent of the country's uranium reserves and accounts for better than 25 percent of the entire uranium market. It operates eight mines at Lake Ambrosia, near Grants, New Mexico. There, a large mill processes 5,000 tons of raw ore a day, turning it into U_3O_8. In addition, Kerr-McGee owns 50 percent of Petrotomics, which mines and mills uranium ore in the Shirley Basin of Wyoming. The other partners in this enterprise are Getty Oil and Skelly Oil.

Kerr-McGee is the only producer integrated through the raw materials end of the nuclear fuels cycle. Kerr-McGee and Allied Chemical are the only two companies which operate plants that change yellow cake into uranium hexafluoride gas, a necessary step before the fuel can be fed into the AEC's gaseous diffusion plants where it is enriched. At other facilities, Kerr-McGee takes the enriched uranium gas and changes it into pellets or powder, the form in which it can be used in building nuclear reactor cores.

The company is increasing its search for more uranium, developing deposits in the northeast Church Rock section of New Mexico and near Rio Puerco, New Mexico. A joint venture of Kerr-McGee and 15 Japanese companies discovered a large deposit of low-grade uranium at Lake Elliott in Canada.

In all, the company holds 1.5 million acres of uranium lands, located principally in New Mexico, Wyoming, Colorado, Montana, South Dakota, Texas, Utah and in Ontario, Canada.

Kerr-McGee is also active in coal, holding leases on 178,000 acres in Oklahoma, Wyoming, North Dakota, Illinois, Colorado, and Arkansas. It operates an underground mine at Choctaw, Oklahoma, where metallurgical coal is produced. The mine is expected to have a capacity of one million tons a year. But most of the company's coal lands remain undeveloped, awaiting introduction of a commercial process that permits changing coal into natural gas.

Through Transworld Drilling Co., a subsidiary, Kerr-McGee is a major contract driller. Transworld has 18 rigs. They operate extensively in the Gulf of Mexico, off South Africa, in the North Sea, etc.

Through Moss-American, another subsidiary, the company owns 260,000 acres of timber land in the West, Midwest, and East. Moss-American is a leading producer of railroad ties. Kerr-McGee produces phosphate, potash, and, through ownership of American Potash & Chemical Corp., is the world's second largest producer of boron.

UNITED NUCLEAR CORPORATION

Grasslands Road, Elmsford, N.Y., 10523.

Basic Company Data

David F. Shaw, Chairman; Douglas M. Johnson, President. Directors: James R. Bancroft, D. Allan Bromley, Kenneth E. Fields, Charles D. Harrington, Robert P. Koenig, W. Latham Leeds, John R. Menke, Henry H. Patton, Talbot Shelton.

Total revenues, 1971 (year ended March 31), $71.1 million; net income, $1.4 million; stock outstanding, 5,055,396 shares.

Interlocks

2 w/ Douglas United Nuclear. 1 ea w/ Adams Properties, Inc.; Smith, Barney & Co.; Adams Western Inc.; Bancroft, Avery & McAlister; Sandvik Special Metals; Atomic Industry Forum; Cerro Corp.; Southern Peru Copper Corp.; Mutual Life Ins. of NY; Atlantic Cement Co.; Cia Minera Andina SA, Ranchers Ex-

plor & Develop Corp.; Yale; Johnson, Bromberg, Leeds & Riggs; Hudson Institute; Ocean Science & Engineering Inc.; Standard Shares Inc.; Vercle Exploration Ltd.; Dearborn Computer Marine; Primary Co., Inc.; Mathematics Park, Inc.; Geokinetics, Inc.; Intl. Geomarine Inc.; Strang's Explorations.

Ownership Information

Mutual Funds: Three funds held 260,800 shares or 5.2 percent of the outstanding stock. Major holdings: National Investors Corp., 137,800; Energy Fund, 75,000; Rowe Price New Era Fund, 48,000.

The company was formed in 1954 as Sabre Uranium Corp., and shortly thereafter created a partnership with Homestake Mining Co. United Nuclear holds 70 percent in the partnership; Homestake, 30 percent. The partnership is the second largest uranium producer in the country, accounting for about 12 percent of the business. It controls about 21,000 acres at Lake Ambrosia and operates five mines. A partnership mill, near Grants, New Mexico, can handle 3,400 tons of uranium ore a day. In addition, United Nuclear operates three other mines. Together the company and partnership control some 12.9 million tons of uranium-bearing materials on their properties. In 1969 the company and partnership together produced 4.4 million pounds of U_3O_8.

Through ownership of Teton Exploration Drilling Co., the firm that carries out all exploration work, United Nuclear participates in a joint venture drilling program in Wyoming with Duval Corp., a subsidiary of Pennzoil United Inc., the big natural gas pipeline company. United Nuclear has leases to 31,000 acres of Navajo lands north of Church Rock, New Mexico, where it hopes to develop uranium. The company is also involved in a joint venture in Australia.

With McDonnell Douglas, the company organized Douglas United Nuclear to manage the AEC's Hanford reactors. To provide the zirconium tube and stainless steel for this operation,

United Nuclear created Sandvik Special Metals Corp., a partnership with Sandvik Steel Works, Sweden.

United Nuclear now fabricates fuel after it is enriched, and in 1971 it announced creation of a joint venture with Gulf Oil Corporation to manufacture and sell commercial nuclear fuel. The venture is called Gulf United Nuclear Fuels Corp., and it is owned 43 percent by United Nuclear.

United Nuclear owns Adams-Western Inc., which is engaged in real estate investment and management in California. Adams-Western owns Summit Mortgage Investors, a Massachusetts trust which owns industrial parks, motels, and mortgage interests in various parts of the country.

THE ANACONDA CO.

25 Broadway, New York, N.Y., 10004

Basic Company Data

John B. M. Place, Chairman; John G. Hall, President. Directors: Charles M. Brinckerhoff, James D. Farley, Robert B. Fulton, Donald D. Greary, Jr., C. Jay Parkinson, William E. Quigley, Robert V. Roosa, Charles A. Siegfried.

Total revenues, 1970, $977 million; net income, $63.8 million; shares outstanding, 1970: 21,891,634.

Interlocks

3 ea w/ Andes Copper Mining Co.; Chile Copper Co.; Chile Exploration Co.; Andes del Peru; Greene Cananea Copper Co.; Santiago Mining Co. 2 ea w/ Chase Manhattan Bank; First Natl. City Bank; Intl. Smelting & Refining; Mines Investment Corp. 1 ea w/ Stauffer Chemical Co.; First Bank System Inc.; Washoe Copper Co.; Chile Steamship Co.; Basic Magnesium, Inc.; Raritan Terminal & Transportation Co.; Silesian Holding Co.; Marine Midland Grace Trust Co.; Brown Brothers Harriman; American Express; Texaco; Rockefeller Foundation; Council on

Foreign Relations; Fleming Suez Brown Brothers Ltd.; Owens Corning Fiberglass; Metropolitan Life Ins. Co.; Lehigh Portland Cement; Celanese Corp.

Ownership Information

Banks: Patman: 2 interlocks each w/ Chase Manhattan and First Natl. City Bank NY. Three funds with investments in Anaconda are managed by Morgan Guaranty, two by First Natl. City Bank, and one by Chase Manhattan.

Insurance: Insurance companies owned 187,200 shares. Major holdings, 1969: Connecticut General, 51,000 shares; Mass Mutual Life, 24,000; Continental Assurance, 16,000.

Foundations: Ford Foundation, 75,000 shares.

Anaconda's copper mines in Chile have been nationalized, thereby cutting off 75 percent of the company's earning power. (In 1969 the company produced about 600,000 tons of copper, nearly 400,000 tons of it coming from Chile. In 1970 there was no production from Chile.)

The remaining operating mines are in the western United States. Most of the production is from Montana (118,333 tons). Other mines are in Arizona, Nevada, British Columbia, and New Mexico. The company is developing new mines in Canada where it works in conjunction with Canadian Pacific Railroad. In Australia, Anaconda develops copper in a joint venture with Rio Tinto Zinc.

The company also produces zinc, lead, silver and gold, cadmium, molybdenum, and bryllium.

Anaconda is a major producer of uranium. In 1970 it produced 3,534,000 pounds of U_3O_8. Its total uranium production is committed to private customers through 1975, when demand is expected to increase. In anticipation of quickened interest, the company activated the dormant Jacpile mine to supplement production from the main Paquate mine.

While Anaconda's business was hurt by the Chilean nationalization, its major strength is believed to lie in large-scale untapped mineral deposits within the United States. However, in
attempting to develop additional copper deposits in Montana,
Anaconda was attacked by conservationists who in 1971 had
apparently succeeded in blocking, at least temporarily, development of new mines. The company fought against passage of a
state law which would require it to fill holes gouged in exploration and require the company to reclaim old mines. The law was
passed, and Anaconda was expected to continue the fight in the
courts.

Like other big mining companies, Anaconda may be forced to
diversify. It has a timber project, and made a bid to purchase
Pacific Northwest Pipeline Co., the natural gas pipeline of which
the courts have ordered El Paso Natural Gas to divest itself.
Anaconda also makes wire and cable, has a major aluminum
operation, and produces brass.

UTAH INTERNATIONAL RESOURCES, INC.
(formerly Utah Construction and Mining Co.)

550 California Street, San Francisco, Calif. 94104.

Basic Company Data

Marriner S. Eccles, Chairman; Edmund W. Littlefield, President. Directors: Ernest C. Arbuckle, Alf E. Brandin, Val A.
Browning, Lawrence T. Dee, George S. Eccles, William R. Kim-
ball, Jr., Arjay Miller, Shepard Mitchell, Albert L. Reeves, Paul
L. Wattis, Alexander M. Wilson.

Gross revenue, 1970: $90.9 million; net income, $30.2 million;
shares outstanding, 1970: 14,100,015.

Interlocks

4 ea w/ First Security Corp.; Marcona Corp.; First Security
Bank of Utah. 3 ea w/ Wells Fargo Bank; Amalgamated Sugar

Co. 2 ea w/ Hewlett-Packard; Eccles Investment Co.; Time Mining Co. 1 ea w/ GE; Chrysler; Union Pacific Corp.; Union Pacific RR; Texas Gulf Sulphur Co.; Ford; Industrial Indemnity; Del Monte Corp.; Cia San Juan; San Juan Carriers, Ltd.; Wattis & Co.; Lakeview Mining Co.; Wattis Construction Co.; Thos. D. Dee Investment Co.; Utah Packers, Inc.; Owens Illinois Castle & Cooke, Inc.; Safeway Stores; Browning Arms; Mountain Fuel Supply; Cabot Corp.; Husky Oil; Oregon Shortline RR; LA & Salt Lake RR; American Bankers Life Assurance Corp.; Farmers Underwriters Assn.; Aubrey G. Lanston & Co.; Ogden Union Ry & Depot Co.; Fibreboard Corp.; Stanford Univ.

Ownership Information

Eccles Investment Co., Salt Lake City, the investment instrument for the Eccles family, held 1,189,285 shares of Utah stock. In 1971, Utah proposed to acquire Eccles by exchanging the company's stock for 1,167,521 shares of Utah. At the same time, Utah proposed to change its name to Utah International Resources, Inc.

Mutual Funds: Twenty-one funds held 1.5 million shares, or 11.2 percent of the outstanding stock. Major holdings: Investors Group, 265,000 shares (Inv. Stock Fund, 165,200; Inv. Variable Payment, 100,000); Price Growth Stock, 266,410.

Insurance: Insurance companies owned 275,000 shares. Major holdings, 1969: INA, 120,000; Prudential, $35 m notes.

Individuals: Marriner S. Eccles, chairman, held 28,659 shares as of January 1971. In addition, Eccles had trustee accounts holding 35,867 shares; holds 100 percent interest in a corporation holding 27,000 shares; and has a 6.2 percent interest in a corporation holding 1.1 million shares. Sara Eccles, his wife, holds 3,500 shares. E. W. Littlefield, president, holds 94,302 shares. In addition, he is custodian or trustee for his children's 55,674 shares. He is trustee for 5,100 shares, and his wife holds 7,848 shares. Lawrence T. Dee, a Utah director, holds 1,050 shares outright, and owns 50 percent of the stock of Thomas D. Dee Investment Co., which holds 253,583 shares. He holds another 16,000 shares in a living trust. George S. Eccles, president of First Security, a bank holding company, has 44,668 shares outright. In addition, he owns all of the stock of a corporation which has 9,182 Utah shares, and has a 1/9 interest in a corporation holding 1.1 million shares. Eccles's wife has 41,382 shares. Paul L. Wattis, a Utah director and president of Wattis & Co., insurance brokers, holds 440,216 shares. In addition, he is trustee of 160,574 shares and co-trustee of 32,400 shares for his children. He is trustee of 600 shares for his grandchildren. He holds 86.08 percent of the stock of Wattis & Co., which owns 318 shares. His wife has 91,014 shares. Shepard Mitchell, a retired attorney, who is also a Utah director, and Wattis together are trustees of 18 trusts established under the will of Ruth Wattis Mitchell which holds an aggregate of 153,908 shares. Littlefield is co-trustee of 16 of these trusts, and beneficiary of the other two trusts holding an aggregate of 17,100 shares.

During its first 40 years of business Utah was mostly engaged in heavy construction within the United States. After World War II the company went into mining. Now most of its income comes from mining, primarily coal and uranium; it also mines copper and iron ore. Either directly or through subsidiaries Utah has holdings in the United States, Peru, Australia, and Canada, and is involved in real estate development, construction, dredging, and shipping.

Utah owns 90 percent of Utah Development Co., an Australian subsidiary; 25 percent of Pima Mining Co., which produces copper; and 45 percent of Marcona Corp., which mines iron ore in Peru and New Zealand, markets iron ore for the Utah organization, and operates a fleet of ore carriers. (Cyprus Mines is the other major holder in Marcona.)

Coal: In 1970 coal displaced iron ore as the principal contributor to the company's profits. The company operates a large strip mine on the Navajo reservation in New Mexico which supplies fuel for the Four Corners power plant, a joint undertaking of 23 utilities. In 1970 coal sales to the plant were 5.5 million tons. The reserves of this mine are estimated to be 1.1 billion tons. The Four Corners plant has been harshly criticized for air pollution. The coal is high in sulphur content, and is said to contain large quantities of mercury as well.

Utah has large-scale coal mining operations in Australia where it is a principal supplier of coking coal for the Japanese steel industry. Utah Development Co. owns Blackwater mine in Queensland. Blackwater produced three million tons in 1970, and the company will expand production to four million tons annually. In addition, Utah is involved in two new mines, which are being developed at Peak Downs and Goonyella in Queensland. Utah owns 85 percent of these projects. The other 15 percent in each is held by Mitsubishi. The mines will provide coal to fulfill a 13-year contract with Japanese buyers for 50.5 million tons of coking coal. In order to place these mines in operation, the company is building new railroads, a port, and a township to house employees. Utah will finance 85 percent of the projected cost, or $180.4 million. This is the largest such project ever undertaken by the company. Utah has rights from the Queensland government to mine and export up to 250 million tons from all the mines. More coal may be taken provided that the total does not exceed 30 percent of recoverable reserves.

Uranium: Until recently the company's primary uranium operation was the Lucky Mc mine in the Gas Hills of Wyoming. Until 1966, the sole customer for that mine and mill's products was the AEC, but since then a wide market has been established. In 1970 the company produced 2.6 million pounds of uranium oxide. A second mine is operating in the Shirley Basin area of Wyoming, and the company is building a new mill there as well. Combined shipments from both mills are expected to exceed four million pounds annually. The Shirley Basin mine is an open pit affair. According to contracts or letters of intent, both mines will be taken up with meeting orders through 1975.

Iron Ore: Utah operates the Iron Spring Mines, outside Cedar City, Utah, and it works CF&I Corp.'s nearby iron deposits. The major customer is US Steel's Provo, Utah, plant. In western Australia, Utah Development, Consolidated Gold Fields Australia, Ltd., and Cyprus Mines each own one-third of the Mount Goldsworthy iron mine. Last year six million tons of ore were mined and shipped to Japan. New Japanese contracts for 52.6 million tons of ore were signed in 1970; the mine is to be expanded.

Marcona Corp.: Utah and Cyprus Mines share voting control of Marcona Corp., a New York corporation. Through Marcona Mining, Marcona Corp. mines iron ore in Peru; through Waverly Mining Co., it engages in mining in New Zealand.

Marcona Mining sells its Peruvian ore to Cia San Juan, SA, a Panamanian subsidiary of Marcona. San Juan then markets the ore products, 80 percent of them going to Japan. San Juan also markets all ore from the Mount Goldsworthy operation. San Juan, in turn, has a shipping subsidiary called San Juan Carriers, Ltd. It is a Liberian corporation, with a fleet of ten ships, nine of them combination ore/oil carriers.

Copper: Utah has a 25 percent interest in Pima Mining Co., which runs an open pit copper mine near Tucson. Other partners are Cyprus Mines, 50 percent; and Union Oil, 25 percent. In addition, Utah plans to begin production soon at the Island Copper mine, now under development on the northern end of Vancouver Island in British Columbia, Canada. Its output will be sold to various Japanese companies.

Other Operations: Utah owns and operates two large dredges. One of them has been at work near Port Hedland, in western Australia at the Mount Goldsworthy iron mine.

Utah has a limited partnership with Haas and Haynie Corp., a commercial construction company. The company has various realty holdings along the San Francisco Bay in Alameda County. It owns part of Alameda Island in San Francisco Bay, and Bay Farm Island off Oakland airport. Barnal Co., a subsidiary, owns an interest in Eden Roc Gardens at Tucson. Utah owns the Work Ranch in Monterey, and a commercial center is planned there. It also owns Mountain Park, a 630-acre spread east of Los Angeles, which is scheduled to be developed for residential purposes. Other holdings include: more than 1,000 acres at Pauma Valley, California; a parcel in Phoenix; 340 acres of South San Francisco, the site of an industrial park; and 1,491 acres south of Vandenberg Air Force Base near Lompoc, California.

UNION CARBIDE CORPORATION

Union Carbide Building, 270 Park Avenue, New York, N.Y., 10017.

Basic Company Data

Birny Mason, Jr., Chairman; F. Perry Wilson, President. Directors: R. Manning Brown, Jr.; John W. Drye, Jr.; Kenneth H. Hannan; J. Victor Herd; James M. Hester; Allen T. Lambert; George H. Love; Robert E. McNeill, Jr.; William S. Sneath; J. Harris Ward.

Total revenues, 1970, $3 billion; net income, $157 million; shares outstanding, 1970: 60,479,000.

Interlocks

4 w/ Continental Insurance Co. 3 ea w/ Continental Corp.; NY Life Insurance Co. 2 ea w/ Manufacturers Hanover Trust Co.; Brooklyn Union Gas Co.; Chrysler; American Title Ins. Co.; New York University. 1 ea w/ Metropolitan Life Insurance; Dominick Fund; Firemans Ins. Co.; Franklin Life Insurance; Diners Club; IBM World Trade Corp.; Boston Old Colony Ins. Co.; Natl. Ben Franklin Insurance; Niagara Fire Ins. Co.; Fidel-

ity & Casualty Ins. Co.; Seaboard Fire & Marine Ins. Co.; Commercial Ins. Co. of NJ; U.S. Export-Import Bank; Glen Falls Ins. Co.; American Intl. Ins. Co.; Capital Finance Corp.; Kelley, Drye, Warren, Clarke, Carr & Ellis; Grocery Store Products Co.; Franklin United Life Ins. Co.; Avon Products, Inc.; Union Camp Corp.; A&P; Louisiana Land & Exploration Co.; Morgan Guaranty; Toronto-Dominion Bank; Dominion Ins. Co.; Canadian Intl. Paper Co.; London Life Ins. Co.; Dome Mines Ltd.; Intl. Nickel Co. of Canada; Midland & Intl. Banks Ltd.; Canada Westinghouse; Hudson Bay Mining & Smelting Co.; IBM, Ltd.; York Univ.; Pacific Ctr., Ltd.; Hiram Walker-Gooderham & Worls; Hanna Mining; GE; Univ. Pittsburgh; Princeton; Conoco; Amer. Smelting & Refining; Fed. Res. Bank, NY; Commonwealth Edison; Intl. Harvester; Northern Trust Co.

Ownership Information

Banks: Patman: 3 interlocks w/ Manufacturers Hanover Trust; 1 ea w/ Northern Trust Co.; Bankers Trust; Mellon Natl. Bank & Trust Co. Manufacturers Hanover manages four funds with investments in Union Carbide.

Insurance: Insurance companies owned two million shares. Major holdings: Prudential, 190,000 common, $220.5 m bonds; Metropolitan Life (one interlock), 60,000 common, $205 m notes; NY Life (three interlocks), 146,000 common.

Mutual Funds: Thirty-nine funds held 5.2 million shares or 8.6 percent of the outstanding stock. Major holdings: Fidelity Group, 647,800 (Fidelity Capital Fund, 406,000; Fidelity Fund, 181,800; Fidelity Trend Fund, 60,000); Affiliated Fund, 563,600; Investors Mutual, 309,250.

Foundations: Ford Foundation, 50,000 shares; Andrew W. Mellon Foundation, 47,000 shares; Carnegie Corp., $2.1 million, bonds and notes; Kresge Foundation, $1 million, notes and debentures.

Universities: Universities owned 207,326 shares. Major holdings: Harvard (June 30, 1970), 69,644; Princeton (June 30, 1969), 34,856 (one director interlock); Univ. Pittsburgh (June 30, 1970), 10,200 (one director interlock).

Union Carbide's business is fairly equally divided between chemicals and plastics, and gases and metals. The company was a pioneer in petrochemicals and maintains a leading position in the field. The company produces ethylene from natural gas and petroleum hydrocarbons. Plastic and chemical products are derived from ethylene. In all, the company makes and sells some 800 chemicals, including solvents used in coatings; plasticizers and stabilizers used in plastics; agricultural chemicals, including Sevin insecticide; chemicals used in aerosol sprays; chemicals used in brake fluids; a variety of silicone products; etc.

Union Carbide is a major producer of thermoplastics, used in such end products as polyethylene film for packaging, wire and cable. It provides industrial gases, mainly oxygen and nitrogen, to the steel industry.

The company occupies an important position in the nuclear industry through its production of uranium and because it operates for the Atomic Energy Commission the gaseous diffusion plants and Oak Ridge National Laboratory.

LEADING U.S. NATURAL GAS PIPELINES

EL PASO NATURAL GAS CO.

2727 Allen Parkway, Houston, Tex., 77001.

Basic Company Data

Howard Boyd, Chairman; Hugh F. Steen, President. Directors: Arthur H. Dean, Alfred C. Glassell, Jr., A. R. Grambling, Paul Kayser, Frank L. King, Leon M. Payne, C. L. Perkins, Willard F. Rockwell, Jr., Franz Schneider, Fred T. Wagner, W. Burney Warren, C. R. Williams, Sam D. Young.

Total revenues, 1970, $926.5 million; net income, $37.5 million; stock outstanding, 1970: 26,381,701 shares.

Interlocks

2 ea w/ Transcontinental Gas Pipeline Corp.; Texas Commerce Bank; Phillips Pacific Chemical Co. 1 ea w/ Geonuclear Nobel-Paso, SA; Beaunit Corp.; Greyhound Corp.; INGAA National Petroleum Council; American Gas Association; Phillips Pacific Chemical Assn.; Armour & Co.; Farah Manufacturing Corp.; Pacific Coast Gas Assn.; Southern Gas Assn.; Fed. Res. Bank, Dallas; Glassell Producing Co.; First Natl. City Bank; Downtown Real Estate; H&K Corp.; Andrews, Kerth, Campbell & Jones; Florida Gas Co.; Florida Gas Transmission; Warren Automatic Tool Co.; Wilson Industries; Western Natural Gas Co.; Pacific NW Pipeline Co.; NW Production Corp.; Westcoast Investment Corp.; Pacific NW Realty Corp.; El Paso Natl. Bank; Texas & Pacific Railway; El Paso Times; Hotel Waldorf-Astoria Corp.; First State Bank; Hilton Hotels Corp.; United California Bank; Western Bancorporation; U.S. Borax & Chemical Corp.; Pacific Mutual Life Ins. Co.; Pacific Indemnity Co.; Wilshire Terr. Corp.; Cyprus Mines Corp.; Rockwell Mfg. Co.; North Amer. Rockwell; Midwest Research Institute; Southwest Research Institute; Mellon Natl. Bank; Merex Argentina; Coleman Co.; Penn State; Wolf Sales Pty. Ltd.; Gas Appliance Mfgs. Assn.; TV Station WOED; Sullivan & Cromwell; ADELA Investment Co. SA; American Bank Note Co.; Bank of NY; American Metal Climax; Cornell; Crown Zellerbach; NW Product Corp.; Campbell Soup; National Union Electric Corp.; Newmont Mining; Phelps-Dodge; Continental Oil; El Can Petroleum Co.; Delphi Management Co.; Pacific Northwest Realty Corp.

Ownership Information

Insurance: Insurance companies owned 493,910 shares. Major holdings: Metropolitan, $296.3 m bonds; Aetna, 30,000 common, 20,000 preferred, $48.8 m bonds; NW Mutual, 100,000 preferred, $25.3 m bonds and debentures; Equitable, 39,180 common, $90.4

m bonds and debentures; Travelers, 39,180 common, 20,000 preferred, $40 m bonds and debentures; John Hancock, $41.8 m
bonds and debentures.

Mutual Funds: Seven funds held 493,000 shares or 1.9 percent
of outstanding stock. Major holdings: Puritan Fund, 203,000
shares.

Other: Among the largest security holders listed by the company
with the FPC included: Merrill Lynch, 709,429; Weber & Co.
(First Natl. City Bank NY for El Paso's Employee Savings Plan),
498,233; Walston & Co. (Chemical Bank NY Trust Co.), 322,240;
Edal & Co. (Natl. Shawmut Bank Boston holding for Puritan
Fund), 202,900; William H. Morley, 300,733; Alfred C. Glassell,
Jr., 229,429; Bache & Co., 169,929; Dean Witter & Co., 153,084;
Hare & Co. (Bank of NY holding for American Inv. Fund, Drey-
fus Investment program, LM Rosenthal Fund, Electronics In-
vestment Corp., Fleetwood Securities Corp., Sherman Dean
Fund, Inc., Fairfield Fund, Inc., First Fund of Virginia), 141,-
735; Kenneth S. Adams, Jr., 141,342; C. R. Williams, 73,818.

El Paso was founded in 1928 by Paul Kayser, a Houston attorney,
to carry gas by pipe from Lea County, New Mexico, 240 miles
to El Paso, Texas. Business floundered during the Depression,
and the company pressed westward, running lines to the copper
operations in Arizona. After World War II pipelines were extended into California, and El Paso became the major supplier
to this important market.

Total gas reserves owned or controlled by El Paso in 1970
were 32.8 trillion cubic feet. Total sales by the company pipelines in that year were 1.75 trillion cubic feet. The company
owned 2,047,082 acres in the United States.

Pipelines: The southern portion of the company's pipes, the
Southern System, extends from the Permian Basin in west Texas
and southeastern New Mexico and the panhandle area of Texas

and Oklahoma, across the southern and northern sections of Arizona and New Mexico to the Arizona-California boundary, with connections to the San Juan Basin of northwestern New Mexico and southwestern Colorado. The Southern System delivers gas to customers in west Texas, New Mexico, Arizona, southern Nevada, and California.

Most of the gas carried by the Southern System is sold under long-term contracts to Southern California Gas Co. (a subsidiary of Pacific Lighting Corp., which supplies gas to the Los Angeles area), to the San Diego gas company, and to Pacific Gas & Electric Co. (which sells electricity and gas to the central and northern parts of California, including San Francisco). Natural gas deliveries to Pacific Lighting subsidiaries averaged 1,513 million cubic feet per day and accounted for 32.5 percent of the company's total revenues from the sale of gas. Gas sold to PG&E amounted to 1,090 million cubic feet per day and amounted to 23.6 percent of the company's gas revenues.

Apart from its California customers, the company's Southern System has 116 active customers, of which 61 are utilities and municipalities; 55 are industrial users served directly by the company.

As of 1969, the Southern System comprised 8,201 miles of main and branch transmission pipes and 8,871 miles of field-gathering and supply pipelines. Total annual sales of gas during 1969 for the Southern System were 1.3 trillion cubic feet.

The northern part of El Paso's pipe system, the Northwest System, extends from the San Juan Basin through Colorado, Utah, Wyoming, Idaho, Oregon, and Washington to a point on the Canadian border near Sumas, Washington. In supplying customers in these states, the Northwest System supplies gas to 25 customers, of which 20 are utilities and municipalities purchasing gas for distribution, and five are industrial users. The Northwest System comprises 3,897 miles of main and branch transmission pipes, and 1,018 miles of field-gathering and supply lines. Total sales were 347 billion cubic feet in 1969. The company is under a Supreme Court order to divest itself of the Northwest

System properties. However, it vigorously resists the divestiture, and congressmen from northwestern states have introduced legislation which would permit the company to continue its operations in that area.

El Paso also owns and operates intrastate gas pipelines in central Utah and west Texas.

Principal sources of the company's gas supply are in the Permian Basin area of west Texas and southeastern New Mexico, the panhandle areas of Texas and Oklahoma, Hugoton field in Kansas, San Juan Basin in New Mexico and Colorado, various fields in the Rocky Mountains and Canada.

Canadian gas is purchased from Westcoast Transmission Co., Ltd., and Pacific Gas Transmission Co., a subsidiary of PG&E.

On December 31, 1969, the company owned gas leasehold rights covering 1,995,524 acres in the continental United States. The company owns 21.8 percent of its gas reserves under leasehold interests and controls 78.2 percent under long-term gas purchase agreements with the major oil companies.

Coal: El Paso is a joint owner with Consolidation Coal Co. (Continental Oil) of a 40,000-acre coal lease located on the Navajo Indian Reservation in northwestern New Mexico. The company recently acquired additional coal leases covering some 42,000 acres in southern Utah. It is estimated that these leases contain recoverable reserves of approximately 900 million tons of coal. In 1971 El Paso announced it would build a commercial plant to make synthetic pipeline gas from coal on these lands. The company said it would use a German process, and expects the plant to be in operation by 1976 providing its system with 250 million cubic feet a day.

Algeria: In 1969 El Paso and the Algerian national gas and oil company, Sonatrach, entered into a 25-year agreement under which Sonatrach would build gas facilities in Algeria and El Paso would purchase LNG equivalent to one billion cubic feet of natural gas daily for importation into the United States at

East Coast ports. Shipments would begin in 1974. El Paso Marine Co., a subsidiary, made commitments to build two LNG tankers in France; others were to be purchased in the U.S. Ten tankers probably will be required to handle the trade; they will cost $50 million each. El Paso has contracts for sale of LNG in the United States with Columbia Gas System, Inc., which will construct the onshore gas facilities. The FPC approved the project, but Algeria and El Paso objected to the proposed terms.

Other Operations: Through El Paso Products Co., a subsidiary, the company makes butadiene and syrene for use in plastics and rubber at Odessa, Texas. El Paso Products and Dart Industries are in a joint venture that manufactures olefin and polyolefin, also at Odessa. El Paso Products has a 50 percent interest in Consolidated Thermoplastics Co., which makes plastic film and sheeting. El Paso Products owns phosphate ore deposits in southwestern Idaho, and runs a fertilizer plant there for the manufacture of phosphate fertilizers. The company also sells ammonia to fertilizer markets.

Another subsidiary, Beaunit Corp., works with El Paso Products in the manufacture of "nylon 6/6" for tire cord, rope, home furnishings, and textile fabrics. Beaunit's main business is the manufacture of rayon, polyester, and nylon fibers for textile and industrial products.

Narragansett Wire Co., another subsidiary, fabricates electric copper wire for the building industry and has major offices and manufacturing facilities at Pawtucket, Rhode Island.

El Paso is engaged in a joint venture with Hecla Mining Co., under which the company transferred a 50 percent interest in Lakeshore copper properties south of Casa Grande, Arizona, to Hecla in return for one million shares of Hecla stock and a share in the projected mining revenues.

El Paso is in a joint venture with Diversified Properties, Inc., for development of a 320-acre residential community in Tempe, Arizona.

El Paso has agreements with the Atomic Energy Commission

and Department of Interior for testing to discover whether nuclear explosions can stimulate and increase ultimate production of underground gas. One test has been carried out under Project Gasbuggy. Opponents of the scheme say the gas is radioactive.

Through a subsidiary, El Paso Europe-Afrique, SA, El Paso has a 50 percent holding in Geonuclear Nobel-Paso, a nuclear engineering company incorporated in Geneva, Switzerland in 1969. Other owners are Nobel Bozel France, 25 percent; Dynamit Nobel Germany, 10 percent; Les Poudreries Reunies de Belgique, 8 percent; and Thompson, Hotchkiss, Brandt France, 7 percent. Geonuclear Nobel-Paso is staffed with technicians drawn from the parent companies and is expected to offer a wide range of services in application of nuclear explosives for the simulation of hydrocarbon production and recovery in mining and earth moving techniques, in the fields of public works and civil engineering, and in the underground storage of gas, water, and polluted effluents.

TENNECO, INC.

P.O. Box 2511, Houston, Texas, 77001.

Basic Company Data

N. W. Freeman, President. Directors: Charles W. Hamilton, H. Malcolm Lovett, Herbert Allen, Simon Askin, W. E. Scott, W. D. P. Carey, Henry U. Harris, Jr., Sydney T. Ellis, B. F. Biaggini, Irvin M. Shlenker, Christopher W. Wilson, R. E. McGee.

Total revenues, 1970, $2.5 billion; net income, $157.8 million; average stock outstanding, 1970: 58,403,761 shares.

Taxes

In 1969 Tenneco paid no federal income tax. In that year the company received a $13.2 million tax credit toward reducing future federal income tax.

Interlocks

3 w/ Southern Pacific Co. 1 ea w/ Farmers Natl. Bank; Bayshore Natl. Bank; Gen. Tel. & Elec.; Allen & Co.; First Natl. Bank Chicago; Ceco Corp.; First Chicago Building Corp.; Natl. Safe Deposit Co.; Scott Foresman & Co.; Univ. Chicago; Harris Upham & Co.; Texaco; Chemical Bank NY Trust; Marineland of the Pacific; Stone & Webster; F. Strauss & Son; Strauss Distributors; Terratex Corp.; Highlands State Bank; Gulf Inland Corp.; Nuodex Canada Ltd.; Nuodex France; Salicilatos de Mexico; British Bewoid Co.; Newport Mexicana; Nuodex Intl., Inc.; General Foam Corp.; Genset Corp.; Butler Chemicals Ltd.; Baker & Botts; Cameron Iron Works.

Ownership Information

Banks: Patman: First Natl. City Bank NY manages funds that hold 10.9, 11.5, 5.8, 6.2 percent of four types of Tenneco preferred stock.

Insurance: Insurance companies owned 373,287 shares. Major holdings: Prudential, 16,450 common, $60.7 m notes; John Hancock, 20,000 preferred, $28.5 m debentures; NY Life, $33.4 m bonds and debentures.

Mutual Funds: Twenty-two funds held 2.2 million shares or 3.5 percent of the outstanding stock. Major holdings: Fidelity Group, 426,300 (Fidelity Fund, 200,000; Fidelity Trend, 226,300); Puritan Fund, 330,000.

Other: Among the ten largest security holders as reported to the FPC were: Cede & Co. (Stock Clearing Corp.), 1,906,531; Thrift & Co. (Houston Natl. Bank), 1,815,152; Merrill Lynch, 1,374,288; Stone & Webster, 1,109,149; Paine, Webber, Jackson & Curtis, 531,411; Tenneco Corp., 385,630; Ferro & Co. (Natl. Shawmut Bank of Boston for Fidelity Fund Inc.), 346,100; Edal & Co. (National Shawmut Bank of Boston for Puritan Fund),

293,300; Olen & Co. (First Natl. Bank Chicago), 286,638; Cummings & Co. (Chemical Bank NY Trust Co.), 235,450.

Gardiner Symonds, who began business as a Chicago banker, built this sprawling conglomerate from a natural gas pipeline. Tenneco began as the Tennessee Gas Transmission Co., and now has interests in natural gas, oil, chemicals, insurance, shipyards, agri-business, farm machinery, and international oil exploration.

The Tennessee Gas Pipeline Co., now a relatively minor subsidiary, is a major pipeline, extending from the gas fields of Texas and Louisiana into the Northeast, servicing the New York metropolitan area. The pipeline has storage reservoirs in Pennsylvania and New York. Its principal customers are Columbia Gas System, Inc., Consolidated Natural Gas Co., and National Fuel Gas Co. They accounted for 44 percent of the company's gas deliveries in 1969.

Total reserves available to the system amounted to 17 trillion cubic feet in 1970. Total gas carried in that year amounted to 1.7 trillion cubic feet.

Tenneco owns two other pipelines which connect with the Tennessee Gas system. Midwestern Gas Transmission Co. operates two pipeline systems with 915 miles of line. Midwestern's southern system connects with the Tenneco pipeline near Portland, Tennessee, and extends 364 miles to the Chicago metropolitan area. The northern system connects with Trans Canada Pipelines Ltd., near Noyes, Minnesota, and extends 551 miles to Marshfield, Wisconsin.

East Tennessee Natural Gas Co. has 1,008 miles of pipe in Tennessee and Virginia, which are interconnected to the Tennessee system.

The company also controls an intrastate operator, Chanel Industries Gas Co., a wholly-owned subsidiary, with 471 miles of pipeline serving industrial customers in the Texas Gulf coast area.

The company principally obtains its gas through long-term contracts from major oil companies in Texas, Louisiana, and Mississippi. In 1960 the company bought an interest in oil and gas leases at the Bastian Bay field in Louisiana. That gas goes into its systems. In addition, gas is imported from Canada through an arrangement with Trans Canada Pipe Lines Ltd.

Tenneco Oil Co., a subsidiary, has oil and gas production interests in 14 states, primarily Gulf Coast, Pacific Coast, mid-continent, and Rocky Mountain areas. It also has interests in three western provinces of Canada. The company owns interests in Venezuelan oil production and is exploring in Argentina, Indonesia, Ethiopia, South Africa, Guatemala, Nigeria, Saudi Arabia, Malagasy Republic, the Netherlands North Sea, British North Sea, Labrador and in the Canadian arctic.

Among Tenneco's most valuable oil and gas interests are its holdings acquired through purchase of Kern County Land Company in California.

Tenneco owns a refinery in New Orleans with a daily capacity of 90,000 barrels. Tenneco sells refined products in the southeastern part of the country and along the Atlantic seaboard, in the United Kingdom, and western Europe.

Tenneco brought in a substantial wildcat oil well in the North Sea in 1970, and is drilling off Indonesia in the South China Sea on a block of 26.1 million acres. Drilling off South Africa found natural gas, but activity was suspended for lack of a market.

Chemicals: Tenneco Chemicals, Inc. owns and operates 23 chemicals plants and is engaged in manufacture of industrial chemicals, plastics, urethane foams, dyes, and printing inks.

Petro-Tex Chemical Corp., 50 percent owned, makes butadiene, principal ingredient in the manufacture of synthetic rubber.

Tenneco owns about 10 percent of the stock of Albright & Wilson, Ltd., London, which produces phosphorus. In 1971 the company loaned Albright & Wilson more money under arrangements that could give Tenneco eventual control of the company.

Packaging: Packaging Corp. of America, another subsidiary, makes containers, paperboard, cartons, pulp products. Containers are principally used in packaging goods, paper and paper products, metal products, rubber and plastics, automotive products, etc. It ran 29 corrugated and solid fiber container plants, 15 paperboard machines at eight locations, eight carton plants, three molded-pulp product plants and two plastics operations. Packaging Corp. buys from independent logging contractors. It has leases or cutting rights to 207,000 acres of Michigan forest land. It also owns Tennessee River Pulp & Paper Co., which produces kraft board. Tennessee has a mill at Counce, Tennessee, and owns, leases, or has cutting rights to over 310,000 acres of timberland in Alabama, Mississippi, and Tennessee.

Agriculture and Land Development: Tenneco has extensive landholdings and an elaborate plan for their development, including the building of new towns and a farm-to-market merchandizing scheme. Landholdings total about twice the size of Rhode Island and operations are grouped under a subsidiary, Tenneco Properties, Inc.

In the late 1960s, Tenneco acquired Kern County Land Company, which has large agricultural holdings. These included control of 401,346 acres in California, 1.1 million acres in Arizona, and 149,000 acres in New Mexico. Of this total (1.6 million acres), Kern County has 121,700 acres devoted to irrigated farm lands. The lands in Arizona and New Mexico and a portion of the acreage in California consist of grazing land and are devoted to ranching. The company has substantial water rights on the Kern River in California and maintains an extensive canal system which services both company and other lands.

In 1970 Tenneco acquired Heggblade-Marguleas Co., the San Francisco agricultural management and marketing concern. This company is in charge of all farmlands where the goal is integration from "seedling to supermarket." This is to include a jet-freight delivery scheme for transporting fruits and vegetables. The company has a food-handling facility for prepackaging fruits and vegetables. Cal Date Co., a subsidiary, owns the largest date processing plant in the world. The company acquired 4,500 acres of grapes, bringing total vineyard acres to 9,000. Through its various subsidiaries Tenneco is the largest grower of table grapes in California. It also produces 1.5 million boxes of strawberries, and large quantities of potatoes and citrus fruits. The company is test marketing food products under a single brand name, Sun Giant.

Various Tenneco agri-business enterprises employ between 3,500 and 5,000 farm workers, most of them nonunion. In the past, Tenneco has refused to negotiate with the farm workers organization.

In land development, two subsidiaries manage varied operations. Tenneco West, Inc., manages all lands in the western part of the United States. The company donated 370 acres for a campus of a state college at Bakersfield, California. The initial enrollment is 1,000 students, and the college is expected to expand to 12,000. According to the Tenneco annual report, "The college enhances the value of 6,500 acres of surrounding company land." Tenneco is preparing a master plan for this area as well as for future development of six residential communities. In addition, Tenneco West supervised final plans for Pine Mountain Club, a 3,200-acre recreational community in Los Padres national forest. The project will include 3,000 home sites, a golf course, club house, equestrian center, bridle paths, and outdoor recreational facilities.

Tenneco Realty, Inc., is responsible for development of the company's Houston properties. This includes development of a two-house/garden apartment complex at Post Oak Park, not far from downtown Houston; Park Towers South, one of the two 19-story office towers planned for Post Oak Park, is near completion. Tenneco Realty is completing plans for a 500-acre residential community at Huntington Park, also in Houston.

Both the subsidiaries described above are, in turn, managed by Tenneco Properties, which had additional responsibilities for the real estate operations of Houston National Co. Tenneco has a 40 percent equity interest and a 13 percent voting interest in Houston National Co., corporate parent of Houston National Bank. Houston National subsidiaries own the 33-story Tenneco building in Houston. Houston National and Pic Realty Corp., a subsidiary of Prudential Insurance, are in a joint venture to construct a three-building complex around the Tenneco headquarters. Included in this scheme is a 29-story Regency Hyatt Hotel. A third partner in the realty development, Bank of the Southwest, is participating in building a 15-story garage.

Finally, Tenneco holds an interest in Palmetto Corp., which owns and develops properties in Texas.

Shipping: Tenneco owns Newport News Shipbuilding & Dry Dock Co., which derives 76 percent of its gross revenues from Department of the Navy contracts. In 1971 Newport News was licensed by French shipbuilders to employ their methods in constructing tankers for transporting natural gas. In 1972 Tenneco was negotiating for purchase of Soviet LNG.

Farm Machinery: Tenneco owns Walker Manufacturing Co., which makes exhaust system parts, jacks, and filters. Walker is allied with Mechanex Corp., a Colorado concern that manufactures truck parts. Tenneco also owns J.I. Case, maker of farm and construction equipment, and the J.I. Case Credit Corp., which finances purchase of Case products.

Other interests include a 24 percent holding in Philadelphia Life Insurance Co., which together with subsidiaries San Francisco Life Insurance Co. and Tennessee Life Insurance Co. has $3.5 billion of insurance in force.

Deepsea Ventures, Inc. is a wholly-owned oceanographic firm, which is developing an ocean mining rig for removing metal-bearing nodules from the ocean floor. (Tenneco hopes to put together an international consortium to mine, process, and market metals).

Tenneco also has interests in Qualitron Aero, a firm which provides support and maintenance services to Air Force bases, and is engaged in remodeling Braniff jets.

In addition, it has a uranium mine in south Texas and is manager of an international group operating in western Australia.

In 1971 Westinghouse and Tenneco announced joint plans to build floating nuclear power plants, which would be positioned at sea within the three-mile limit.

/

TEXAS EASTERN TRANSMISSION CORP.

Southern National Bank Building, Houston, Tex. 77002.

Basic Company Data

George R. Brown, Chairman; B.D. Goodrich, President. Directors: John R. Beckett, John F. Lynch, Marsh A. Cooper, Ralph S. O'Connor, George F. Kirby, Herbert J. Frensley, E.H. Tollefson.

Total revenues, 1970, $652.5 million; net income, $59.3 million; average common shares outstanding, 1970: 20,033,662.

Interlocks

Two ea w/ Brown & Root, Inc.; Highland Resources, Inc. 1 ea w/ ITT; Southland Paper Mills Inc.; Halliburton Co.; First City Natl. Bank of Houston; Louisiana Land & Exploration Corp.; Armco Steel; Fannin General Ins. Co.; Gordon Jewelry Corp.; Highland Insurance; Southwestern Pipe Inc.; Baylor College of Medicine; Brown Foundation, Inc.; Gibraltar Savings Assn.; Joe D. Hughes, Inc.; Transamerica Corp.; Occidental Life Ins. Co.; Delaware Turbine Inc.; Transamerica Development Co.; American Life Ins. Co. of NY; Transamerica Ins. Co.; United Artists Corp.; Trans Intl. Airlines; Bank of America; Corpus Christi State Natl. Bank; Southern Natl. Bank, Houston; McIntyre Porcupine Mines Ltd.; Granby Mining Co.; Jefferson Lake Petrochemicals of Canada; Granisle Copper Mines; Jedway Iron Ore Ltd.; Natural Resources Growth Fund; Hardwicke Investment Corp. Ltd.; Wentworth Investment Corp. Ltd.; Maqul of Ireland Ltd.; Bridge & Tank Co. of Canada Ltd.; Home Oil Co.; Crown Life Ins. Co.; Belrust Investment Corp. Ltd.; Falconbridge

Nickel Mines Ltd.; National Trust Co. Ltd.; Canadian Imperial Bank of Commerce; Mining Assn. of Canada; James Buffam & Cooper.

Ownership Information

Banks: Patman: Morgan Guaranty manages one fund which holds 6.7 percent of Texas Eastern preferred stock.

Insurance: Insurance companies owned 265,658 shares. Major holdings: Northwestern Mutual Life, 50,000 shares.

Mutual Funds: Nineteen funds held 22 million shares or 8.3 percent of the outstanding stock. Major holdings: Dreyfus Fund, 482,100; Investors Stock Fund, 278,000; Putnam group, 215,000 (Putnam Fund of Boston, 150,000; Putnam Income Fund, 65,000).

Foundations: Carnegie Corp., $910,000 notes and bonds.

Other: Among the ten largest security holders reported to the FPC, were: Merrill Lynch, 490,706; First Natl. Bank, Shreveport (trustee for employee stock purchase plan), 490,626; Brown Foundation, 368,042; George P. Brown, 350,489; Lerche & Co. (1 Bank of N.Y. for Dreyfus Fund, Lazard Fund), 296,800; John F. Lynch, 219,723; Varley & Co. (Bank of NY), 197,900; Edal & Co. (Natl. Shawmut Bank of Boston holding for Puritan Fund), 153,500; William A. Smith, 152,286; Sail & Co. (State Street Bank & Trust Co. for Putnam Fund group), 150,000.

Texas Eastern was formed in 1947 by a group of Texans, and was successful in bidding for ownership of the government's Big Inch and Little Big Inch pipelines, which had carried petroleum from Texas to the Northeast during World War II. After the war the pipelines were in demand to carry natural gas. The original group included George and Herman Brown. George Brown provided a substantial portion of the initial capital. In 1971 he was chairman and fourth largest stockholder. The Brown Foundation was third largest stockholder, and together they own more stock than any of the other ten largest holders. Brown is also chairman of Brown & Root, the engineering and construction company which si a division of Hallburton. Herbert J. Frensley, a Texas Eastern director, is president of Brown & Root and vice-president of the Brown Foundation. Much of the engineering and construction work for Texas Eastern and its subsidiaries was done or supervised by Brown & Root.

The company operates three major pipeline systems in the United States. Two of them transport natural gas and one moves liquid petroleum products.

The eastern natural gas system involves 8,750 miles of pipelines extending from the Texas and Louisiana Gulf coasts northeastward to the eastern seaboard at New York City. Texas Eastern has a 28 percent holding in Algonquin Gas Transmission Co. Algonquin is the company's second largest customer, and it supplies about half the total New England market, servicing such cities as Boston, New Haven, and Providence.

The company's western natural gas system, operated through Transwestern Pipeline Co., is composed of 3,042 miles of pipelines from West Texas and Oklahoma, across the southwestern states to a connection with a pipeline serving Los Angeles and other cities in southern California. The 3,238-mile liquid petroleum pipeline system, which entends from the Texas Gulf coast to Chicago and eastern New York state, transports a range of products from light heating oils to liquified petroleum gases. Texas Eastern's propane sales organization, Pyrofax Gas Corporation, distributes through 510 sales outlets in 21 states, eastern Canada and Bermuda.

Texas Eastern is part of a group studying the prospects for an arctic gas pipeline. (The other members are Alberta Gas Trunk Line Co. Ltd.; Columbia Gas Systems Inc. and Northern Natural Gas Co.) The pipeline under study would bring gas from Alaska's Prudhoe Bay through Canada to U.S. markets. In North America, Texas Eastern holds a 25 percent interest in a gas well venture in Texas, and is a bidder for offshore Louisiana territories. Together with Pacific Lighting Corp. of Los Angeles, the company is involved in a three-year gas exploration program in West Texas, Arizona, New Mexico, and western Oklahoma. It hit substantial oil and gas deposits in the Atlantic off Nova Scotia. It conducts exploratory drilling in Appalachia and is involved in seismic evaluation of vast offshore regions along the Atlantic coast. Texas Eastern was one of several companies negotiating for Soviet LNG.

In the North Sea Texas Eastern has a 15.38 percent interest in the Gas Council/Amoco Group's Leman Bank Field, which is making steadily increasing gas deliveries to Britain. The group also has the Indefatigable gas field in the North Sea where development drilling is under way. Texas Eastern is part of an Amoco-Noco group which has interests in the Norwegian sector of the North Sea. In 1970 Texas Eastern acquired two concessions aggregating 1.7 million acres on the Atlantic continental shelf offshore from Morocco.

PENNZOIL UNITED INC.

900 Southwest Tower, Houston, Tex., 77002.

Basic Company Data

J. Hugh Liedtke, Chairman; William C. Liedtke, Jr., President. Directors: W.L. Lyons Brown, E. Cockrell, Jr., George L. Coleman, J.D. Stetston Coleman, Boyd N. Everett, James G.S. Gammell, R.B. Gilpatrick, Jr., R.U. Haslanger, Leland F. Johnson, Baine P. Kerr, W.P. Morris, Ed Parkes, Allen M. Shinn.

Total revenues, 1970, $742.4 million; net income, $70 million; outstanding stock, 1970: 19,476,143 shares.

Interlocks

5 w/ Duval Corp. 3 w/ Atlas Processing Co. 2 w/ Ashcraft-Wilkinson. 1 ea w/ Penn Grade Assn.; First Natl. Bank Midland;

Capital Natl. Bank, Houston; Texas Mid-Continental Oil & Gas Assn.; National Petroleum Refiners Assn.; Rice Univ.; U.S. Naval Foundation; Baylor College of Medicine; First Natl. Bank, Shreveport; CNA Financial Corp.; Continental Assurance Co.; Harvard Industries; Mellon Natl. Bank; British Assets Trust, Ltd. (Edinburgh); Ivory & Sime; Whiting Corp.; Western Pacific RR; Morlan Pacific Corp.; Transcontinental Insurance Co.; Sulphur Institute; Potash Institute of N. Amer.; New Mexico Mining Assn.; Brown-Foreman Distillers Corp.; Jack Daniel Distillery; Ashbourne Realty & Land Development Corp.; Commercial Solvents Corp.; Baker & Botts; Bank of the Southwest NA; Riviana Foods, Inc.; First Natl. Bank, Miami (Oklahoma).

Ownership Information

Banks: Patman: State Street Bank & Trust Co., Boston, manages funds which control 7.7 percent of Pennzoil common stock.

Insurance: Insurance companies owned 194,173 shares. Major holdings, 1969: Connecticut General Life, 71,800 shares; 1970: Aetna, $9.2 m debentures; John Hancock, $19 m. debentures.

Mutual Funds: Eighteen funds held 1.3 million shares or 7.1 percent of the outstanding stock. Major holdings: United Group, 351,300 (United Accumulative, 296,300; United Income, 55,000).

Two-thirds of Pennzoil's revenues derive from United Gas Pipe Lines, a natural gas pipeline engaged in interstate commerce. Although the FPC requires that such companies file annual reports revealing the ten largest security holders, United gets around the rules by reporting it is a wholly-owned subsidiary of Pennzoil. Pennzoil files nothing.

The company grew out of a merger in 1968 of Pennzoil Co. and United Gas Corp. The merged company basically explores for and produces oil and gas, markets Pennzoil oil products, and operates a major natural gas pipeline. The pipeline supplies two-thirds of the firm's revenues.

United Gas Pipe Lines and its subsidiary, Pennzoil Pipeline Co., gather and distribute gas in the southeastern part of the country—Louisiana, Mississippi, Alabama, and Florida. The system comprises 10,500 miles. Total gas reserves in 1970 available to the company were 18.4 trillion cubic feet. In 1970 the pipelines transported 1.8 trillion cubic feet. The company also operates a large undersea pipeline, Sea Robin, in the Gulf of Mexico.

Pennzoil's oil reserves are estimated at 126 million barrels. The company produced 12.6 million barrels in 1970. It owns and operates four refineries, in Pennsylvania, West Virginia, and Louisiana. Pennzoil has a 52 percent interest in Eureka Pipeline Co., which has a crude gathering system in West Virginia. It also has a 91 percent interest in National Transit Co., which runs a crude gathering system in Pennsylvania and New York. A new subsidiary explores for oil and gas in the Gulf of Mexico.

Pennzoil is expanding its foreign activities. The company holds 1.6 million acres of leaseholds in Indonesia; 6.1 million acres in Paraguay; 42,500 acres in southern England; 236,000 acres in Brunei, Borneo; 139,824 acres in the Norwegian North Sea; and 109,350 acres in the Dutch North Sea.

Duval, another subsidiary, owns and processes copper, molybdenum, silver, gold, potash, and sulphur deposits in Arizona, Nevada, New Mexico, Texas, and Saskatchewan, Canada.

TRANSCONTINENTAL GAS PIPE LINE CORP.

3100 Travis Street, Houston, Tex., 77001.

Basic Company Data

E. Clyde McGraw, Chairman; James B. Henderson, President. Directors: John F. Burton, Alfred C. Glassell, Jr., Norman V. Kinsey, R.D. Ricketts, Benno C. Schmidt, Franz Schneider, Joseph J. Snyder.

Total revenues, 1970, $399.6 million; net income, $46 million; common stock outstanding, 1970: 22,227,438 shares.

Interlocks

2 w/ El Paso Natural Gas. 1 ea w/ Trans-Southern Pipeline Corp.; Bank of the Southwest; Texas Compressor Corp.; Trans-Jeff Chemical Corp.; Transcontinental Production Co.; J.H. Whitney & Co.; Espurance Land & Development Co. (Australia); Freeport Sulphur; Marine Colloids Inc.; Global Marine, Inc.; Ternaki Offshore Petroleum Co.; Colonial Management Assoc., Inc.; MIT; Michigan Seamless Tube Co.; Boston 5¢ Savings Bank; Gulf States Tube Corp.; Arthur D. Little, Inc.; Liberty Mutual Ins. Co.; Colonial Fund, Inc.; Glassell Producing Co.; First City Natl. Bank; Downtown Real Estate; H&K Corp.; El Paso Products Co.; Newmont Mining; Phelps-Dodge; Univ. Pittsburgh, Continental Oil.

Ownership Information

Insurance: Insurance companies owned 182,747 shares. Major holdings, 1969: Home Ins., 96,940 common. 1970: Metropolitan Life, $65.5 m bonds; NY Life, $17.8 m bonds and debentures; Aetna, 7,200 preferred, $12.9 m bonds and debentures.

Foundations: Kresge Foundation held $1 million in Transco bonds.

Universities: Universities owned 167,349 shares. Major holdings: MIT (September 1969), 62,884 shares; Univ. of Pennsylvania (June 30, 1970), 40,000 shares.

Other: Among the largest security holders as reported to the FPC were: Stone & Webster, 1,991,609; Hamill & Co. (First City Natl. Bank, Houston), 888,831; Salkeld & Co. (Bankers Trust Co. for Gen. Amer. Inv. Co., United Funds Inc., United Science Fund, Petroleum Corp. of America, Johnston Mutual Fund), 366,054; Merrill Lynch, 327,430; Alfred C. Glassell, Jr., 211,394; Mrs. Bess N. Fish, 145,408; R.D. Ricketts, 138,100;

Bid & Co. (New England Merchants Natl. Bank for Boston Fund Inc.), 95,661; Secnato (Bank of the Southwest), 94,973; White, Weld & Co., 94,873; Norman V. Kinsey, 75,000; Kinsey also controls 116,700 shares as trustee of various wills.

Newmont Mining, which has one director interlock with Transco, reported in 1969 ownership of 363,205 shares of Transco common, then worth $6.2 million and representing 1.6 percent of the outstanding stock.

As of July 1, 1970, the company had control of gas reserves totaling 11.9 trillion cubic feet. Gas sales in the year ended June 30, 1970, were 963.8 billion cubic feet.

Transco owns and operates an interstate pipeline system which extends 1,842 miles from the Texas and Louisiana Gulf coasts to the New York-New Jersey-Philadelphia metropolitan areas. The company buys 80 percent of its gas in southern Louisiana; most of the remainder comes from south Texas, with a little from Mississippi. It has an extensive gathering system, including some 650 miles of pipes laid underwater to gas wells offshore Texas and Louisiana in the Gulf of Mexico. Major suppliers of gas to Transco are South Texas Natural Gas Gathering Co., Union Oil Co. of California, Gulf, and Mobil. Most of the gas is sold by Transco to 15 major customers. The largest include Public Service Electric & Gas Co., Newark; Consolidated Edison and Brooklyn Union Gas in New York. The others are Piedmont Natural Gas; Atlanta Gas Light; Long Island Lighting; Philadelphia Gas Works of UGI Corp.; Philadelphia Electric; Pub Service Co. of NC; South Jersey Gas Co.; Elizabethtown Gas Co.; North Carolina Natural Gas; Washington Gas Light; Pennsylvania Gas & Water Co.; Delmarva Power & Light Co.

Alfred C. Glassell, Jr., a director and fifth largest stockholder in the company, also is a director and sixth largest stockholder in El Paso Natural Gas. El Paso's pipelines are from the Southwest to California, with one line going up through the mountain states. The company also plans to import liquified natural gas to

East Coast U.S. ports from Algeria. Imported LNG might eventually compete with gas piped by Transco from the Gulf of Mexico.

The single largest stockholder in Transcontinental is Stone & Webster, the New York securities firm, which also runs a management consulting company for utilities. Stone & Webster also has substantial investments in natural gas. G. Montgomery Mitchell, vice-president of Stone & Webster Management Consultants, was made executive vice-president of Transco in 1971. Stone & Webster is listed as fourth largest stockholder of Tenneco, another major natural gas pipeline which also services the Northeast from Texas and Louisiana.

MAJOR JAPANESE COAL AND IRON ORE SUPPLIER

KAISER INDUSTRIES CORP.

Kaiser Center, 300 Lakeside Drive, Oakland, Calif., 94604.

Basic Company Data

Edgar F. Kaiser, Chairman; E.E. Trefethen, Jr., President. Directors: S.A. Girard, Jack L. Ashby, Clay P. Bedford, Jack J. Carlson, Lloyd N. Cutler, Peter S. Haas, James N. Land, Jr., George E. Link, William Marks, Rudolph A. Peterson, T.J. Ready, Jr., Walter A. Rosenblith, George D. Woods.

Total revenues, 1970, $313.2 million; net income, $23.2 million; average shares outstanding, 1970: 25,882,610.

Interlocks

2 ea w/ First Boston Corp.; Myers Drum; Kaiser Foundation. 1 ea w/ Bank of America; Firearms Fund Ins. Co.; Calif. Inst. Technology; Bancamerica Corp.; Time, Inc.; DiGiorgio Corp.; Standard Oil of Calif.; Kaiser Foundation Health Plan, Inc.;

Kaiser Jeep Corp.; American Motors Corp.; Mahindra & Mahindra, Ltd.; E. Ilin Industries (Israel); Hammersley Iron Pty. Ltd. (Australia); Hammersley Holdings, Ltd.; Thelen, Marrin, Johnson & Bridges; Wilmer, Cutler & Pickering; MIT; Comalco Industries Pty., Ltd.

Ownership Information

Mutual Funds: Fifteen funds held 4.3 million shares or 13.2 percent of the outstanding stock. Major holdings: Investors Stock Fund, one million shares; Windsor Fund, 597,310; Lexington Fund, 312,100; Investment Fund, 312,120.

Foundations: The Henry J. Kaiser Family Foundation in 1970 owned 15,429 shares of preferred stock (and 6,411,231 shares of common stock).

Universities: Universities owned 276,291 shares. Major holdings: Harvard (June 30, 1970), 102,075.

Kaiser Industries and its associated companies are of particular interest because they supply the Japanese with large portions of iron ore and coking coal used in the manufacture of steel. In doing so, the company has established a large-scale operation in Australia and Canada.

Kaiser Industries divisions are engaged in engineering and construction, aerospace and electronics, broadcasting, sand and gravel. In addition, the company has controlling interests in Kaiser Aluminum & Chemical Corp., third largest domestic aluminum company; Kaiser Steel, tenth largest U.S. steel firm; Kaiser Cement & Gypsum Corp., major West Coast producer of cement; and holds 5.5 million shares (22 percent) in American Motors.

Kaiser Aluminum & Chemical owns 45 percent of Comalco, Ltd., which is a major aluminum producer in Australia. It also holds a 37.3 percent interest in Queensland Alumina, Ltd., an aluminum processing plant in Queensland. The other major partner in both projects is Rio Tinto Zinc. Together these two companies literally established the aluminum industry in Australia. Other major aluminum activities are in Jamaica, Ghana, West Germany, Belgium, United Kingdom, and Switzerland. Kaiser has interests in companies that are constructing aluminum plants in Argentina, Bahrain, Brazil, Canada, Japan, Korea, Singapore, Sweden, Thailand, Turkey, and India.

Kaiser Aluminum & Chemical is partners with Aetna Life & Casualty in real estate and land development schemes in various places, including Riverside, California; Hawaii; Ventura County, California; Arizona; and in the San Fernando Valley, California.

The company supplies Japanese steel makers with iron ore from a mine in British Columbia held through Texada Mines Ltd. The company also mines nickel in New Caledonia in a 50 percent partnership with Société le Nickel.

Kaiser Steel owns the only fully integrated steel plant on the West Coast. In connection with operations there, Kaiser Steel mines coal in Utah and New Mexico. The company consumes 80 percent of the coal production and sells the remainder. It recently agreed to provide the Japanese with 650,000 tons of coal from the Utah mine, and from its U.S. operations, Kaiser Steel provides the Japanese with both iron ore and pellets.

Kaiser Steel owns a 34.5 percent interest in Hammersley Holdings, Ltd., which has mining rights in western Australia where reserves are estimated at five billion tons of ore. Kaiser's other major partner is Rio Tinto Zinc. Hammersley has contracts worth $2 billion for delivery of iron ore and pellets to Japan, Europe, and the United States through 1986.

In addition, Kaiser Resources, Ltd., owned 75 percent by Kaiser Steel, has substantial coal holdings in the Crowsnest section of British Columbia. That company has entered into a 15-year contract with the Japanese under which it will provide five million tons of coal.

Both Kaiser Steel and Kaiser Aluminum hold the stock of United International Shipping Corp., which maintains a charter fleet of 15 ships. It also owns 50 percent of National Steel & Shipbuilding Co., a shipbuilding company.

MAJOR WORLD URANIUM PRODUCER

RIO TINTO ZINC CORPORATION, LTD.

6 St. James's Square, London, SW1, England.

Basic Company Data

Sir Val Duncan, Chairman and chief executive; Roy W. Wright, deputy chairman and deputy chief executive. Directors: Sir Mark Turner, R.J.L. Atham, R.D. Armstrong, Hon. R.J. Assheton, Hon. E.L. Ballieu, Rt. Hon. Lord Byers, Rt. Hon. Lord Clitheroe, Gerald Coke, D.R. Colville, A.G. Davies, L.A. Devaux, D.A.C. Dewdney, D. Fredjohn, Sir Basil Goulding, S. Harris, E.S.W. Hunt, M. Littman, Captain J.R.B. Longden, Sir Maurice Mawby, W.D. Mulholland, J.A. Paterson, A.J. Rew, J.R. Robinson, Baron Guy de Rothschild, S. Piro, N.J. Travis.

Total revenues, 1970, £439.4 million ($1 billion); net profit, £48.7 million ($99.3 million); outstanding ordinary shares, 1970: 218,672,270.

Interlocks

2 ea w/ Midland & Intl. Banks, Ltd.; New Broken Hill Consol. Mines; N.M. Rothschild and Sons. 1 ea w/ Commercial Union Assurance Co.; Wm. Mallinson & Sons Ltd.; Whitebread Inn Co.; Nuclear Develop, Ltd.; National Cash Register Co.; Toronto-Dominion Bank; Borax Holdings, Ltd.; Natl. Westminster Bank; John Brown & Co.; Tube Investments, Ltd.; Coutts & Co.; BBC; Rio Algom Mines; Bank of England; Mercantile Investment Trust; Anglesey Aluminum; W&H.M. Goulding Ltd.; Natl. Bank of Ireland; Hibernian Ins. Co. Ltd.; Irish Pensions Trust; British Steel Corp.; Iron & Steel Corp.; Comalco Industries; Interstate Oil Ltd.; Hamersley Holdings Pty. Ltd.; New Court Securities

Corp.; European Property Co. Ltd.; Anglo American Corp. of S.A.; Charter Consolidation; Discount House of South Africa; First Union General Investment Trust Ltd.; General Mining & Financing Corp.; Huletts Sugar Corp.; Industrial Finance Group; Highveld Steel & Vanadium Corp.; Banque Rothschild; Natl. Provincial and Rothschild Intl. Ltd.

Rio Tinto Zinc Corporation (RTZ) is a British-based international group of companies with interests in metals and fuels. The current company is an amalgam of three original enterprises. One was the Rio Tinto Co., which controlled copper/pyrite mines in Spain since the latter part of the nineteenth century. More recently it developed copper in Zambia, and uranium and hydropower in Canada. In 1962 Rio Tinto Co. merged with Consolidated Zinc Corporation. Consolidated Zinc was founded on zinc and lead deposits at Broken Hill in New South Wales, Australia, and had joined Kaiser Industries in building an aluminum industry in Australia. In 1968 the Rio Tinto group merged with Borax Holdings, Ltd., which controlled the world's most valuable borax holdings in California and Nevada.

The resulting combination, RTZ, is a multinational operation functioning as a sort of broker among other giant corporations and governments in seeking to develop the world's natural resources. These relationships involved affiliation with Kaiser Industries in steel and aluminum, an important interest in British Petroleum, longstanding involvements with the Rothschilds, and interconnections with the Anglo American Corporation of South Africa.

The table (pp. 363–365) indicates prominent subsidiaries and affiliates. These other connections should be noted:

RTZ has a 3,876,923 stock unit investment in British Petroleum.

Two RTZ directors, D.R. Colville and Baron Guy de Rothschild are partners of N.M. Rothschild & Sons. In January 1970 Rothschild held 609,398 ordinary RTZ shares, 85,501 cumulative preferred shares, 5,160 CRA shares, and 9,250 Hammersley

Principal Subsidiary and Associated Companies and Investments as of December 31, 1970

RTZ Group

Company and country of principal operations	Class of shares held	Proportion of class held %	RTZ interest in equity capital %	Principal locations	Principal activities
AUSTRALIA					
Conzinc Riotinto of Australia Limited	Ordinary shares of A50c	80·6	80·6	Melbourne, Victoria	Holding and management company
The Zinc Corporation Limited	Ordinary shares of $A2.50	100	80·6	Broken Hill, New South Wales	Lead, zinc and silver mining
New Broken Hill Consolidated Limited [1] Incorporated in the United Kingdom	Shares of 5s (25p)	33·2	26·8	Broken Hill, New South Wales	Lead, zinc and silver mining
Sulphide Corporation Pty. Limited	Ordinary shares of $A2	75	67·2	Cockle Creek, New South Wales	Zinc smelting and refining and lead smelting and sulphuric acid production
The Broken Hill Associated Smelters Pty. Limited [1]	Shares of $A1	50	40·3	Port Pirie, South Australia	Lead smelting and refining: zinc fuming and electrolytic zinc reduction; production of sulphuric acid
Comalco Limited [1]	'B' shares of $A1	100	36·3	Melbourne, Victoria Weipa, Queensland Bell Bay, Tasmania Yennora, New South Wales Perth, Western Australia Adelaide, South Australia, and Brisbane, Queensland	Bauxite mining; primary aluminum smelting; aluminum fabrication
Queensland Alumina Limited [1]	Shares of $A2	—	5·8	Gladstone, Queensland	Alumina production
Hamersley Holdings Limited	Shares of $A25c	54	43·5	Hamersley Ranges and Dampier, Western Australia	Iron ore mining
Bougainville Copper Pty. Limited	Shares of $A1	80	50·1	Bougainville Island, Papua & New Guinea	Development of copper deposit
Mary Kathleen Uranium Ltd.	Ordinary stock	51	41·1	Mary Kathleen, Queensland	Uranium mining (operations suspended at present)

Principal Subsidiary and Associated Companies and Investments as of December 31, 1970 (continued)

RTZ Group

Company and country of principal operations	Class of shares held	Proportion of class held %	RTZ interest in equity capital %	Principal locations	Principal activities
CANADA					
Tinto Holdings Canada Limited	Shares of of no par value	100	100	Ontario	Holding company
Rio Algom Mines Limited	Common shares of no par value	59·5	51·1	Head office: Toronto, Ontario	Holding and management company
				Mining division: Elliot Lake, Ontario	Uranium and copper mining, uranium refining and rare earth chemical production
				Steel division: Welland, Ontario, and Tracy, Quebec	Stainless and specialty steel and alloy manufacture
Lornex Mining Corporation Limited [1]	Common shares of Can $1	50	25·6	Highland Valley, British Columbia	Development of copper/molybdenum deposit
Preston Mines Limited	Class 'A' shares of Can $1	100	—	Timmins, Ontario	Holding company
British Newfoundland Corporation Limited [1]	Common shares of no par value	80·9	80·9	Montreal, Quebec, and St. John's, Newfoundland	Holding and management company:
	Common shares of no par value	49·0	42·7		Mining and mineral exploration
Churchill Falls (Labrador) Corporation Limited [1]	Common shares of no par value	—	24·3	Churchill Falls, Labrador	Hydroelectric power development
Allan Potash Mines	(40% participation in joint venture)			Saskatoon, Saskatchewan	Potash mining and refining
Indal Canada Limited	Common shares of no par value	64·7	64·7	Ontario	Holding and manufacturing company
NETHERLANDS ANTILLES					
Rio Tinto Zinc Finance NV	Shares of US $1,000	100	100	Curaçao	Finance company
SOUTH AFRICA					
Palabora Mining Company Limited	'A' shares of R1	64·8	38·9	Phalaborwa, northeast Transvaal	Copper mining, smelting and refining; vermiculite mining; production of sulphuric acid

Company				Location	Business
Compañía Española de Minas de Rio Tinto SA [1/3]	Shares of Ptas 1,000	33·3	33·3	Near Huelva, southwest Spain	Pyrites mining and sulphuric acid production; oil refining and petrochemicals production
UNITED KINGDOM					
Imperial Smelting Corporation Limited [2]	Ordinary shares of £1	100	100	Bristol	Holding and management company
Imperial Smelting Corporation (NSC) Limited	Ordinary shares of £1	100	100	Avonmouth, Swansea and Burry Port	Zinc smelting and refining and lead smelting, sulphuric acid and chemical manufacture
British Titan Limited [1]	Ordinary shares of £1	30·4	30·4	(Various)	Titanium pigments production
Anglesey Aluminum Limited	Ordinary shares of £1	70	43	Holyhead	Production of primary aluminum
R.T.Z. Pillar Limited [2]	Ordinary shares of 2s (10p)	100	100	London and Cheltenham	Holding and management company
Borax Consolidated Limited	Ordinary shares of £1	100	100	London, Belvedere and Chessington	Borax refining, marketing and research
Capper Pass & Son Limited [2]	6% Cumulative Preference shares of £1	100	—	North Ferriby	Tin smelting and refining; production of solders and alloys'
	Ordinary shares of £1	100	100		
Rio Tinto Finance & Exploration Limited [2]	Ordinary shares of £1	100	100	London (and overseas centers)	Holding of short-term investments: mineral exploration
The British Petroleum Company Limited [1]	Ordinary stock	1·1	1·1	(Various)	Oil production, refining and distribution
UNITED STATES OF AMERICA					
United States Borax & Chemical Corporation	Common shares of US $1	100	100	Los Angeles and Boron, California	Borax mining, refining, marketing and research
Rio Tinto Zinc Corporation of America	Shares of no par value	100	100	Delaware	Holding company

NOTES

1. Companies marked [1] are associated companies or investments. Associated companies are those in which RTZ holds 25 percent or more of the ordinary shares and plays a significant part in the management of the company's affairs, or where the investment is in the nature of a partnership.
2. Holdings in companies marked [2] are held directly by RTZ or its nominees. All others are held by subsidiaries of RTZ or their nominees.
3. As of December 31, 1970, the exchange of shares resulting from the merger between Compañía Española de Minas de Rio Tinto SA and Union Española de Explosivos had not been completed.
4. The companies listed above include those whose results or assets, in the opinion of the directors, principally affected the profits or assets of the Group. Except where otherwise stated, all companies are incorporated in the countries in which they principally operate.

SOURCE: Annual Report, Rio Tinto Zinc Corp., Ltd., 1970.

shares. In December, 1970, Colville held 44,068 ordinary shares, 1,102 Hammersley shares.

Charter Consolidated Co., an affiliate of the Anglo American Corporation of South Africa, has a major undisclosed holding in Rio Tinto Zinc. This is of interest because both RTZ and Anglo American are deeply involved in uranium markets.

RTZ's major operations are in Australia, where 44.5 percent of its assets are committed; North America, with 24.1 percent; and Great Britain, with 20.9 percent. In terms of industries, iron accounts for 23.9 percent of the business; copper, 18.9 percent; aluminum, 12.8 percent; lead and zinc, 10.2 percent, and borax, 10 percent.

Iron ore: Hammersley Iron Pty. Ltd., based in Western Australia, is the single largest supplier of iron ore and pellets to the Japanese steel industry, with long-term contracts worth $1.4 billion. There are also contracts to supply iron ore to the United Kingdom, West Germany, Holland, Italy, France, Belgium, Greece, and the United States. The company installed a deep water port to handle ships up to 100,000 tons at Dampier, built a 182-mile railway to service the port, and constructed two townships to house workers. Hammersley is owned 54 percent by CRA (the local RTZ company) and 36 percent by Kaiser Steel Corp., a subsidiary of Kaiser Industries. RTZ's other major steel operation is in Canada where Atlas Steels, a division of Rio Algom, supplies specialty steels for both the U.S. and Canadian markets.

Copper: In northeast Transvaal, RTZ has a 39 percent interest in Palabora open-cast copper mine, which produces 80,000 short tons a year. Half of that production is sold to West Germany. In addition to RTZ, other companies with an interest in Palabora mine include Newmont Mining Corp., Selection Trust (in which Anglo American has a substantial holding), and Union Corp., as well as other South African investors. On Bougainville Island in Papua and New Guinea, Bougainville Copper Pty. Ltd., an affiliate, is putting into operation a new copper mine expected to produce 150,000 tons of copper a year. It will supply Japanese copper smelters, and West German and Spanish markets. In Canada both Rio Algom and British Newfoundland Corporation, Ltd. (Brinco) control and manage various copper deposits. In the United States, Pyrites Co., Inc., based in Delaware, produces copper from leach liquors supplied by Bethlehem Steel.

Aluminum: RTZ and Kaiser Aluminum & Chemical Co. own equally Comalco Industries Pty. Ltd., which in turns controls one of the world's largest bauxite deposits at Weipa, in the northern tip of Queensland, Australia, with reserves of over two billion tons. About half the bauxite is exported to Japan and Europe. The other half is refined in Australia. The most important refining plant is operated by Queensland Alumina Ltd. Its ownership is 16 percent Comalco, with other partners, including Kaiser Aluminum, Alcan Aluminum of Canada, and Pechiney of France. Comalco plans to increase its production in Australia by establishing a new consortium, and to begin a plant in Sardinia where it has a 16.7 percent interest in a consortium.

A new company, RTZ-BICC Aluminum Holdings, Ltd., owned by RTZ and British Insulated Callenders Cables Ltd., will build an aluminum reduction plant at Anglesey. This project will be owned by RTZ-BICC and Kaiser Aluminum and called Anglesey Aluminum Ltd.

Uranium: Through Rio Algom Mines, Ltd., RTZ is at the heart of the Canadian uranium industry, at one point running seven of 11 integrated mining and milling operations around Elliot Lake in Ontario's Algoma district. Deposits in this area form the single largest concentration of uranium reserves in the West. Since the formation of Rio Algom, in 1960, the company produced nearly 38 million pounds of uranium oxide. Long-term commitments are close to 50 million pounds.

In the United States, Rio Algom is developing a uranium mine at Moab, Utah, with anticipated annual output of 1.2 million pounds of uranium oxide. This will establish Rio Algom Corporation, a subsidiary of Rio Algom Mines, Ltd., as a supplier in the United States, a market that has previously been closed to foreign interests. A first contract for part of the mine's production is with Duke Power Co. Rio Algom is also drilling for uranium in Wyoming with Mitsubishi. In Canada Rio Algom and other RTZ affiliates are pressing the search for uranium in Elliot Lake, Labrador, and northern Quebec. In South Africa, RTZ is engaged in pilot tests at Rossing in South West Africa.

In Australia, RTZ controls and manages Mary Kathleen Uranium, which was taken out of uranium production in 1963. However, the government approved an export contract for 5,000 tons of uranium oxide. Finally, RTZ has investments in nuclear-industry companies in Britain, Germany, Belgium, and Austria.

Oil and Gas: RTZ has a substantial investment in British Petroleum. In Australia RTZ participates through Interstate Oil and other companies. In the United Kingdom, five production licenses are held by RTZ in conjunction with Hamilton Brothers and two other British companies for exploration in the North Sea. One discovery of natural gas has been made.

Coal: Through its Australian affiliated CRA, RTZ has a majority holding in and manages the Blair Athol group of companies, which control a coal deposit estimated at 250 million tons in Queensland.

Hydroelectric Power: In Canada RTZ has a 40 percent equity in Brinco through Thornwood Investments, Ltd., its joint holding company with Bethlehem Steel. Brinco's major project, operated through its subsidiary Churchill Falls (Labrador) Corporation, Ltd., is developing a 7-million-horsepower hydroelectric plant for supply of electricity from the Churchill Falls in Labrador. Construction began in 1967, and first power deliveries are scheduled for 1972. This is one of the largest power projects ever undertaken, and involved the raising of Canadian $1 billion. (Half of that was raised through sale of first mortgage bonds in the United States, and $300 million in Canada.)

Brinco is also interested in developing a uranium enrichment plant. Uranium enrichment requires vast amounts of electric power, and this combine has the power necessary to supply such an installation.

MAJOR WORLD URANIUM PRODUCER

ANGLO AMERICAN CORPORATION OF SOUTH AFRICA

44 Main Street, Johannesburg, South Africa.

Basic Company Data

H.F Oppenheimer, Chairman; Sir Keith Acutt, W.D. Wilson, joint deputy chairmen. Directors: D.O. Beckingham, F.S. Berning, E.T.S. Brown, Sir Frederick Crawford, G.C. Fletcher, W.S. Gallagher, M.B. Hofmeyr, Sir Philip Oppenheimer, G.W.H. Relly, Sir Albert Robinson, M.W. Rush, J.W. Shilling, S. Spiro, J. Ogilvie Thompson, G.H. Waddell, D.A.B. Watson.

Interlocks

7 w/ De Beers Consol. Mines. 4 ea w/ Discount House of SA; Charter Consolidated, Ltd.; S. Oppenheimer & Sons, Ltd. 3 ea w/ Baart & Hard Metal Products SA; Rand Selection Corp. 2 ea w/ General Mining & Finance Corp.; African Explosive & Chemical Industries; Hudson's Bay Mining & Smelting Co., Ltd.; Ultra High Pressure Units Ltd.; Highveld Steel & Vanadium Corp.; Industrial Finance Corp. of SA; Johannesburg Consol. Invest. Co.; Orange Free State Investment Trust; West Rand Investment Trust. 1 ea w/ De Beers Holdings, Ltd.; Capetown Univ.; Williamson Diamonds; Barclays Bank; Banque de Paris et des Pays-Bas; Canadian Imperial Bank of Commerce; Free State Geduld Mines, Ltd.; Industrial Distributors Ltd.; Banque Belge Ltd.; British Diamond Distributors; British S. African Co., Canadian Rock Co.; Central Mining & Investment Corp.; Consol. African Selection Trust; Diamond Corp., Ltd.; Facts; Gardner Steel Ltd.; Shannon Diamond & Carbide Ltd.; Sierra Leone Selection Trust; First Union General Investment Trust; Swaziland Iron Ore Develop. Co.; Huletts Sugar Corp.; Pacific Corp. Ltd.;

Rio Tinto Zinc; Rustinberg Platinum Mines; Argus Printing & Publishing Co.; Standard Bank SA; Rand American Investment Fund; Rand Mines Ltd.; African & European Invest. Co.; Natl. Finance Corp.

Ownership Information

Anglo American Corporation of South Africa is the lead company in a group of investment, mining, and industrial concerns, and it is the main vehicle for the activities of Harry F. Oppenheimer, the gold magnate. Anglo American is the leading gold producer in the world; historically it has been the Oppenheimer family firm. From time to time Oppenheimer engaged in ventures with his American friend, Charles W. Engelhard, the New Jersey businessman and politician. In 1969 Oppenheimer bought a majority interest in Engelhard Hanovia, the Engelhard family's holding company. That purchase gave the Anglo American group control over Engelhard Minerals and Chemicals Corp., the New Jersey concern which is the world's leading producer of precious metals. Until his death in 1970 Engelhard himself maintained sizable investments in the Anglo American group and was a director of the South African company.

The Anglo American group consists of a large number of firms which depend on it for management and administration but in which Anglo American has less than 50 percent interest. In addition, the corporation is closely associated with Charter Consolidated in London, through which the group channels its international investments outside Africa, and De Beers Consolidated Mines, the diamond mining enterprise in South Africa.

Investments are made mainly through specialized investment arms: Orange Free State Investment Trust and West Rand Investment Trust for gold mining companies in those areas; Anglo American Investment Trust for diamond mining and marketing; Anglo American Industrial Corporation for industrial and commercial holdings, etc.

In 1970 the group mines were responsible for 40 percent of

South Africa's gold production, which amounted to 31 percent of the world production. Anglo American mines provided 30 percent of South Africa's coal and uranium. In Zambia, mines managed by the company produced 58 percent of that country's copper, equivalent to 6 percent of the world's supply.

More than half the shares of the corporation are held in South Africa. About 42 percent are in Great Britain and other European countries.

Fuels: Production of uranium oxide by group mines in 1970 totaled 1,178 metric tons, and while there was a glut of uranium on the market, the company expects demand to increase by the mid-1970s.

The group operates 12 collieries in southern Africa and has important interests in five others. In addition to supplying coal for electricity in South Africa, the group mines will supply 10 million tons of a 27.8 million ton contract with the Japanese.

Anglo American's position in the fuels industry is enhanced because of its interconnection with General Mining & Finance. The latter company provides about one-third of all uranium and is active in coal as well.

Charter Consolidated: Administered outside the group in London, Charter Consolidated has assets of $800 million and is the major vehicle for spearheading the group's investments outside Africa. For example, Charter has an 8 percent holding in Rio Tinto Zinc. That share is augmented by two million shares of RTZ held by other investment trusts which Charter controls.

Charter has a 24.7 percent interest in Anglo American Corp. of Canada, Ltd., a mining finance company, which owns 28 percent of Hudson's Bay Mining & Smelting Co., Ltd. The latter company is involved in copper and zinc production and has oil and gas interests. Charter also holds 44.7 percent of Western Decalta Petroleum, Ltd., also engaged in Canadian oil and gas ventures. In Australia, Charter has several exploration ventures, including a 30 percent interest in a merchant banking company, International Pacific Corp., Ltd.

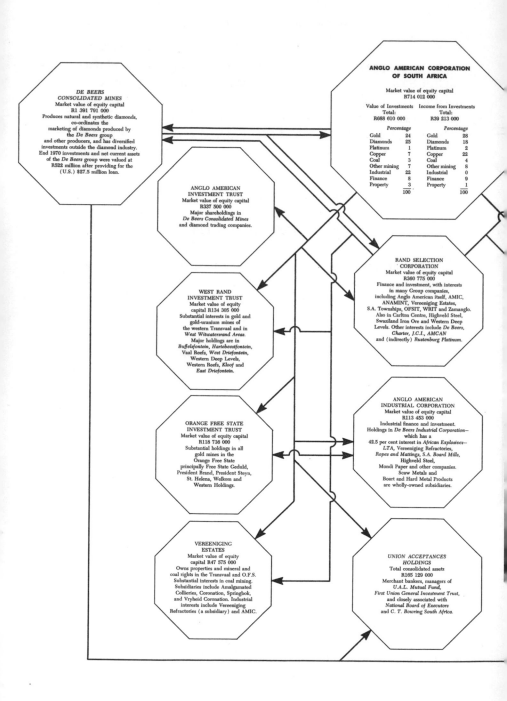

DE BEERS CONSOLIDATED MINES
Market value of equity capital
R1 391 791 000
Produces natural and synthetic diamonds,
co-ordinates the
marketing of diamonds produced by
the De Beers group
and other producers, and has diversified
investments outside the diamond industry.
End 1970 investments and net current assets
of the De Beers group were valued at
R522 million after providing for the
(U.S.) $27.5 million loan.

ANGLO AMERICAN CORPORATION OF SOUTH AFRICA
Market value of equity capital
R714 012 000

	Value of Investments Total: R688 610 000	Income from Investments Total: R39 213 000
	Percentage	Percentage
Gold	24	Gold 28
Diamonds	25	Diamonds 18
Platinum	1	Platinum 2
Copper	7	Copper 22
Coal	3	Coal 4
Other mining	7	Other mining 8
Industrial	22	Industrial 0
Finance	8	Finance 9
Property	3	Property 1
	100	100

ANGLO AMERICAN INVESTMENT TRUST
Market value of equity capital
R337 500 000
Major shareholdings in
De Beers Consolidated Mines
and diamond trading companies.

RAND SELECTION CORPORATION
Market value of equity capital
R360 775 000
Finance and investment, with interests
in many Group companies,
including Anglo American itself, AMIC,
ANAMINT, Vereeniging Estates,
S.A. Townships, OFSIT, WRIT and Zamanglo.
Also in Carlton Centre, Highveld Steel,
Swaziland Iron Ore and Western Deep
Levels. Other interests include De Beers,
Charter, J.C.I., AMCAN
and (indirectly) Rustenburg Platinum.

WEST RAND INVESTMENT TRUST
Market value of equity
capital R134 305 000
Substantial interests in gold and
gold-uranium mines of
the western Transvaal and in
West Witwatersrand Areas.
Major holdings are in
Buffelsfontein, Hartebeestfontein,
Vaal Reefs, West Driefontein,
Western Deep Levels,
Western Reefs, Kloof and
East Driefontein.

ANGLO AMERICAN INDUSTRIAL CORPORATION
Market value of equity capital
R113 453 000
Industrial finance and investment.
Holdings in De Beers Industrial Corporation—
which has a
42.5 per cent interest in African Explosives—
LTA, Vereeniging Refractories,
Ropes and Matting, S.A. Board Mills,
Highveld Steel,
Mondi Paper and other companies.
Scaw Metals and
Boart and Hard Metal Products
are wholly-owned subsidiaries.

ORANGE FREE STATE INVESTMENT TRUST
Market value of equity capital
R118 736 000
Substantial holdings in all
gold mines in the
Orange Free State
principally Free State Geduld,
President Brand, President Steyn,
St. Helena, Welkom and
Western Holdings.

VEREENIGING ESTATES
Market value of equity
capital R47 575 000
Owns properties and mineral and
coal rights in the Transvaal and O.F.S.
Substantial interests in coal mining.
Subsidiaries include Amalgamated
Collieries, Coronation, Springbok,
and Vryheid Coronation. Industrial
interests include Vereeniging
Refractories (a subsidiary) and AMIC.

UNION ACCEPTANCES HOLDINGS
Total consolidated assets
R165 129 000
Merchant bankers, managers of
U.A.L. Mutual Fund,
First Union General Investment Trust,
and closely associated with
National Board of Executors
and C. T. Bowring South Africa.

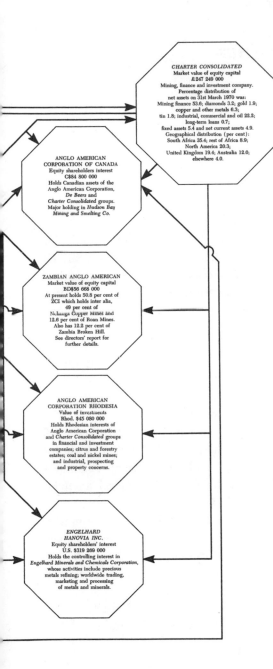

CHARTER CONSOLIDATED
Market value of equity capital
£247 249 000
Mining, finance and investment company.
Percentage distribution of
net assets on 31st March 1970 was:
Mining finance 53.6; diamonds 3.2; gold 1.9;
copper and other metals 6.3;
tin 1.8; industrial, commercial and oil 22.2;
long-term loans 0.7;
fixed assets 5.4 and net current assets 4.9.
Geographical distribution (per cent):
South Africa 35.4; rest of Africa 8.9;
North America 20.3;
United Kingdom 19.4; Australia 12.0;
elsewhere 4.0.

ANGLO AMERICAN
CORPORATION OF CANADA
Equity shareholders interest
C$84 800 000
Holds Canadian assets of the
Anglo American Corporation,
De Beers and
Charter Consolidated groups.
Major holding in Hudson Bay
Mining and Smelting Co.

ZAMBIAN ANGLO AMERICAN
Market value of equity capital
BD$56 668 000
At present holds 50.8 per cent of
ZCI which holds inter alia,
49 per cent of
Nchanga Copper Mines and
12.6 per cent of Roan Mines.
Also has 12.2 per cent of
Zambia Broken Hill.
See directors' report for
further details.

ANGLO AMERICAN
CORPORATION RHODESIA
Value of investments
Rhod. $45 080 000
Holds Rhodesian interests of
Anglo American Corporation
and Charter Consolidated groups
in financial and investment
companies; citrus and forestry
estates; coal and nickel mines;
and industrial, prospecting
and property concerns.

ENGELHARD
HANOVIA INC.
Equity shareholders' interest
U.S. $319 269 000
Holds the controlling interest in
Engelhard Minerals and Chemicals Corporation,
whose activities include precious
metals refining; worldwide trading,
marketing and processing
of metals and minerals.

MAJOR ELECTRIC UTILITIES

TENNESSEE VALLEY AUTHORITY

Knoxville, Tenn.

Basic Company Data

Aubrey J. Wagner, Chairman. Directors: Frank E. Smith, Don McBride.

In fiscal 1971 (July 1, 1970 to June 30, 1971) TVA sold 90.6 billion kilowatt-hours, about the same as the previous year. Of that amount 55.5 billion kilowatt-hours went to 160 municipal and cooperative electric systems distributing TVA power to two million customers in parts of seven states, including homes, farms, business, and industry.

About 40 large industries are served directly by TVA. Sales to industry totaled 21.3 billion kilowatt-hours. Sales to federal installations, including the AEC, TVA's biggest single customer, were 12.4 billion kilowatt-hours. Sales to electric utilities accounted for another 1.4 billion kilowatt-hours.

In fiscal 1971, the TVA markets broke down as follows: 1.9 million residential customers purchased 27,291 billion kwh for $332.5 million; 236,687 industrial and commercial customers bought 45.5 billion kwh for $381.2 million; 11 federal agencies purchased 12.4 billion kwh for $65 million.

One of TVA's major campaigns is to add all-electric homes in its districts. There are 637,000 homes using TVA power for space heating, or one out of every three residential customers in the region. Nationally only about one of every 14 homes is heated electrically.

The largest industrial customers include Air Reduction Co., Inc.; Alcoa; Consolidated Aluminum Corp.; Reynolds Metals

Co.; Monsanto Co.; Satuffer Chemical Co.; Union Carbide; Texas Eastern Transmission.

About three-quarters of TVA power comes from coal-fired plants. TVA began installing coal-fired plants during the 1950s when the hydroelectric potential of the Tennessee River had been developed, and during a period of rapid expansion by its biggest single customer, the AEC.

TVA is the largest coal purchaser in the nation, accounting for about 10 percent of the utility coal markets. TVA burned 32.5 million tons of coal at its steam plants in 1971 and expects to require between 35 and 40 million tons each year during the remainder of this decade. Coal contracts totaled $325 million during the fiscal 1971, "most of it representing awards during the period from July to December 1970, when the need for coal to rebuild stockpiles was critical. Prices during that period were generally 50 to 100 percent above 1968 levels."

Coal deliveries to TVA plants during the year included 22.3 million tons from west Kentucky, 4.8 million tons from Illinois, 4.5 million tons from east Kentucky, 4.4 million tons from Tennessee, about one million tons from Alabama, 766,000 tons from Virginia, and 371,000 tons from Indiana.

Ten leading coal suppliers accounted for 75 percent of coal. They are by rank: Peabody Coal (Kennecott), 22.7 percent; Island Creek (Occidental), 11.8 percent; Kentucky Oak Mining (Falcon Seaboard), 9.1 percent; American Metal Climax, 7.6 percent; Pittsburgh & Midway (Gulf Oil), 6.2 percent; Old Ben Coal (Sohio), 5.6 percent; Ben & Zollar Coal Co. (Zeigler Coal Co.), 6.3 percent; Arch Minerals (Ashland Oil), 3.7 percent; Freeman Coal(General Dynamics), 2 percent; Webster County Coal (Mapco), 1.9 percent.

Partly because of difficulty in persuading coal companies to bid on long-term contracts, TVA is mining its own coal reserves. Of the 16 million megawatts of power under construction or planned, 11 megawatts are to be nuclear, thus signifying a major shift away from coal. TVA and the Commonwealth Edison of

Chicago together will build a breeder reactor financed by the government. The utility is also investigating the possibility of arranging for its own supplies of uranium through control of leases and is also looking into the possibility of gasifying coal.

CONSOLIDATED EDISON CO. OF NEW YORK, INC.

4 Irving Place, New York, N.Y., 10003.

Basic Company Data

Charles F. Luce, Chairman; Louis H. Roddis, Jr., President. Directors: E. Virgil Conway, John Doar, Frederick M. Eaton, Grayson L. Kirk, Hobart D. Lewis, Milton C. Mumford, J. Wilson Newman, Richard K. Paynter, Jr., Richard S. Perkins, William S. Renchard, Lawrence A. Wien, James D. Wise.

Total revenues, 1970, $1.1 billion; net income, $94.2 million; common shares outstanding, 1970: 42.4 million.

Interlocks

4 w/ New York Life. 3 w/ Chemical Bank NY Trust Co. 2 each w/ First Natl. City Bank NY; Seamans Bank. 1 ea w/ Shearman & Sterling; Monsanto Co.; Commonwealth Fund; IBM; Mobil; Dividend Shares; Nation-wide Securities; Greenwich Savings Bank; Bigelow-Sanford Inc.; Wien, Lane & Malkin; Hammermill Paper Co.; Borden Inc.; Armstrong Rubber; Foote Mineral Co.; ITT; Southern Pacific; Hospital Corporation of America; Allied Chemical Corp.; Delaware & Bound Brook RR; Otis Elevator; Penn-Reading Seashore Lines; Dun & Bradstreet; Atlantic Mutual Insurance Co.; General Foods Corp.; Mutual Life Insurance; Reuben H. Donnelley Corp.; Fidelity Union Trust Co.; Lever Brothers; Equitable Life Assurance; Crown Zellerbach; Federal Reserve Bank NY; Unilever Ltd.; Thomas J. Lipton Inc.; Natl. Securities & Research Corp.; Reader's Digest; Bedford Stuyvesant Develop. & Services Corp.

Ownership Information

Banks: Patman: First Natl. City Bank NY, Morgan Guaranty, and Chemical Bank NY Trust each manage one trust with investments in Con Ed. First Natl. City Bank owns 6.1 percent of preferred 4.65 stock; Morgan Guaranty owns 7 percent of preferred 5.75 stock.

Insurance: Insurance companies owned 409,794 shares. Major holdings: Metropolitan, 569,000 shares (five kinds of preferred stock), $40.6 million bonds; Equitable, 200,000 shares (two kinds preferred), $6 million bonds; NW Mutual, 350,000 shares (two kinds preferred), $939,120 bonds; Aetna, $14.3 million bonds; Prudential, $11.4 million bonds; NY Life, 229,500 shares (three kinds preferred), $29.6 million bonds.

Mutual Funds: Three funds held 110,000 common shares or 0.3 percent of the outstanding stock.

Foundations: Ford Foundation, $2 million bonds; Carnegie Corp., $1 million bonds and notes; Kresge Foundation, $1.4 million bonds and notes; Kellogg Foundation, $300,000 bonds and notes.

Other: The largest security holders as reported to the FPC included: Cede & Co. (Stock Clearing Corp.), 1,971,692 common shares; Merrill Lynch, 916,108 common shares, 30,032 preferred shares; Sigler & Co. (Manufacturers Hanover holding for Canadian Intl. Growth Fund, Channing Funds, Gen. Pub. Serv. Corp., Institutional Growth Fund group, U.S. & Foreign Securities Corp.), 155,348 common shares, 20,373 preferred shares; Bache & Co., 144,483 common shares, 6,137 preferred shares; Loeb Rhoades & Co., 114,143 common shares, 3,418 preferred shares; Gunther & Co. (for Swiss Bank Corp.), 105,733 common shares; NV Administratiekantoor Opgericht Door Heldring & Pierson

En Broekmans Effectenkantoor, 104,910 common shares; Egger & Co. (Chase Manhattan Bank), 102,070 common shares; Cudd & Co. (Chase Manhattan Bank for Amer. Mutual Fund, Chemical Fund, Equity Fund, Intl. Resources Fund, Investment Co. of America), 91,914 common shares, 9,123 preferred shares; Salkeld & Co. (Bankers Trust Co. for Gen. Amer. Investors Co., Johnston Mutual Fund, Petroleum Corp. of America, United Funds), 94,575 common shares, 4,170 preferred shares; Atwell & Co. (United States Trust Co.), 84,146 common shares, 6,721 preferred shares.

Con Ed supplies electric service throughout the five boroughs of New York City and in about 70 percent of Westchester County. Gas service is supplied in Manhattan and the Bronx, in parts of Queens, and in the more populous parts of Westchester County. Steam service is supplied in part of Manhattan. About 84 percent of operating revenue is derived from electricity, 11 percent from gas, and 5 percent from steam.

As of February 1, 1971, the net generating capacity of the company was 8,989,000 kilowatts. Of this capacity, 7,486,000 kilowatts represented fossil fuel plants; 260,000 kilowatts from Indian Point, which is nuclear and oil-fired; and 1,243,000 kilowatts from gas turbines.

During 1970, 65 percent of the fuel used by Con Ed was oil, 19 percent was gas, 15 percent coal, and 1 percent nuclear. Since then the company phased out its coal-fired plants.

Major suppliers of oil are New England Petroleum, Jersey Standard, and Hess. Natural gas is supplied from three pipelines —Transcontinental, Texas Eastern, and Tenneco.

The single largest customer for electricity is New York Transit Authority. Other major users are office building complexes.

Con Ed's 20-year plan (1971–1990) envisions growth of about 450,000 kilowatts per year. "The new program recognizes the very serious delays that are besetting the licensing of nuclear plants by postponing until the next decade the construction of nuclear unit 4 which in our 1969 plan had been scheduled for this decade."

Con Ed predicts demand for electricity will grow from the 7,950,000 kilowatts peak in 1971 to more than 17 million kilowatts by 1990. The company estimates a 5.7 percent growth in peak demand next year, declining to an average 4.2 percent in the 1975–1980 period and 3.9 percent in the 1980–1985 period.

In an effort to encourage customers to conserve electricity Con Ed discontinued its sales program, proposed revisions in the rate structures to reduce quantity discounts, and engaged in educational campaigns.

Facilities under construction for the early 1970s included two 350,000 kilowatt peaking gas turbines on barges at the Brooklyn waterfront; 800,000 kilowatts in two units at Haverstraw; 1,840,- 000 kilowatts at Indian Point units two and three; 480,000 kilowatts representing the company's share in two units at Newburgh; 800,000 additional capacity at Astoria. The company is also making a 500,000 kilovolt (kv) connection to Pennsylvania-New Jersey-Maryland (PJM) system, a 345 kv tie with Public Service Electric & Gas, and a 345,000 kv tie to upstate utilities.

During the second half of the 1970s and early 1980s, the company plans to construct a two million kilowatt pumped storage hydroelectric project at Cornwall; a 1.2 million oil-fired station on the lower Hudson, and 700,000 kilowatts of additional peaking gas turbines. For the latter part of the 1980s, "We presently foresee as new sources of electric energy a series of base load plants, probably nuclear, possible island-based or barge-mounted, together with advanced design gas turbines, and perhaps a beginning on fuel cells, MHD [magnetohydrodynamics generation], and breeder reactors."

The company is participating in studies that could lead to the importation of 500,000 kilowatts from Hydro Quebec in 1977, either by straight purchase or through seasonal exchange. There has been some indication that Quebec might have additional power for sale from new projects such as James Bay.

In 1972 Con Ed will spend $7 million on research and development compared to $2.2 million in 1971.

COMMONWEALTH EDISON CO.

72 West Adams Street, Chicago, Ill., 60690.

Basic Company Data

J. Harris Ward, Chairman; Thomas G. Ayers, President. Directors: Norris A. Aldeen, John A. Barr, Joseph L. Block, Lowell T. Coggeshall, Gordon R. Corey, Albert B. Dick, III, George E. Johnson, Brooks McCormick, Morgan F. Murphy, Edward Byron Smith, Joseph S. Wright.

Total revenues, 1970, $881.8 million; net income, $134.3 million; common shares outstanding, 1970; 42,487,648.

Interlocks

4 w/ Northern Trust Co. 2 ea w/ Inland Steel; First Natl. Bank Chicago; Univ. Chicago; Continental Illinois Natl. Bank & Trust; Illinois Institute of Technology; Swift & Co.; Intl. Harvester. 1 ea w/ S. C. Johnson & Son; Stewart-Warner Corp., Marlennan Corp.; Zenith Radio Corp.; Standard Oil Indiana; NY Life Insurance; Union Carbide; Illinois Tool Works; Federal Reserve Chicago; Western Reserve Life Assurance Co.; Talman Federal Savings & Loan Assn. Chicago; Central Natl. Bank Chicago; Pioneer Western Corp.; Amerocke Corp.; Stanley Works; First Natl. Bank & Trust Co.; A. B. Dick Co.; Chicago & Illinois Midland Railway; Conhill Corp.; Abbott Laboratories; Field Foundation; Visual Information Systems Inc.; Joseph T. Ryerson & Son; Chicago Board of Trade.

Ownership Information

Banks: Patman: 3 interlocks w/ Northern Trust Co.; 3 w/ First Natl. Bank Chicago; 2 w/ Continental Illinois Natl. Bank.

Insurance: Insurance companies owned 2,473,255 shares. Major holdings, 1971: Prudential, 207,000 common shares, $34.1 million bonds; NY Life, 136,000 common shares, $27.5 million bonds; Aetna, 31,925 common shares, $15.8 million bonds and debentures; Travelers, 100,325 common shares; $6.8 million debentures and bonds; Equitable, $19.8 million bonds; Metropolitan Life, $42.7 million bonds; John Hancock, $9.9 million bonds.

Mutual Funds: Seventeen funds held 1,813,275 shares or 4.3 percent of the outstanding stock. Major holdings: Wellington Fund, 427,300 shares; Mass Investors Trust, 374,100 shares.

Foundations: Kresge Foundation, $1 million bonds and notes; Andrew W. Mellon Foundation, 13,000 shares, $2 million bonds; Kellogg Foundation, 7,293 shares, $300,000 bonds and notes.

Universities: Universities owned 362,105 shares. Major holdings: Univ. California (June 30, 1969), 87,902 shares; Harvard (June 30, 1970), 63,984 shares; Univ. Texas (August 31, 1969), 62,370 shares; Northwestern (May 31, 1970), 68,014 shares (one interlock).

Other: Ten largest security holders as reported to the FPC included: How & Co. (Northern Trust Co., trust department), 626,310 common shares, 6,016 preferred shares; Cede & Co. (Stock Clearing Corp.), 592,490 common shares; Finat & Co. (First Natl. Bank Chicago), 514,431 common shares, 4,958 preferred shares; Touchstone & Co. (Wellington Fund), 427,300 common shares; Park & Co. (State Street Bank & Trust Co., Boston, investment company department), 424,100 common shares; Olen & Co. (First Natl. Bank Chicago, trust department), 394,065 common shares, 3,194 preferred shares; Eagle & Co. (First Natl. Bank Chicago), 339,263 common shares, 32,373 preferred shares; Thomas & Co. (First Natl. City Bank), 339,864 common shares; Sigler & Co. (Manufacturers Hanover Trust Co. for Canadian Intl. Growth Fund, Channing Funds, Gen. Pub.

Service Corp., U.S. & Foreign Securities Corp., Institutional Growth Fund, Institutional Shares, Institutional Investors Fund), 246,502 common shares, 52,433 preferred shares; King & Co. (First Natl. City Bank for Leon B. Allen Fund, Axe-Houghton Fund A and B, Broad Street Investing Corp.), 219,624 common shares, 10,342 preferred shares.

The company produces, purchases, transmits, and distributes electricity in a 13,000-square-mile area of northern Illinois, extending from Lake Michigan to the Mississippi River, including the city of Chicago. Population of the area totals 7.8 million. The company operates 14 fossil fuel plants, one nuclear, three peaking facilities, and three small hydroelectric plants. Its subsidiaries include Commonwealth Edison Co. Indiana; Chicago & Illinois Midland Railway Co.; Mid-Illinois Gas Co.

Under Chairman J. Harris Ward, Commonwealth Edison gambled that by 1973, 40 percent of its entire generating capacity would be nuclear. Ward hired nuclear engineers to help run an all-nuclear company, and laid plans for subsidiaries which could mine, process, and transport uranium. But by 1969 costs for nuclear power were moving up, not down as projected by the AEC, and it appeared cheaper and more efficient to build fossil fuel plants. Thus, Ward had to abandon his nuclear plan and build a coal power plant. The result of this planning fiasco was to place the company in a tight squeeze which was passed along to consumers in the form of higher rates. Moreover, the company was not able to meet pollution standards.

In 1969 Commonwealth Edison had declared, "Commonwealth Edison is complying and will continue to comply in full with all government laws and regulations on air pollution, including Chicago's air pollution ordinance." Actually the company had applied to the Air Pollution Control Appeal Board for an exemption from the law, so that it could continue burning high-sulphur coal.

Commonwealth Edison declared, "We account for less than five percent of all contaminants in the air you breathe. Included in this five percent figure are sulphur oxide emissions. We account for less than one-tenth of these." But a report by Argonne National Laboratory said, "Commonwealth Edison Company is responsible for 65.58 percent of the total sulphur oxide emissions in Chicago." In August 1969 the company applied for a 6.1 percent rate increase, citing increased costs (taxes, labor, etc.), making it necessary to raise additional monies in order to maintain and improve service. But the company told *The Wall Street Journal* that if it got the money, then profits would go up. "If the rate increase is approved," he [J. Harris Ward, chairman] said, "we might have a five to eight percent gain in earnings."

Major coal suppliers to Commonwealth Edison include Peabody, Jersey Standard, and Consolidation. In 1970 the company spent $3.4 million on research and development.

Revenues were broken down in 1970 as follows: $340.4 million residential; $313.6 million commercial; and $155.2 million industrial.

In 1970 the company's net after-tax profit as percent of gross revenue was 15.15 percent. Return on common equity was 13.6 percent.

PACIFIC GAS & ELECTRIC CO.

245 Market Street, San Francisco, Calif., 94106.

Basic Company Data

Robert H. Gerdes, Chairman; S. L. Sibley, President. Directors: John F. Bonner, Ransom M. Cook, James F. Crafts, Charles de Bretteville, Alfred W. Eames, Jr., Walter A. Haas, James M. Hait, Elliott McAllister, Leon S. Peters, Richard H. Peterson, Porter Sesnon, Emmet G. Solomon, Carl F. Wente.

Total revenues, 1970, $1.1 billion; net income, $166.2 million; common shares outstanding, 1970: 59,728,000.

Interlocks

3 ea w/ Bank of California; Mills College. 2 ea w/ Wells Fargo

Bank; Del Monte; Cyprus Lawn Cemetery Assn.; Pacific Gas Trans.; Alberta Natural Gas Co.; Alberta & Southern Gas Co. 1 ea w/ Stanford Univ.; United Calif. Bank; Shell Oil; Bank of America; Metropolitan Life Ins.; Pacific Tel. & Tel.; Univ. Calif.; Crocker-Citizens Natl. Bank; Fibreboard Corp.; Clorox Co.; Foremost McKesson; Calif. Water Service Co.; Porter Estate Co.; Watkins-Johnson Co.; Litton Industries; Industrial Indemnity; Cutter Labs; FMC Corp.; Varian Associates; Georgia-Pacific; Arthur D. Little; Interpace Corp.; Levi Strauss Co.; Pacific Intermountain Express; Iris Securities; Canadian Canners Ltd.; Safeway; Western Union; Ridder Publications; Fireman's Fund Ins.; Natl. Newark & Essex Bank; Amex Holding Co.; Deltona Corp.; Marco Island Development Corp.; Fund American Cos.; Standard Pacific Gas Lines Inc.; Natural Gas Corp. Calif.; Pacific Gas Communications Co.

Ownership Information

Banks: Patman: National Shawmut Bank (Boston) owned 5.5 percent of the preferred stock.

Insurance: Insurance companies owned 2,678,053 shares. Major holdings, 1970: John Hancock, 124,800 common shares; Metropolitan Life, 251,446 preferred shares, $22 million bonds; Equitable, 99,000 common shares, 760,475 preferred shares, $20.1 million bonds; NW Mutual, $10.5 million bonds; Travelers, 56,750 preferred shares, $10.5 million bonds; Conn. General, 25,000 common shares, 4,100 preferred shares, $6.6 million bonds; Aetna, $16.1 million bonds; Prudential, 355,000 common shares, 234,275 preferred shares, $756,500 bonds; NY Life, 127,140 common shares, 764,005 preferred shares, $34 million bonds.

Mutual Funds: Fifteen funds held 2,682,252 common shares or 4.4 percent of the outstanding stock. Major holdings: Investors Group, 787,800 (Inv. Mutual, 387,800; Inv. Variable Payment, 100,000; Inv. Stock Fund, 300,000); Investment Co. of America, 675,000; Wellington Fund, 370,600.

Foundations: Ford Foundation, 263,000 shares, $500,000 bonds; Carnegie Corp., 90,000 shares; Kellogg Foundation, 10,800 shares, $300,000 bonds and notes; Kresge Foundation, 5,000 shares, $900,000 bonds.

Universities: Universities owned 187,179 shares. Major holdings: Univ. California (June 30, 1969), 134,795.

Other: Ten largest security holders reported to FPC: Safund & Co. (Bank of California), 2.6 million common shares; Cede & Co. (Stock Clearing Corp. NY), 1.2 million common shares; Cudd & Co. (Chase Manhattan Bank for American Mutual Fund, Chemical Fund, Equity Fund, Intl. Resources Fund, Investment Co. America), 1.8 million common shares; Equitable Life, 99,000 common shares, 760,475 preferred shares; NY Life, 63,570 common shares, 764,000 preferred shares; Merrill Lynch, 414,535 common shares, 173,687 preferred shares; Prudential, 353,600 common shares, 234,275 preferred shares; Emp & Co. (Harris Trust & Savings, trust department), 575,111 common shares; Touchstone & Co. (Wellington Fund), 370,600 common shares; Carson & Co. (Morgan Guaranty), 328,350 common shares, 12,856 preferred shares.

PG&E serves over two million people in northern California. Part of the company's success, according to its critics, comes from a policy of buying public power at relatively low rates, then reselling it at higher prices to its own customers. The company has successfully fought off efforts by public power groups to sell power direct to consumers. In the early part of the century Congress passed the Raker Act, which allowed the city of San Francisco to obtain public power by damming the Hetch Hetchy River in the Yosemite Mountains, and then to string a power line from the dam site to the city. The idea was to provide San Francisco with a plentiful supply of inexpensive electricity. San Francisco went ahead and built the transmission lines from the dam site to the edge of the city, but existing utilities, including

PG&E, refused to handle the power. At that point, the city authorities buckled, and instead of seizing private utility assets under the right of public domain, it allowed PG&E to buy the public power at low rates. As a result the Hetch Hetchy power is sold at low prices to PG&E and then resold at higher rates to other customers, including irrigation districts. PG&E provides other power for the city of San Francisco at its own rates, estimated by some critics to be $30 million more than the cost of the power were it taken direct from Hetch Hetchy. PG&E shrewdly takes advantage of public power projects in other ways. For instance, the company buys power from the California water plan's Oroville Dam for about $20 million, then resells it for some $42 million.

Over the years company officials have been well represented on the board of regents at the University of California, where PG&E provides large amounts of electricity for the Radiation Laboratory. According to independent estimates provided the university, it would have been cheaper by $5 million over ten years to buy this electricity direct from the Central Valley Project. But rather than discomfit PG&E, the university never did so.

The company is an important natural gas pipeline operator through ownership of Pacific Gas Transmission Co., which buys natural gas at the Canadian border from a Canadian subsidiary, Alberta Natural Gas Co. Alberta sells gas in Canada. But most of PG&E basic gas supplies come from El Paso Natural Gas Co., which historically has dominated the California gas markets.

In 1970 PG&E spent $6.1 million in advertising including $2.2 million to Batten, Barton, Dursten & Osborne in San Francisco. At the same time, it laid out $4 million for research and development. Of that $4 million, about $250,000 went to research on environment related subjects.

In 1970 revenues from residential sales amounted to $260 million; revenues from commercial and industrial sales were $397.7 million.

In addition to hydroelectric produced power, PG&E electricity is produced from natural gas and fuel oil, with one nuclear plant.

In 1970 the company's net after-tax profit as percent of gross revenue was 15.07 percent. In that year return on common equity was 10.6 percent.

SOUTHERN CALIFORNIA EDISON CO.

601 West Fifth Street, Los Angeles, Calif., 90053.

Basic Company Data

Jack K. Horton, Chairman; T. M. McDaniel, Jr., President. Directors Norman Barker, Jr., Arnold O. Beckman, Edwin W. Carter, William B. Coberly, Jr., Terrell C. Drinkwater, Stanton G. Hale, Daniel J. Haughton, Frederick G. Larkin, Jr., John V. Newman, Fred Oldendorf, Jr., Gerald H. Phipps, Richard R. Von Hagen, Vaile G. Young.

Total revenues, 1970, $720.6 million; net income, $127.4 million; average common shares outstanding, 1970: 40,482,950.

Interlocks

4 ea w/ United California Bank; Pacific Mutual Life Ins. Co. 2 ea w/ Lockheed Aircraft Corp.; Security Pacific Natl. Bank; Western Bancorporation. 1 ea w/ Northrop Corp.; American Mutual Fund; Investment Co. of America; Bank of America; Huntington Library; Bank America Corp.; Lloyd Corporation Ltd.; Buffums (dept. stores); Broadway Hale Stores; AT&T; Del Monte; Gerald H. Phipps Inc.; Belcaro Realty; First Natl. Bank of Denver; First Natl. Bancorporation; Denver & Rio Grande Western RR; Denver Dry Goods; Empire Sports; Western Federal Savings & Loan Assn.; Getty Oil; North American Rockwell; Western American Bank; Stanford Univ. Bus. School; Carnation Co.; Lockheed Aircraft Intl.; Transcontinental Lines; Olson Brothers; Santa Anita Foundation; Emporium Cepnell Co.; Union Bank; Unionamerica Ind.; Western Air Lines Inc.; Calif. Cotton Oil Corp.; Kube Inc.; Coberly-West Co.; Forest Lawn; American Security & Fidelity; Beckman Instruments;

Stanford Research Institute; Security First Natl. Bank; System Development Corp.; Continental Air Lines.

Ownership Information

Banks: Patman: National Shawmut Bank (Boston) owned 6 percent of preferred 4.75 stock and First Natl. City Bank NY owned 8.2 percent of preferred 4.24 cumulative stock.

Insurance: Insurance companies owned 5,887,009 shares. Major holdings, 1970: John Hancock, 120,000 shares common, 110,000 shares preferred, $1.9 million bonds; Equitable, 150,000 shares common, 634,925 shares preferred, $6.9 million bonds; North West Mutual, 100,000 shares common, 115,000 shares preferred, $8.1 million bonds; Prudential, 384,000 shares common, 211,630 shares preferred, $1.9 million bonds; NY Life, 172,000 shares common, 143,000 shares preferred, $31.4 million bonds.

Mutual Funds: Twenty-two funds held 3,121,880 shares or 7.7 percent of outstanding stock. Major holdings: Investors Group, 612,000 shares (Investors Mutual, 250,000; Investors Stock Fund, 362,000); Dreyfus Fund, 503,700 shares.

Foundations: Ford Foundation, 235,000 shares, $200,000 bonds; Kresge Foundation, $2.6 million bonds; Mellon Foundation, $1 million bonds and notes, 27,032 shares.

Universities: Universities owned 439,926 shares. Major holdings: Harvard (June 30, 1970), 127,472; Univ. California (June 30, 1970), 102,200 shares; Univ. Texas (August 31, 1969), 71,-742 shares; California Institute Technology (December 31, 1969), 31,496 shares (one interlock).

Other: Ten largest security holders listed by the company with the FPC included: Equitable, 154,000 shares common, 1,904,775 shares preferred; Kane & Co. (Chase Manhattan Bank), 1.3 million shares common, 8,000 shares preferred; Prudential,

384,000 shares common, 634,890 shares preferred; Cudd & Co. (Chase Manhattan for American Mutual Fund, Inc., Chemical Fund, Inc., Equity Fund, Intl. Resources Fund, Inc., Investment Co. of America), 868,016 shares common, 77,382 shares preferred; Hep & Co. (United Calif. Bank, trust department), 771,-978 shares common; Thomas & Co. (First Natl. City Bank NY for DeVegh Inv. Co. and United Corp.), 736,140 shares common; Sabat Co. (Savings Banks Trust Co.), 500 shares common, 720,650 shares preferred; Cede & Co. (Stock Clearing Corp.), 663,563 shares common; Carson & Co. (Morgan Guaranty Trust Co.), 541,179 shares common, 11,500 shares preferred; NY Life, 86,000 shares common, 429,000 shares preferred.

Southern California Edison provides electricity to the southern part of California, including the Los Angeles metropolitan area. At the end of 1970 Edison's effective operating capacity totaled 10,904,845 kilowatts. Construction projects scheduled for completion during the next three years will add 2.5 million additional kilowatts. The company owns 48 percent in coal-fired generating units at Four Corners in New Mexico from which it draws 768,-000 kilowatts. In addition, Edison is a 56 percent participant in two coal-fired plants at Mohave, Nevada. Edison's share of these two projects will total 885,000 kilowatts.

The company has one nuclear unit in operation at San Onofre and it produces 450,000 kilowatts. The new proposed units each will have a capacity of 1.1 million kilowatts.

To provide the company with anticipated additional amounts of uranium over the next 20 years, Mono Power Co., a subsidiary, has entered into a joint exploration program with Union Pacific Railroad Co. Under this program, the partners will drill on Union Pacific properties in Wyoming, Colorado, and Utah over the next five years.

To meet increased demands for natural gas the company bought into Mountain Pacific Pipeline Ltd., which is seeking to develop a project to buy natural gas from recent petroleum discoveries in the North Slope area of Alaska and transport it to

California, as well as from British Columbia and the Northwest territories of Canada. In this connection, Pacific States Pipeline Co., a new U.S. corporation in which Edison has a 25 percent holding, was organized to transport Mountain Pacific gas from the United States-Canada border southward to California markets.

Southern California Edison is taking a fresh look into geothermal potentials in the Imperial Valley, and Mono Power Co. has applied for leases on about 25,000 acres.

The 1970 sales breakdown: Industrial, 16 billion kilowatts for revenues of $142.3 million; commercial, 13.5 billion for $250.2 million; residential, 11.1 billion for $271.1 million.

The company adds to its revenues through various realty projects. It leases rights of way to 18 cities for different projects, ranging from trails, Little League ball parks, farms, commercial parks, etc. Southern California and Bechtel Corp. jointly are developing Calabasas Park, an all-electric new town outside Los Angeles. The company has developed a sort of all-electric camping site, Camp Edison-Shaver Lake, along artificial lakes made from its hydroelectric projects in the high Sierra. The campsites are equipped with plugs for electric blankets, frying pans, etc.

Southern California Edison subsidiaries include: Associated Southern Investment Co., which makes miscellaneous nonpublic utility investments; Electric Systems Co., primarily engaged in financing of applications of electric energy; Energy Services Inc., which furnishes heating and cooling services; Calabasas Park Co. invests in and manages real estate; Calabasas Communications Co. develops, operates, and maintains CATV systems; Calabasas Developers Inc., realty development; Mono Power Co., real estate acquisition and development.

SOUTHERN COMPANY

Perimeter Center East, P.O. Box 720071, Atlanta, Ga., 30346.

Basic Company Data

Alvin W. Vogtle, Jr., President. Directors: Peyton T. Anderson,

Harllee Branch, Jr., William J. Cabaniss, James V. Carmichael, Robert F. Ellis, Jr., Joseph M. Farley, Edwin I. Hatch, Robert T. Jones, Jr., J. D. Lewis, Clyde A. Lilly, Jr., Earl M. McGowin, William S. Morris, III, M. G. Nelson, Robert H. Radcliff, Jr.; Alfred M. Shook III, W. C. Vereen, Jr.; A. J. Watson, Jr.

Total revenues, 1970, $738 million; net income, $100.6 million; common shares outstanding, 1970: 55,449,500.

Interlocks

4 w/ Southern Services, Inc. 3 ea w/ Southern Electric Generating Co.; Protective Life Ins. Co.; Gulf Power Co.; Alabama Power Co.; First Natl. Bank (Birmingham). 2 ea w/ Georgia Power Co.; Mississippi Power Co. 1 ea w/ Louisville & Nashville RR Co.; Southeastern Newspapers Corp.; General Reinsurance Corp.; US Steel; General Motors; Hayes International Corp.; Star Automobile Co.; Knight Newspapers; Citizens & Southern Natl. Bank; Georgia Southern & Florida RR Co.; Macon Telegraph Publishing Co.; Scripto Inc., Lockheed Aircraft Corp.; Trust Co. of Georgia; Emory Univ.; Georgia Intl. Life Ins. Co.; Alabama Property Co.; Southern Research Institute; Knox Development Corp.; Liberty Natl. Life Ins. Co.; Alabama Great Southern RR; Foundation Life Ins. Co.; Federal Reserve Bank Atlanta; Home Ins. Co.; Seaboard Coastline RR; Seaboard Coastline Industries; City Investing Co.; Shook & Fletcher Supply Co.; Appalachia Natl. Life Insurance; Birmingham Realty Co.; Southern Industries Corp.; Commercial Bank (Panama City, Fla.); Springfield Commercial Bank; Atlantic & St. Andrews Bay Ry Co.; Nelson Buick Co.; Moultrie Textiles; Riverside Mfg. Co.; Riverside Industries; Riverside Uniform Rentals; Bema Uniform Rentals; Hancock Bank, Mississippi Business & Industrial Development Corp.; Union Camp Corp.; Southern Pine Inspection Bureau; American Sand & Gravel Co.; Jones, Bird & Howell; Canton (Ga.) Cotton Mills; Jones Mercantile Co.

Ownership Information

Insurance: Insurance companies owned 2,984,818 shares. Major holdings: Prudential, 523,400; John Hancock, 150,000; Equitable, 130,000.

Mutual Funds: Twenty-five funds held 2,993,570 shares or 5.4 percent of the outstanding stock. Major holdings: Institutional Investors Mutual, 475,300; Dreyfus Fund, 440,500; Affiliated Fund, 433,900.

Foundations: Rockefeller Foundation, 342,000 shares; Ford Foundation, 254,000 shares; Hartford Foundation, 50,000 shares; Mellon Foundation, 33,000 shares; Sloan Foundation, 52,000 shares.

Universities: Universities held 302,059 shares. Major holdings: Univ. Texas (August 31, 1969), 121,700 shares.

Southern Company owns all the outstanding stock of Alabama Power Co., Georgia Power Co., Gulf Power Co., and Mississippi Power Co., each of which is an operating public utility. Alabama and Georgia each own 50 percent of the outstanding common stock of Southern Electric Generating Company (SEGCO).

The companies serve most of Alabama and Georgia together with the northwest portion of Florida and southeastern Mississippi. The territory has an area of approximately 120,000 square miles and an estimated population of 8.1 million. Principal cities served are Atlanta, the major distributing center in the Southeast, Birmingham, a heavy industrial center and a major steel-producing area, and Mobile, the big Gulf port.

In Georgia, Georgia Power serves 646 communities with a population of 4.2 million; Alabama Power serves 639 communities with 2.8 million population; Gulf Power, 70 communities with 450,000 population; Mississippi Power, 137 communities with 650,000 people. The Southern Company system is interconnected, and there are connections with TVA.

In 1970 residential business accounted for approximately 35 percent of total revenues; commercial sales, 28 percent; industrial, 27 percent. Sales to nonaffiliated systems were 10 percent. Percentages of total power revenues from industry during the 12-month period ended June 30, 1970, by industrial classification were: textile mill products, 18 percent; chemicals and allied products, 13 percent; primary metal industries, 8 percent; paper and allied products, 8 percent; food and kindred products, 6 percent; stone, clay, and glass products; 6 percent; and 41 percent for all other classifications.

The fuel electric plants on the system during 1970 burned coal and natural gas at the ratio of approximately 85 percent coal to 15 percent natural gas. Both Alabama and SEGCO own and operate coal reserves adjacent to steam plants. Alabama mines supplied about a quarter of the coal it consumed during 1970. It is negotiating for purchase of 27 million tons of reserves. SEGCO owns 300 million tons of coal reserves in the Cahaba field. The Southern system companies have long-term contracts for annual purchase of 17 million tons of coal. Consolidation Coal is one major supplier.

In 1970 one plant was converted to oil, and oil may become a much larger factor in the future.

Coal and gas will continue to be the principal fuels over the next few years. By 1973 the system will have a total capacity of about 16.4 million kilowatts, of which some 12.7 million kilowatts will be fossil fuel (coal or gas); hydroelectric, 1.8 million kilowatts; combustion turbines, 1.1 million kilowatts; and nuclear, 800,000 kilowatts.

The system's first two nuclear units are scheduled to begin operation in 1973 and 1975. By the mid-1980s, it is probable that about half of the new generation installed on the system will be nuclear.

In 1970 Southern Company's net after-tax profit as percent of gross revenue was 13.64 percent. In 1970 return on common equity by the system companies was as follows: Alabama, 12.1 percent; Georgia Power, 12 percent; Mississippi Power, 13.2 percent; Gulf Power, 15.1 percent; Southern Electric Generating, 13.5 percent.

AMERICAN ELECTRIC POWER CO.

2 Broadway, New York, N.Y., 10004.

Basic Company Data

Donald C. Cook, President. Directors: Malcolm P. Aldrich, John E. Amos, William W. Boeschenstein, Courtney C. Brown, Herbert B. Cohn, Richard M. Dicke, Richard G. Folsom, James M. Gavin, Walter O. Menge, George V. Patterson, W. J. Rose, Nelson Schaenen, Frank Stanton.

Total revenues, 1970, $665.7 million; net income, $116.9 million; average number of common shares outstanding, 1970: 50,833,000.

Interlocks

4 ea w/ Appalachian Power Co.; Franklin Real Estate Co.; Indiana Franklin Realty Co.; Indiana & Michigan Electric Co.; Kanawha Valley Power Co.; Kentucky Power Co.; Kingsport Power Co.; Ohio Power Co.; Twin Branch RR Co.; Wheeling Electric Co. 3 ea w/ Ohio Valley Electric Corp.; West Pa. Power Co.; Michigan Power Co.; Captina Operating Co. 2 ea w/ American Electric Power Services Corp.; Indiana-Kentucky Electric Corp.; Central Appalachian Coal Co.; Cardinal Operating Co.; Beech Bottom Power Co.; Central Coal Co.; Central Operating Co.; South Bend Mfg. Co.; Windsor Power House Coal Co.; Lincoln National Corp.; Michigan Gas Exploration Co.; Arthur D. Little Inc.; CBS. 1 ea w/ Central Ohio Coal Co.; Simpson Thacher & Bartlett; ABC; Diebold Computer Leasing Inc.; Amos & Brotherton; Owens-Corning Fiberglass Corp.; Pan American; NY Life Ins. Co.; Diebold Ventures Capital Corp.; RPI; Air Reduction Co.; Troy Savings Bank; Bendix Corp.; Research Analysis Corp.; Potter Instrument Corp.; Magnavox Co., Lincoln Natl. Life Ins. Co.; Smith, Barney & Co.; Associated Dry Goods Corp.; Columbia Univ. Business School; Borden Inc., Intl. Exec. Services Corp.; Union Pacific RR; Uris Bldg. Corp.; Chemical

Bank NY Trust Co.; Southern Pacific Co.; Equitable Life Assurance Society; Commonwealth Fund.

Ownership Information

Insurance: Insurance companies owned 3,344,884 shares of American Electric Power Co. Major holdings included, INA, 288,772 shares; Continental Ins. N.Y., 193,242 shares; Equitable Life, 132,500 shares (one interlock); NY Life, 119,818 shares.

Mutual Funds: Fourteen mutual funds held 884,500 shares or 1.6 percent of outstanding stock. Major holdings: Mass Investors Trust, 180,000 shares.

Foundations: Ford Foundation, 165,000 shares; Hartford Foundation, 40,000 shares; Mellon Foundation, 38,174 shares.

Universities: Universities owned 347,686 shares worth $9 million. Major holdings: Harvard (June 30, 1969), 76,510 shares; Princeton (June 30, 1969), 66,627 shares; Univ. Texas (August 31, 1969), 62,875 shares.

Through seven major operating companies American Electric Power manages the largest privately owned utility network in the nation. It also owns coal companies, a short-haul railroad, and other power subsidiaries.

Operating subsidiaries of the AEP holding company network include: Appalachian Power Co., Roanoke, Virginia, serving more than 500,000 customers in western Virginia, southern and western West Virginia; Indiana & Michigan Electric Co., Fort Wayne, Indiana, serving 358,000 customers in eastern and northern Indiana and southwestern Michigan; Kentucky Power Co., Ashland, Kentucky, serving 105,080 customers in eastern Kentucky; Kingsport Power Co., Kingsport, Tennessee, serving 27,716 customers in northeastern Tennessee; Michigan Power Co., Three Rivers, Michigan, serving 23,706 customers in southwestern Michigan; Ohio Power Co., Canton, Ohio, serving about 500,000 customers in eastern, central, southern and northwestern Ohio; Wheeling Electric Co., Wheeling, West Virginia, serving 36,970 customers in the Wheeling area.

Other subsidiary companies: Beech Bottom Power Co., jointly owned with the Allegheny Power System; Captina Operating Co.; Cardinal Operating Co., jointly owned with Buckeye Power, Inc.; Central Appalachian Coal Co.; Kanawha Valley Power Co.; Sewell Valley Utilities Co.; Twin Branch Railroad Co.; West Virginia Power Co.; Windsor Power House Coal Co.; Central Coal Co.; Central Ohio Coal Co.; Central Operating Co.

In 1970 operating revenues were broken down as follows: 11.2 billion kilowatt hours residential sales producing revenues of $203 million; 6.3 billion kilowatt hours commercial for $115.7 million; 30.6 billion kilowatt hours industrial for $241.7 million.

In 1971 the system had 12 million kilowatts of power supply. It is expected to double by the end of the 1970s.

Most of the system's generating facilities are located in or nearby the Appalachian coal fields, and are fired by coal. In Michigan, where transportation costs are a factor, AEP is building two nuclear units. When these two nuclear units are completed, nuclear energy will represent about 15 percent of the system's total capacity.

Through subsidiaries AEP now provides 20 percent of its own coal supplies. The company is actively buying coal reserves and within five to seven years expects to produce 50 percent of its coal supply. Consolidation Coal (Continental) and Peabody (Kennecott) are two major suppliers.

AEP is investigating the possibility of gasifying coal, with an eye to providing fuel in areas where there are strict regulations over sulphur content of fuel. The company is investigating the possibility of hauling coal to the plant site, then turning it into gas and creating electricity through burning gas.

The companies of the AEP system are interlinked with one another. In addition, the system is connected to other systems that buy or exchange power with AEP. Links to the Chicago metropolitan area are provided through a 345 and 765 kv line;

the system maintains a loop through the state of Michigan; it has ties to the eastern seaboard through the Allegheny and Keystone systems. A 765 kv line hooks into the TVA system to the South. AEP has a line to VEPCO on the East.

Wholesale power sales to other systems are increasing, and in 1970 amounted to 15 percent of the company's total revenues.

The company's net after-tax profit as percent of gross revenue in 1970 was 17.56 percent.

PUBLIC SERVICE ELECTRIC & GAS CO.

80 Park Place, Newark, N.J., 07101.

Basic Company Data

Edward R. Eberle, President. Directors: William H. Blake, C. Malcolm Davis, Jess H. Davis, W. Robert Davis, Donald B. Kipp, Joseph D. Scheerer, Carrol M. Shanks, Clifford D. Siverd, Robert I. Smith, Edwin H. Snyder, W. Paul Stillman, Watson F. Tait, Jr.

Total revenues, 1970, $741.2 million; net income, $93.4 million; common stock outstanding, 1970: 35,974,638 shares.

Interlocks

2 ea w/ First Natl. State Bank N.J.; Mutual Benefit Life Ins. Co.; Prudential; Natl. Biscuit Co.; U.S. Savings Bank; First Jersey Natl. Bank; Pennwal Corp.; Fidelity Union Trust. 1 ea w/ Newark Milk & Cream Co.; Driver-Harris Co.; P.S. Coordinated Transport Co.; Firemans Ins. Co. Newark; Commercial Ins. Co. Newark; Washington General Ins. Corp.; Tri-Continental Corp.; Union Camp Corp.; C. F. Mueller Co.; Food Fair Stores Inc.; Bekin Dickinson & Co. Inc.; Shanks Davis & Remer; Bigelow Sanford Inc.; Skyline Oil Co.; Waltham Industries Corp.; American Cyanamid Co.; Pitney Hardin & Kipp; Camden Trust Co.; Potomac Insurance Co.; Pa. Gen. Ins. Co.; Bank of New Jersey (Camden); General Acceptance Group; Stevens Institute of

Technology; Phillip Morris; Carrier Corp.; Bethlehem Steel; Fidelity Union Trust Co.; Lowe Paper Co.; Fidelity Union Bancorporation.

Ownership Information

Banks: Patman: First Natl. City Bank NY owns 7.3 percent of preferred stock.

Insurance: Insurance companies owned 2.2 million shares. Major holdings, 1970: Prudential, 331,000 common, $1 m bonds; NY Life, 263,550 common, 86,500 shares of three types of preferred, $17.3 m bonds; Aetna, 5,600 preferred, $11.1 m debentures and bonds.

Foundations: Rockefeller Foundation, 100,000 common; Carnegie Corp., $1.4 m bonds and notes; Mellon Foundation, $1 m bonds and notes; Sloan Foundation, 68,000 common, $1.2 m debentures; Kresge Foundation, $990,000 bonds and debentures; Duke Endowment, $200,000 bonds.

Universities: Universities held 152,334 shares. Major holdings: Univ. Texas (August 31, 1969), 59,050; Univ. Penn (June 30, 1970), 40,314.

Other: Ten largest securities holders reported to the FPC included: Merrill Lynch, 1,333,297 common shares; Kane & Co. (Chase Manhattan Bank), 726,555 shares; Sigler & Co. (Manufacturers Hanover Trust Co. for Canadian Intl. Growth Fund, Channing Funds, Gen. Pub. Serv. Corp., Institutional Funds, U.S. & Foreign Securities Corp), 441,886 shares; Elm & Co. (Pittsburgh Natl. Bank) 435,507 shares; Reing & Co. (Morgan Guaranty Trust Co.), 391,059 shares; Prudential Insurance Co., 386,000 shares; Carson & Co. (Morgan Guaranty Trust Co.), 356,107 shares; Cudd & Co. (Chase Manhattan Bank for American Mutual Fund, Chemical Fund, Equity Fund, Intl. Resources Fund, Investment Co. of America), 282,536 shares; Genoy & Co. (Morgan Guaranty Trust Co.), 281,564 shares; N.Y. Life Insurance, 263,550 shares.

The company provides gas and electricity to about 5.5 million people in New Jersey, representing about three-quarters of the state's population. Its service area extends from New York to Philadelphia and includes the cities of Newark, Jersey City, Camden, Trenton, Paterson, and Elizabeth. Of the total revenue, about two-thirds comes from sale of electricity, the remainder from gas.

In electrical sales, 36 percent of revenues came from residential customers, 28 percent from industrial, and 33 percent from commercial. Gas revenues: 64 percent from residential customers, 23 percent from commercial, and 13 percent from industrial.

In generating electricity the company uses 65 percent oil, 25 percent coal, and 10 percent gas.

Edwin H. Snyder, the chairman who retired in 1971, drew a salary of $110,000. Edward R. Eberle, president, received $80,-000. The company spent $3.6 million in sales expenses, including $337,439 to Williams & London, a Newark advertising agency. According to its annual report to the Federal Power Commission, the company spent about $400,000 for research and development. Of that total the biggest item was $130,000 for research into fuel cells. Public Service said it spent $414 for research into air pollution and $549 on research into underground transmission lines.

The company plants, fueled variously with coal, gas, and oil, are equipped with precipitators, but do not have any desulphurization equipment.

Public Service reported extensive financial dealings with companies where Public Service directors are officers. It guaranteed an $8 million loan to Rochester & Pittsburgh Coal Co., a major supplier, made by Manfacturers Hanover Trust and Mutual Benefit Life Insurance. W. Paul Stillman, a Public Service director, is chairman of Mutual Benefit, and Watson F. Tait is a director of both Public Service and the insurance firm.

In 1970 Prudential, sixth largest security holder in the company, received $3.4 million in insurance premiums for life and health insurance for Public Service employees. Public Service directors and former directors C. Malcolm Davis, Jess H. Davis, Donald C. Luce and, before his death, Charles Engelhard were all directors of Prudential. (Luce is no longer listed as a Public Service director.)

First National State Bank of New Jersey made an unsecured 8.5 percent loan of $7 million to Public Service in 1969, and an unsecured 8 percent loan of $10 million in 1970. Public Service director Stillman is chairman of the bank. Public Service director Tait is a bank director.

Fidelity Union Trust Co. made an 8.5 percent unsecured loan of $7 million to Public Service in 1969, and an 8 percent $10 million loan in 1970. C. Malcolm Davis is chairman of the bank, and Luce, another Public Service director, is a bank director as well.

The National Newark & Essex Bank made an 8.5 percent $4 million loan in 1969, and an 8 percent $4 million loan in 1970. Engelhard (deceased) was a director and Donald B. Kipp is a director.

The First Jersey National Bank made an 8.5 percent $2 million loan in 1969 and an 8 percent $2 million loan in 1970. Edward Eberle, Public Service president, is a director of the bank; Jess H. Davis is a director of both the bank and Public Service.

The Trust Co. of New Jersey made an 8.5 percent $1 million loan in 1969, and an 8 percent $1 million loan in 1970. Stewart G. Stalnecker is a director of the bank and vice-president and treasurer of Public Service.

The Bank of New Jersey made an 8.5 percent $1.5 million loan in 1969. W. Robert Davis, a Public Service director, is president of the bank.

The People's Trust of New Jersey made an 8 percent $3 million loan in 1970. Robert Baker is a director of the bank and executive vice-president of Public Service.

Public Service is involved in building four nuclear power plants, and is planning two others. Of the four now in the process of construction, two are in Salem County, in southern New Jersey. Two others, to be managed by Philadelphia Electric Co., are to be at Peach Bottom, Pennsylvania. Two future units are planned for Newbold Island in the Delaware River below Trenton.

Public Service also owns as a subsidiary Public Service Coordinated Transport, New Jersey's biggest bus company and operator of Newark's subway system. The transportation subsidiary carries upward of 750,000 riders daily, including about 90,000 commuters from northern New Jersey to New York, has a fleet of 2,500 buses and 30 subway systems. According to the transportation company's recently appointed chairman, John J. Gilhooley, the company was facing bankruptcy by 1972. Gilhooley is former commissioner of the New York City Transit Authority. In July of 1970, Gilhooley, then representing an investment group, offered to buy the transport concern for $29 million. He was joined in this offer by Claude Jessup, former chairman of Continental Trailways. The offer was withdrawn in February 1970. Both Gilhooley and Jessup joined the board of the existing company.

The company's net after-tax profit as percent of gross revenue in 1970 was 12.60 percent. Return on common equity that year was 10.7 percent.

DETROIT EDISON COMPANY

2000 Second Avenue, Detroit, Mich., 48226.

Basic Company Data

Walker Cisler, Chairman; William Meese, President. Directors: Richard C. Andreae, Robert F. Bacher, H. Glenn Bixby, James Boyd, Prentiss M. Brown, Charles T. Fisher, III, Edwin O. George, Harlan Hatcher, George M. Holley, Jr., Joseph L. Hudson, Jr., Frederick H. Mueller, Kenneth D. Nichols, Raymond T. Perring, Alan E. Schwartz, Boylston A. Tompkins.

Total revenues, 1970, $529.2 million; net income, $62.6 million; common shares outstanding, 1970: 31 million.

Interlocks

3 w/ Manufacturers Natl. Bank of Detroit. 2 w/ Natl. Bank Detroit. 1 ea w/ California Inst. of Technology; Yale Woolen Mills; Natl. Steel; Burroughs Corp.; Fruehauf Corp.; Chemical Bank NY Trust; Atomic Power Development Association; Power Reactor Develop. Co.; Eaton Yale & Towne; Detroit Institute Technology; Ex-Cell-O Corp.; Michigan Chrome & Chemical; Detrex Chemical Industries; Michigan Bell Tel.; Micromatic Industries; Cooper Range Co.; White Pine Mining Co.; Dashaveyor Co.; Felmont Oil; White Pine Copper Co.; First Natl. Bank; Arnold Transit Co.; Union Terminal Piers; Mackinac Bridge Authority; Univ. Michigan; Holloy Carburator; J.L. Hudson Co.; Assoc. Merchandizing Corp.; Dayton Hudson Corp.; Detroit Bank & Trust Co.; McGregor Fund; Chrysler Corp.; Reliance Ins.; Federal Reserve Bank Chicago; Honigman, Miller, Schwartz & Cohen; SOS Consolidated Inc.; Macoid Industries; Allied Supermarkets; Cunningham Drug Stores; Handelman Co.; Teleflex Inc.; Bowery Savings Bank; General American Investors; Babcock & Wilcox; Natl. Aviation Corp.; Flintkote Co.; Percolator Inc.

Ownership Information

Banks: Patman: 2 interlocks ea w/ National Bank Detroit; Detroit Bank & Trust. 1 interlock w/ Manufacturers Natl. Bank Detroit. Bankers Trust Co. NY manages one fund with investments in Detroit Edison.

Insurance: Insurance companies owned 790,363 shares. Major holdings: Metropolitan Life, $20.9 m bonds; NY Life, $6.7 m bonds; John Hancock, $4.2 m bonds.

Mutual Funds: Three funds held 177,600 shares or 0.6 percent of the outstanding stock.

Foundations: Andrew W. Mellon Foundation, $2.5 million in bonds and notes; Carnegie Corp., $1 million bonds and notes; Ford Foundation, $800,000 in bonds; John A. Hartford Foundation, $930,000 bonds; Kresge Foundation, $700,000.

Universities: Universities owned 89,090 shares. Major holdings: Univ. Texas (August 31, 1969), 41,500 shares; Harvard (June 30, 1970), 32,632 shares.

Other: Among the ten largest security holders as reported to the FPC were: Cede & Co. (Stock Clearing Corp.), 933,560; Trussal & Co. (Natl. Bank of Detroit Trust Dept. for Mutual Income Foundation), 241,950 common shares; Forwash & Co. (Detroit Bank & Trust Co.), 142,586 common; Merrill Lynch, 139,119 shares; Calhoun & Co. (Manufacturers Natl. Bank Trust Dept.), 103,861 common; Sloyan & Co. (Manufacturers Hanover Trust Co.), 100,000 common; Hamilfund & Co. (First Natl. Bank Denver for Hamilton Funds Inc.), 100,000 common; Spicer & Co. (Detroit Bank & Trust Co.), 84,167 common; Bache & Co., 80,178 shares.

Detroit Edison serves approximately 1,538,000 customers in southeastern Michigan, an important industrial, commercial, and agricultural area consisting of both urban and rural communities. During 1970 the company derived about 37 percent of its electric revenues from sales to residential customers, 30 percent from industrial sales, and 24 percent from commercial sales. Principal industries served include automobile and other transportation equipment firms, steel, chemical, cement industries, and manufacturers and fabricators of machinery and other metal products. During 1970 the 20 largest industrial customers accounted for approximately 18 percent of utility revenues, with no one customer accounting for more than 4 percent.

The company had a total capability of 6.1 million kilowatts, and of that 5.3 million were accounted for by fossil fuels plants. Most of the fossil fueled plants are coal-fired. Major coal contracts have been with Consolidation (Continental) and more recently Eastern Gas & Fuel Associates.

An additional 5.5 million kilowatts of capacity is under construction. Of that total, 3.2 million is to be fossil fueled and 1.1 million nuclear.

Since 1955 Detroit Edison has been a member of two nonprofit atomic power research and development organizations—Atomic Power Development Associates, Inc. and Power Reactor Development Company. The former firm designed the Fermi nuclear reactor, and Power Reactor owns and operates the nuclear facilities of the Fermi plant. The Fermi plant was closed for four years prior to 1970 because of an accident, and has operated periodically since then.

In 1970 Detroit Edison spent $5.3 million on advertising, and $3.8 million on research and development.

In 1970 the company's net after-tax profit as percent of gross revenue was 11.84 percent. The company had a 10.1 percent return on common equity.

Walker Cisler, who joined the company and continues as chairman until he becomes 77 (in 1976), draws a salary of $137,390. In addition, he owns 9,019 shares of stock in Detroit Edison. William Meese, president and chief executive officer, was paid $63,727.

FLORIDA POWER & LIGHT CO.

4200 Flagler Street, P.O. Box 3100, Miami, Fla., 33101.

Basic Company Data

McGregor Smith, Chairman; R.C. Fullerton, President. Directors: George F. Bennett, George W. English, Robert H. Fite, Benton W. Powell, Will M. Preston, Harry T. Vaughn, Sr.; Lewis E. Wadsworth, William A. Shands.

Total revenues, 1970, $416 million; net income, $97.4 million; common shares outstanding, 1970: 14.6 million.

Interlocks

1 ea w/ State Street Investment; Middle South Utilities; Harvard; New England Electric System; Commonwealth Oil Refining; Federal St. Fund; John Hancock Life Insurance; Second Federal St. Fund; U.S. & Foreign Securities; Hewlett-Packard; English, McCaughan & O'Bryan; First Natl. Bank Fort Lauderdale; First Federal Savings & Loan Assn. (Broward Co.); First Natl. Bank (Margate); First Natl. Bank (North Broward); First Natl. Bank (Pompano Beach); Guaranty Natl. Bank (Fort Lauderdale); Plantation First Natl. Bank; Caulley Steel & Aluminum Co.; Wright & Putnam Inc.; Harbor Beach Co.; Utilities Operating Co.; U.S. Sugar Corp.

Ownership Information

Banks: Patman: one interlock with Manufacturers Hanover Trust; Morgan Guaranty manages one fund with investments in Florida Power & Light. Morgan owns 10 percent of preferred ($4.75) and 5.3 percent of 4½ preferred stock.

Insurance: Insurance companies owned 1.1 million shares. Major holdings, 1970: Prudential, 50,000 common, $4.1 m bonds; Equitable, 50,000 common, 35,000 of three types of preferred, $3.8 m bonds; NY Life, 60,000 three types of preferred, $3.6 m bonds; John Hancock (one interlock), $5.8 m bonds.

Mutual Funds: Twenty-six mutual funds owned 1.5 million shares, or 10.2 percent of the outstanding stock. Major holdings: Dreyfus Fund, 369,800; Investors Group, 322,600 (Inv. Mutual, 71,700; Inv. Stock Fund, 200,900; Inv. Variable Payment, 50,-000); Wellington Fund, 233,000.

Foundations: Ford Foundation, 145,000 shares; Sloan Foundation, $1 million bonds; Kresge Foundation, 2,500 shares.

406   A GUIDE TO THE ENERGY INDUSTRY

Universities: Universities owned 217,279 shares. Major holdings: Harvard, (June 30, 1970) (one interlock), 105,209.

Other: Among the ten largest security holders as reported to the FPC were: Thomas & Co. (First National City Bank for DeVegh Inv. Co., United Corp.), 430,800 common shares; Lerche & Co. (Bank of N.Y. for Dreyfus Fund, Lazard Fund), 286,150 shares; Cudd & Co. (Chase Manhattan Bank for American Mutual Fund, Chemical Fund, Equity Fund, Intl. Resources Fund, Investment Co. of America), 251,837 shares; Touchstone & Co. (State Street Bank & Trust Co. for Wellington Fund), 250,600 shares; Atwell & Co. (U.S. Trust Co. of N.Y.), 211,933 shares; Sigler & Co. (Manufacturers Hanover Trust Co. for Canadian Intl. Growth Fund, Channing Funds, Gen. Pub. Service Corp.; Institutional Growth Fund, U.S. & Foreign Securities Corp.), 199,472; Kane & Co. (Chase Manhattan Bank), 195,277 shares; Carson & Co. (Morgan Guaranty Trust Co.), 189,200 shares; Don & Co. (Old Colony Trust Co.), 182,620 shares; Firjer & Co. (First Jersey Natl. Bank for Anchor Capital Fund, Westminster Fund, Fundamental Investors, Washington Natl. Fund), 165,100 shares.

Florida Power & Light Co. supplies electricity along the east and lower west coasts of Florida, including the Miami area, Palm Beach, the agricultural area around Lake Okeechobee, portions of central and north central Florida. Because of the tourist industry there are peak demands year round.

Fifty-four percent of operating revenues come from residential service, 31 percent from commercial, and 15 percent from other sources. The company owns 10 fossil fuel power plants with a gross capacity of 5.9 million kilowatts.

In 1971 the Justice Department said the company had agreed in a dissent decree to begin extensive construction to halt discharge of heated water into Biscayne Bay. The decree was filed to terminate a water pollution suit brought against Florida Power & Light on March 30, 1970. The suit charged that hot water discharged from the plant damaged marine life in the bay. Under the decree the utility agrees to construct a cooling system within five years. The system will recycle water used.

In 1970 the company spent $7.6 million to increase its sales. Florida Power & Light spent $750,143 for research, most of it going into studies for control of air pollution.

The company's net after-tax profit as percent of gross revenue in 1970 was 14.24 percent. Return on common equity in 1970 was 11.9 percent.

GENERAL PUBLIC UTILITIES CORPORATION

80 Pine Street, New York, N.Y., 10005.

Basic Company Data

William G. Kuhns, President. Directors: Homer M. Chapin, Kenneth L. Isaacs, George H. Lanier, Jr., Albert F. Tegen, Donald A. Henderson, Ferdinand K. Thun, Charles B. Stauffacher, John H. DeVitt.

Total revenues, 1970, $416.7 million; net income, $51.8 million; average stock outstanding, 1970: 28,387,705 shares.

Interlocks

1 ea w/ with Jersey Central Power & Light Co.; Metropolitan Edison Co.; New Jersey Power & Light Co.; Penn Electric Co.; Marine Midland Grace Trust Co.; Home Life Insurance; Coca Cola Bottling Miami; Cenco Instruments Corp.; Central Vermont Public Service Co.; Novo Corp.; Grow Chemical Corp.; Esterline Corp.; Loral Corp.; Mass Mutual Life Ins. Co.; Continental Can Co.; American Manufacturers Mutual Ins. Co.; Vulcan Materials; Chase Manhattan Bank; General American Investors; Lumberman's Mutual Casualty Co.; Physics Intl. Co.; Turner Halsey Co., Inc.; Lanier Textile Co.; Wehadkee Yarn Mills; Mt. Vernon Mills Inc.; Hammermill Paper Co.; American Sterilizer; First Natl. Bank Pennsylvania; Twentieth Century Fox Film Corp.;

Mass. Financial Services; Southern Pacific Co.; Fiduciary Exchange Fund; Leverage Fund; Suffolk Franklin Savings Bank; Phelps-Dodge; Canada General Fund Inc.; Depositors Fund Boston; Diversification Fund; Capital Exchange Fund; Thun Investment Co.

Ownership Information

Insurance: Insurance companies owned 982,799 shares. Major holdings: INA 130,700 shares.

Mutual Funds: Four funds held 387,408 shares or 1.3 percent of outstanding stock.

Foundations: Andrew W. Mellon Foundation, 15,000 shares.

Universities: Universities held 338,090 shares. Major holdings: Harvard (June 30, 1970), 117,375 shares; California Institute of Technology (December 31, 1969), 84,930 shares; Univ. Pennsylvania (June 30, 1970), 65,678 shares.

General Public Utilities is a holding company that owns the outstanding stock of four major subsidiaries serving customers in New Jersey and Pennsylvania. They are Jersey Central Power & Light Co. and New Jersey Power & Light Co. in New Jersey, and in Pennsylvania, Metropolitan Edison Co. and Pennsylvania Electric Co.

GPU subsidiaries are physically interconnected and serve an area of 24,000 square miles in the east central, north coastal, and northwestern area of New Jersey and in western, northern, central, and southeastern Pennsylvania, with an estimated population of 3.8 million. This area extends from the Atlantic Ocean to Lake Erie and includes more than 1,200 communities, the largest of which is the city of Erie, Pennsylvania. Subsidiaries serve approximately 1.3 million customers with a net integrated hourly peak load of about 1.4 million kilowatts.

Approximately 60 percent of the revenues of the system come

from Pennsylvania customers and the balance from New Jersey customers. In 1970 residential sales accounted for about 42 percent of total operating revenues and 33 percent of total kilowatt sales; commercial sales, 23 percent of revenues and 19 percent of kilowatt sales; and industrial sales, 28 percent of revenues and 43 percent of total kilowatt sales.

The company's net after-tax profit as percent of gross revenue in 1970 was 12.43 percent. Return on common equity for the subsidiaries in that year was as follows: Jersey Central Power & Light Co., 12.8 percent; New Jersey Power & Light Co., 2.4 percent; Metropolitan Edison, 7.5 percent; Pennsylvania Electric Co., 10.8 percent.

10: FINANCIAL INSTITUTION CONTROL OF ENERGY COMPANIES

Aetna Life & Casualty

Company Name	Interlock	Common Stock	Preferred Stock	Bonds, Debs., Notes	Funds Managed
AMER ELEC POWER		8,490			
ANACONDA				$ 2.9 m bonds	
ARCO		31,925		$876,000 bonds	
COMMONWEALTH ED				$15.8 m bonds & debs.	
CON ED				$14.3 m bonds	
CONOCO				$210,000 debs.	
DETROIT ED		30,000		$ 5.2 m bonds	
EL PASO			20,000	$48.8 m bonds & debs.	
FLA P&L				$ 3.8 m bonds	
GE	one	79,500			
GULF		59,300		$ 9.2 m debs. & trust agreement	
PENNZOIL				$16.1 m bonds	
PG&E					
PHELPS-DODGE	one		5,600	$11.1 m bonds & debs.	
PUB SERV ELEC & GAS			27,500 (3 types)	$ 4.1 m bonds	
SO CAL ED				$ 5.6 m bonds	
SONJ			1,250	$ 8.4 m bonds	
TENNECO			6,000	$17.9 m bonds & debs.	
TEXAS EASTERN		82,908		$ 1.2 m bonds	
TEXACO			7,200	$12.9 m bonds & debs.	
TRANSCO					
US STEEL	one				
WESTINGHOUSE			64,800 (2 types)	$597,100 debs.	

Bankers Trust Company

Company Name	Interlock	Common Stock	Preferred Stock	Bonds, Debs., Notes	Funds Managed
CONOCO	three				
DETROIT ED	one				one
MOBIL					two
SONJ					one

California Institute of Technology

Company Name	Interlock	Common Stock	Preferred Stock	Bonds, Debs., Notes	Funds Managed
DETROIT ED	one				
GEN PUB UTILITIES		84,930			
KAISER	one				
KERR-MC GEE	one				
SO CAL ED	one	31,496			
SOCAL	one				
TENNECO		71,322			
US STEEL	one				

Chase Manhattan Bank
(Nominees—Egger & Co., Kane & Co.)

Company Name	Interlock	Common Stock	Preferred Stock	Bonds, Debs., Notes	Funds Managed
ANACONDA	two				one
ARCO	one	102,070			
CON ED	one				
CONOCO	one	195,277			
FLA P&L					
GE	one				
GEN PUB UTILITIES	one				
MOBIL					one
PUB SERV ELEC & GAS		726,555	2,342		
ROYAL DUTCH	one				
SO CAL ED		1.3 million	8,000		
SONJ	one				one
WESTINGHOUSE	one				two

Chemical Bank New York Trust

(Nominees—Walston & Co., Cummings & Co.)

Company Name	Interlock	Common Stock	Preferred Stock	Bonds, Debs., Notes	Funds Managed
AMER ELEC POWER	one				
CON ED	three				one
DETROIT ED	one				
EL PASO		322,240			
KENNECOTT	one				
MOBIL	one				
PITTSTON	one				
SONJ	one				
TENNECO	one	235,450			
TEXACO	one				two
US STEEL	two				

Connecticut General Life Insurance Co.

Company Name	Interlock	Common Stock	Preferred Stock	Bonds, Debs., Notes	Funds Managed
AMER ELEC POWER		40,000			
COMMONWEALTH ED				$ 5.7 m bonds	
CON ED				$5.9 m bonds	
DETROIT ED				$ 4.7 m bonds	
EL PASO		19,590		$24.7 m bonds	
GE	one	10,000			
OCCIDENTAL				$ 1.7 m bonds	
PENNZOIL				$ 1.0 m debs.	
PG&E		25,000	4,100	$ 6.6 m bonds	
PHELPS-DODGE	one				
PITTSTON				$ 2.2 m bonds	
PUB SERV ELEC & GAS				$620,320 bonds	
SO CAL ED		30,000		$523,200 bonds	
SOUTHERN CO		60,000	33,353 (6 types)	$ 8.9 m debs. & bonds	
TENNECO				$ 6.7 m bonds	
TEXACO				$ 3.9 m debs.	
TEXAS EASTERN				$11.9 m bonds	
TRANSCO				$ 3.8 m bonds	
UNION CARBIDE					
WESTINGHOUSE		15,795			

Equitable Life Assurance Society

Company Name	Interlock	Common Stock	Preferred Stock	Bonds, Debs., Notes	Funds Managed
AMER ELEC POWER					
ARCO	one	80,000		$ 5.4 m debs.	
BABCOCK-WILCOX		20,000			
COMMONWEALTH ED				$19.8 m bonds	
CON ED	one	39,180	200,000 (2 types)	$ 6.0 m bonds	
EL PASO				$90.4 m bonds & debs.	
FLA P&L		50,000	35,000 (3 types)	$ 3.8 m bonds	
GE	one				
GULF		230,000		$22.0 m notes	
KENNECOTT				$14.4 m notes	
MOBIL					
PG&E		70,000	760,475 (4 types)	$20.1 m bonds	
PUB SERV ELEC & GAS		99,000	50,000		
SO CAL ED		150,000	634,925 (3 types)	$ 6.9 m bonds	
SOCAL		84,000			
SONJ		130,000			
SOUTHERN CO		130,000			
TENNECO				$ 5.7 m debs	
TEXACO		264,000			
TEXAS EASTERN				$ 1.7 m debs.	
UNION CARBIDE		117,200			
US STEEL		20,670			
WESTINGHOUSE		92,000		$13.3 m debs.	

First National City Bank of New York

Company Name	Interlock	Common Stock	Preferred Stock	Bonds, Debs., Notes	Funds Managed
ANACONDA	two				two
COMB ENG					one
CON ED	two		6.1%		one
EL PASO	one				
GE	one				
KENNECOTT	one				
MOBIL	one				
PHELPS-DODGE	two				one
PUB SERV ELEC & GAS			7.3%		
SO CAL ED			8.2%		one
SONJ					
TENNECO			10.9%, 11.5%, 5.8%, & 6.2% (4 types)		
TRANSCO	one				
US STEEL	two				
WESTINGHOUSE	one		6.6%		two

NOTE: Where stock holdings in percentages, information is from Patman Bank Report. All other statistics from company portfolios.

Ford Foundation

Company Name	Interlock	Common Stock	Preferred Stock	Bonds, Debs., Notes	Funds Managed
AMER. ELEC POWER		165,000			
ANACONDA		75,000			
ARCO		67,000		$1.3 m bonds	
BABCOCK-WILCOX				$939,000 bonds	
CON ED				$2m bonds	
CONOCO		115,000			
DETROIT ED				$800,000 bonds	
FLA P&L		145,000			
GE		76,000			
GULF		250,000			
MOBIL		139,000			
PENNZOIL				$10.4 m bonds	
PG&E	one	263,000		$500,000 bonds	
ROYAL DUTCH		293,000			
SO CAL ED		235,000		$200,000 bonds	
SOCAL		15,000			
SONJ		400,000			
SOUTHERN CO		254,000			
TEXACO		252,000			
UNION CARBIDE		50,000			
US STEEL		45,000			
WESTINGHOUSE	one	137,000		$4.1 m bonds	

John Hancock Mutual Life Insurance Co.

Company Name	Interlock	Common Stock	Preferred Stock	Bonds, Debs., Notes	Funds Managed
AMER ELEC POWER		100,000		$ 2 m notes	
ARCO				$ 9.9 m bonds	
COMMONWEALTH ED				$ 3.3 m bonds	
CON ED				$ 4.2 m bonds	
DETROIT ED				$41.8 m bonds & debs.	
EL PASO	one			$ 5.8 m bonds	
FLA P&L					
GE		70,000			
GULF		290,000			
OCCIDENTAL				$ 5.8 m notes	
PENNZOIL				$19 m debs.	
PG&E		124,800		$10.4 m bonds	
PUB SERV ELEC & GAS				$ 1.9 m bonds	
SO CAL ED		120,000	110,000 (2 types)	$ 1.9 m bonds	
SONJ		32,063		$17.5 m notes	
SOUTHERN CO		150,000			
TENNECO			20,000	$28.5 m debs.	
TEXACO		300,000			
TEXAS EASTERN				$28 m bonds & debs.	
TRANSCO				$14.3 m bonds	
UNITED NUCLEAR				$291,690 debs.	
UTAH INTL.		62,000			
WESTINGHOUSE		86,800		$ 3.6 m debs.	

Harvard

Company Name	Interlock	Common Stock	Preferred Stock	Bonds, Debs., Notes	Funds Managed
AMER ELEC PWR		76,510			
COMM ED		63,984			
CONOCO		220,356			
DETROIT ED		32,632			
FLA P&L	one	105,209			
GE		99,039			
GEN PUB UTILITIES		117,375			
GULF		671,187			
KAISER		102,075			
KENNECOTT		71,082			
MOBIL		242,010			
PHELPS-DODGE		50,208			
ROYAL DUTCH		113,217			
SO CAL ED		127,472			
SOCAL		190,380			
SONJ	one	245,914			
TEXACO		770,259			
UNION CARBIDE		69,644			
WESTINGHOUSE		60,449			

Investor's Funds Group

Company Name	Interlock	Common Stock	Preferred Stock	Bonds, Debs., Notes	Funds Managed
BABCOCK-WILCOX		400,000			
CONOCO		942,100			
FLA P&L		322,600			
GE		964,600			
GULF		1,685,900			
KAISER		1,020,000			
MOBIL		1,153,500			
PG&E		787,800			
ROYAL DUTCH		1,022,744			
SO CAL ED		612,000			
SOCAL		416,600			
TEXACO		1,915,900			
TEXAS EASTERN		278,400			
UNION CARBIDE		309,250			
UTAH INT'L		265,200			
WESTINGHOUSE		403,200			

Massachusetts Institute of Technology

Company Name	Interlock	Common Stock	Preferred Stock	Bonds, Debs., Notes	Funds Managed
GULF		96,056			
SOCAL		54,425			
SONJ		143,592			
TRANSCO	one	62,884			
WESTINGHOUSE		18,197			

Massachusetts Mutual Life Insurance Co.

Company Name	Interlock	Common Stock	Preferred Stock	Bonds, Debs., Notes	Funds Managed
COMB ENG			100		
CON ED				$1.4 m bonds	
CONOCO			24,000		
DETROIT ED			5,334		
FLA P&L				$8.7 m bonds & debs.	
GEN PUB UTILITIES	one				
MOBIL		20,000			
OCCIDENTAL				$9.5 m notes	
PG&E				$36,500 bonds	
PHELPS-DODGE		28,400			
PITTSTON				$4.2 m notes	
PUB SERV ELEC & GAS		52,600		$1.9 m bonds	
SO CAL ED			10,000		
SONJ		40,874			
TENNECO		40,505	28,950 (3 types)		
TEXACO		50,000		$1.8 m debs.	
TEXAS EASTERN			9,750	$722,244 bonds	
TRANSCO			10,750 (2 types)	$3.1 m bonds & debs.	
UNITED NUCLEAR				$219,240 debs.	
WESTINGHOUSE				$1 m debs.	

Mellon National Bank & Trust Co.

Company Name	Interlock	Common Stock	Preferred Stock	Bonds, Debs., Notes	Funds Managed
CONOCO	one				four
EL PASO	one				ten
GULF	four	17.1% (1968)			
PENNZOIL	one				
PHELPS-DODGE	one				
US STEEL	two				one
WESTINGHOUSE	two				

Metropolitan Life Insurance Company

Company Name	Interlock	Common Stock	Preferred Stock	Bonds, Debs., Notes	Funds Managed
ANACONDA	one				
ARCO		100,000		$ 25.9 m notes	
BP					
COMMONWEALTH ED				$10 m notes	
CON ED			569,000 (5 types)	$ 42.7 m bonds	
CONOCO		40,000		$ 40.6 m bonds	
DETROIT ED				$ 20.9 m bonds	
EL PASO				$296.3 m bonds	
GE		50,000			
GULF		50,000		$176.9 m notes	
KERR-MC GEE		47,500			
MOBIL	one	40,000			
PG&E	one		251,446 (2 types)	$22 m bonds	
PUB SERV ELEC & GAS		85,000			
SO CAL ED			62,500		
SOCAL		26,250			
SONJ		41,600		$ 21.2 m notes & debs.	
SOUTHERN CO		70,000			
TEXACO		40,000		$8 m debs.	
TEXAS EASTERN				$ 55.3 m debs. & bonds	
TRANSCO				$ 65.5 m bonds	
UNITED NUCLEAR	one	60,000		$205 m notes	
US STEEL				$ 9.4 m debs.	
WESTINGHOUSE				$23.5 m debs.	

Morgan Guaranty Bank and Trust Company

(Nominees—Carson & Co., Genoy & Co., Reing Co.)

Company Name	Interlock	Common Stock	Preferred Stock	Bonds, Debs., Notes	Funds Managed
ANACONDA					three
ARCO	one				two
COMB ENG			7%		one
CON ED					one
CONOCO	two	189,200			one
FLA P&L			10% & 5.3% (2 types)		one
GE	two	17.5%			three
KENNECOTT	three				one
MOBIL		328,350			
PG&E		6%	12,856		one
PHELPS-DODGE	one				
PUB SERV ELEC & GAS		391,059 (Reing) 356,107 (Carson) 281,564 (Genoy)			
ROYAL DUTCH	one		11,500		
SO CAL ED	two	541,179			two
SONJ			6.7%		
TEXAS EASTERN	one				
UNION CARBIDE	one				
US STEEL	two				

New York Life Insurance Company

Company Name	Interlock	Common Stock	Preferred Stock	Bonds, Debs., Notes	Funds Managed
AMER ELEC POWER	one	119,818		$5.8 m notes	
ANACONDA				$24.5 m debs.	
ARCO		76,311		$27.5 m bonds	
COMMONWEALTH ED	one	136,000		$29.6 m bonds	
CON ED	four		229,500 (3 types)	$541,667 notes	
CONOCO		60,000		$ 6.7 m bonds	
DETROIT ED				$33.5 m debs.	
EL PASO					
FLA P&L			60,000 (3 types)	$ 3.6 m bonds	
GE		245,000			
GULF		370,796			
KENNECOTT		169,000			
MOBIL		201,850			
OCCIDENTAL				$ 9.5 m notes	
PG&E	one	127,140	764,005 (5 types)	$34 m bonds	
PHELPS-DODGE		22,000			
PITTSTON				$ 2.2 m bonds	
PUB SERV ELEC & GAS		263,550	86,500 (3 types)	$17.3 m bonds	
SO CAL ED		172,000	143,000 (2 types)	$31.4 m bonds	
SOCAL		81,556			
SONJ		259,000			
TENNECO				$33.4 m bonds & debs.	
TEXACO		247,978			
TEXAS EASTERN				$12.6 m bonds & debs.	
TRANSCO				$17.8 m bonds & debs.	
UNITED NUCLEAR	three	146,000			
US STEEL	one				
WESTINGHOUSE		125,400	15,000	$13 m debs.	

Northwestern Mutual Life

Company Name	Interlock	Common Stock	Preferred Stock	Bonds, Debs., Notes	Funds Managed
ANACONDA				$ 1.8 m debs.	
ARCO			10,000	$ 3.5 m bonds	
COMMONWEALTH ED			20,000	$939,120 bonds	
CON ED			350,000 (2 types)	$ 2.0 m bonds	
CONOCO				$ 5.2 m bonds	
DETROIT ED				$25.3 m bonds & debs.	
EL PASO			100,000		
GE		31,000			
KENNECOTT		92,500			
MOBIL		96,000		$ 4.7 m bonds	
OCCIDENTAL			67,950		
PENNZOIL				$10.5 m bonds	
PG&E		128,000			
PHELPS-DODGE				$ 4.3 m bonds & debs.	
PUB SERV ELEC & GAS		31,112			
ROYAL DUTCH		100,000	115,000 (3 types)	$ 8.1 m bonds	
SO CAL ED		81,520			
SONJ		90,000			
SOUTHERN CO			25,000	$ 1.6 m bonds	
TENNECO		171,000			
TEXACO		50,000	48,230 (2 types)	$ 2.5 m bonds	
TEXAS EASTERN			28,365 (2 types)	$ 2.5 m bonds & debs.	
TRANSCO				$ 1.9 m debs.	
WESTINGHOUSE		66,000			

The Prudential Insurance Co.

Company Name	Interlock	Common Stock	Preferred Stock	Bonds, Debs., Notes	Funds Managed
AMER ELEC POWER		82,000			
COMMONWEALTH ED		207,000		$ 34.1 m bonds	
CON ED				$ 11.4 m bonds	
EL PASO				$ 4.5 m notes	
FLA P&L		50,000		$ 4.1 m bonds	
GE		155,000			
GULF		560,000		$21 m notes	
KERR-MC GEE		60,000		$ 70.5 m notes	
MOBIL		350,000			
PG&E	four	355,000	234,275 (2 types)	$756,500 bonds	
PUB SERV ELEC & GAS	two	331,000		$1 m bonds	
ROYAL DUTCH		245,850			
SO CAL ED		384,000	211,630 (2 types)	$ 1.9 m bonds	
SOCAL	one	175,000			
SONJ	one	410,000		$ 5.3 m debs.	
TENNECO		16,450		$ 60.7 m notes	
TEXACO		480,000			
TEXAS EASTERN				$ 8.5 m bonds	
UNION CARBIDE		190,000		$220.5 m bonds	
UTAH INTL				$35 m notes	
WESTINGHOUSE		292,000			

Rockefeller Foundation

Company Name	Interlock	Common Stock	Preferred Stock	Bonds, Debs., Notes	Funds Managed
ANACONDA	one				
GE		189,600			
MOBIL		600,000			
PUB SERV ELEC & GAS		100,000			
SONJ		3 million			
SOUTHERN		342,000			
TEXACO	one				

Travelers Life

Company Name	Interlock	Common Stock	Preferred Stock	Bonds, Debs., Notes	Funds Managed
ANACONDA					
COMMONWEALTH ED		100,325		$ 2.9 m notes	
CON ED			56,400 (3 types)	$ 6.8 m bonds & debs.	
DETROIT ED				$ 4.7 m bonds	
EL PASO		39,180	20,000	$ 1.2 m bonds	
FLA P&L				$40.0 m bonds & debs.	
GULF				$ 2.4 m debs.	
PENNZOIL				$530,000 bonds	
PG&E			56,750 (3 types)	$ 3.8 m debs.	
PUB SERV ELEC & GAS				$10.5 m bonds	
SO CAL ED			60,000 (2 types)	$ 2.0 m bonds	
SOCAL				$ 1.0 m bonds	
SONJ		25,500		$ 4.0 m debs.	
TENNECO				$ 7.5 m notes	
TEXACO				$ 9.1 m bonds & debs.	
TEXAS EASTERN				$28.3 m notes	
TRANSCO				$ 7.3 m bonds & debs.	
WESTINGHOUSE				$ 8.7 m bonds	
				$ 1.4 m bonds	

University of California

Company Name	Interlock	Common Stock	Preferred Stock	Bonds, Debs., Notes	Funds Managed
ARCO		66,995			
COMMONWEALTH ED		87,902			
GE		75,802			
OCCIDENTAL	one				
PG&E	one	134,795			
SO CAL ED		102,200			
SOCAL		75,918			
TEXACO		92,303			

Wellington Fund (Touchstone & Co.)

Company Name	Interlock	Common Stock	Preferred Stock	Bonds, Debs., Notes	Funds Managed
COMM ED		427,300			
FLA P&L		233,000			
KENNECOTT		341,400			
PG&E		370,600			
ROYAL DUTCH		1,077,099			
SONJ		605,800			
TEXACO		589,600			

INDEX

Canadian Petroleum Association, 163
Canadian Superior, 183
Canpac Minerals, 212
Capline, 221
Captive mines, 18
Carameros, George D., Jr., 152
Cardinal River Coals, 213
Carnegie Corp., 274
Carter Oil, 55
Cascade Pipe Ltd., 213
Caudill, Harry, 34
Central del Rio, 183
Central Intelligence Agency, 270
Central Queensland Coal Associates, 214
Charter Consolidated, 126, 197
Chase Manhattan Bank, 413
Chemical Bank New York Trust Co., 181, 414
Chemical production from sea water, 255-258
Chesapeake & Ohio Railroad, 30, 118, 226-227
Chevron, 271
Chih-yuan, An, 151
China, 109, 112-115, 128, 151, 158, 269-272
 coal industry, 269-270
 electric power industry, 271-272
 oil industry, 270-271
China Sea, 165
Chinese Petroleum Corp., 271
Chrysler International, 131
Churchill, Winston, 99
Churchill Falls Corporation, 98-99, 100, 150
Cities Service Co., 162, 165, 166, 220
Claiborne County, Tennessee, 38
Clark Oil, 221
Cleveland Electric Illuminating Co., 228
Clifford, Clark, 136
Clinton Oil Co., 271
Clutha Development Corporation, 122, 214

Coal, 205-216
 control of, 7, 58, 77-78
 gasification of, 11, 74-76, 209-212, 268
 hydrogenation of, 49-51
 leading U.S. producers of, 307-322
 major Japanese supplier of, 358
 reserves, 3, 59, 140, 205, 212, 215
 transportation of, 226-228
Coal gasoline cartel, 48-52, 66
Coal industry
 Australia, 213-215
 Canada, 212-213
 China, 269-270
 control of, 206, 207
 depletion allowance, 28-29
 health and safety of workers, 38-48
 mechanization of, 19, 22, 23, 39
 profitability of, 27
 reorganization of, 14-16
 Rocky Mountain area, 58-61
 Soviet Union, 215-216
 strikes and, 17
 TVA and the, 20-23, 78-83
 United States, 205-212
 West Virginia, 30-33
Coal Lessors Association, 28
Coal Mine Health and Safety Law (1969), 44
Coal Research, Office of, 209-210, 211, 268
Cochran, Neil, 211
Colonial Oil & Gas Co., 162, 220
Colonial Pipeline Co., 220
Columbia Gas, 184, 189, 232
Columbia Gas Transmission System, 220, 223
Columbia LNG Corporation, 152
Columbia River treaty, 100-102, 150
Colville, D., 125
Combustion Engineering, 62, 196, 198
Coming Water Famine, The (Wright), 103

About the Author

JAMES RIDGEWAY was born in Auburn, New York. He was a contributing editor of *The New Republic*, and an editor and founder of *Hard Times*, the radical weekly paper. Mr. Ridgeway is the author of two previous books, *The Closed Corporation* and *The Politics of Ecology*. He is married and lives in Washington, D.C.